DICKENS'S S

Charles Dickens, generally regarded as the greatest novelist of the Victorian age, was known as 'The Inimitable', not least for his distinctive style of writing. This collection of twelve essays addresses the essential but often overlooked subject of Dickens's style, with each essay discussing a particular feature of his writing. All the essays consider Dickens's style conceptually, and they read it closely, demonstrating the ways it works on particular occasions. They show that style is not simply an aesthetic quality isolated from the deepest meanings of Dickens's fiction, but that it is inextricably involved with all kinds of historical, political and ideological concerns. Written in a lively and accessible manner by leading Dickens scholars, the collection ranges across all Dickens's writing, including the novels, journalism and letters.

DANIEL TYLER is a Leverhulme Postdoctoral Research Fellow in English at Oxford University and a Lecturer in English at Lincoln College, Oxford.

Nineteenth-century British literature and culture have been rich fields for interdisciplinary studies. Since the turn of the twentieth century, scholars and critics have tracked the intersections and tensions between Victorian literature and the visual arts, politics, social organisation, economic life, technical innovations, scientific thought – in short, culture in its broadest sense. In recent years, theoretical challenges and historiographical shifts have unsettled the assumptions of previous scholarly synthesis and have called into question the terms of older debates. Whereas the tendency in much past literary critical interpretation was to use the metaphor of culture as 'background', feminist, Foucauldian and other analyses have employed more dynamic models that raise questions of power and of circulation. Such developments have reanimated the field. This series aims to accommodate and promote the most interesting work being undertaken on the frontiers of the field of nineteenth-century literary studies: work that intersects fruitfully with other fields of study such as history, or literary theory, or the history of science. Comparative as well as interdisciplinary approaches are welcomed.

A complete list of titles published will be found at the end of the book.

DICKENS'S STYLE

EDITED BY
DANIEL TYLER

CAMBRIDGE
UNIVERSITY PRESS

CAMBRIDGE
UNIVERSITY PRESS

University Printing House, Cambridge CB2 8BS, United Kingdom

Cambridge University Press is part of the University of Cambridge.

It furthers the University's mission by disseminating knowledge in the pursuit of education, learning and research at the highest international levels of excellence.

www.cambridge.org
Information on this title: www.cambridge.org/9781107527430

© Cambridge University Press 2013

First published 2013
First paperback edition 2015

A catalogue record for this publication is available from the British Library

Library of Congress Cataloguing in Publication data
Dickens's Style / edited by Daniel Tyler.
pages   cm. – (Cambridge Studies in Nineteenth-century Literature and Culture ; 86)
Includes bibliographical references and index.
ISBN 978-1-107-02843-2 (hardback)
1. Dickens, Charles, 1812–1870–Literary style.   2. English language–19th century–Style. I. Tyler, Daniel, 1981– editor of compilation.
PR4594.D54 2013
823'.8–dc23
2012051608

ISBN 978-1-107-02843-2 Hardback
ISBN 978-1-107-52743-0 Paperback

Contents

Contributors

MATTHEW BEVIS is University Lecturer and Tutorial Fellow at Keble College, Oxford. His books include *The Art of Eloquence: Byron, Dickens, Tennyson, Joyce* (2007) and *Comedy: A Very Short Introduction* (2012), and, as editor, *Some Versions of Empson* (2007) and *The Oxford Handbook of Victorian Poetry* (2013).

JOHN BOWEN is Professor of Nineteenth-Century Literature at the University of York. He has written widely on Dickens, including a study of Dickens's early works, *Other Dickens: Pickwick to Chuzzlewit* (2000).

ROBERT DOUGLAS-FAIRHURST is Fellow and Tutor in English at Magdalen College, Oxford. His biography *Becoming Dickens: The Invention of a Novelist* won the 2011 Duff Cooper Prize. He has also produced editions of *Great Expectations* and *A Christmas Carol* for Oxford World's Classics and acted as Historical Adviser on the 2011 BBC television adaptation of *Great Expectations*. He writes regularly for publications including the *Times Literary Supplement* and the *Daily Telegraph*.

JENNIFER GRIBBLE is Honorary Associate Professor of English at the University of Sydney. She has written extensively on fiction (especially of the nineteenth century) and her books include an edition of George Eliot's *Scenes of Clerical Life* (1998). She is currently working on a study of Dickens and the Bible.

PHILIP HORNE is Professor of English at University College London. He has written widely on nineteenth- and twentieth-century fiction, especially on Henry James, and on film. He has edited *Oliver Twist* (2002). His book *Henry James and Revision: The New York Edition*, was published in 1990; *Henry James: A Life in Letters* in 1999.

FREYA JOHNSTON is University Lecturer and Tutorial Fellow at St Anne's College, Oxford. She works on eighteenth- and nineteenth-century

English and comparative literature. Her publications include *Samuel Johnson and the Art of Sinking* (2005) and, as co-editor, *Samuel Johnson: The Arc of the Pendulum* (2012).

CLARE PETTITT is Professor of Nineteenth-Century Literature and Culture at King's College London. She has written articles on Dickens and on other Victorian novelists. Her book *Patent Inventions: Intellectual Property and the Victorian Novel* (2004) includes a chapter on *Little Dorrit*.

REBEKAH SCOTT is the Plumer Junior Research Fellow in English at St Anne's College, Oxford. She has published essays on Henry James's style and has co-authored (with Adrian Poole) the chapter on Dickens in *Great Shakespeareans: Scott, Dickens, Eliot, Hardy* (2011).

HELEN SMALL is Professor of English Literature and Tutorial Fellow of Pembroke College, Oxford. She has written widely on Dickens and on Victorian literature. Her book *The Long Life* (2007) won the Truman Capote Award for Literary Criticism, 2008, and includes a chapter on *The Old Curiosity Shop*.

GARRETT STEWART is James O. Freedman Professor of Letters at Iowa University. He is a fellow of the American Academy of Literature and the Arts. He has written widely and influentially on style in Dickens and in others. His many books include *Dickens and the Trials of Imagination* (1974), *Death Sentences: Styles of Dying in British Fiction* (1984), *Dear Reader: The Conscripted Audience in Nineteenth-Century British Fiction* (1996) and *Novel Violence* (2009).

BHARAT TANDON is Lecturer in the School of Literature, Drama and Creative Writing at the University of East Anglia. His first book was *Jane Austen and the Morality of Conversation* (2003), and his forthcoming study, *Ghosts of Sound: Haunting Figures in Victorian Writing*, considers how various Victorian writers, including Dickens, employed textual figures of echoing and haunting in order to understand their relations to time and history.

DANIEL TYLER is Leverhulme Postdoctoral Research Fellow in English, Oxford University, and Lecturer in English at Lincoln College, Oxford. His book *A Guide to Dickens's London* was published in 2012. He has written on Dickens for the *Times Literary Supplement* and the *Dickens Quarterly*.

Acknowledgements

I am grateful to Robert Douglas-Fairhurst, and also to Matthew Bevis, Oliver Herford, Philip Horne and Helen Small, for their advice and help as this volume took shape. Several of the ideas and arguments were first presented at a conference on Dickens's style in Oxford, and I would like to extend my thanks to the English Faculty for supporting and hosting the event and to all those involved in the occasion, particularly Simon J. James, David Paroissien, Corinna Russell and George Yeats. I am grateful to the anonymous readers for Cambridge University Press for their insights and to my editors there, Anna Bond, Maartje Scheltens and especially to Linda Bree. I would like to thank the Leverhulme Foundation for the award of a postdoctoral fellowship, during the tenure of which I have completed the work on this volume. Heartfelt thanks also to Johanna, for her encouragement and support.

Editions and abbreviations

Where possible, we have used the Clarendon edition of the novels. Where there is no Clarendon, the latest Oxford World's Classics edition has been used, unless otherwise stated. The Penguin editions of *Pictures from Italy* and *American Notes* have been used. *Sketches by Boz*, *The Uncommercial Traveller* and other short pieces are taken from the Dent edition of the *Journalism*. Abbreviations and bibliographical details are given below. Quotations from these works are incorporated parenthetically within the text. For ease of reference, we have given chapter and page numbers for quotations in the form ([book], chapter, page).

AN	*American Notes*, edited by Patricia Ingham, with introduction and notes (Harmondsworth: Penguin, 2000)
BH	*Bleak House*, edited by Stephen Gill with an introduction and notes (Oxford University Press, 2008)
BR	*Barnaby Rudge*, edited by Clive Hurst, with an introduction and notes by Ian McCalman and Jon Mee (Oxford University Press, 2008)
CC	*A Christmas Carol*, in *A Christmas Carol and Other Christmas Books*, edited by Robert Douglas-Fairhurst with an introduction and notes (Oxford University Press, 2006)
CH	Philip Collins (ed.), *Dickens: The Critical Heritage* (London: Routledge & Kegan Paul, 1971)
Chimes	*The Chimes*, in *A Christmas Carol and Other Christmas Books*, edited by Robert Douglas-Fairhurst with an introduction and notes (Oxford University Press, 2006)
'CT'	'A Christmas Tree', in *Charles Dickens: Selected Journalism*, ed. David Pascoe (London: Penguin, 1997)
DC	*David Copperfield*, edited by Nina Burgis (Oxford: Clarendon Press, 1981)

DS	*Dombey and Son*, edited by Alan Horsman (Oxford: Clarendon Press, 1974)
ED	*The Mystery of Edwin Drood*, edited by Margaret Cardwell (Oxford: Clarendon Press, 1972)
GE	*Great Expectations*, edited by Margaret Cardwell (Oxford: Clarendon Press, 1993)
HM	*The Haunted Man*, in *A Christmas Carol and Other Christmas Books*, edited by Robert Douglas-Fairhurst with an introduction and notes (Oxford University Press, 2006)
HT	*Hard Times*, edited by Paul Schlicke with an introduction and notes (Oxford University Press, 2008)
Journalism	*Dent Uniform Edition of Dickens's Journalism*, vols. I–III, ed. Michael Slater (London: Dent, 1994–9) and vol. IV, ed. Michael Slater and John Drew (London: Dent, 2000)
LD	*Little Dorrit*, edited by Harvey Peter Sucksmith (Oxford: Clarendon Press, 1979)
Letters	*The Pilgrim Edition of the Letters of Charles Dickens*, ed. Graham Storey, Kathleen Tillotson and Madeline House, et al., 12 vols. (Oxford: Clarendon Press, 1982–2002)
Life	John Forster, *The Life of Charles Dickens*, Library Edition, 2 vols. (London: Chapman & Hall, 1876)
MC	*Martin Chuzzlewit*, edited by Margaret Cardwell (Oxford: Clarendon Press, 1982)
MHC	*Master Humphrey's Clock* (Philadelphia, PA: Lee & Blanchard, 1841).
MJG	*Memoirs of Joseph Grimaldi*, 2 vols. (London: Bentley, 1838)
NN	*Nicholas Nickleby*, edited by Paul Schlicke with an introduction and notes (Oxford University Press, 2008)
OCS	*The Old Curiosity Shop*, edited by Elizabeth M. Brennan (Oxford: Clarendon Press, 1997)
OMF	*Our Mutual Friend*, edited by Michael Cotsell with an introduction and notes (Oxford University Press, 2008)
OT	*Oliver Twist*, edited by Kathleen Tillotson (Oxford: Clarendon Press, 1966)
PI	*Pictures from Italy*, edited by Kate Flint, with introduction and notes (Harmondsworth: Penguin, 1998)
PP	*The Pickwick Papers*, edited by James Kinsley (Oxford: Clarendon Press, 1986)

SB   *Sketches by Boz*, in the *Dent Uniform Edition of Dickens's Journalism*, vol. I, edited by Michael Slater (London: Dent, 1994–9)

Speeches   *The Speeches of Charles Dickens*, edited by K. J. Fielding (Oxford: Clarendon Press, 1960)

TTC   *A Tale of Two Cities*, edited by Andrew Sanders with an introduction and notes (Oxford University Press, 2008)

UT   *The Uncommercial Traveller*, in the *Dent Uniform Edition of Dickens's Journalism*, vol. IV, ed. Michael Slater and John Drew (London: Dent, 2000)

Introduction

Daniel Tyler

Dickens was a great prose stylist and yet criticism has frequently disregarded or undervalued his style. Striking but elusive, at once entirely a property of his prose and yet apparently superfluous, style has often evaded the attention of scholarship that is focused on the qualities of Dickens's fiction it considers more meaningful. Whether understood as a set of local verbal details or larger narrative modes, as an imaginative habit or an occasional flourish, as a way of writing peculiar to the author or shared within periods and genres, style has sometimes been deemed incidental, as if it is a merely playful, self-delighting distraction from the plain meaning of the work. Such a view has been fostered implicitly through the crowding out of attention to style in preference for other interests in Dickens's writing, but also explicitly through the kind of attention it has been granted. Early readers who lamented the irregularity of Dickens's prose and its deviations from contemporary standards of correctness, and subsequent scholars who have analysed the techniques and rhetorical features of Dickens's writing, have regarded style, helpfully but limitingly, as an end in itself, cut off from matters of plot and theme and from the deepest interests and values of the fiction. These perspectives have long been accompanied by another view: that Dickens's unruly style runs at odds with the central aims of his writing, whether productively or self-defeatingly. The many purposeful, cooperative contributions of his highly stylised prose to his fiction have been under-represented. This volume seeks to redress this imbalance by exploring the workings of Dickens's style, that is, its inner mechanisms and its outward effects. The chapters demonstrate that the attention of the critic may be rewardingly directed towards the way Dickens writes inseparably from what he writes about.

Dickens looks at the world aslant, and his innovative, narrative style responds to and enables that vision. His sharp observations, combined with his fanciful reimaginings, are registered by his style. It is through style, by its verbal surprises, its arresting effects, that we are made to look

I

again at what we thought we knew: at places, characters, behaviours, speech patterns, turns of event, at our own sympathies and expectations. Among the most prominent transformational aspects of his writing is his attention-grabbing use of figurative language, often introduced by the promising 'as if', whereupon a bravura act of imagination ensues, unearthing unexpected connections or similarities. Just as noticeable is his habit of anthropomorphism, of bestowing life upon inanimate objects, often by means of as little as an ambivalent adjective or two ('blunt, honest piece of furniture' [*SB*, 177], 'rebellious poker' [*PP*, 35, 537]), and, equally, the converse move of subtracting life from his characters, with a deadening adjective or simile. Dreamlike effects often come upon Dickens's prose when, as he habitually does, he moves into blank-verse rhythms, into repetitions of word or sentence structure, as in the mounting anaphora of his rhetorical sallies, or when he exploits the possibilities of the present tense in long conspicuous passages of it.

So performative a prose has been suspected to operate according to the impulsive, opportunistic forces of comedy, sound and habit, to the detriment of reason and precision. Without doubt, this stylised prose is not self-effacingly subservient to other creative aims. It flaunts itself and makes itself felt as part of the work. Indeed, Dickens's imagination does not exist apart from the style that renders it, for, as Robert Alter has said, style's 'unique enchantments' are 'a privileged vehicle of insight, even of vision'.[1]

Dickens's insights not only penetrate the world around him, but they also access the contingencies and opportunities of language. Geoffrey Hill, who has written discerningly on the responsibilities of a literary style and the circumstances that may bear upon it, has suggested that, 'The more gifted the writer the more alert he is to the gifts, the things given or given up, the *données*, of language itself', and Dickens's gifts certainly include a generous receptivity to the treasures and pleasures of a bountiful language.[2] He is alert to the latent meanings in words, to buried etymologies that prompt, in an instant, a lively wordplay that activates a second comic or subterranean chain of thought. His prose is rich with acoustic effects, such as the linkages of alliteration, assonance and internal rhymes, chimes that build connections of their own amid the representation of a fragmented reality. The gifts of language go far beyond the abundance of near-synonyms for many words, but they include that, and one aspect of Dickens's style is his ability to run through a set of lexical variations for a single thing or trait. His recognition of language's abundant provision is matched by Major Bagstock, in *Dombey and Son* (1846–8), when he calls his 'Native' servant 'so many new names as must have given him great occasion to marvel at the resources of the English language' – an observation that comes just as his author is about to turn out yet another phrase for Carker's smile: his 'dental treasures' (*DS*, 26, 363).

The accounts of Dickens's style in this volume consider the large-scale, self-advertising representational effects, such as conspicuous figurations and rhetorical structures, and they take us beyond those into the more mysterious intricacies of his prose, into the submerged logic of his verbal play, which have not always been so apparent to critics. Early claims about the looseness of Dickens's prose,[3] or longer lasting claims about its irregularity and its disproportion[4] can conceal the attributes of verbal care and precision, the judicious selection of the apposite word, the sharp ear for nuance and polysemy that also characterise his writing. Passages of fine lexical ingenuity are the surest sign that Dickens's achievement does not lie in some imagined realm of meaning existing prior to, or beyond, the verbal expression, but that it is located in the verbal, stylised writing itself. Style, for Dickens, does not somehow come subsequently to meaning, as if it is just a set of after-effects. It participates in, produces and performs meaning.

The best sense we get of the way Dickens conceived of his own verbal style – alongside the prefaces and the letters of advice to his journals' contributors – is in his fiction, and with special prominence in the short essays and papers of the 1850s and 1860s, often stylistic cameos in themselves. There, Dickens frequently seeks out dramatically innovative perspectives on the familiar world both to incite and to represent his heightened style.

The well-known example of Dickens's fanciful invention in *Hard Times* (1854), where the great factories of industrial Coketown are seen as 'Fairy palaces', is cast as the perspective of rail passengers: 'the travellers by express-train said so' (*HT*, 1, 10, 84). The link between train travel and Dickens's imaginative style is played out in full his 1851 essay, 'A Flight', which describes the experience of travelling by train from London to Paris (with a ferry connection between Folkestone and Boulogne), a route then newly passable in eleven hours.[5]

Dickens adapts his style to the defamiliarising effects of train travel, working up a flexible syntax and an inventive grammar that can keep pace with the rapidity of his journey and the strangely visionary perspectives it affords:

> Now a wood, now a bridge, now a landscape, now a cutting, now a – Bang!
> a single-barrelled Station – there was a cricket-match somewhere with two

white tents, and then four flying cows, then turnips – now, the wires of
the electric telegraph are all alive, and spin, and blur their edges, and go
up and down, and make the intervals between each other most irregular:
contracting and expanding in the strangest manner. Now we slacken. With
a screwing, and a grinding, and a smell of water thrown on ashes, now we
stop! ('A Flight', *Journalism*, III, 29)

The energetic and uneven prose meets a specific representational need, as
the syntax itself contracts and expands in irregular intervals and the rhythmical last sentence grinds to a halt, like the steam engine. But with its syntactical and grammatical irregularities, its temporal confusions and shifts of
tense, its rhythms, its clipped sentences, its combination of detailed realism
and hallucinatory vision ('four flying cows'), its odd collocations ('then turnips'), this is Dickensian prose with many of its long-practised habits.

In its last paragraph, the essay provides its clearest indication that it
has been not only an expression of Dickens's style, but a dramatised, con-
ceptualised representation of it. Dickens's narrative persona retires for the
night, 'blessing the South-Eastern Company for realising *The Arabian
Nights* in these prose days, murmuring, as I wing my idle flight into the
land of dreams' ('A Flight', 35). The wonderful strangeness of the Arabian
Nights, frequent paradigm of Dickens's imaginative practices, is made real
by the estranging, unsettling experience of rapid locomotion. The pun on
'prose' days – plain and commonplace, but hinting at a piece of writing –
underscores the analogy, as the pun of the tale's title, 'A Flight', is realised:
at once a mode of rapid transportation and an imaginative flight of fancy,
such as Dickens's flexible style can effect.

The imaginative, transformational effects of Dickens's visionary style
are again prominent in his essay on 'Chatham Dockyard', where they
are all the more conspicuous amid the grim, industrial conditions of the
shipbuilders' yard.[6] In the sketch, published in the second series of *The
Uncommercial Traveller* (1868), Dickens's fanciful narration tends to tame,
to prettify and to subdue the massive machinery at work in the construction of a warship. The powerful machine that cuts and shapes the iron is
thought to be an 'obedient monster' ('Chatham Dockyard', *Journalism*,
IV, 292). The wood-cutting machines that blow woodshavings into the
air around them are 'large mangles with a swarm of butterflies hovering
over them' ('Chatham Dockyard', 293). The machine that picks up the
logs is recast, recalling a circus or pantomime stage prop,[7] as a 'Chinese
Enchanter's Car'. Under the influence of Dickens's style, no less than the
Traveller's idle musings, the industrial dockyard is 'Quite a pastoral scene'
('Chatham Dockyard', 295).

As often happens in Dickens's shorter pieces, the essay conceives of its characteristic, transformational style as the product of a dreamy, out-of-the-ordinary mental state – in this case 'a state of blissful indolence':

> Sauntering among the ropemaking, I am spun into a state of blissful indolence, wherein my rope of life seems to be so untwisted by the process as that I can see back to very early days indeed, when my bad dreams – they were frightful, though my more mature understanding has never made out why – were of an interminable sort of ropemaking, with long minute filaments for strands, which, when they were spun home together close to my eyes, occasioned screaming. ('Chatham Dockyard', 295)

Dickens's style romanticises the world, and it entertains, but its strangeness can also be disturbing. Here, as elsewhere, blissful indolence coexists with the terrors of childhood, or opens up access to them. Childhood fears attend characters from Oliver Twist, through Smike, Little Nell and Paul Dombey, to David Copperfield and Pip, but they are as often brought into the narrative style itself, as Dickens's descriptions combine the 'mature understanding' of the adult with the instinctive, unaccountable fears of the child. Many critics have noticed the proximity of Dickens's visionary mode to some form of psychological disturbance, in a line of reading inaugurated by G. H. Lewes's severe critique of the 'vividness of imagination approaching so closely to hallucination' in Dickens's writing, where '*revived* images have the vividness of sensations'.[8]

Such effects are products of style in this passage. Dickens sustains the overlaid image of ropemaking, opportunistically turning it to different ends: moving it into the figuration of metaphor and on to an actual occurrence of his remembered dream. The ropemaking is not so much a well-wrought, bounded metaphor as an image, vivid to the author's mind, in which he apprehends and half-realises latent metaphorical possibilities. It is a feature of Dickens's style that owes much to the poetic faculty by which, contrary to ordinary expectations, words precede and impel the ideas. D. W. Harding once wrote of this quality in Shakespeare, where 'half-activated images … gain their effect through not being brought to the full definition of an exact metaphor'.[9] Something similar happens in Dickens's image of ropemaking here. His sentences are characteristic in their precise verbal agility, for it is the quick play on 'spun' – joining ropemaking and head-spinning confusion – that triggers the metaphor of his rope of life. Later, the impersonal voice of the grammatically isolated phrase 'occasioned screaming' deftly suggests that the strands, which are disturbingly spun home, rather than comfortingly home-spun, recall at once the lively fear of his earlier self and his safe distance from it now. It strikes a balance between immediate experience and safe recollection that is characteristic of his first-person narratives.

Dickens knew that the series of imaginative recreations in his sketch of Chatham Dockyard amounted to an investigation into his habitual transformational mode of writing. He hints as much to his readers when he mentions the Chinese Enchanter's Car:

> When I was a child (the Yard being then familiar to me) I used to think that I should like to play at Chinese Enchanter, and to have that apparatus placed at my disposal for the purpose by a beneficent country. I still think that I should rather like to try the effect of writing a book in it. ('Chatham Dockyard', 295)

Given that style is inseparable from Dickens's artistic vision, it is surprising how often criticism, throughout the history of Dickens scholarship, deems it peripheral or considers it a matter of technique detachable from other concerns. One reason for this is the elusive, evasive nature of style as a critical concept. It is often assumed that style is an aspect of writing that is superadded to the plain sense of a passage, and yet it is far from clear that these two things can ever be separated. Style may be what distinguishes a particular writer or what any number of writers can strive to obtain. It may be a property of the writing – features of grammar, syntax and vocabulary – or the product of reading, identifiable only through recurrent usage. It may draw attention to itself by its idiosyncrasy or it may be precisely that aspect of writing that goes unnoticed because of its familiarity. For Dickens's first readers, style was as likely to be an objective standard of correct writing, teachable and transferable, as otherwise, whereas more recent accounts regard style as a mark of individuality, perhaps instinctive as well as distinctive. This volume opens out some of the complications of style as a concept, as the essays assess the handling of language, grammar, syntax and rhetoric that seems distinctively, identifiably, Dickens's.

A legacy of the conceptual separation of style from other aspects of literary achievement has been a long trend of reading it as part of a critical category of its own. This is true, as I have said, of early concerns that Dickens's prose contravenes agreed norms of correctness, deriving from eighteenth-century ideals of rhetorical prose. It was against such criticisms that John Forster, among others, defended Dickens. The idea that style is a formal feature set apart from the ideological and other involvements of Dickens's fiction has persisted. George Orwell's influential essay on

Dickens treats his ideology separately from his style. He focuses on the paraphraseable, translatable meaning of the fiction, until the essay moves onto more aesthetic concerns in its final section, in what looks like an awkward shuffle: 'I have been discussing Dickens simply in terms of his "message", and almost ignoring his literary qualities', perpetuating the sense that style has little to do with the purposive, ideological work of a novel.[10] In 1970, G. L. Brook's useful study of Dickens's style investigated his language largely in isolation from other creative inclinations.[11] Brook's study recasts some of the early complaints against Dickens's writing when it laments his lack of restraint and the author's illusion-defeating intrusions into his fiction.[12]

Attention to Dickens's style has not been prominent in academic criticism in recent years. Scholarship has tended to focus on Dickens's relation to culture: to the ideological biases and blinds of his own culture, to Victorian material and popular cultures, and to mass culture today. It has often been driven by ideological concerns in its interest in his representations of women, the home, slavery and empire or in his perceived buttressing of middle-class values. It has demonstrated his remarkable investment in and studied depiction of a minutely realised material culture. And it has investigated his continuing presence as a cultural phenomenon, first in his own day and then in the Dickens 'industry' of the twentieth and twenty-first centuries.[13] Notwithstanding the conceptual complexity and value of many of these approaches, Dickens's style of writing has rarely been of the first importance.

When critics have attended to Dickens's style, the tendency has been to read it as being at odds with the essential meaning of his work. It is thought to betray the contradictions or tensions in his ideology, which he is able to resist more deliberatively in other aspects of his writing, such as plotting and characterisation, which are seen to be less instinctive. Orwell's essay contains an early version of this kind of response. He observes that, 'The outstanding, unmistakable mark of Dickens's writing is the *unnecessary detail*', and it is the apparently superfluous nature of the detail that causes a problem for Orwell's interest in the political purposes of fiction.[14]

For Orwell, style could seem superfluous and, strictly speaking, 'irrelevant' as far as the political and moral commitments of a work were concerned.[15] Other critics have seen it to be more actively troublesome. Marxist readings in the 1960s and 1970s found in Dickens's fiction contradictions and self-contestations that were judged creative, productive responses to the contradictions of nineteenth-century ideology. Often more attuned to structure (and to narrative or plot) than to style, such accounts found in the sum total of Dickens's fiction, especially in their habits of excess and unruliness, which are as evident in his style as elsewhere, points of welcome resistance to the dominant ideologies of the nineteenth century.

This habit of mind took a more doubtful, mistrustful turn in later criticism – in the heyday of deconstructive readings of Dickens and, still, in the ongoing ideological critiques of his fiction. In many of these accounts, the uncontrolled energies of the novels, which includes their style, unsettle and resist the texts' attempts to bolster bourgeois ideology. Steven Connor has drawn attention to the way in which the 'unbounded "energetics" of Dickens's writing' compromise various normative Victorian power relations, even though the narrative may also replicate official structures or economies: 'the excessiveness of Dickens's writing ... manifests itself in the problematic overflowing of categories, the blurring of boundaries, and the promiscuous commingling of what official ideologies wish to promote as naturally distinct.'[16] The excessive, anarchic principle of Dickens's fiction disturbs the orthodoxies that his fiction is otherwise thought to reinforce.[17] For such critics, style is a rogue element, confounding Dickens's polemical purposes. Their accounts respond to the waywardness of his style, such characteristics as its pleasure in superfluous detail, its digressions and its uncontrolled energies, and they find that these energies complicate the ideological intentions of the fiction.

Dickens's narratives are frequently confronted by embodiments of their own unruly energies. One example of this is his essay 'Gone Astray', written for *Household Words* in 1853.[18] The nine- or ten-year-old Dickens (supposedly) is lost in London, and he wanders around aimlessly, and occasionally fearfully, marvelling at the great city. Recounted from the perspective of the forty-year-old man, the essay thematises aspects of Dickens's characteristic visionary mode, as it conflates innocence and wonder with experience and cynicism.[19] As the boy anticipates various careers – joining the army as a drummer, becoming a chimney sweep or seeking his fortune like Dick Whittington – the essay sets the pleasures of purpose over against the attractions of digression, impulses of both plot and style throughout Dickens's career. This is a narrative in search of a plot, then, when the boy, sitting down to eat a small German sausage while he anticipates his next steps, encounters, all of a sudden, 'a dog with his ears cocked':

> He was a black dog, with a bit of white over one eye, and bits of white and tan in his paws, and he wanted to play – frisking about me, rubbing his nose against me, dodging at me sideways, shaking his head and pretending

to run away backwards, and making himself good-naturedly ridiculous, as if he had no consideration for himself, but wanted to raise my spirits. ('Gone Astray', *Journalism*, III, 158–9)

The playful energies of the dog call up the playful energies of Dickens's prose, in the run of present participles, 'frisking', 'rubbing', 'dodging' and so on, which energises the writing, even as it creates a digression. So, too, the language knowingly bestows upon the dog unexpectedly human characteristics: that he can 'pretend' to do anything, or that he has the complexity of character to be 'good-naturedly ridiculous'.

The boy believes that 'things were coming right' and that with the dog by his side he would recover his situation, for the dog 'would help me seek my fortune'.

> I considered by what name I should call him. I thought Merrychance would be an expressive name, under the circumstances; and I was elated, I recollect, by inventing such a good one, when Merrychance began to growl at me in a most ferocious manner.
>
> I wondered he was not ashamed of himself, but he didn't care for that; on the contrary he growled a good deal more. With his mouth watering, and his eyes glistening, and his nose in a very damp state, and his head very much on one side, he sidled out on the pavement in a threatening manner and growled at me, until he suddenly made a snap at the small German, tore it out of my hand, and went off with it. He never came back to help me seek my fortune. From that hour to the present, when I am forty years of age, I have never seen my faithful Merrychance again. ('Gone Astray', 159)

Style misbehaves like this. It has a life of its own, and it runs away with itself under its own impulses. It refuses to be constrained by the intended plot. Style slips the leash. Some critics have found it threatening, too, for all its good-natured appearance and its attempts to raise our spirits. Dickens's short story itself worries that the cheerful, playful, childlike vision is only a fiction; that the brisk realities of life may be darker and more threatening (although with exact comic effect the last epithet, 'faithful', resists complete disabusement). Even the dog's name, Merrychance, signals the anxiety in much of Dickens's later fiction that happy accident might be only a product of irresponsible imagination, not of lived reality.

Dickens's figurative language is particularly prone to this kind of reading. *Hard Times* is the *locus classicus* for ideological suspicion of Dickens's unruly metaphorical style. For example, in an influential discussion of that novel, Catherine Gallagher writes that metaphors, 'especially when they attempt to disguise an ugly reality, are useless even pernicious things'.[20] In an insightful introduction to the novel, Kate Flint considers the 'double movement at work in [its] rhetoric'.[21] She writes that Dickens's 'portrayal of the working classes and their environment' is not 'immune to his own rhetorical effects' and goes on to indicate that he 'cannot quite escape from the habits of his own transformative imagination, turning the town into a giant-inhabited fairy-land'.[22] Implicit in this vocabulary is a sense that Dickens's polemical intentions are compromised (albeit knowingly) by his writing, for they are not 'immune to' or able to 'escape from' the habits of his metaphor-making.

Despite the critical suspicion, Dickens was aware that his transformative effects, such as those in the 'Chatham Dockyard' piece, were not always innocent or harmless. He knew that fictional illusions had the potential to unfit his readers for real life. To put it bluntly, wandering around the heavy machinery of a Victorian dockyard in a state of blissful indolence could be dangerous:

> Having been torn to pieces (in imagination) by the steam circular saws, perpendicular saws, horizontal saws, and saws of eccentric action, I come to the sauntering part of my expedition, and consequently to the core of my Uncommercial pursuits. ('Chatham Dockyard', 294)

Dickens's imagination conjures up the fatal violence of which the machinery is capable, and his prose carries the threat into his imaginative pursuits, as 'saw' resounds in 'sauntering'. Dickens's ear hears the blades despite the daydreaming that seems to quieten them, for the threat echoes through the passage: 'torn', 'saw', 'core'. Dickens's transformative style may seem to take the sting out of a threatening world, but he knew as well as his critics that this might only be a trick of the mind, a trick of the text.

The emphasis in most of the critical accounts I have been discussing is on the independent life of Dickens's style, on its divergence from the sense-making functions of his fiction. Certainly Dickens's style is able and often willing to run away from meaning, to fail to perform as required. But that this is not the whole case is best illustrated by one further example.

Eight months after writing that he would 'never see his faithful Merrychance again', Dickens and his readers might be permitted a double-take as the second and third installments of *Hard Times* featured a dog called Merrylegs. Comprising one of the lesser known doubles in Dickens's fiction, the second dog is surprisingly like the first. Like Merrychance, Merrylegs runs away. The novel sustains a question for most of its length about whether we are likely to see him again – indeed whether he will prove to be faithful Merrylegs.

Merrylegs is the dog belonging to Sissy Jupe's father, the failing circus performer. Both disappear early in the novel. Although it is feared that Sissy has been deserted, she never gives up hope that they will return. An uncertainty hangs over Signor Jupe and Merrylegs equally throughout the book. We wonder whether Sissy's hope for their homecoming is misplaced or to be vindicated, whether the outcome will prove or defy the possible pun on her name: Sissy Dupe.

Unlike Merrychance, Merrylegs comes back. In the penultimate chapter we learn that he catches up with the circus in Chester, though the dog's appearance without his master reveals that Jupe has died, leaving unresolved the question of whether he selfishly abandoned his daughter or took himself off to avoid dragging her down with him. Sleary, the circus-master, sees in this return a parable about the supremacy of love over calculation, which is also an ethical principle at the heart of the novel.

The episode not only balances up the public record of Dickens's thoughts about dogs, but it also speaks to another set of possibilities for the way in which his style behaves. The anarchic, disruptive vitality of Merrylegs, and of style, can be brought to heel. The performative energies of Dickens's style (like those of Merrylegs) need not be thought of as wayward or contradictory; they can work in conjunction with the plot and embody and reinforce the novel's central values.

Dickens's style frequently, typically, cooperates with his intentions. In most of his writing, certainly at his best, style is enlisted to perform meaning. Its effects are involved in the total sense of a passage. My examples so far have already attested to the participation of local stylistic effects in larger meanings, showing that Dickens often marshals attributes of his style – his figurative language, his wordplay, his sound effects – to the immediate thematic ends of each fiction.

This is not to say that the effects are always proportionate to the aims, nor is it to deny that style can have an independent life, but it is to say that Dickens's style is meaningful and pertinent, more frequently than criticism tends to grant. It may still be wayward and unruly at times. It may retain a fondness for superfluous detail, for playful digression, for flights of metaphorical fancy, but these effects are, at least as often as not, productive and knowing. They also coexist with other qualities: Dickens's flexible, multifaceted style, can also be chastened, plain, subtle, precise.

It has been suggested that Dickens's style coincides with his broader intentions to a greater degree in his later fiction. S. J. Newman's *Dickens at Play* (1981) tracks the work of style from *Sketches by Boz*, where it emits 'thematically irrelevant imaginative spasms', to *Martin Chuzzlewit* (1843–4), which he regards as Dickens's finest comic novel, where the author's 'art participates in the condition it describes', namely that real life is 'mercurial and improvisational' (to borrow Lionel Trilling's phrase).[23] The chapters in this volume do not insist on a developmental narrative of Dickens's style but seek to take the measure of Dickens's variously playful and productive signature prose wherever it is found. His style, diverse and flexible all along, is shown to be significantly involved in his work's total effects from the start. Garrett Stewart's recognition in his lastingly valuable study, *Dickens and the Trials of Imagination* (1974), that there are in Dickens's style 'small moments of almost impossible insight and rightness … sudden illuminations that take our breath away [which] frequently collapse into a single disclosure the largest themes of their books', is not confined to the late novels.[24]

Reading style in this way across Dickens's writing career does not, and should not, imply a turn away from politics, ideology, history or culture. Indeed, a full account of these forces in Dickens's fiction must address his style, because style itself is responsive (or resistant) to the circumstances of the time. For example, in his study of Dickens's rhetorical prose in *The Art of Eloquence: Byron, Dickens, Tennyson, Joyce* (2008), Matthew Bevis demonstrates how often style is complicit in the political responsibilities of the fiction, arguing that critical attempts to separate Dickens's lively imagination from political engagement are misplaced. There are occasions when the writing seems to deflect its own political intentions. The vague generalities of the satire on the Circumlocution Office, for example, in *Little Dorrit* (1855–7) compromise the political message: 'the exaggerated, enjoyable forcefulness of the writing weakens the force of the political statement.'[25] But Bevis shows how often Dickens 'brings the workings of his imagination to bear on his socio-political enquiries' and that even in *Little Dorrit* his writing 'practices a reflective and potentially enabling politics from within the very exaggerations of its style'.[26] Dickens assimilated forms of political debate and reportage into his prose, which enabled an astute, thoughtful and politically responsible circumspection on his part.

Similarly, the chapters that follow here show that Dickens's style was inflected by numerous nineteenth-century ideas and debates, ranging through such topics as time, ghosts, historiography, national diction, grand narratives of creation and apocalypse from geology and theology, and historical arguments about literary style itself. Dickens himself believed his mode of writing was adapted to the needs of his generation. He claimed that the 'fanciful treatment' of his subjects was just what was required 'in these times, when the tendency is to be frightfully literal and catalogue-like'.[27]

Even this obliquely, style could be historically contingent. The metaphorical transformations in Dickens's novels could bring imaginative relief to an industrial world that was seen to be stiflingly mechanical. This interconnection of aesthetics and ethics is why Arthur Quiller-Couch's claim that the merit of Dickens's writing is ethical, rather than stylistic, is not as unpromising for a volume on Dickens's style as it might at first appear. He argues that Dickens's supreme achievement is his spirit of charity. This is his value:

> It is Charity; the inestimable gift of Charity that Dickens flings over all things as his magic mantle: so that, whether there be prophecies, they shall fail; whether there be tongues, they shall cease; whether there be knowledge, it shall vanish away; and whether there be little critics tormented about Dickens' style, in the folds of that mantle they shall be folded and hushed.[28]

Quiller-Couch was writing in the wake of the rhetoricians and grammarians early in the twentieth century who found fault with Dickens for his departures from a high style, and in fact he goes on to lay out a case, as well, for the merits of Dickens's prose style. But it is the combined argument of the chapters in this volume that this style is not a separate matter from the inestimable gift of charity that Dickens's fiction bestows or, more pressingly, from any other of its ethical or representational aims.

A few examples will show the features of Dickens's style turned to meaningful, thematic ends, and they will also serve to introduce recurrent themes of the chapters in this volume.

There was little that called upon as much of Dickens's stylistic repertoire as did his scenes of dying. Some of his habitual stylistic manoeuvres are enlisted in the face of death. He makes use of blank verse rhythm, prose rhymes, adjectives that animate or deanimate their nouns, shifts of tense, metastasis, ellipsis and pronomial alterations.[29] Such ingenuity is necessary because the fact of death is an affront to language's capacity of representation: for example, when we hesitate between past and present tenses when speaking of a recently deceased friend, or struggle for the right pronoun, like Pip, who, returning to the forge upon the death of Mrs Joe, 'began to wonder in what part of the house it – she – my sister – was' (*GE*, II, 16, 278).

The demands placed upon Dickens's writing by the proximity of death, and his style's ability to rise to its challenges, are readily evident in the short piece, 'A December Vision' (1850), written for *Household Words*.[30]

Dickens's narrative is gifted, or cursed, with a vision of the spirit of death. The spirit's inexorable work finds its stylistic keynote in a passage that tends towards regular rhythm and enlists rhyme for its purposes:

> It had its work appointed; it inexorably did what was appointed to it to do; and neither sped nor slackened. Called to, it went on unmoved, and did not come. Besought, by some who felt that it was drawing near, to change its course, it turned its shaded face upon them, even while they cried, and they were dumb. ('A December Vision', *Journalism*, II, 306)

Here, the metrical regularity of the prose is suited to the spirit of death that 'neither sped nor slackened'. The predictability of the metre meets the inevitability of death, as it 'went on unmoved', where there is an unobtrusive pun on 'unmoved', indicating that death is not deflected from its course but also that it must seem heartless and uncaring.

Dickens makes extensive use of rhyme throughout this vision, whether in unexpected internal rhymes that indicate the chancy, unexpectedness of death or predictable end rhymes that reflect its inevitable, inexorable progress. Both are evident here: 'to do' is suddenly echoed in 'called to', and the last word of 'and did not come' is rhymed immediately and surprisingly with 'some', before the sound is taken up into the determined rhythm of the line to end rhyme, as if inevitably, with 'and they were dumb'.

These acoustic effects are extended throughout the piece, to the degree that Dickens cannot feasibly be thought unwitting of them, and they combine with other verbal tricks:

> But, whether the beholder of its face were, now a King, or now a labourer, now a Queen, or now a seamstress; let the hand it palsied be on the sceptre, or the plough, or yet too small and nerveless to grasp anything: the Spirit never paused in its appointed work, and, sooner, or later, turned its impartial face on all. ('A December Vision', 307)

Here, too, Dickens marshals the unexpectedness of prose rhyme, as when the repeated 'now' is echoed in 'plough' to match the unexpectedness of death, while rhyme's ability to fall in with the rhythm of the passage suggests the inevitable sweep of death, as 'small' is end-rhymed with 'all'. The brutal equality of death afflicts even those whose hands are 'too small and nerveless' – not 'nervous', though there is reason for trepidation, as the prose invites us to hear the near homophone – 'to grasp anything', with its latent figurative suggestion of the baffling incomprehensibility of death.

And yet, these rhythms and rhymes also play out, amid the immediate affliction and surprise of death, the narrative's loftier perspective that acknowledges its inevitability. Although death triumphs across the city and 'in the proudest and most boastful places, most of all', the cumulative effect of the rhymes, of 'most' and 'boast', or more protractedly of 'boastful' and 'most of all', and another rhyme in 'I saw innumerable hosts fore-doomed', is to suggest that a replicating pattern can be discerned in death's operations. The unpredictability yields to a larger, graspable pattern.

In the province of death, Dickens's stylistic ingenuity is liable to turn towards one of his characteristic modes: sentimentality. Critics have long found the sentimental passages one of the most disconcerting or faintly embarrassing aspects of Dickens's style. Such scenes as the death of Little Nell or Paul Dombey Jnr. are thought to be excessive and insincerely calculated to coerce emotional responses from their readers. In such critical accounts, the prose is considered loose and overwritten; as, for example, H. M. Daleski's judgement that the death of Paul Dombey shows 'a preoccupation ... with emotion for its own sake that betrays itself in an imprecision of detail in the description'.[31] There has been an equally long tradition, starting with some of Dickens's first readers, of considering these passages as among his most genuinely moving, and some critics have attempted to do justice to these responses.[32] Any such attempt must include a demonstration of the full range of the effects of Dickens's sentimental style by refusing to overlook as 'merely sentimental' prose which is thoughtfully and feelingly adapted to the occasion.

G. L. Brook singles out the description in *Nicholas Nickleby* (1838–9) of Newgate Prison, site of public executions, as an instance of Dickens's overly sentimental style, of his 'lack of restraint' and of his making 'too strong an appeal to the emotions':[33]

> There, at the very core of London, in the heart of its business and animation, in the midst of a whirl of noise and motion: stemming as it were the giant currents of life that flow ceaselessly on from different quarters and meet beneath its walls: stands Newgate; and in that crowded street on which it frowns so darkly – within a few feet of the squalid tottering houses – upon the very spot on which the venders of soup and fish and damaged fruit are now plying their trades – scores of human beings, amidst a roar of sounds to which even the tumult of a great city is as nothing, four, six, or eight strong men at a time, have been hurried violently and swiftly from the world, when the scene has been rendered frightful with excess of human life; when curious eyes have glared from casement, and house-top, and wall and pillar; and when, in the mass of white and upturned faces, the dying wretch, in his all-comprehensive look of agony, has met not one – not one – that bore the impress of pity or compassion. (*NN*, 4, 29–30)

Brook observes: 'The idea of a public execution is horrible enough without any heightening of effects, and probably many readers will feel that [this] vivid description of Newgate would have been more, and not less, effective without the emotional repetition in the last two lines.'[34] And yet, this passage forestalls, exactly and sympathetically, its deepest regret. Its lament is that though these men are 'hurried violently and swiftly from the world' in front of many onlookers, even this does not arrest the uncaring, onrushing speed of urban life, which is conveyed through the heightened style of incremental description, the parallelism of the 'when' clauses, and impelled by the internal rhymes of 'score', 'roar' and 'four'. As Philip Davis has shown, Victorian sentimental prose often calls a halt to the inexorable progress of its own medium in a way that focuses attention on the unproclaimed pains of the ordinary life it describes.[35] Here, the sentimental repetition of 'not one – not one' enacts precisely the desired effect. It punctuates the rapid flow of the sentence in order to concentrate attention upon the horrors in its midst. It is at once a rhetorical effect and a disavowal of rhetoric, reminding us that style can draw attention to itself and yet might equally be heedlessly passed over as a typical trait. The wry choice to repeat the words 'not one', so that they are written not once, calls attention to the verbal artistry, and since it might require a reader to draw back from the immediate concern of the passage to notice it, the sentimental prose tests the reader's own response to the pathetic scene. Nor should the effect of the 'all-comprehensive look of agony' be missed, for by this touch the description has become the dying man's vision, and, by a half-heard pun on 'all-comprehensive', what he comprehends, as if in a moment of final illumination, and we realise we have been drawn into his vision and his understanding. Dickens's sentimental style, here as often elsewhere, itself aims to comprehend, in both senses, the stirring scene; it grapples with its significance and seeks to calibrate as well as to effect the due emotional response.

One other thing that happens here is that the repetition of 'not one' calls up a rhetorical, human voice out of the flattened tone, or the regular rhythm, of the written prose. It is a beseeching human voice. Dickens has a remarkable sensitivity to patterns of speech, a sharp ear for idiolects whether they be those of politicians or the London poor, and these voices transfer into his writing, increasingly blending with the narrative voice, into (as Ian Watt and Robert Golding have shown)[36] a distinctive oral style, a style of writing so flexible that it can accommodate the mannered voices of innumerable characters, without ceasing to be distinctively itself. Golding identifies the potency and resourcefulness of this style in its most versatile forms from the 1850s onwards: 'The ensuing all-pervasive, multi-functional, highly expressive rhetorical mode proved to be of exceeding flexibility, subtlety and dramatic expressiveness. It now conveyed with far greater precision and concentration biting satire, gentle irony or finer shades of feeling.'[37]

The many voices that are accommodated in Dickens's fiction and even in his own narrative voice have been regularly approached through Bakhtin's term, 'heteroglossia' – the multi-vocal style of writing that keeps a text open to rival interpretations. And yet the frequent proximity of Dickens's narration to the rhythms and devices of speech enables it to play host to a wider range of ancillary, meaningful effects than has sometimes been accounted for. These include his fondness for apostrophe, often-intrusive interjections in a voice that his readers took for his own, and, more sophisticatedly, the techniques associated with his handling of reported speech and free indirect style.

Although Bakhtin's discussion has been taken as paradigmatic of the multi-voiced quality of novels – partly because he offers it as such – his examples show Dickens turning the peculiarly sophisticated oral quality of his own style to the particular needs of his satire in *Little Dorrit*.[38] All the examples Bakhtin gives relate to Merdle and the aristocratic Barnacles, where Dickens ventriloquises public sentiment in order to point up its hypocrisy and to puncture its cant. Consider Bakhtin's first example:[39]

> The conference was held at four or five o'clock in the afternoon, when all the region of Harley Street, Cavendish Square, was resonant of carriage-wheels and double-knocks. It had reached this point when Mr. Merdle came home, from his daily occupation of causing the British name to be more and more respected in all parts of the civilised globe, capable of the appreciation of world-wide commercial enterprise and gigantic combinations of skill and capital. For, though nobody knew with the least precision what Mr. Merdle's business was, except that it was to coin money, these were the terms in which everybody defined it on all ceremonious occasions, and which it was the last new polite reading of the parable of the camel and the needle's eye to accept without enquiry. (*LD*, 1, 33, 386)

This is an example of Dickens's blurring of free indirect style and reported speech. His tendency to mimic the pompous rhetoric of some of his characters, or some parts of society, is recast as reported speech by the specific attribution, after the fact, of the words to their originators, however vaguely they are identified: 'these were the terms in which everybody defined it on all ceremonious occasions.' What is involved in the slide from free indirect style to reported speech is a greater distancing of the

authorial viewpoint from the public rhetoric. It exacts a judgement on
what is now understood to be not merely pomposity but hypocrisy, and
this is a matter of technique and style that is ethically charged in the satiric
presentation of Merdle and his set. With remarkable frequency, the tricks
of style serve the sense of the writing.

The chapters that follow consider one or more aspects of Dickens's style.
At times philosophical and theoretical, they all read style closely, combining conceptual thinking with alert readings of the enjoyable operations
of these features in his prose. It is precisely this plural methodology that
unites the chapters. The aim is determinedly not that an attention to 'style'
should supplant historical or political enquiry but that such readings will
consider these interests inseparably from the textures of Dickens's prose.
The collection argues that for any writer, but for Dickens especially, close
attention to the intricate operations of style will productively underpin
critical enquiry.

    In the first chapter, John Bowen opens out some of the conceptual dif-
ficulties facing the critic of style by looking at that strangely ubiquitous
Dickensian prop: the umbrella. Umbrellas pop up throughout Dickens's
career, from his first published fiction, 'Mr Minns and his Cousin' (1833),
throughout his novels – *The Old Curiosity Shop* (1840–1) and *Martin
Chuzzlewit* are discussed here – and into the late essay 'Please to Leave
Your Umbrella' (1858). The chapter shows that they have 'a close affinity with the question of style' and teases out their shared characteristics.
They are shown to inspire passages of stylistic verve, as well as embodying
questions about the way style operates. As John Bowen puts it, bravura
moments of writing about umbrellas 'act as both brilliant feats of style in
themselves and repeated testings both of the limits and internal regularities of style and of the conceptual and critical tools that we use to get a
handle on it'. In particular, the curious self-divisions of umbrellas (essen-
tial/superfluous, present/absent, aggressive/defensive) are replicated in the
displays of style that they prompt. These self-divisions remind us of the
paradox that Dickens's style is multiple and contradictory, while always
still itself. As such, this first chapter goes to show that while this volume
describes hallmarks of Dickens's style, building a practical and detailed
account of it, nevertheless his style, or his styles, can at the same time
remain multiple, elusive and resistant to definition.

    As his imaginative preoccupation with umbrellas suggests, Dickens was
fascinated by things, by the stuff of everyday life. These things are sometimes emblematic, and John Bowen's focus on umbrellas as an emblem

of Dickens's style is followed by Matthew Bevis's interest in clocks and watches as 'emblems of – and enquiries into – the committed vagrancy of his own style'. This chapter reminds us that the vagaries of time are also sources of humour for Dickens, and it builds a case for the significance of his carefully timed prose in a way that only close attention to the style of Dickens's writing about time and clocks across several occasions can achieve. It looks at instances spanning Dickens's career but has special regard for *A Christmas Carol* (1843), *Dombey and Son* and *Great Expectations* (1860–1). It shows that Dickens was repeatedly drawn to the comic possibilities of finding time out of joint.

The timing of Dickens's prose is one of his style's most delicate responses to the circumstances of his age and, more privately, of individual experience. Robert Douglas-Fairhurst's chapter considers the timing that is intrinsic to Dickens's rhythms and shows how resourceful this aspect of his writing proves to be. Indeed, Dickens's rhythms are not only affected by both public and private concerns but they can also test one against the other, by setting, for example, the idiosyncrasies of personal experience against the patterns and compulsions of the social group. In this context, the chapter reveals that the critical histories of 'rhythm' and 'style' are shared, as both are seen to involve a tussle between writing as a form of self-revelation and as an expression of social agreement. The chapter focuses especially on Dickens's much discussed (and much maligned) habit of turning to blank verse, which he does most famously in *The Old Curiosity Shop*, but also on many other occasions, especially as his prose confronts scenes of death.

After three chapters that range across Dickens's career and conceptualise style in ways that inform the rest of the volume, there is an approximate chronological drift to the chapters that follow. If Dickens's fiction, and his style, are persistently occupied with the material world, then my own chapter explores their equal fascination with the immaterial world, as well as some curious transitions from one to the other. The chapter considers Dickens's ghost stories and, in particular, his manner of writing them. It investigates those aspects of his style – particularly his tendency to animate the inanimate – that are prominent and thematically central in the ghost stories and suggests that Dickens's finest experiments with the genre, *A Christmas Carol* foremost among them, furnish us with investigations into the mysterious operations of a style that, across his career, seems so intrinsically ghostly.

Clare Pettitt's chapter considers the distortions of time in the Christmas books, especially *The Chimes* (1844), and in other writing of the 1840s.

Moving from *Barnaby Rudge* (1841) through to *A Tale of Two Cities* (1859), it surveys Dickens's thinking and writing about history between these two historical novels and in the 1840s in particular, a decade of international political unrest, as well as of extensive foreign travel on Dickens's part. It shows that Dickens was keenly aware of the difficulties of grasping the historical significance of the present moment and that he searched for a style able to confront these complications. The chapter addresses his use of the historic present tense, which reached its apogee in *Dombey and Son* (1846–8), and shows that it provided a way of writing about events that had not yet settled into the neat chronologies of history.

Freya Johnston's chapter investigates Dickens's habit of exaggeration. She notes that a historical understanding of what it is to exaggerate includes not only magnification or intensification but also accumulation and aggregation, so it is closely related to Dickens's fondness for material detail. It is a style of writing that combines 'vigilant attention to minutiae' and an 'excess of oratory'. As such, her chapter finds in this central aspect of Dickensian style a mode of responding to the world that requires us to move beyond familiar binaries in Dickens criticism between romance and realism, between 'close fidelity' to life and 'rampant infidelity', even between style's prodigality and its precision. Contesting the critical tendency to isolate relevance and excess as irreconcilable principles of style, the chapter recovers Dickens's style of exaggeration from its detractors and shows that a style of exaggeration, of accumulation and enlargement, is an appropriate mode of expression for characters and novels concerned with matters such as poverty and memory – especially significant in *David Copperfield*.

Philip Horne's chapter also comes to focus on *David Copperfield*, because it examines the way that styles of speaking and narrating imply character, and while, as many of the chapters show, the narrative style in most of the novels presents an authorial personality that we might identify as Dickens, it is in the semi-autobiographical novel that this is most demonstrably the case. The chapter offers examples from several novels of how much is at issue in writing the voices of characters and narrator, demonstrating 'the inextricability of style from other matters – of memory, imagination, responsibility and judgement'. It considers the adjustments, at once of style and character, that Dickens made to the interpolated passages of autobiography in *David Copperfield*. Throughout, the chapter shows the importance of the detailed verbal life of Dickens's characterful narration, from intricate wordplay to the use of punctuation.

The personality invested in Dickens's many voices owes much to his expertise in handling diction – particularly his calculated deployment of Latinate and English vernacular registers. Several of the chapters in this volume point to his well-known fondness for Latinate circumlocutions and aggrandisements. Rebekah Scott's chapter, in particular, explores Dickens's use of imported and native words against a backdrop of writing in the popular periodical press, especially in the 1850s, that called for maintaining the supposed purity of the English language. The chapter shows how often the collocational couplings which have long been recognised as a feature of Dickens's style are admixtures of Latinate and English vernacular words, producing an 'aural grotesque'. In particular, her chapter considers Saxon gutturals and growls on the part of Dickens's many sub-literate, sub-vocal speakers and shows that, for Dickens, style is not the same as eloquence and that grunting, mumbling and growling on the part of his characters could constitute a stifled eloquence, a form of stylistic restraint to counterpoint his frequently excessive style.

The guiding authorial presence which Philip Horne detects in *David Copperfield*'s narrative voice is again felt at the level of style in Dickens's next novel, *Bleak House* (1852–3). It announces itself showily in the first chapter through what Jennifer Gribble's chapter identifies as 'the metaphor, metonymy and synecdoche unfolding in its dense figural play'. Her chapter discusses Dickens's figurative style in a fresh reading of the novel's well-known opening chapter. Although, as I have been discussing in this introduction, this aspect of Dickens's writing is often thought to compromise more serious, thoughtful intentions, Jennifer Gribble's discussion demonstrates that Dickens's playful, ostentatiously figurative style is compatible with knowing engagement with contemporary debates in science and theology, 'effectively challenging the view that the world of thought lay beyond his horizon'.

During the last decade of his writing career, Dickens could be identified from a style that was distinctly his own. By 1859, David Masson observed that 'the Public have caught what is called his mannerism or trick' but, far from predictably, in his late fiction Dickens both explores and extends his characteristic style.[40] A shared aspect of the final three chapters in this volume, amid their wider concerns, is a recognition that Dickens's style had become, in Helen Small's words, 'as much an object of attention in its own right as a vehicle for the narrative'. For example, Bharat Tandon's chapter shows that the question of how distinctively personal a writing style can be, raised by Philip Horne and Jennifer Gribble, has an added dimension in the late *Uncommercial Traveller* essays (1861), since there the

Uncommercial's lively reading of London brings him face to face with a city that has long been associated with and transformed by Dickens's style. The chapter identifies a continuity of style between Dickens's fiction and his late journalism which is replicated by the Uncommercial's encounter with a city firmly associated with Dickens's earlier writing. Dickens himself is a part of the city as London has become inseparable from its life in the pages of his novels.

Garrett Stewart's chapter focuses on a single chapter of *Our Mutual Friend* (1864–5) to address two hallmarks of Dickens's writing: the set-piece death scene and the stylistic habit of syllepsis. The remarkably stylised, present-tense chapter in which Rogue Riderhood is carried into the Jolly Six Porters on a bier, on the brink of death, illustrates the breath-taking possibilities of the grammatical and syntactical ambiguities associated with syllepsis in Dickens's prose – although it turns out to be not a death scene but a resurrection, another of Dickens's long-standing pre-occupations, as Riderhood is recalled to life. The usual twinning of literal and figurative signifiers in the rhetorical trope considered here proves a resourceful device in a scene where Riderhood struggles to regain an actual bodily presence rather than succumbing to the kind of absence that can only be represented figuratively. It suits, indeed, a scene in which the crux of the interest involves general metaphysical questions, as well as personal loyalties and grudges. So much so that Stewart shows this chapter to operate under a 'sylleptic paradigm' as it includes specific examples of the rhetorical figure and occasions where the same kind of double-thought implies unrealised alternatives, by way of a counterfactual grammar. The chapter brings to light the hidden logic and unvoiced insights that are submerged into Dickens's style in this scene, as they so often are in his writing. It reveals what Stewart calls 'the incomparable dexterity of Dickens as a syntactician' and so provides the most sustained demonstration of this volume's case for attending to the tactics of syntax in Dickens's writing.

Helen Small's chapter, 'Dispensing with Style', shows that for all the stylistic excesses that make up Dickens's characteristic style or styles, many of which are explored in this collection, there is a coexistent, perhaps unexpected, reaching for plainness in his writing. This is apparent as a principle throughout his career, especially in his comments to other writers and to contributors to his journals, and it becomes more evident in practice in his late work. This is most compellingly the case in *Edwin Drood* (1870), which, Small argues, sees Dickens holding up to scrutiny his signature prose and putting in a new effort towards plainness. The volume's last chapter, then, reminds us of the versatility of Dickens's style, and it provides a fitting culmination to a series of chapters that show how frequently that style is controlled, even when it is flamboyant and showy, to the point where, in his final novel, a rejection of excess might suggest not only a measure of reserve about his own stylistic exuberance but also a natural development of a style that has always been capable of simplicity, restraint and subtlety.

NOTES

1 Robert Alter, 'Reading Style in Dickens', *Philosophy and Literature*, 20 (1) (1996): 130–7, at 130.
2 Geoffrey Hill, 'Unhappy Circumstances', *The Enemy's Country* (1991), in *Collected Critical Writings*, ed. Kenneth Haynes (Oxford University Press, 2008), 176–91, at 188.
3 Samuel Warren thought *American Notes* was written 'in a very careless, slip-shod style' (1842). David Masson noted that 'Mr Dickens's language' was (ordinarily) 'loose and redundant' (1851). Margaret Oliphant's stern judgement was that 'Mr Dickens is the careless, clever boy who could do it twice as well, but won't take pains' (1862), *CH*, 122, 252, 442.
4 For example, Mowbray Morris wrote of his 'want of proportion and control' and his 'want of perception and proportion' (*CH*, 606, 607). Much later, Arthur Clayborough claimed that 'deliberate disproportion between subject matter and style – in a word, ... incongruity – is too central in Dickens's work to be ignored', *The Grotesque in English Literature* (Oxford: Clarendon Press, 1967), 242.
5 'A Flight' (1851), first published in *Household Words*, 30 August 1851, collected in *Journalism*, III, 26–34.
6 Charles Dickens, 'Chatham Dockyard', first published in *All the Year Round*, 29 August 1863; reprinted in *The Uncommercial Traveller*, Second Series (1868); collected in *Journalism*, IV, 287–325.
7 As noted by John Drew in *Journalism*, IV, 288, with reference to D. Mayer, *Harlequin in his Element: The English Pantomine, 1803–1836* (Cambridge, MA: Harvard University Press, 1969).
8 George Henry Lewes, review of Forster's *Life of Charles Dickens*, I, *Fortnightly Review*, 17 (February 1872): 141–54; reprinted in *CH*, 569–77, 571.
9 D. W. Harding, *Experience into Words: Essays on Poetry* (Cambridge University Press, 1982), 181.
10 George Orwell, 'Charles Dickens' (1939), in *The Collected Essays, Journalism and Letters of George Orwell*, vol. I: *An Age Like This, 1920, 1940*, ed. Sonia Orwell and Ian Angus (London: Secker & Warburg, 1968), 413–60, at 448.
11 G. L. Brook, *The Language of Dickens* (London: André Deutsch, 1970).
12 Brook, *The Language of Dickens*, 46–53.
13 According to one recent account, nowadays 'scholars tend to examine the novelist in relation to such issues as gender, sexuality, empire, race, visual culture,

politics, economics and science.' Toru Sasaki, 'Major Twentieth-Century Critical Responses', in Sally Ledger and Holly Furneaux (eds.), *Charles Dickens in Context* (Cambridge University Press, 2011).

14 Orwell, 'Charles Dickens', 450.

15 George Orwell, 'Why I Write' (1946), in *The Collected Essays*, I, 1–7, at 6.

16 Steven Connor (ed.), 'Introduction', *Charles Dickens* (London: Longman, 1996), 1–33, at 28.

17 D. A. Miller's work on Dickens comprises one of the most influential arguments for the complicity of Dickens's writing with 'official' Victorian ideologies, particularly the behavioural norms that are regulated by the police. His interest in Dickens's writing is often concerned with structural and narrative representations rather than specifically with a politics of style, but it is instructive to note his reading of style in Jane Austen as characterised by evasion and self-effacement: 'For all along, shame has been style's encrypted alter ego – its alternate form as ego – and style, the unremitting labor of managing and masking this encryption.' *Jane Austen; or, The Secret of Style* (Princeton University Press, 2002), 48. Similar suspicions are common in ideological critiques of Dickens.

18 Charles Dickens, 'Gone Astray', *Household Words*, 13 August 1853, collected in *Journalism*, III, 155–65.

19 For a discussion of the stylistic significance of this essay, see Robert Douglas-Fairhurst, 'Charles Dickens: Going Astray', in Adrian Poole (ed.), *The Cambridge Companion to English Novelists* (Cambridge University Press, 2010), 132–48.

20 Catherine Gallagher, *The Industrial Reformation of English Fiction: Social Discourse and Narrative Form, 1832–1867* (Chicago University Press, 1985), 162.

21 Kate Flint, Introduction to *Hard Times* (London: Penguin, 1995), xi–xxxiii, at xix.

22 Flint, Introduction, xix.

23 S. J. Newman, *Dickens at Play* (London: Macmillan, 1981), 17, 106.

24 Garrett Stewart, *Dickens and the Trials of Imagination* (Cambridge, MA: Harvard University Press, 1974), xv–xvi.

25 Matthew Bevis, *The Art of Eloquence: Byron, Dickens, Tennyson, Joyce* (Oxford University Press, 2008), 128.

26 Bevis, *The Art of Eloquence*, 129.

27 *Life*, II, 349–50.

28 Arthur Quiller-Couch, *Charles Dickens and Other Victorians* (Cambridge: The University Press, 1925), 72.

29 Garrett Stewart, *Death Sentences: Styles of Dying in British Fiction* (Cambridge, MA: Harvard University Press, 1984), especially Chapter 2.

30 Charles Dickens, 'A December Vision', *Household Words*, 14 December 1850, collected in *Journalism*, II, 305–9.

31 H. M. Daleski, *Dickens and the Art of Analogy* (London: Faber, 1970), 138. Other adverse responses include Samuel Philips in 1851 lamenting that 'in any

passage of sentiment Mr Dickens lets the sentiment run away with him' (*CH*, 262) and John Carey suggesting that sentimentality was 'always threatening to kill Dickens' art', *The Violent Effigy: A Study of Dickens' Imagination* (London: Faber, 1973), 28.

32 For example, Fred Kaplan, *Sacred Tears: Sentimentality in Victorian Literature* (Princeton University Press, 1987), and Nicola Bown (ed.), *Rethinking Victorian Sentimentality*, special issue of *19: Interdisciplinary Studies in the Long Nineteenth Century*, 4 (2007), available online at http://19.bbk.ac.uk/index.php/19/issue/view/67 (accessed 4 January 2013). For a precursor to these responses, see Steven Marcus, *Dickens: From Pickwick to Dombey* (London: Chatto & Windus, 1965), 160: 'Sentimentality, like self-pity, can be as amenable to the qualities of genius, both affective and intellectual, as any of our more primitive responses.'

33 Brook, *The Language of Dickens*, 46.

34 Brook, *The Language of Dickens*, 47.

35 Philip Davis, 'Victorian Prose and Sentimentality', in Alice Jenkins and Juliet John (eds.), *Rereading Victorian Fiction* (Basingstoke: Macmillan, 2000), 13–28.

36 Ian Watt, 'Oral Dickens', *Dickens Studies Annual*, 3 (1974): 165–81; and Robert Golding, *Idiolects in Dickens: The Major Techniques and Chronological Development* (London: Macmillan, 1985).

37 Golding, *Idiolects in Dickens*, 217.

38 Mikhail Bakhtin, 'Discourse in the Novel' (1935), in *The Dialogic Imagination: Four Essays*, ed. Michael Holquist, trans. Caryl Emerson and Michael Holquist (Austin, TX: University of Texas Press, 1981), 259–442.

39 Quoted in Bakhtin, 'Discourse in the Novel', 303.

40 David Masson, *British Novelists and Their Styles: Being a Critical Sketch of the History of British Prose Fiction* (Boston, MA: Lincoln & Gould, 1859), 257.

CHAPTER ONE

Dickens's umbrellas

John Bowen

The idea of style is complicated, as the twenty-seven separate senses, many subdivided, listed in the *OED* show. Many of these are linked to practices of writing and inscription, from the word's earliest meaning of 'an instrument made of metal, bone, etc., having one end sharp-pointed for incising letters on a wax tablet, and the other flat and broad for smoothing the tablet and erasing' to 'the rules and methods, in regard to typography, display, etc., observed in a particular printing office'.[1] But if the idea of 'style' points (and style seems always to point) to the materiality of writing and to its kinship with 'a weapon of offence, for stabbing, etc.', it equally gestures to less tangible qualities, such as mode, manner or form.[2] Style is not one of Raymond Williams's *Keywords*, but it could well be, for its rich tangle of meanings covers a wide range of cultural experience and description and both rests upon and binds together some fundamental philosophical oppositions in an apparently untroubled way. In its central meaning for literary criticism, style is what gathers 'those features of literary composition which belong to form and expression rather than to the substance of the thought or matter expressed'.[3] There is a dense sediment of philosophical assumptions behind this understanding of style, but it is not at all clear whether readers and critics can ever decisively separate questions of 'form and expression' from those of 'thought or matter', even if they were to think that desirable. It seems as difficult to dispense with the idea of style as to accept the conceptual baggage and assumptions that it carries with it.

This is not just a conceptual matter though, for everyday usages of the term are equally problematic and Janus-faced. Style in ordinary literary-critical usage points on the one hand to questions of literary singularity, particular moments of felicity and grace in writing, and on the other to identifiable structures of repetition or regularity, the signs of a particular authorial thumbprint. Much of both the usefulness and difficulty of the term stems from that double (and more than double) quality.[4] This is compounded in discussing Dickens's work by the rich mass of particulars that his writing compasses. There is something so monstrous about the topic of Dickens's style, in its variety, daring and invention, that to offer a reasonably full account of even a single work would be an immense task. There is a fear of being deluged by the sheer bulk of material, particularly if one wishes to discuss not just Dickens's fictional style but also some of the trickier questions for stylistic analysis raised by his letters and journalism. But the plethora of possible examples may hide a difficulty that is not merely quantitative. When F. R. Leavis wrote that Dickens 'was no more a stylist than Shakespeare', it was intended as the highest of compliments.[5] For Leavis, only lesser writers were stylists, and to be as great a writer as Dickens or Shakespeare was to exceed or surpass the very category of style. Flaubert, say, may be a greater 'stylist' than Dickens but for Leavis, a lesser writer. How does one map a style that exceeds the very idea of style?

A 'guerrilla' approach to the problem rather than a frontal assault may be the best option, and umbrellas are my weapon of choice. This may seem at first a capricious, arbitrary or affected choice of topic. But umbrellas, I want to argue, have a close affinity with the question of style. Like an umbrella, a style can be a humble material object, a probe, pin or engraving tool. An umbrella, like that kind of style, has a sharp point and a smooth surface. Umbrellas, like styles, can be used for stabbing or pointing as well as for inscribing and writing. Like styles, they pop up in many places, in many different ways and for many different purposes. Like theatrical props that support character or characterisation, umbrellas have a probing ability that in Dickens's work is used particularly by women (as when Mrs Gamp's umbrella in *Martin Chuzzlewit* 'thrust out its battered brass nozzle from improper crevices and chinks, to the great terror of the other passengers' [*MC*, 29, 468]) but one that is at least partly veiled by their fabric or skirts. Like an iceberg or a literary style, most of the point of an umbrella is hidden, something that looks unimportant but which is invested with a great deal of psychic and textual importance. Umbrellas in Dickens's work, then, are both an instance or set of instances of style and an analogy for it, neither a concept nor simply an occasional metaphor but a term that can be used both to illustrate and to exemplify my argument about his style and, when necessary, to waylay and distress it. As G. K. Chesterton said in his introduction to *Hard Times*, 'If we take a thing frivolously we can take it separately, but the moment we take a thing seriously, if it were only an old umbrella, it is obvious that that umbrella opens above us into the immensity of the whole universe.'[6]

Umbrellas are a recurrent feature of Dickens's writing, with more than 120 uses or mentions in the fiction and several appearances in his letters and journalism. They often occur at moments of particular writerly felicity or force, as in the Fleet Prison, the ethical and narrative turning point of *The Pickwick Papers*, when Jingle tells Pickwick that he 'Lived on a pair of boots – whole fortnight. Silk umbrella – ivory handle – week – fact – honour – ask Job – knows it' (*PP*, 42, 658) or in *Nicholas Nickleby* when Wackford Squeers delights in having caught Smike with 'only one cast of the umbrella, as if I had hooked him with a grappling-iron' (*NN*, 38, 496). However decisive, moving or absurd such umbrella moments are, they would not be normally thought of as essential features of Dickens's writing or style, and it is perfectly possible to imagine a work of his with no umbrellas at all, although in fact all his novels do contain at least one, with the sole exception of *A Tale of Two Cities*. This gives us a particularly apposite corpus to discuss the question of style, for style too must rest upon recurrent features but not be readily predicted or foreseen. The ability to be recurrent but to appear (and disappear) in unforeseen ways is also umbrella-like, in that an umbrella usually belongs to a particular person but is always in danger of being mislaid or lost or turning up in the wrong place, or doing something that seems inappropriate or surprising, or simply being borrowed or used by others. Umbrellas often stage in Dickens's work little performances, theatres of absence and presence. As with Dickens's style, there is always something self-divided and potentially comic about umbrellas, which lies in their ability to be lost and found, to be turned inside out, to be both 'masculine' and 'feminine' and to make one look stylish or unstylish. The self-divisions of Dickens's style are particularly revealing and seem deeply linked to the simultaneous acting out and warding off of certain kinds of memory and memorialisation. My three major examples explore how that self-division occurs (1) between characters in fiction; (2) in two voices in the same letter; and (3) within a single narrating voice.

This chapter is not intended to be an anthology, comic or otherwise, of the many umbrellas in Dickens's work, but it is a good idea to gain a sense of the variety of ways in which he and his characters use umbrellas. They are weapons and shields most often, but also ingredients in soup and gruel. They are compared to birds, cabbages and leaves and appear in a wide array of inventive and surprising contexts, both indoors and outside, in places that include courtrooms, Parliament, prisons, palaces, bedrooms and omnibuses. Sometimes they resemble detachable, mobile prostheses: Silas Wegg in *Our Mutual Friend* has both a wooden leg and an umbrella. Like Wegg's leg, they are often strangely invested with erotic desire in a distinctly bisexual or hermaphroditic, rather than simply phallic, way.

Jacques Derrida, who has written provocatively on an umbrella in (or not quite in, or problematically in) Friedrich Nietzsche's work, describes an umbrella as an 'hermaphroditic spur encased in veils', which catches well its sexual ambivalence.[7] Many of Dickens's most powerful, preternatural or disturbing figures, including Elijah Pogram, Quilp, Wackford Squeers, Mrs Gamp, Mrs Joe Gargery and Mr F's aunt are equipped with and deploy umbrellas. In his 1858 article 'Please to Leave Your Umbrella', Dickens identifies the loss of memory, of knowledge and of the ability to make aesthetic judgements with the handing over of one's umbrella.[8] If one hands over an umbrella in that essay, one hands over with it the most prized and intimate sense of self. The marginal, multiple and contradictory qualities of umbrellas, which can act as containers, grappling irons, disguises and writing instruments, which have inner and outer sides that are liable to be confused or turned the wrong way round, and which are often most noticeable when they are lost or absent, inspire some of Dickens's most remarkable acts of fictional and epistolary impersonation. They act as both brilliant feats of style in themselves and repeated testings both of the limits and internal regularities of style and of the conceptual and critical tools that we use to get a handle on it.

Spurs: Nietzsche's Styles, Jacques Derrida's enigmatic meditation on the question of style, intermittently comes to settle or focus on a passage in a manuscript by Nietzsche that reads 'I have forgotten my umbrella.'[9] Derrida at one point says of Nietzsche, 'this style-spur ... it must not be forgotten ... is also an umbrella.'[10] Derrida's phrasing, through reminding us to remember, compelling us not to forget, links umbrella to style. It is a mysterious remark, but perhaps less so than at first appears, for Derrida wants to deploy the idea of style without allowing it to settle into a concept regulated by ideas of coherence, property, expression and the self, to which many theories of the topic seem, intentionally or not, to subordinate themselves. The umbrella, a thing that has all sorts of improperness about it, is a useful tool or instrument to achieve this, although umbrellas never seem to settle willingly into being tools, instruments or objects. As a casual manuscript jotting, for example, Nietzsche's remark does not seem properly to belong to Nietzsche's oeuvre or indeed to philosophical exposition at all. In bringing out the odd bisexual energies of Nietzsche's work, with its simultaneous 'feminism' and 'misogyny', Derrida shows how an umbrella resembles literary style through two key aspects: the ability to attack on the one hand and to ward things off on the other. These two qualities are also important in Dickens's work. A style, like an umbrella, is both aggressive and apotropaic; it is both self-divided and never properly belongs to anyone.

Spurs is by any standards a very odd account of style, which Derrida wants to reformulate as a more general structure of writing, iterability or the trace, freed from the idea of proper, coherent and male self-identity.[11] He does not simply wish to reject the idea of style for a more extended sense of iterability or the trace but rather to loosen it from those ideas about property, belonging, identity and masculinity that have inter-twined themselves so thoroughly with the history of thinking about style. Derrida does this partly through the question of 'the woman' in Nietzsche and partly through his own text's complex relationship to parody. *Spurs*, I want to argue, is a quasi-parodic and self-parodic text, and this quality points to one of the persistent dangers, lures or hopes that haunts analysis of literary or philosophical style. The most stylish writers, those with the most identifiable styles, are those who seem most in danger of being par-odied or of falling into self-parody, as the writing and critical receptions of both Dickens and Derrida themselves confirm. There is a complex enactment and warding off of that danger in Dickens's work, through its intimate relationship to parody from at least the opening sentence of *The Pickwick Papers* onwards. An earlier and better symbolic opening to Dickens's career is the first paragraph of his very first published piece of fiction, 'A Dinner at Poplar Walk' (retitled in *Sketches by Boz* as 'Mr Minns and his Cousin') which begins:

> Mr. Augustus Minns was a bachelor, of about forty as he said – of about eight-and-forty as his friends said. He was always exceedingly clean, pre-cise, and tidy; perhaps somewhat priggish, and the most retiring man in the world. He usually wore a brown frock coat without a wrinkle, light inexplicables without a spot, a neat neckerchief with a remarkably neat tie, and boots without a fault; moreover, he always carried a brown silk umbrella with an ivory handle. ('Mr Minns and His Cousin', *SB*, 306)

Dickens begins his career as a writer of fiction with Mr Minns, who arrives carrying an umbrella, the loss of which impels the story that follows. In the first of Dickens's many lists, the umbrella is both attached to its sen-tence through the repetitions of 'with' and 'without' and semi-detached, hooked on after and by the semicolon. In the course of the story, the search for the umbrella causes Minns to arrive home from visiting his rela-tives in a filthy temper at three in the morning, determined never to see them again. At the very opening of Dickens's career, the umbrella, like a literary style, both enfolds and dominates the story while simultaneously being forgotten both within it and by it.

Dickens, like Nietzsche, is a writer distinguished both by the power – an often aggressive, dominating, not to say phallic, power – and the plurality of his styles. The questions of the relation of style to aggression and the apotropaic, to memory, sexual identity and parody, that are raised by Derrida's account of Nietzsche's work emanate constantly from Dickens's work and may be pointed to, prised open, enfolded or shut up tight by the presence or absence of umbrellas. Their mediating power, their pro-miscuous belonging, their movement in and out of domestic space, their ability to be both a prosthetic limb and a kind of portable private space or container, their belonging to and movement between different genders, all seem to feed a surprisingly intense psychic investment and stylistic inven-tion in Dickens's work. They seem particularly to appear at moments when erotic desire is interwoven with violence and the stirrings of mem-ory. That triad of erotic desire, violence and memory is at the heart of many of Dickens's greatest moments and structural to his novels, most perfectly in *Great Expectations*.

Umbrellas, then, those strange transitional objects, give both a reason-ably limited corpus of Dickens's writing to discuss and a jauntily and per-sistently troubling one. They can also be taken as a figure for criticism: a critical umbrella can both ward off the avalanche of potential examples of Dickens's style and be used to poke about in some of its odder corners. Mr Davis in *Pictures from Italy* (1846)

> always had a snuff-coloured great-coat on, and carried a great green umbrella in his hand, and had a slow curiosity constantly devouring him, which prompted him to do extraordinary things, such as taking the covers off urns in tombs, and looking in at the ashes as if they were pickles – and tracing out inscriptions with the ferrule of his umbrella, and saying, with intense thoughtfulness, 'Here's a B you see, and there's a R, and this is the way we goes on in; is it? …' His antiquarian habits occasioned his being infrequently in the rear of the rest; and one of the agonies of Mrs. Davis, and the rest of the party in general, was an ever-present fear that Davis would be lost. This caused them to scream for him, in the strangest places, and at the most improper seasons. And when he came, slowly emerging out of some sepulchre or other, like a peaceful Ghoul, saying 'Here I am!' Mrs. Davis invariably replied, 'You'll be buried alive in a foreign country, Davis, and it's no use trying to prevent you!' (*PI*, 130)

Like Mr Davis, the critic of style seems condemned to take the covers off the urns of the dead in order to retrace letters and inscriptions with the tip of his or her umbrella, curious and incorrigible as a ghoul.

In one of the relatively few explicit discussions of Dickens's style, Robert Alter follows Saul Bellow in seeing style as being able 'to unearth bur-ied essences'.[12] It may be more complicated than that, though, and raise

more troubling questions about the relationship between the particular-
ities of literary style and the presence or absence of essences, buried or
otherwise. This is particularly so of Dickens's extraordinarily various and
inventive oeuvre, which seems to produce effects much odder, harder to
name and less simply assimilable to Alter's ready-to-hand metaphysical
essentialism. Style, like umbrellas, in Dickens's work, I want to argue, is
often used to point or attack on the one hand and to ward things off on
the other in three particular ways: first, threats or taints of class difference
and criminality; second, anxieties about masculinity and sexual difference;
and third, questions about identity, property and the law more generally.
The main examples that I want to discuss, all in different ways, have this
simultaneously aggressive and apotropaic quality and an intimate if somewhat oblique relationship with memory, parody and the law. And they all
feature umbrellas. In *Great Expectations*, when Mrs Joe goes to visit Miss
Havisham, she carries with her

> a basket like the Great Seal of England in plaited straw, a pair of pattens, a
> spare shawl, and an umbrella, though it was a fine bright day. I am not quite
> clear whether these articles were carried penitentially or ostentatiously; but,
> I rather think they were displayed as articles of property. (*GE*, I, 13, 99)

John Carey saw umbrellas in Dickens's work as indicators of class discomfort and hierarchy: 'Elaborately undignified, they immediately locate their
owner in the lower class.'[13] It is an acute remark, but Mrs Joe's umbrella
is not simply a badge of class standing and discomfort. As Pip's relations
both to Magwitch and Wemmick remind us, the novel is deeply concerned with the power, penitence and ostentation of portable property.
This basket of random domestic goods – a shawl, a pair of pattens and
an umbrella, carried in a basket like the Great Seal of England – encap-
sulates the aggressive self-protection that so characterises Mrs Joe, at one
of the few moments in the book when she leaves home, a poor woman,
self-styled and sealed, going to see a rich one on a fine bright day, umbrella
at the ready to prod or to shield.

One of the most powerful and explosive scenes in all of Dickens's writing occurs in Chapter 49 of *The Old Curiosity Shop*. Shortly before, Little
Nell has arrived at the village at which she will die, but her progress to
death is punctuated by an episode in which Quilp, who is thought to be
dead, is discovered to be alive. In a novel full of scenes of mourning, the
chapter stages a fake wake for Quilp. Like all those in which he appears,
it contains a remarkable amount of aggression, violence and comedy,
built around the question of how one remembers the dead. Manically

triumphant in his escape from death – whistling, laughing, giving out a shrill scream as he walks down the street – the intensity of Quilp's 'flow of spirits' is overwhelming (*OCS*, 49, 378). There is a rather different flow of spirits at his house where his family and friends are mourning him or, rather, showing 'a faint assumption of sentimental regret', which 'struggled but weakly with a bland and comfortable joy' as they drink his whisky (49, 380). His lawyer, Sampson Brass, rather than Mrs Quilp or his mother-in-law Mrs Jiniwin, is at the centre of the scene, which we see through Quilp's eyes, as he silently returns to watch and listen through a crack in the door. Brass and the family are writing an advertisement for Quilp, trying to decide whether his legs are better described as 'crooked' or 'very crooked'. Just before the moment when he famously bursts in and bursts out the words 'aquiline, you hag', after they have decided to describe his nose as 'flat', Sampson Brass remembers him:

> This is an occupation … which seems to bring him before my eyes like the Ghost of Hamlet's father, in the very clothes that he wore on work-a-days. His coat, his waistcoat, his shoes and stockings, his trousers, his hat, his wit and humour, his pathos and his umbrella, all come before me like visions of my youth. (*OCS*, 49, 382)

Brass, at a moment of memorialisation in a novel obsessed with memory and the remembering of the dead, is trying to articulate what Quilp's style is or was. As he does so, he encounters a difficulty that any such project encounters: that of maintaining the distinction between what is essential and what is merely trivial or superfluous. In Dickens's work, it is a particular challenge because we often want to value and notice precisely its superfluous details. George Orwell saw 'The outstanding, unmistakable mark of Dickens's writing' – what makes it stylistic, as it were – as 'the *unnecessary detail*'.[14] For Orwell, it is the detail that we get hold of or that hooks itself, like an umbrella's handle, to us.

Brass settles on Quilp's wit, humour, pathos and, climactically, his umbrella: it is an odd collocation, as odd in its way as that between the living and the dead. Sampson brings together the affective and ethical on the one hand with the banally material on the other: waistcoats, shoes, stockings, umbrella and, slightly later, the colour of Quilp's linen. Qualities that we might want to remember as being an essential aspect or accomplishment of the dead, such as wit, pathos and humour, are suddenly punctuated by a thing that seems merely contingent, occasional, easily detachable or lost. The umbrella, as umbrellas so often do, seems to have got itself into the wrong place. It is a characteristically funny bit of comic bathos, but also an especially revealing moment because of the particular play or battle of literary styles at work between Quilp and Brass. Quilp, as Garrett Stewart puts it in his rich discussion of style in *The Old Curiosity Shop*, is 'almost a parody of the mimetic novelist'.[15] What contemporaries would have thought of as Dickens's most characteristic modes – wit, humour and pathos – are here at a defining moment ascribed to Quilp, an identification that, lest it seem too strong, is immediately deflated and held at bay by the umbrella that interposes itself as it passes from comic aggressor to memorialising lawyer and back again. 'When we laugh with Quilp', Stewart notes, 'we are in part responding to a comic style': a style of phallic aggression and dominance.[16] Sharply contrasted with it at this moment is Brass's style, explicitly that of a lawyer, indeed of the law, whose purpose, in which it invariably seems to fail in Dickens's work, is to regulate social aggressivity. For, as Stewart puts it, Brass is 'the most fully drawn hypocrite of language so far' in Dickens's work and one who preens himself that he is 'styled gentleman by act of Parliament'.[17] For Stewart, his 'faith in legal "style" becomes a kind of fanatical religious certainty'.[18] But it is also a claim of class distinction and of class power that enables him both to frame Kit Nubbles and so cruelly to exploit the Marchioness.

The passage is also of course a parody: a double or triple parody of a scene of mourning. Brass is not really sad, but is imitating or parodying grief, and Quilp is not really dead but is listening outside the door, awake at his own wake, so that even if Brass were sincere he would not really be mourning. Brass's speech is a parody of Hamlet's 'My father – methinks I see my father – ... In my mind's eye, Horatio' and a proleptic parody of the emotions that we readers will be asked to feel at Nell's death; Brass and the others are mourning a fictional death, as we will shortly be expected to, just as they hope to profit from the death, as Dickens will from that of Nell.[19] On the one hand, then, across the umbrella and through the parody, we see the meeting of a lawless, radically uninhibited, phallic and violent comic style and a legal, hypocritical parasitic style, both of which have an intimate relationship with the literary: Quilp as mimetic novelist, Brass as Shakespearian parodist. It is an opposition that will run throughout Dickens's work.

On 7 June 1843, as he was in the middle of writing *Martin Chuzzlewit*, Dickens wrote a letter to Augustus Tracey, Governor of Tothill Fields Prison in London. It was a prison that Dickens admired, which he had just recently visited and which was run in ways of which he clearly approved. Philip Collins gives an excellent account in *Dickens and Crime* of how positively Dickens felt about Tracey and his prison regime, which was run on the silent system.[20] They clearly had a warm and lasting friendship. But reading the surviving letters addressed to Tracey with an attention to their style and their often strikingly aggressive comedy tells a rather different and more complex story, one that seems intimately linked to Dickens's memories of his childhood and his father's imprisonment and his own consequent simultaneous attraction towards and repulsion from carceral institutions. A simple invitation to dinner, for example, ends with the threat: 'If you tell me you are engaged, I shall attack you savagely in some public Journal, for having poured boiling water over that man's Thigh … I shall head the article "Inhuman atrocity in Tothill Fields Prison. – Ferocious cruelty of the Governor."'[21]

The 7 June letter is one that Dickens writes from home as if his home were a prison to Tracey whose home is a prison; an umbrella links the two, as both property and theft. As in the passage from *The Old Curiosity Shop*, the letter is one that counterposes through parody and self-parody two very different styles: an unlicensed aggressivity on the one hand (even more violent, if that were possible, than Quilp's) and a protective official hypocrisy. They are marked by very different lexical and grammatical choices which create radically different voices, styles or writings, and again concern the fate of an umbrella.

1 Devonshire Terrace | York Gate Regents [sic] Park | Seventh June 1843. Governor.

Now, we don't want none of your sarse – and if you bung any of them tokes of yours in this direction, you'll find your shuttlecock sent back as heavy as it came. Who wants your Bridewell umberellers? Do you suppose people can't perwide theirselves with crooked handles, without axing *you*? Who ever see your umbereller? *I* didn't. Go and look for it in the Gruel; and if it an't there, search the Soup. It an't so thick, but wot you'll find three and sixpence worth of ginghum among the ox heads as you pave your garden with. Ah. Oh. Yes. No. Yor'ne too cheekish by half Governor. That's where it is. You'd better take it out of yourself by a month and labour, on the Mill. If that don't answer, let off one of them blunderbusses in the office agin your weskut. *That's* what your complaint wants.

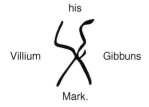

Memorandum added by the Chaplain

P.S. The unfortunate man forgot to state that the umbrella was Found in his possession while he penned the above – that his wretched wife was as well as could be expected; also her sister – that he had determined not to ask the Governor in Dr Howe's behalf, for a ticket to the St. Giles's Lions (thinking the said Doctor troublesome in that respect) but had conferred with Mr. Crea according to the Governor's kind suggestion; and would write the Governor when the Night was fixed.[22]

There is much to say about the style of this letter, whose immediate cause seems to be an umbrella that Dickens has taken by accident or which Tracey has left at his house. That slight mishap releases an extraordinary fictional and epistolary energy. On the one hand, the letter is marked by aggression, as Dickens or Gibbuns sends back what he calls this 'shuttlecock' (a shuttlecock which resembles a miniature pointless umbrella) which is then batted back by the chaplain. On the other hand, it is deeply defensive against a (presumably non-existent) accusation. Dickens writes to Tracey in two styles: against and in defiance of the law, on the one hand, and for it, in the shape of the chaplain, on the other. The two parts or two letters radically contradict or delete each other, rather like the letter which Micawber writes to David Copperfield in which, having threatened suicide in the body of the letter, 'for mental torture is not supportable beyond a certain point', he then adds in a postscript that his debts are settled and that 'myself and family are at the height of earthly bliss' (*DC*, 54, 671). The letter to Tracey is a text full of performative complexity, neatly encapsulated in its magnificently self-erasing, 'Ah. Oh. Yes. No', successively and simultaneously exhalation, exclamation, affirmation and denial.

Villium Gibbuns's part of the letter is full of imperatives and rhetorical questions, containing no fewer than sixteen sentences, some no longer than a single word, in eleven lines of print; the postscript, by contrast, has a single sentence over seven lines of print. Gibbuns's grammar is very simple: his writing lacks subordination in every sense. It is chock-full of what Dickens's contemporaries took as most characteristic of his own style: of linguistic innovation and hyperbole, highly informal in its diction and full of jargon and street language, including 'bung', 'gingham' (meaning umbrella), 'tokes' and the exquisite 'too cheekish by half', as if cheek or cheeky had simultaneously diminished and extended itself by a half. 'Cheekish', like other words here, is newish, as Dickens's usage either precedes or coincides with the earliest listed in the *OED*. There is some telling alliteration in 'Go and look for it in the gruel; and if it ain't there search the soup', a pair of tetrameters that could be the chorus to a music-hall song. There is an insistent aggression in the phrasing ('asking' becomes 'axing') and in the repetitive particularity of its address to 'you ... you ... you ... you ... you ... you ... your', followed by the emphatic '*I* didn't' and then again 'you ... you ... You've'. The whole passage hinges and rotates on that violently negating '*I* didn't'. An umbrella – or rather the slightly opened-out or extended 'um*ber*eller' – is the centre of this, it's 'ell' looking back to 'Bridewell' and its 'er' to 'perwide'. As in *The Old Curiosity Shop*, the umbrella is linked to questions about eating and drinking, the possession of someone else's property, the threat of imminent death and the force of the law, written in a style of simultaneous and hyperbolic defence ('*I* didn't') and attack: 'You'd better take it out of yourself by a month and labour, on the Mill.'

The 'oral' qualities of Dickens's writing are a commonplace of nineteenth-century accounts of his style, but this text's relationship to orality is a more complexly conflicted one. Tracey's prison was run on the silent system, and prisoners were punished (most commonly by deprivation of food) for speaking. His regime was a very punitive one, and over one-third of all the punishments in the whole prison system at this time were inflicted at Tothill Fields or at Coldbath Fields Prison, which was also run by a friend of Dickens, who approved and supported his work.[23] Punishments were most usually for infringing the silence rule, as an oral transgression, speech, was punished by an oral deprivation, hunger. Dickens is voicing, speaking for, someone who is not allowed to speak, and certainly not like this to the governor of the prison, and he does so by both hiding the umbrella and thrusting it down the governor's throat in the soup or gruel. It is hard not to think of Oliver Twist at this point: the governor politely asks for something and gets something very different from what he expected back. Like Oliver's asking for more, Tracey's polite request is answered with a beating or its equivalent: hard labour on the treadmill, followed by an encouragement to shoot himself with his own blunderbuss, in order to let out the umbrella that he has already taken in. But if this is an oral text in one sense, it is also a written one. The oral is foregrounded in the idiom of Gibbuns, who seems not to be able to write (he has to sign his name with an extraordinary cross that looks like two crossed umbrellas or a nest or tangle of hooks and sticks) but then is described as having 'penned the above' by the chaplain. It is, then, a text that is written by and not written by Dickens, written by and not written by Gibbuns, both signed by and not signed by Dickens and by Gibbuns, both oral and written.

The letter ends with an arrangement or failure to make an arrangement to see 'the St. Giles's Lions'. Those who live in the notorious criminal slum are like the inhabitants of a zoo but also like a group of literary lions, of the sort that Dickens had satirised a few years before in Mrs Leo Hunter in *The Pickwick Papers* and the article 'Some Particulars Concerning a Lion' in *Bentley's Miscellany* (*PP*, 15).[24] Criminals might become celebrities, as in Harrison Ainsworth's fiction or, as Thackeray and others had accused *Oliver Twist* of doing, through making crime seem glamorous and stylish.[25] Literary celebrity and criminal life thus seem to have a deep if occult affinity. In the chaplain's section, there is one deletion in Dickens's manuscript: the words 'I forgot' are replaced by 'The unfortunate man forgot', as Dickens changes his mind about signing the postscript that rests below the signature. He has to erase or forget the words 'I forgot' in reply to a letter about forgetting. The memory, like the umbrella, may be hidden in all sorts of places, such as in a prison or in the gruel and soup it perwides. It is hard at such a moment not to think of the passage in the 'Autobiographical Fragment' in which Dickens wrote that 'but for the mercy of God, I might easily have been, for any care that was taken of me, a little robber or a little vagabond', a passage that raises the possibility that he might have been lionised not as a literary celebrity but as a St Giles criminal.[26] The umbrella of the prison governor, like this remarkable and self-divided feat of literary style, simultaneously links, attacks and wards off the memory of self, of prison and of hunger. Criminality and literary celebrity are radically divided and yet linked by letter, signature, parody and umbrella in the writing of someone who cannot write and who signs with a mesh of crossed umbrellas. Dickens himself has, as a literary celebrity, gone lion-hunting at Tracey's prison and has found a style to be carried and lost between prison and home and the two or three identities (chaplain, author, criminal) that could both protect and attack: a voice, style or writing not unlike an umbrella. The question of the umbrella's return remains open at the end. It is not restored to its proper owner with this letter.

If one significant characterisation of Dickens's style by his contemporaries was its 'orality' and closeness to speech, another was its sexual ambivalence. David Masson in an 1851 review in the *North British Review*, for example, rather positively discerned in Dickens's work the 'keen and feminine sensibility of a fine genius'.[27] More negatively, James Fitzjames Steven, in one of a series of violent attacks on Dickens's fiction, claimed that there was 'a sex in minds as well as in bodies, and Mr Dickens's literary progeny seem to be of the most part of the feminine gender, and to betray it by most unceasing flirtations, and by a very tiresome irritability of nerve'.[28] From

Stevens's misogynistic perspective, even Dickens's male characters (and by implication Dickens himself) are marked by a kind of mental hermaphroditism that troubles the forms and boundaries of sexual differentiation.

There are many strange and strangely eroticised umbrellas in Dickens's work. Henrietta Petowker in *Nicholas Nickleby* knows that she is admired at the theatre by the jauntily phallic appearance of 'a most persevering umbrella in the upper boxes' (*NN*, 25, 320); Wackford Squeers in the same novel takes his umbrella to bed with him (12, 134); Miss Mowcher appears to David Copperfield to possess so much occult sexual knowledge which she both displays (by offering to 'put up the scaffolding' for David to grow a pair of whiskers) and hides (in acting as a go-between in the seduction of Emily by Steerforth) that she has to carry an umbrella so large it 'would have been an inconvenient one for the Irish Giant' (*DC*, 32, 393). In *Little Dorrit*, Mrs F's aunt, probably the single most linguistically violent of all Dickens's women ('He has a proud stomach ... Give him a meal of chaff') at one point rubs 'her esteemed insteps with her umbrella, and vindictively glared' at the innocent Arthur Clennam (*LD*, 1, 23, 393). The 'affectionate lunacy' of Mrs Bagnet in *Bleak House* is shown by her repeatedly giving Trooper George 'a great poke between the shoulders with her umbrella' (*BH*, 55, 783). The self-pleasure, affection and aggression of these sexually knowing women – actress, beautician, widow and wife – are all signified by the style of their umbrella work.

Shortly after the letter to Tracey and probably written in the same month, one of Dickens's most powerful and knowing women and his best-known wielder of the umbrella, Mrs Gamp, appeared for the first time in *Martin Chuzzlewit*. Her umbrella became so famous that it entered the language: a 'gamp' is both a kind of nurse and a kind of umbrella, two things admitted to the bourgeois home that are meant to protect you from harm but which may in fact have the opposite effect, as Mrs Gamp's 'he'd make a lovely corpse' reminds us (*MC*, 25, 410). Mrs Gamp's umbrella, appropriately for a leaved object, is the colour of 'a faded leaf, except where a circular patch of a lively blue had been dexterously let in at the top' (*MC*, 19, 315). It is like a miniature portable landscape, with a patch of blue sky over a plantation. That leafiness is picked up in *Our Mutual Friend* in the form of Silas Wegg's umbrella that resembles 'an unwholesomely-forced lettuce' (*OMF*, 1, 5, 44). Betsey Prig, appropriately, given her role in puncturing the fiction of Mrs Gamp's imaginary friend Mrs Harris, reverses the trope, possessing as she does a lettuce (or possibly a cabbage) 'of such magnificent proportions that she was obliged to shut it up like an umbrella' (*MC*, 49, 747). Lettuces, letters and umbrellas: as many-leaved as a literary style, and Mrs

Gamp's umbrella is a particularly self-multiplying one, for she 'so often moved it, in the course of five minutes, that it seemed not one umbrella but fifty' (*MC*, 29, 468). Mrs Gamp is a prime example of the strangely sexualised inflexions of Dickens's style. Her umbrella is linked to a specifically feminine knowledge of the two ends of human life, for without it, 'neither a lying-in nor a laying-out could by any possibility be attempted' (*MC*, 49, 757). But the umbrella's importance, sexual knowledge and erotic energy are more pervasive and ambivalent even than that, for at any moment in one of Gamp's many journeys it is liable to 'thrust out its battered brass nozzle from improper crevices and chinks, to the great terror of the other passengers' (*MC*, 29, 468). Derrida's description of the umbrella as an 'hermaphroditic spur of a phallus which is modestly enfolded in veils' is more than anticipated here by Dickens; indeed, it is made more intense through the explicitly hermaphroditic figure of a nozzle which thrusts itself out from 'improper crevices or chinks'.[29] 'Nozzle' is particularly felicitous because it implies that this may be an umbrella that squirts liquid out rather than protects one from it, just as the earlier description in *Sketches by Boz* of 'great, dropsical, mildewed umbrellas' suggests that they had produced or absorbed the fluid that they were designed precisely to repel.[30]

The most important umbrella in all of Dickens's work is also the only one that he claims as his own. It is an umbrella in which his whole being is said to be at stake and comes from a text that has a good deal of affective importance in biographical understandings of his life and work, as it was written during the very height of the spectacular break-up of Dickens's marriage and the beginnings of his relationship with Ellen Ternan. 'Please to Leave Your Umbrella', first published in *Household Words* in May 1858, is one of the very few texts by Dickens that explicitly discusses the nature of aesthetic judgement. It is also markedly unusual in that it explicitly imitates a named author and text, the Lawrence Sterne of *A Sentimental Journey*. The article or essay does not form part of a group or sequence of articles and was never gathered by Dickens for volume publication. It is a distinctive and singular text, for these reasons and for its teasing, indeed self-teasing, style and mode of address. Like the letter to Tracey, it is marked by sharp internal divisions both in its many generic affiliations – successively and simultaneously satire, essay, memoir, anecdote, adaptation, pastiche and confession – and its style.

'Please to Leave Your Umbrella' records a trip to an almost deserted Hampton Court Palace that the narrator makes with what he calls 'this little reason in my bosom'.[31] A reason in a bosom is a striking phrase: two bodies locked together or the most intimate and private thought, a figure both of heartfelt desire and rational secrecy. The 'little reason' is usually taken by critics to be a way for Dickens to speak about his feelings for Ellen Ternan, but the essay constantly plays literal and figurative possibilities against each other to the despair of any simple-minded biographical reading. The article begins by lamenting that the 'little reason is neither here (ah! I wish it were!) nor there' ('Please to Leave Your Umbrella', *Journalism*, III, 484). The parenthetic punctuation or exhalation within the phrase invests the unimportant figure of no importance with the breath of present desire. She is not there at the scene of writing, but the text will not localise or identify her in any other place either. It is characteristic of the Sternean mode, in its repeated incitement and withdrawal of possible erotic or romantic interpretations. The text swathes itself like an umbrella in veils, to tease itself and us with the play of its erotic, narrative and stylistic possibilities, simultaneously internal monologue, dialogue and pastiche.

However one reads the biographical backstory or tries to furl or unfold its veils, the major relationship within the diegesis is that of the narrator to his umbrella. The umbrella is also the text's central figure for what is most proper to the subjectivity of the narrating self and a privileged way, I want to argue, to understand its mode of narration and style. Let us follow it. As he goes into Hampton Court, the narrator is asked by a policeman to leave his 'very wet' and dripping umbrella at the threshold, which he willingly does ('Please to Leave Your Umbrella', 484). Its relinquishment releases an erotic quasi-domestic fantasy of the writer and his little reason staying in the empty palace 'until the grisly phantom on the pale horse came at a gallop up the staircase ... I and my little reason, Yorick, would keep house here, all our lives in perfect contentment and when we die, our ghosts should make of this dull palace the first building ever haunted happily!' ('Please to Leave Your Umbrella', 485). It is a strangely haunted, melancholy fulfilment of a non-domestic domestic desire in which happiness is figured as death.

But the umbrella, which had at first appeared to be a mere quotidian detail, turns out to be the pivot on which the text turns, both essential to the narrator's being and the text's privileged signifier. The fantasy of romantic bliss is suddenly arrested by an encounter with an artwork that resembles 'a stagnant pool of blacking in a frame' ('Please to Leave Your Umbrella', 485). Blacking, we know, has deep psychic significance for Dickens, a privileged figure of deeply sorrowful memory.[32] At the moment of encounter with an artwork that looks like blacking, he exclaims 'Good Heaven! ... now I think of it, what a number of articles that policeman below stairs required me to leave with him' (485). Once the law has taken the umbrella, he is undefended from the sense that

> the whole material and immaterial universe [is] to be sticky with treacle and polished up with blacking. That policeman demanded of me, for the time being, all the best bumps in my head. Form, colour, size, proportion, distance, individuality, the true perception of every object on the face of the earth or the face of the Heavens, he insisted on my leaving. ('Please to Leave Your Umbrella', 485)

This, he says, makes him 'filled with terror', a castrating anxiety at the hands of the law. Aesthetic judgement is thus intrinsically linked by Dickens to the possession of an umbrella, and its loss entails the loss also of taste, reason and aesthetic judgement.

> Leave your umbrella-full of property which is not by any means to be poked at this collection, with the police, and you shall acknowledge, whether you will or no, this hideous porcelain-ware to be beautiful, these wearisomely stiff and unimaginative forms to be graceful, these coarse daubs to be masterpieces. Leave your umbrella and take up your gentility. Taste proclaims to you what is the genteel thing; receive it and be genteel! ('Please to Leave Your Umbrella', 486)

Without his umbrella, without 'Form, colour, size, proportion, distance, individuality ... true perception', the narrator is in a domain of fulfilled desire, on a sentimental journey with his little reason. Such fulfilment only exists, however, in a world which is genteel and in which he can see nothing but blacking. The umbrella, like the writing, wards off both these possibilities: both fulfilled desire and a flooding of memory with the past and darkness. In one way, the narrator wants to leave the umbrella and his own style behind, to stay within his happy Sternean fantasy until death comes up the stair. But if he does so, he will have a world painted in blacking.

The ending of 'Please to Leave Your Umbrella' is the only time that the text portrays the two figures together, narrator and little reason, with their back towards us, shrouded in an umbrella, sheltered, warding off, walking away from us. It is a beautiful modulation: what has been so hyperbolically one's own, identified with one's own unique singular identity, becomes a shared portable shelter for two. The article ends with the words: 'and then I and my little reason went dreaming away under its shelter through the fast-falling rain, which had a sound in it that day like the rustle of the coming summer' ('Please to Leave Your Umbrella', 488). It is, one can safely say, a scene of wit, humour, pathos and an umbrella. It is also one of the very few times that an umbrella is used in Dickens's work to keep off the rain. Like literary style, the recovered umbrella, which once carried with itself taste, judgement and discrimination, those essential qualities of bourgeois subjectivity and independence of mind, now acts as a shelter in which, like a bed, one can dream, partly revealing and partly concealing Dickens and his little reason, and whether it was human or not, whether sexed or not, indeed, whether there was anything there at all.[33]

NOTES

1 *OED* sense 1; *OED* sense 21d.
2 *OED* sense 2. On the question of pointing in relation to the work of art, see Jacques Derrida, 'Restitutions of the Truth in Pointing [Pointure]' in *The Truth in Painting* (University of Chicago Press, 1987), 255–382.
3 *OED* sense 14.
4 There is a substantial literature on the philosophy of style, in both 'analytic' and 'Continental' traditions. On the former, see, in particular, Richard Wollheim's distinction between 'general' and 'individual' style, most succinctly expressed in *Painting as an Art* (Princeton University Press, 1990). For an account of style as 'expression of personality', see Jenefer M. Robinson, 'Style and Personality in the Literary Work', *Philosophical Review*, 94 (2) (1985): 227–47. Robinson's argument rests on an uncritical and ahistorical assertion of a coherent psychological 'personality' underlying all artistic acts and an assumption of a consensual 'knowledge of persons and human nature' ('Style and Personality', 245) on which we can base our understanding of them. Her corpus of material rests on distinctions between sincere acts of style and 'pretending, imitating, or acting the part' ('Style and Personality', 229) and between 'normal' and 'parasitic' ('Style and Personality', 236) cases that seem to me untenable. On the former, see the debate between John Searle and Jacques Derrida, partly collected in Jacques Derrida, *Limited Inc* (Evanston, IL: Northwestern University Press, 1988). On the latter, see J. Hillis Miller, 'The Critic as Host', in *Theory Now and Then* (Durham, NC: Duke University Press, 1991), 143–70. A development of Robinson's 'act-based' (as opposed to feature-based) account of style as a 'way of doing something' concerned with 'emergent or gestalt properties' is Peter Lamarque's 'Imitating Style' in *Work and Object: Explorations in the Metaphysics of Art* (Oxford University Press, 2010), 139–53, which has a more plural sense of the 'underlying psychological states or processes' that underlie style. But I am not sure that an expressive model captures the complexity of the topic, as I try to show in my analyses of Dickens, nor that when we read, for example, Max Beerbohm's parody of Henry James we 'laugh at the Beerbohm … but not at James himself', nor that this account of parody has the ability to explain the kind of artistic self-parody that we sometimes encounter.
5 F. R. Leavis, *The Great Tradition* (Harmondsworth: Penguin 1972), 282.
6 G. K. Chesterton, *The Collected Works of G. K. Chesterton*, vol. xv: *Chesterton on Dickens*, ed. Alzina Stone Dale (San Francisco, CA: Ignatius, 1989), 171.

A contrasting view of Dickens and umbrellas is Mark Twain's, whose 'The Approaching Epidemic' fears that after Dickens's death 'the nation is to be lectured to death' by 'the man who has a "Toothpick once used by Charles Dickens" ... the man who "once rode in an omnibus with Charles Dickens;" and the lady to whom Charles Dickens "granted the hospitalities of his umbrella during a storm"'; 'The Approaching Epidemic', in *Collected Tales, Sketches, Speeches and Essays* (New York: The Library of America, 1992), 447–8, at 448.

7 Jacques Derrida, *Spurs: Nietzsche's Styles* [*Éperons: les styles de Nietzsche*] (University of Chicago Press, 1979).

8 Charles Dickens, 'Please to Leave Your Umbrella', *Household Words*, 1 May 1858, reprinted in *Journalism*, III, 483–8.

9 Derrida, *Spurs*, 123.

10 Derrida, *Spurs*, 41.

11 On the trace, see Jacques Derrida, *Of Grammatology* (Baltimore, MD: Johns Hopkins University Press, 1976), 65: '*The trace is in fact the absolute origin of sense in general. Which amounts once again to saying that there is no absolute origin of sense in general*' (italics in original). See also 'Translator's Preface', ix–lxxx, at lxx. On writing, see Geoff Bennington, *Jacques Derrida* (Chicago University Press, 1993), 42–64.

12 Robert Alter, 'Reading Style in Dickens', *Philosophy and Literature*, 20 (1) (1996): 130–7, at 130.

13 John Carey, *The Violent Effigy: A Study of Dickens' Imagination* (London: Faber, 1973), 128.

14 George Orwell, 'Charles Dickens', in *The Collected Essays, Journalism and Letters*, vol. I: *An Age Like This, 1920–1940*, ed. Sonia Orwell and Ian Angus (Boston, MA: D. R. Godine, 2000), 450–504, at 493. Emphasis in original.

15 Garrett Stewart, *Dickens and the Trials of Imagination* (Cambridge, MA: Harvard University Press, 1975), 91.

16 Stewart, *Dickens and the Trials of Imagination*, 100.

17 Stewart, *Dickens and the Trials of Imagination*, 94–5.

18 Stewart, *Dickens and the Trials of Imagination*, 94.

19 William Shakespeare, *Hamlet*, I, ii, 183–5. For John Ruskin, Nell 'was simply killed for the market, as a butcher kills a lamb'; 'Fiction, Fair and Foul', in *The Library Edition of the Works of John Ruskin*, ed. E. T. Cook and Alexander Wedderburn (London: George Allen, 1903–12), XXXIV, 275 n.

20 Philip Collins, *Dickens and Crime* (London: Macmillan, 1965), 52–4, 65–7.

21 Letter of 23 March 1846, in *Letters*, IV, 526.

22 Letter of 7 June 1843, in *Letters*, III, 503–4.

23 Collins, *Dickens and Crime*, 61.

24 Charles Dickens, 'Some Particulars Concerning a Lion', *Bentley's Miscellany*, I, May 1837, 515–18, reprinted in *Journalism*, I, 508–12.

25 William Makepeace Thackeray, 'Catherine: A Story', *Fraser's Magazine*, May 1839–February 1840.

26 *Life*, I, 29–30.

27 David Masson, 'Pendennis and Copperfield: Thackeray and Dickens', *North British Review*, May 1851, xv, 57–89, reprinted in *CH*, 249–59, 251.

28 From an unsigned review of the Library Edition of the Works, *Saturday Review*, 8 May 1858, v, 474–5, reprinted in *CH*, 383–6, 385–6.

29 Derrida, *Spurs*, 129.

30 Charles Dickens, 'Shabby-Genteel People', *SB, Journalism*, I, 261–4, at 264. See also Robert Douglas-Fairhurst, *Becoming Dickens: The Invention of a Novelist* (Cambridge, MA: Belknap Press of Harvard University Press, 2011), 117.

31 Charles Dickens, 'Please to Leave Your Umbrella', *Household Words*, 1 May 1858, collected in *Journalism*, III, 483–8, at 484.

32 For Dickens's own account of his year in the blacking warehouse, see *Life*, I, 22–39. For an excellent recent account see Rosemarie Bodenheimer, *Knowing Dickens* (Ithaca, NY: Cornell University Press, 2007), 66–80.

33 The greatest authorities on Dickens's life differ concerning the text and the visit to Hampton Court that it seems to commemorate. For Michael Slater, 'Ellen Ternan ... may well have accompanied Dickens on a jaunt to Hampton Court during the spring of 1858': *Journalism*, III, 483. See also Michael Slater, *Dickens: A Life in Writing* (New Haven, CT: Yale University Press, 2009), 448. For the editors of Dickens's letters, however, 'he was clearly alone': *Letters*, VIII, xiv n. In the same volume, see also the letter to an unknown correspondent, probably dating from the end of 1857, in which Dickens offers 'cordial thanks for the elegant umbrella' (*Letters*, VIII, 500). The Pilgrim editors note that Dickens's tone 'suggests a present from a lady, possibly ... Mrs Ternan' (*Letters*, VIII, 500, n7).

CHAPTER TWO

Dickens by the clock

Matthew Bevis

No one looks at us while we plait and weave these words.
Clock-mending again.

Charles Dickens ('Tramps', The Uncommercial Traveller)

'In a novel there is always a clock', observed E. M. Forster in 1927.[1] A year later, Virginia Woolf noted that 'the extraordinary discrepancy between time on the clock and time in the mind is less known than it should be and deserves fuller investigation.'[2] Several investigations have been undertaken since then, although their focus has tended to be more on clocking than on clocks. (Forster's comment was itself made in a chapter on 'The Story', where the clock figured as symbolic shorthand for the novel's commitment to the portrayal of 'life by time'.) Other theorists and critics have studied this commitment in different ways – from Georg Lukács, say, on the novel's relation to 'the historico-philosophical position of the world's clock',[3] to Ian Watt on the mode's interest in tracking things 'minute-by-minute' and its 'insistence on the time process'.[4] Clocking is what the novel does. Frank Kermode argued that 'we use fictions to enable the end to confer organization and form on the temporal structure.'[5] 'We ask what [a clock] *says*: and we agree that it says *tick-tock*. By this fiction we humanize it, make it talk our language ... The clock's *tick-tock* I take to be a model of what we call a plot, an organization that humanizes time by giving it form.'[6] According to Kermode, *tock* is our word for 'an end'; it is 'the time of the novelist'.[7]

A shift of attention from the time of the novelist to the timing of a few novels, or from the world-historical clock to a handful of specific clocks, might seem like an unpromising lowering of ambition, but perhaps these clocks have other stories to tell – and to resist.[8] Their sound might sometimes be a modulation rather than a model of plot. Dickens's clocks have a style of their own, one which is linked to how he conceives the pleasures and the responsibilities of writing itself. The *OED*'s first recorded instance in English of 'tick-tock' offers an instructive starting place: 'They were both so silent that the ticktock of the Sacrifice of Iphigenia clock on the mantelpiece became quite rudely audible' (Thackeray, *Vanity Fair*, 1848). Tick-tock here speaks of a dark denouement, but it's also registered as an awkward filler, a pause or hiatus in storytelling. Dickens was as intrigued by this rude disruption to narrative as he was by narrative itself. There is always a clock in his novels, but it is not always easy to see what time it is telling. This uncertainty can be related to a desire in his writing to evade demands for an onwardly clocked narrative – and to an accompanying concern about whether this desire should be indulged or curbed. The *OED* points out that 'tick-tick' was just as common in the nineteenth century as 'tick-tock', and Dickens opts for the former when describing the sound of clocks (as far as I know, the word 'tock' never appears in his fiction). Tick-tick brings into view a recalcitrant force that needn't develop along with the plot. Early reviewers said things which are still being said over and over: 'Dickens's characters ... are nearly always furnished with some peculiarity, which, like the weight of a Dutch clock, is their ever gravitating principle of action'; 'Most of them actually have nothing inside them, they are poetic automata which perform a certain number of motions by clockwork'.[9]

Granted, Dickens's characters often go like clockwork. But clocks often go wrong. Although William Paley saw the watch as a handy stepping stone from what is made to an argument for an intelligent maker, when Dickens thought about timepieces he often thought about *mis*timings and mistakes: 'everything is right here, and going like a clock – a great deal more like a clock than this thing he bought me for my room here, which is an utterly unreliable, unreasonable, and incomprehensible beast.'[10] In *Pamela*, Samuel Richardson, praised by Dickens for 'that wonderful genius for the minutest details in a narrative',[11] has Mr B investigate the character-as-clockwork trope with a sharp eye: 'He is a regular Piece of Clockwork, will they joke, and all that: And why, my Dear, should we not be so? For Man is as frail a Piece of Machinery as any Clockwork whatever; and, by Irregularity, is as subject to be disorder'd.'[12] Novelistic clockwork may be subject to the same irregularities, especially when dealing with so frail a machine as Man.

In contrast to structuralist and narratological calculus ('author X takes 5 pages to describe 5 seconds', and so on), it's noteworthy how often writers have tended towards clocks when mulling over inner lives, rather than plotted actions. In his life of Dickens, Forster recalled Dr Johnson's comparison between Richardson and Fielding: 'there was as great a difference between them', Johnson said, 'as between a man who knew how a watch was made, and a man who could tell the hour by looking on the dial-plate.'[13] In *Middlemarch*, George Eliot's narrator asserts that 'the human mind' is much subtler 'than the outside tissues which make a sort of blazonry or clock-face for it',[14] but the sense of the clock-*face* as 'tissues' keeps in play the idea of the human as a kind of clock. Franz Kafka would later sense that even the mind is chronometric, speaking of 'the block and tackle of the inner being': 'A small lever is somewhere secretly released, one is hardly aware of it at first, and at once the whole apparatus is in motion. Subject to an incomprehensible power, as the watch seems subject to time, it creaks here and there, and all the chains clank down their prescribed path one after the other.'[15] It's as though the *tick-tick* of Dickensian character is being felt from the inside, rather than just attributed from a study of the clock-face.

Instead of thinking with Kermode and others, then, about the humanising of time and the conferring of overarching structures and grand narratives through the machinations of *tick-tock*, what might be gained by thinking about the temporalising of the human and the possible resistances to plotting from within Dickens's style itself? Kafka's awareness of something being 'secretly' released leads him to imagine a 'prescribed path', but the pre-scribed in Dickens is frequently en route to strange detours, detours which might be considered in relation to what Graham Greene once referred to as 'the tone of Dickens's secret prose, that sense of a mind speaking to itself with no one there to listen, as we find it in *Great Expectations* ... the sense that even the author was unaware of what was really going on'.[16] A story is a 'going on' of sorts, but some of Dickens's most interesting goings-on are headed elsewhere. Greene made his observations whilst recalling G. K. Chesterton's view that the novelist's atmospheres often eclipse his stories: 'The secrecy is sensational; the secret is tame ... The surface of the thing seems more awful than the core of it.'[17] This is true all the way to *The Mystery of Edwin Drood*, where a watch is meant to house the secrets of the tale, yet where – along the way – clocks keep shtum: 'Edwin glanced at his face, uncertain whether or no he seriously objected ... But Edwin might as well have glanced at the face of a clock' (*ED*, ii, 92). In Dickens's writing, clocks might be seen as presenting an echo of the problem of other minds. They arrive at moments when the narrative stops and stares, as though trying to get a read on the characters who inhabit it, wondering what kind of depth the surface may portend.

Dickensian clocks keep secrets as well as time. They house, hide and half-say things. Master Humphrey puts his manuscripts inside his clock and confesses of his 'very books' that 'I can scarcely bring myself to love even these last like my old clock' (*MHC*, 11). Maybe because the secrets of the books – and of writing itself – are stored there. The author's own clocks certainly gave him pause for thought:

My Dear Sir,

    Since my hall clock was sent to your establishment to be cleaned it has gone (as indeed it always had) perfectly well, but has struck the hours with great reluctance, and after enduring internal agonies of a most distressing nature, it has now ceased striking altogether. Though a happy release for the clock, this is not convenient to the household. If you can send down any confidential person with whom the clock can confer, I think it may have something on its works that it would be glad to make a clean breast of.

Faithfully yours,
Charles Dickens[18]

On another occasion he wrote: 'Dear Sir, I have the pleasure to enclose you a cheque (payable to Order) for £21. The clock goes reasonably well, but always loses something. Faithfully yours, Charles Dickens'.[19] In letters like this, 'Faithfully yours' has an extra glint: the human goes like clockwork – running to order, keeping good faith, acknowledging debts – whilst the clock proves all too human, always at a slight loss, quietly bearing the mark of its fallible maker. So the clock is conceived not just as human but as a way of enquiring what it is to be human, and it is in need of a 'confidential' person to share its experience. What Dickens hears in and around clocks is not exactly the signifier of order but rather a portent of a kind of unruliness or unpredictability from *within* perceived order. In *Nicholas Nickleby*, when Kate is told that 'appetite is the best clock in the world' (*NN*, 55, 725), the phrase gestures towards an unnervingly accurate yet also a strangely disorienting sense of what makes people tick. This chapter looks at a range of timekeepers in Dickens – and at some larger models of timing that his writing both entertains and resists – before focusing in detail on *Great Expectations*.[20] Attention to watches and clocks can help to tease out some of the odd things his 'secret prose' is trying to say, although I should concede at the outset that, in an effort to keep faith with the obliquity of Dickens's clocks, this essay's plot line will only be clarified much later on, when Pip and Magwitch enter the story.

In 1858, Dickens was presented with a gold watch made by the craftsmen of Coventry. It was inscribed with a tribute to his 'eminent services in the interests of humanity', so when Dickens thanked them for the gift and hoped that 'this little voice will be heard scores of years hence', he was hoping for the endurance of his expressive services as well as that of his watch.[21] Privately, he wrote, 'The Coventry people have given me a seventy five Guinea Watch, which is chronometer, Repeater, and every other terrible Machine that a watch *can* be. It was very feelingly and pleasantly given, and I prize it highly.'[22] The ambiguous nature of this prizing might be linked to the novelist's fraught, intimate relationship with his own gifts as a stylist. Dickens is himself something of a repeater, drawn to building up stories through refrain, echo and reiteration. Indeed, the gift of the watch was apt because the novelist's reading in Coventry a year earlier had been from *A Christmas Carol*, a story with a recurring interest in timings and timepieces – and in restating the obvious ('you will therefore permit me to repeat, emphatically, that Marley was as dead as a door-nail' [*CC*, I, 9]). At the opening of the tale the children avoid asking Scrooge 'what it was o'clock' (I, 10); by the end of it, the man's reform is marked by the fact that clock-watching is now an occasion for practical jokes. When Bob Cratchit arrives a 'full eighteen minutes and a half' late for work, his master pretends to take him to task: 'What do you mean by coming here at this time of day?' (V, 82).

The moral of the story is clear enough, but between these two temporal bookends something less straightforward is going on. We are initially told that the old grouch is 'secret, and self-contained … he carried his own low temperature always about with him. External heat and cold had no influence on Scrooge; he iced his office in the dog-days' (*CC*, I, 10). Maybe the secret is that his self-containment is itself a pose. Perhaps this is why he delights 'to edge his way along the crowded paths of life, warning all human sympathy to keep its distance' (I, 10); he feels a deep need for an audience to whom he can perform his immunity from this very need. Later, he wakes up and listens for the chimes of the neighbouring church:

> To his great astonishment the heavy bell went on from six to seven, and from seven to eight, and regularly up to twelve; then stopped. Twelve! It was past two when he went to bed. The clock was wrong. An icicle must have got into the works. Twelve!
> He touched the spring of his repeater, to correct this most preposterous clock. Its rapid little pulse beat twelve; and stopped. (*CC*, II, 26–7)

Picking up on a disordered pulse *beating* here, perhaps what Scrooge is sensing is not so much a freezing up but the early signs of a thawing out from his own investment in maintaining a 'low temperature'. This would make the clock a kind of disturbed, surrogate heartbeat as he wakes to a new, surprising knowledge of himself. Reading for a plot, we could say that he's a changed man. But to put it this way would be to overlook another possibility. He was always this man; he just tried for a while to evade the difficulties and uncertainties which came with being him. From this perspective, the subterranean power of the tale comes not from reading it as a steadily clocked progress narrative but from our being privy to the revisiting of a past self that had so carefully been iced over. We are told of Scrooge that 'his mind flew back again, like a strong spring released, to its first position, and presented the same problem to be worked all through' (*CC*, II, 27). This is a picture of a mind speaking to itself with no one there to listen and of a mind running like clockwork. Just like the clocks at this moment in the tale, it must be felt to go back, not forwards, in order to go *through*. Scrooge's touching of the spring is Dickens's way of touching on the springs of the character's actions, maybe even discovering them *as* he writes by going back over them – as though the writer comes to understand Scrooge as he creates and then observes the process of Scrooge coming to understand himself. The novelist often marvelled at the 'surprising processes of the mind' which occurred during composition and at the odd, unexpected ways in which his characters 'opened out' before him whilst writing: 'Given what one knows, what one does not know springs up.'[23]

Clocks often spring up in Dickens at those moments when the writing is skirting around the limits of the knowable. 'You are a clock. How is it that you always know?', asks one character in *Little Dorrit*, but the reply is one that a clock might give: 'How can I say!' (*LD*, I, I, 5). The *OED* credits Dickens with the first citation of an apposite phrase: '*To know (also find) what o'clock it is*: to know (or discover) the real state of things: 1835 Dickens, *Sketches by Boz* (1836), "Our governor's wide awake, he is … He knows what's o'clock".' A 'governor' is also the name of a clock part, so character is again being read as a kind of tic. But, like 'the real state of things', the knowing here (or finding, or discovering) is shrouded in secrecy. The governor knows what's o'clock, but we don't quite know what he knows (and, perhaps, neither does he). Just as when Scrooge finds himself wide awake, it is not made wholly clear what he has awoken *to*. The shuttling back and forth between the inanimately timed and the organically tensed in Dickens's style is frequently accompanied by the feeling that something is being shown whilst also being left inscrutable. When Master Humphrey listens to St Paul's clock, he observes, 'Its very pulse, if I may use the word, was like no other clock … the fancy came upon me that this was London's Heart' (*MHC*, 361). He then imagines the surrounding area which this heart serves: 'In that close corner … there are such dark crimes

... as could hardly be told in whispers ... does it [the clock] not express the city's character well?' (361). A clock also accompanies reflections on a submerged and shady character in *Bleak House*. When Miss Hortense has 'her arms composedly crossed, but with something in her dark cheek beating like a clock' (*BH*, 54, 768), the pulsing beat hints at a back story lying just beneath the surface. These biological clocks may be read as portents of what William Carpenter would call 'unconscious chronometry' later in the century.[24] They allude to the secrets that bodies might divulge if only they could speak: telltale without exactly telling the tale, they offer oblique signs of buried life. In *The Lazy Tour of the Two Idle Apprentices* (1857), one speaker confesses: 'At One in the morning, I am what you saw me when the clock struck that hour – One old man. At Two in the morning, I am Two old men. At Three, I am Three.'[25] It would seem that, when Dickens uses clocks to think with, plot lines drag their heels and characters multiply.

The bearing of these clocks on Dickens's weirdly conflicted attitude to storytelling needs to be understood in relation to his culture's own stories about clocks. As Lewis Mumford famously pronounced: 'the clock, not the steam engine, is the key machine of the modern industrial age.'[26] The 1780s saw the invention of the pocket chronometer, and a few years later, the word 'timekeeper' began to refer not just to an object but also to a person. The new century witnessed working-class ownership of watches and clocks, which, in turn, raised questions about whether people were taking possession of time or being possessed by it – merely cogs in a capitalist machine, as it were. Dickens's clocks sometimes beat in time to elements of this narrative. Stuck in the Fleet in *The Pickwick Papers*, Sam Weller says to his master: 'There's a Dutch clock, Sir ... And a bird-cage, Sir ... Veels vithin veels, a prison in a prison. Ain't it, Sir' (*PP*, 40, 626). In *Little Dorrit*, 'There was a grave clock, ticking somewhere up the staircase; and there was a songless bird in the same direction, pecking at his cage as if he were ticking too' (*LD*, 1, 13, 138).

Moments like this stress the lock in *clock*, and the *cage* that surrounds the age. In *Nicholas Nickleby*, Kate is asked, 'Vere's your govvernor?' – '"My what – did you say?" asked Kate, trembling; for she thought "governor" might be slang for watch or money' (*NN*, 21, 260). This is shorthand for an emerging plot line of modernity, what E. P. Thompson saw as the unholy trinity of 'Time, Work-Discipline, and Industrial Capitalism'.[27] Time is the 'governor' because time is money. The clock and the watch help to shape and regulate the rhythms of nineteenth-century industrial life. This is the age, after all, in which one's job is first described as 'full-time'. Time is no longer simply passed, it is spent. Daylight will soon be savings. Dickens's style sometimes has its own kind of grim fun with all this. In *Sketches by Boz*, Mr Watkins Tottle receives his annuity 'in periodical payments on every alternate Monday; but he ran himself out, about a day after the expiration of the first week, as regularly as an eight day clock; and then, to make the comparison complete, his landlady wound him up, and he went on with a regular tick' (*SB*, 415). So he lives 'on tick' – cash-strapped and pushed for time. In *Hard Times*, 'the deadly statistical clock' runs the show: 'Time went on in Coketown like its own machinery' (*HT*, I, 14, 88). 'Its' here is gruesomely timed to point in two directions: towards 'Coketown', primarily, but also towards 'Time' itself, because Time has its own machinery – clocks and watches, which are now a parody of the *deus ex machina*. The image is of a revolution turning in on itself – 'veels' within 'veels', a vicious circle rather than an upward progress.

According to Benedict Anderson, print capitalism aids and abets this modern sense of timing. Building on Walter Benjamin, Anderson links the rise of newspapers and novels to the need to forge an imagined community, one which feels placed and plotted within the same story: 'The date at the top of the newspaper, the single most important emblem on it, provides the essential connection – the steady onward clocking of homogenous, empty time.'[28] And, so Anderson's story goes, the novel works in a similar way: 'Consider the structure of the old-fashioned novel … It is clearly a device for the presentation of simultaneity in "homogeneous, empty time", or a complex gloss upon the word "meanwhile".'[29] But Dickens's devices sometimes seem to have a life of their own. In *Dombey and Son*, the word 'meanwhile' is glossed thus: 'meanwhile the clocks appeared to have made up their minds never to strike three any more' (*DS*, 6, 76). Just after a fascinated Paul Dombey has watched a clock-mender strip and fix his father's old clock, he hears the workman whisper something to the footman on his way out, 'in which there was the phrase "old-fashioned". What could that old fashion be, that seemed to make the people sorry! What could it be!' (*DS*, 14, 192). Anderson may be right about the newspaper, but not about the novel. Talk of an 'old-fashioned device' does not allow enough for the complexity of the fashioning.

From the start, Dickens was hammering out a style that explored, without quite succumbing to, equations between journalistic and imaginative readings of time. The first clock to appear in his writing is published in a newspaper (the *Evening Chronicle*): 'Thoughts about People' mentions 'the clock at The *Chronicle* Office'.[30] This is certainly the clock as *chronos*, as 'steady onward clocking' – to recall Anderson's phrase. Dickens would praise the newspapers later as 'the clock of the world',[31] and writing to the moment was a vital part of his own success (as an early reviewer in *Illustrated London News* noted of his serial form: 'The course of Dickens's narrative seemed to run on, somehow, almost simultaneously with the real progress of events').[32] Yet the writer's narratives themselves cast side-glances at the need to be up to date, as 'The Full Report of the Second Meeting of the Mudfog Association for the Advancement of Everything' makes clear:

> *Saloon of Steamer, Thursday night, half-past eight*
> … 'I am happy to say that I am the first passenger on board, and shall thus be enabled to give you an account of all that happens in the order of its occurrence.'
>
> …
>
> *Ten minutes past nine*
> 'Nobody has yet arrived … I write down these remarks as they occur to me, or as the facts come to my knowledge, in order that my first impressions may lose nothing of their original vividness. I shall dispatch them in small packets as opportunities arise.'
>
> *Half-past nine*
> 'Some dark object has just appeared upon the wharf. I think it is a travelling carriage.'
>
> *A quarter to ten*
> 'No, it isn't.'[33]

A consciousness wholly intent upon clocking things in real time and upon its corollary – The Advancement of Everything – may have lost the plot through too highly developed a need to find it. One way of linking the action of a printed text to that of a clock would be to say that both structures provide ways of spatialising time. With this idea in play, 'some dark object has just appeared' can be read in relation to the words on the page as well as to the things looming into view on the wharf. Yet these dark objects are vehicles for Dickens's voyages towards other apprehensions of time, towards a vision of prose not so much as a 'travelling carriage' but as the re-seeing, the re-marking, of 'the remarks' it makes. The need for a story or a scoop is, for many of Dickens's readers, a need for news, but there's an enquiring energy in the prose which is centrally concerned with tracking how facts may 'come to' knowledge in spite of our attempts at knowingness.

The clock at the *Chronicle* Office may have been the first to appear in Dickens's fiction, but it was also the first to disappear. When he revised 'Thoughts about People' for *Sketches by Boz*, Dickens cut the detail, and the first clock to appear in volume form is a different type of creature:

'Another time he took to pieces the eight-day clock on the front land-ing, under pretence of cleaning the works, which he put together again, by some undiscovered process, in so wonderful a manner, that the large hand has done nothing but trip up the little one ever since.'[34] This is an oblique portrait of the artist as a young man. Under the guise of doing something useful with his time, his real pleasure lies in tinkering with time – seeing how it's put together and how it might be made to go differ-ently. Many strange clocks – and people – after this one seem unflustered by the human need for them to get from tick to tock. In *Dombey and Son*, Florence is surrounded by 'clocks that never told the time, or, if wound up by any chance, told it wrong, and struck unearthly numbers, which are not upon the dial' (*DS*, 23, 312). Dickens's clocks play up, or play around, and in doing so they become emblems of – and enquiries into – the com-mitted vagrancy of his own style. To borrow a resonant phrase from *David Copperfield*, in his writing it is 'as if Time had not grown up himself yet, but were a child too, and always at play' (*DC*, 3, 32).

As time grew up in the nineteenth century, so did 'horology'. The year after Dickens was born, according to the *OED*, the word began to mean 'the art or science of measuring time', although the dictionary's source also points to 'the construction of horologues': 'The term horology is at present more particularly confined to the principles upon which the art of making clocks and watches is established' (1813). 'Art *or* science.' Dickens's style situates itself in relation to this 'or' and to questions about how time was to be conceived and controlled as well as measured. (How much, for example, is to be left to 'art', and how much to 'principles', when mak-ing fictional clocks and watches?) George Eliot began *Daniel Deronda* by drawing attention to the oversights of the art–science division. Even 'a beginning' is a kind of 'make-believe':

> Even science, the strict measurer, is obliged to start with a make-believe unit, and must fix on a point in the stars' unceasing journey when his sidereal clock shall pretend that time is at Nought. His less accurate grand-mother Poetry has always been understood to start in the middle; but on reflection it appears that her proceeding is not very different from his; since Science, too, reckons backward as well as forward, divides his unit into bil-lions, and with his clock-finger at Nought really sets off *in medias res*.[35]

Dickens's beginnings are especially attentive to the need to clock backward as well as forward, and many of his opening gambits tease out the impli-cations of Eliot's gentle pun on 'proceeding'. (Edging towards noun, it encompasses the sense of 'a piece of conduct or behavior'; edging towards

adjective, it takes on the sense of something 'following, ensuing', *OED*.)
The opening sentence from the first piece of fiction Dickens ever published goes like this: 'Mr Augustus Minns was a bachelor, of about forty
as he said – of about eight-and-forty as his friends said.'[36] Perhaps the joke
is on Minns, but the prose is not about to confirm things either way. The
writing's meaning unfolds in time but without exactly cancelling out the
first impression. (It's not quite deciding that he's *not* forty.) It begins *in
medias res* and in middle age, and with the feeling that a 'make-believe
unit' may be as real as anything surrounding it. You're only as old as you
feel, as Minns might say.

Dickens's novels open with a less certain sense of the imagined community than Anderson offers in his discussion of the temporal symbiosis
between novels and newspapers. The first sentence in *Oliver Twist* ends:

> and in this workhouse was born: on a day and date which I need not trou-
> ble myself to repeat, inasmuch as it can be of no possible consequence to
> the reader, in this stage of the business at all events: the item of mortality
> whose name is prefixed to the head of this chapter. (*OT*, 1, 1)

The insistence on a day and a date ('the single most important emblem
on the newspaper') is withheld so that the person, not the date, may go at
the top. Notwithstanding Dickens's enduring love affair with repetition of
many kinds, the narrator's unwillingness to 'repeat' the day and date here
is his way of avoiding becoming merely a 'chronometer, Repeater, and
every other terrible Machine that a watch *can* be'. The opening chapter
times Oliver's first cry at exactly 'three minutes and a quarter' (*OT*, 1, 4)
after his birth, but the narrative clock in this first sentence stays true to an
ambivalence that runs throughout the novel – and throughout much of
Dickens's writing.

It has been often said that time is ineffective as well as coercive in *Oliver
Twist*. (The hero is unsullied by time while others are creatures of time
and circumstance.) From the novel's opening sentence, though, Dickens's
style itself becomes a form of mediation between these two points of view.
The day and date will not be repeated, 'inasmuch as it can be of no possible consequence to the reader, [*pause*] in this stage of the business at all
events.' For a moment, the punctuation and pacing of the sentence implies
that time is of no importance, before the development of the syntax hints
at a revision of first impressions. The style needs to be read as both a line
and as a loop – unfolding chronologically in time and doubling back on
itself over time. To read in this way is to apprehend the present – in the
words of one recent study of temporality in narrative – as 'the object of a

future memory'.[37] What is of consequence is both confirmed and belied by temporal sequence, because the meaning of any single moment – in sentences as in life – is in part created by what we bring to it and what we expect or want from it. Readers experience things here not only as Anderson suggests, as the embodiment of a 'steady onward clocking', but also as a temporality that clocks itself in two directions at once, a temporality in which we can be encouraged to resist the self-fulfilling prophecies of apparently mechanistic chains of consequence. '*In this stage* of the business *at all events*': the sentence has whispered that *this stage* may be informed by, not isolated from, *all events*, whilst also steering clear of any definitive sense of cause and effect.

Dickens continued to make his grand entrances with ambiguous forms of clocking:

> Whether I shall turn out to be the hero of my own life, or whether that station will be held by anybody else, these pages must show. To begin my life with the beginning of my life, I record that I was born (as I have been informed and believe) on a Friday, at twelve o'clock at night. It was remarked that the clock began to strike, and I began to cry, simultaneously. (*DC*, I, I)

This looks back to other clocks and beginnings. Sterne's Tristram Shandy was born in 1718, 'betwixt the first *Sunday* and the first *Monday* in the month of *March*'.[38] So, which was it, Sunday or Monday? That novel, it will be recalled, begins with trouble with clocks – '*Pray, my dear ... have you not forgot to wind up the clock?*' (I, I, 5) – and Tristram will later confess that 'I wish there was not a clock in the kingdom' (III, 18, 151). Given David's fussiness, readers might wonder on which day he was born if he was born *exactly* at midnight (Friday or Saturday?). Like Tristram, he records only what he has been told, so the opening is meant to keep us guessing about time – and about what time could possibly tell. Later beginnings are also clocked and unclear: 'Thirty years ago, Marseilles lay burning in the sun, one day' (*Little Dorrit*, I, I, I). 'In these times of ours, though concerning the exact year there is no need to be precise' (*Our Mutual Friend*, I, I, I). 'One day thirty years ago' might have passed unnoticed, but the shift from a specific to a strangely nebulous sense of the moment seems to demand to be noticed. It's as though the novels' clocks are not simply marking time but biding or brooding over it.

Dickensian style is on the lookout for how exact temporal measurement compels an awareness of that which evades measurement – or, more precisely, an awareness of something left out or behind. As, for instance, when

Mr Pickwick listens to the church clock striking twelve – 'when the bell ceased the stillness seemed insupportable – he almost felt as if he had lost a companion' (*PP*, 11, 158) – or when David Copperfield recalls that 'I sat counting the ticking of the clock ... deepening my sense of the solemn hush around me' (*DC*, 30, 379). The clock brings into earshot a silence, or a stillness, with which the writing often wants to tarry. For the novelist and his audience, 'these times of ours' were not 'homogenous', but irreducibly plural – part of a debate about the values and dangers of simultaneity itself, and about what designs simultaneity might have on the individuals who were subject to it.[39] In *Dombey and Son*, the narrator says that 'there was even railway time observed in clocks, as if the sun itself had given in' (*DS*, 15, 218), but the sun was not giving in without a fight. In the 1840s, many town clocks had two minute hands, one for local time (based on sunrise) and one for railway time (based first on the London time kept by St Paul's, and later on Greenwich Mean Time [GMT]). The dissemination of print certainly had a major part to play in the journey towards conformity; the first issue of the *Illustrated London News*, published in 1842, carried the headline: 'Important to Railway Travellers. Uniformity of Clocks through-out Great Britain'.[40] Yet, in the same month in which *Dombey and Son* was finishing its serial run, *Blackwood's Magazine* carried a piece entitled 'Greenwich Time: The Time Is Out of Joint – Oh Cursed Spite' which defended local time against calls for standardisation. A meeting of the Plymouth Town Council witnessed the following reply to the recommen-dation that a move to railway time would lead to increased productivity: 'MR. W. F. COLLIER remarked that it would be well if the Mayor could, at the same time, cause Railway trains to arrive at the hours at which they were due (*hear, hear*).'[41] 'At the same time' can be heard as a wry reflec-tion, perhaps, on the trickiness of simultaneity in practice even when it has been agreed upon in principle. Although by the mid 1850s nearly all public clocks in Great Britain were set to GMT, during Dickens's lifetime there was nothing on the statute book defining what time was for legal purposes. A piece in *Household Words* in 1859 reminded readers that 'if we frisk by rail-way ... at every mile, at every furlong that we proceed westwards, there is really and truly a different "What o'clock?", although for convenience sake and uniformity of business, we may agree to regulate our watches by rail-way time, Saint Paul's time, or any other cathedral time.'[42]

Dickens's timings take their bearings from this mixed state of affairs. Paul Dombey asks the clock-mender 'what he thought about King Alfred's idea of measuring time by the burning of candles; to which the workman replied, that he thought it would be the ruin of the clock trade if it was to come up again' (*DS*, 14, 192). Onward and upward, then. But when the man sets to work on the clock, we are informed that he 'had taken its face off, and was poking instruments into the works by the light of a candle!' (*DS*, 14, 192). So this miniature sun still has a part to play in the maintenance of modern temporality. The novel itself also remains committed to a range of temporal orders, for although *Dombey and Son* is frequently wheeled out as the novel in which Dickens's own drive towards plotting and order assumes new, increasingly coherent shapes (it is the first novel for which he wrote out detailed plans in advance), some of those number plans acted not as prompts for grand designs but as reminders of cherished yet unruly objects. Take two notes in particular: 'clock' and 'Captain Cuttle's Big Watch' (838, 840). When Cuttle offers his watch to Walter, he advises, 'Put it back half an hour every morning, and about another quarter towards arternoon, and it's a watch that'll do you credit' (*DS*, 19, 266). Clocks, then, should be watched lest they encourage you to get ahead of yourself. This organised yet open-ended approach to time (*about* another quarter) makes Cuttle a worthy associate of Solomon Gills:

> [Captain Cuttle] became silent, and remained so, until old Sol went out into the shop to light it up, when he turned to Walter, and said, without any introductory remark:
> 'I suppose he could make a clock if he tried?'
> 'I shouldn't wonder, Captain Cuttle,' returned the boy.
> 'And it would go!', said Captain Cuttle, making a species of serpent in the air with his hook. 'Lord, how that clock would go!'
> For a moment or two he seemed quite lost in contemplating the pace of this ideal timepiece, and sat looking at the boy as if his face were the dial.
> (*DS*, 4, 44)

Cuttle is enthused by an artistry that doesn't just keep time but creates it. His own serpentine flourish is a way of joining in with the temptation to play with time, and it is not entirely clear whether he envisages this ideal timepiece as something which would 'go' in the sense of going accurately or going exuberantly. Dickens's own light brushwork in the last sentence shares the imaginative pace of his character: 'For a moment or two' is timed, after all, but not overly so. Once again, narrative action is stilled to a moment of psychological contemplation; the clock would no doubt *go*, but Cuttle sits looking – as though the clock were a catalyst for a more searching gaze into the boy's character.

It is fitting that Sol goes out here 'to light up' the shop because – as old Sol – he is a kind of surrogate sun in the novel, a compound figure

of old-fashioned variable and newly fashioned standardised timing. He is
introduced like this:

> He wore … a tremendous chronometer in his fob, rather than doubt which
> precious possession, he would have believed in a conspiracy against it on
> part of all the clocks and watches in the City, and even of the very Sun
> itself.
>   … It is half-past five o'clock, and an autumn afternoon, when the reader
> and Solomon Gills become acquainted. Solomon Gills is in the act of see-
> ing what time it is by the unimpeachable chronometer. (*DS*, 4, 37–8)

The timepiece is in competition with both clocks and the sun, refusing to
be beholden to either. Sol's faith in it is, I think, a gently comedic version
of Dickens's faith in his own artistry, and perhaps his way of humouring
that artistry. It intimates the novelist's belief in the value of his own creative shapings of time, and it is sensed here in the claim that 'It is half-past
five o'clock … when the reader and Solomon Gills become acquainted.'
Whilst in America, Dickens wrote to Forster: 'We are never tired of
imagining what you are all about. I allow of no calculation for the difference of clocks, but insist on a corresponding minute in London. It is
much the shortest way, and best.'[43] Like Cuttle, Dickens insists upon putting the clock back in order to indulge in the tireless work of imagining.
His letter hints at how his plotting takes its cue from character (rather
than vice versa), and the narrator of *Dombey and Son*, following old Sol's
lead, also allows of no calculation for the difference of clocks. The novel's
time becomes ours ('*it is* half-past five o'clock') and so becomes the narrator's oblique way of getting us to imagine what Sol is all about. Like the
form in which he appears, Sol is both subject to the clock and an obstacle
to its power – at once subservient to the force of time and a force that
imposes imaginative demands on time.

When Henri Bergson considered the nature of the comic in relation
to character, he referred to what he called 'the ready-made element in our
personality, the mechanical element which resembles a piece of clockwork
wound up once for all and capable of working automatically'.[44] But this
element also points to something beyond the mechanical – something more
like a person's insistence on building a style of experience. Call it an individual's way of impinging on life. Sol doesn't just look at his watch; we see
him 'in the act of seeing what time it is'. The slowing up of the prose invites
an appreciation of this act as at once a kind of make-believe and reconfigur-
ing of the real itself. Northrop Frye observed that 'The obstructing humors
in Dickens are absurd because they have overdesigned their lives. But the
kind of design that they parody is produced by another kind of energy, and

one which insists, absurdly and yet irresistibly, that what is must never take final precedence over what ought to be.'[45] The same might be said for the humour of Dickens's narrative voice. When this narrator explains that 'it is half-past five o'clock', the word 'is' itself has been permeated by what ought to be. Readers arrive late on the scene, but this fact is not allowed to take final precedence over the time which has passed yet which never seems to pass. That time – absurdly, yet irresistibly – is the right time. Like the style for which they stand as figures, Dickens's clocks go by going back.

Far back, there is a clock that meant a great deal to Dickens, one that can still be heard ticking below the surface of *Great Expectations*. It can be approached by way of a piece he published a few years earlier about difficulties he was having with writing:

> I had scarcely fallen into my most promising attitude, and dipped my pen in the ink, when I found the clock upon the pier – a red-faced clock with a white rim – importuning me in a highly vexatious manner to consult my watch, and see how I was off for Greenwich time. Having no intention of making a voyage or taking an observation, I had not the least need of Greenwich time, and could have put up with watering-place time as a sufficiently accurate article. The pier-clock, however, persisting, I felt it necessary to lay down my pen, compare my watch with him, and fall into a grave solicitude about half-seconds.[46]

Sue Zemka has recently read Dickens's clocks as guardians of an isolated moment which is registered as significant before then being satirised by the plot's momentum; the clock appears, she suggests, only as a prelude to narrative making its 'long, perambulatory pull away from momentariness'.[47] But this perspective is reliant upon a model of Dickens's style as peripatetic, and it might be countered by noting that many of the clocks in his fiction appear whilst somebody is sitting still or 'having no intention of making a voyage'. Here, clocking the time gets in the way of writing, yet it has led to *this* writing; a grave solicitude about half-seconds is both displacement activity and a way of burrowing deeper into the moment by expanding it – and expanding upon it. The juggling acts between the animate and inanimate to which Dickens is so often drawn are felt more obliquely than usual (he writes 'How I was off', not 'how it [the watch] was off' for Greenwich time; the clock is not an 'it' but a 'him'), but they can be felt nonetheless. One inspiration for this way of seeing and writing is hinted at by the clock itself: 'a red-faced clock with a white rim'. A peculiarly clown-like clock, then, one that ushers into view the time of pantomime.

Dickens recalled as a child having an 'intense anxiety' to know what clowns 'did with themselves out of pantomime time, and off the stage'.[48] In his *Memoirs of Joseph Grimaldi* he drew attention to the relations between imagined and real time by telling a story in which Joe's violent and abusive father faked his own death in order to see how his two sons would take it. Joe's brother (glad of the release) says, 'Oh! Never mind … we can have the cuckoo-clock all to ourselves now' (*MJG*, II, 35). At this point, the act becomes too much for the deceased to bear, and he jumps up to beat the boy in front of Joe. As Dickens tells it, the story has all the slapstick hallmarks of a pantomimic raising from the dead but with a gruesome twist that brings the thing off stage and uncomfortably close to home. This blurring of the edges between on-stage funny business and off-stage reality would become a vital aspect of Dickens's style; in *American Notes*, he remembers Boston: 'every thoroughfare in the city looked exactly like a scene in a pantomime … As to Harlequin and Columbine, I discovered immediately that they lodged … at a very small clockmaker's one story high, near the hotel; which … had a great dial hanging out – to be jumped through, of course' (*AN*, I, 3, 34). This is the essence of 'pantomime time' as it took a hold of Dickens's imagination. He is probably thinking here of the most renowned pantomime of all:

> *The comic business begins here …* [CLOWN *and* PANTALOON] *endeavour to secure* HARLEQUIN, *who eludes their grasp, and leaps through the face of the clock, which immediately presents a* SPORTSMAN *with his gun cocked. The* CLOWN *opens the clock door, and a little* HARLEQUIN *appears as the pendulum, the* CLOWN *saying 'Present! Fire!' The* SPORTSMAN *lets off his piece, the* CLOWN *falls down, during which period* COLUMBINE *and* HARLEQUIN, *who had previously entered through the panel, escape. After some tricks, the* CLOWN *runs off in pursuit.*[49]

In 'pantomime time', clocks are used to evade the exigencies of the moment, paradoxically becoming the vehicles by which time itself is resisted. As a hoop to be jumped through, the clock stands as a transformative threshold, a catalyst that turns people into timepieces as a way of keeping them safe from harm. Pantomime time borrows from reality in order to revise it; later in *Mother Goose*, the famous clock of St Dunstan's Church (the first clock in London to have a minute hand) makes an appearance, but the appendage for accuracy here is the means of transcendence: 'PANTALOON *mounts the dial and the* CLOWN *clings around it – ascending in this situation.*'[50] As the clown's hands seek out a communion with the hands of the clock, the staging now suggests that time is on his side. Pantomime, it would seem, can stop the clock.

Dickens's writings on pantomime frequently lead him to a particular word (my emphasis below). In *Sketches by Boz*, he talks of 'the *secret* cause' of an audience's 'amusement and delight' at the shows.[51] In 1852, he says that 'the *secret* of this enjoyment lies in the temporary superiority to the common hazards and mischances of life' because – despite all the rough and tumble – there's no harm done.[52] In another article he writes:

> every one … is so superior to all the accidents of life, though encountering them at every turn, that I suspect this to be the *secret* (though many persons may not present it to themselves) of the general enjoyment which an audience of vulnerable spectators, liable to pain and sorrow, find in this class of entertainment.[53]

One of the accidents of life is time itself, encountered at 'every turn' of the clock. It's an accident waiting to happen – and waiting to be overcome – in pantomime, where time is of no consequence. Like its clock, the mode's secret shares a deep affinity with what Greene called Dickens's 'secret prose': it gestures towards that aspect of his style which on occasion seems to step outside, or aside from, its duties to clocked cause and effect. The impulse remains secret, I think, because it is felt as irresponsible as well as irresistible – at once a guilty pleasure and a source of consolation. In *Great Expectations*, the subplot of the novel is not just the one about the real causes and consequences that shape Pip's life. It is also the story about the insights and evasions of Dickens's comic, pantomimic style itself – about the fantasies that style can encourage, and the ones it may need to rethink.

As he started to write the novel, Dickens wrote excited letters to Forster: 'I can see the whole of a serial revolving … in a most singular and comic manner … I have got in the pivot on which the story will turn too … [a] grotesque tragi-comic conception.'[54] The story will turn and revolve like a clock, but a peculiar kind of clock – one that never quite lets comic manner get the upper hand over tragicomic conception. Late in the novel, Pip goes to see Wopsle play in a pantomime. The show is preceded by a piece that features 'an honest little grocer with a white hat, black gaiters, and red nose, getting into a clock, with a gridiron, and listening, and coming out, and knocking everybody down from behind' (*GE*, iii, 8, 381). This sort of thing is often good clean fun in Dickens, but in this novel connections between stage-clowning and life off-stage are unsettling. (Orlick later tells Pip how he dealt with Mrs Joe: 'I come upon her from behind, as I come upon you to-night. *I* giv' it her!' [iii, 14, 423].) Next comes the 'new grand Comic Christmas pantomime', but Pip is perturbed to find that Wopsle, even whilst on stage, has 'a good deal of time on his hands', enough time to look into the audience at Pip whilst he's playing the part: 'I could not make it out. I sat thinking of it, long after he had ascended to the clouds in a large watch-case, and still I could not make it out' (III, 8, 382). It feels as though the protagonist might – unbeknownst to himself – be *part* of a pantomime.

Edwin Eigner has argued that *Great Expectations* is the first novel by Dickens in which a leading clown figure is absent and suggests that this may be as a result of his father's horrific death in 1851. (Eigner reads John Dickens as a model for Micawber and the clowns of the earlier novels.)[55] But Clown is still alive and kicking (much as Joe Grimaldi's father was) as a faintly discernible yet disquieting presence. When Pip casts himself as the lead part in his own Great Expectations, he imagines that Miss Havisham has called upon him to 'set the clocks a going and the cold hearths a blazing … and marry the Princess' (*GE*, II, 10, 232). So he is a kind of Harlequin, a transformative hero. After his first visit to Miss Havisham's house, Pip whispers an aside to the audience and brings stage-time into real time:

> That was a memorable day to me, for it made great changes in me. But, it is the same with any life. Imagine one selected day struck out of it, and think how different its course would have been. Pause you who read this, and think for a moment of the long chain of iron or gold, of thorns or flowers, that would never have bound you, but for the formation of the first link on one memorable day. (*GE*, I, 9, 73)

Many readers have sensed that the 'chains' allude to the memorable day that really makes great changes to Pip – the one on the marshes – and to the chain that shackles Magwitch. But the last occurrence of the word 'chain' itself in the novel before this paragraph referred to the fact that Miss Havisham's 'watch and chain were not put on' (*GE*, I, 8, 58), and the next comes in reference to a man with 'a large watch-chain' (I, 2, 83). According to Partridge's *Dictionary of Slang*, from around 1860 the term 'chain-gang' was slang for 'watch-chain makers'. The link between criminality and temporality is strengthened when Wemmick mulls over Jaggers's gold watch: 'there are about seven hundred thieves in this town who know all about that watch; there's not a man, a woman, or a child, among them, who wouldn't identify the smallest link in that chain' (II, 6, 205–6). A couple of convicts turn Pip's way in the pub later on: 'his eye appraised my watch-chain … they laughed and slued themselves round with a clink of their coupling manacle, and looked at something else' (II, 9, 227).

These chains lead closer to the secret, 'tragi-comic conception' at the heart of the novel: the clown. In pantomime, the clown is a criminal, a pickpocket, a thief (often, a stealer of watches) – the underdog who rebels and who makes the best of situations through seemingly absurd manip- ulations of time. Dickens recalled his childhood as 'the period when I believed the Clown was being born into the world with infinite pockets',[56] and Pip's formative memory features a man who, 'after looking at me for a moment, turned me upside down, and emptied my pockets' (*GE*, 1, 1, 4). This is the man who plays Clown to Pip's Harlequin, the man who brings to a head Dickens's enduring fascination with clocking and shady charac- ter: Pip recalls of Magwitch that 'Something clicked in his throat, as if he had works in him like a clock, and was going to strike' (1, 3, 19). 'Works' surreptitiously refers to 'deeds' as well as to 'inner mechanisms'. Magwitch is going to strike – not now, but much later, as the clown would, and in a way that calls into question the authority of the timepieces by which Pip measures his life.

In *Mother Goose*, Clown is got out of the way as Harlequin runs off for adventures with the girl, before he rises up again and makes a spectacular comeback. Most pantomimes proceed to what is usually termed the 'dark scene', where the magic wand is eventually snatched from Harlequin's grasp and flourished in triumph by Clown. In *Great Expectations*, Pip's last childhood vision of Magwitch is as he sees him 'disappear ... as if it were all over with him' (*GE*, 1, 5, 41). But the novel's dark scene arrives when Magwitch returns. Here, though, the wand is a watch:

> I read with my watch upon the table, purposing to close my book at eleven o'clock. As I shut it, Saint Paul's, and all the many church-clocks in the City – some leading, some accompanying, some following – struck that hour. The sound was curiously flawed by the wind; and I was listening, and thinking how the wind assailed and tore it, when I heard a footstep on the stair.
>
> ... As he ascended the last stair or two, and the light of my lamp included us both, I saw, with a stupid kind of amazement, that he was holding out both his hands to me.
>
> ... 'Look'ee here!' he went on, taking my watch out of my pocket, and turning towards him a ring on my finger, while I recoiled from his touch as if he had been a snake, 'a gold 'un and a beauty: *that's* a gentleman's, I hope!'
>
> ... 'Don't you mind talking, Pip,' said he, after again drawing his sleeve over his eyes and forehead, as the click came in his throat which I well remembered.

> ... I tried to collect my thoughts, but I was stunned. Throughout, I had seemed to myself to attend more to the wind and the rain than to him; even now, I could not separate his voice from those voices, though those were loud and his was silent.
>
> ... the wretched man, after loading wretched me with his gold and silver chains for years, had risked his life to come to me, and I held it there in my keeping! (*GE*, ii, 20, 311–20)

Even before Magwitch's arrival, Pip's attempt to read by the clock is subject to a dim awareness that the clocks in his life are not quite in sync. Once Magwitch takes the stage, Pip will continue to be horrified and fascinated by his hands (he comes back to them again and again throughout the chapter), and, given that Magwitch 'has works in him like a clock', these hands might then be seen as the works on the clock face. They are a grotesque reminder to Pip that he must finally come into visceral contact with time. The scene opens with his awareness of how the sound of the clocks mingles with that of the weather so that when he says that '*even now*, I could not separate his voice' from the wind and rain, the subterranean hint of the prose is that Magwitch's voice will always be linked to a clock – and to a click that is linked to his past. Clown is again up to his old tricks – taking watches from pockets, turning time over in his hand to see what magic might be made with it – only now the pantomime tricks portend real trouble. For Pip to hold Magwitch's life in his 'keeping' (along with all the gold and silver chains) is to hold a life as one might hold an inherited and precious timekeeper. What this broken-down yet back-from-the-dead clown is bringing home is the idea that some clocks are not there merely 'to be jumped through, of course'.

Here might be a good place to clarify my own plot line. A secret, long-standing yearning in Dickens's style for an escape from onwardly plodding narrative, from plot, from consequence, was always there in pantomime and its clock. That yearning helped to nurture many of his writing's great strengths: its ability to hint at what can lie beneath a character and a moment (as in his depiction of Scrooge); its willingness to resist some versions of determinism (as in his treatment of Oliver); and its insistence on seeing timeless fantasy as a kind of replenishment (as in his handling of Captain Cuttle and Old Sol). But this yearning may on other occasions shade into a refusal to countenance what is owed to time and to what one's time is beholden. When thinking through his plans for the final part of *Great Expectations*, Dickens wrote to Forster that 'the general turn and tone of the working out and winding up, will be away from all such things as they conventionally go'.[57] To wind something up can be to start as well as to end a process. Dickens's figuring of his own formal audacity here as a clock-like motion tells of his need in this particular novel to unwind, or to re-wind, some of the ways we might have thought it would go – towards a happy-ever-after, say, or towards a swerving away from unwanted cause and effect (what Dickens had earlier seen as pantomime time's immunity from 'the common hazards and mischances of life'). If pantomime informs much of his fiction, in *Great Expectations* the clock that resembles that mode's ludic time most closely is now seen as a danger. Pip recalls that, at Miss Havisham's, 'I felt as if the stopping of the clocks had stopped Time in that mysterious place, and, while I and everything else outside it grew older, it stood still ... It bewildered me, and under its influence I continued at heart to hate my trade and to be ashamed of home' (*GE*, 1, 17, 124). In these surroundings, the need to step outside or to freeze time is both the cause and consequence of the wrong kind of secret. In pantomime, a stopped clock is momentary respite from everyday cares and consequences; in this novel, it is a harbinger and cause of shame.

As if to atone for his negligence about clocking the significance of his own life story, Pip spends the later parts of the novel paying attention to keeping the clock moving. The plan to effect Magwitch's escape relies on tide times, and, as the detective work of critics has shown, *Great Expectations* is probably Dickens's most systematically dated and clocked. The author's working plans for the novel reveal the pains he took to get things right: 'Tide ... Up at 3 PM – till 9. P.M. Wednesday | Down at 9 PM. till 3 AM Thursday Morning | Up at 3 AM. till 9. AM Thursday morning | when the boat starts' (*GE*, 487). Dickens, like Pip, times things meticulously behind the scenes (although we wouldn't know the author's care, so guardedly does the prose style keep its own counsel). Unlike Pip, though, the author takes these measurements even though he knows the plan will fail; it is as though he were looking to clocks for the sense of an ending which he knows his novel cannot provide. As a clown with a new, hard-won experience, Magwitch offers another way of thinking through time. Time as flowing, variable river – not as segmented, isochronous, clock – is a way of acknowledging the value of one moment whilst refusing to unhook it from others. When Magwitch is told by a newly assiduous Pip as they row down the river that in a few hours he will be free, he responds like this:

> He dipped his hand in the water over the boat's gunwale, and said, smiling with that softened air upon him which was not new to me:

'Ay, I s'pose I think so, dear boy. We'd be puzzled to be more quiet and easy-going than we are at present. But – it's a flowing so soft and pleasant through the water, p'raps, as makes me think it – I was a thinking through my smoke just then, that we can no more see to the bottom of the next few hours, than we can see to the bottom of this river what I catches hold of. Nor yet we can't no more hold their tide than I can hold this. And it's run through my fingers and gone, you see!' holding up his dripping hand. (*GE*, III, 15, 434)

This is a lovely, light revision of the clown's hand as the hand of the clock. Magwitch has time on his hands, only they are dripping now with another feeling for temporality. No amount of clocking tide times is adequate preparation for what happens next, yet it also feels as if Magwitch is in on a secret with his creator as he touches the element in which he will soon be immersed. And, of course, Pip is also looking back in time, so he is now privy to the wisdom and the foresight of Magwitch's words. It is as though – through the timed amplitude of Dickens's fictional form – Harlequin has finally come to an understanding with Clown by rethinking the pleasures of pantomime. *Great Expectations* has become a way for Dickens to carve out a space between a frantic need to 'set the clocks a-going' and a desire to stall them, or to jump through them as if they don't exist. Nobody is 'superior to the accidents of life' in this novel, yet the grace with which Magwitch concedes the unfathomable nature of the moment makes him equal to it.

Whilst defending a vision of pantomime as 'animated action or gesture' and linking this to a defence of fictional writings that draw attention to the 'surface' of things, Chesterton once observed that 'psychological things are not less psychological because they come to the surface in pantomime. The argument amounts to saying that a really delicate piece of clockwork exists only when the clock stops.'[58] In Dickens's art, pantomimical action is a spur to psychological investigation, and the delicacy of the author's clockwork is sensed in the play between stalled and restarted clocks. Dickens's timepieces increasingly come to speak of and from a moment that won't seem to 'stop'; they betoken a need to return to a scene that is not quite ever finished with (the writing on the watch in *Little Dorrit* says as much: 'D.N.F.' – Do Not Forget [I, 30, 349–50]). Indeed, his clocks and watches to some extent allegorise the journeyings of his style by refusing to give up on what has gone before, by looking to make use of the past even as the story keeps ticking over. These clocks are partly historical – part of a literary and cultural narrative about the possibilities for modern narrativity itself – but they are also deeply personal. In his 'Autobiographical Fragment' – first published in Forster's biography – Dickens recalled a moment after the blacking-factory episode that came on the back of his father's insolvency. He was called before the official appraiser to ensure that his clothing and personal effects did not 'exceed twenty pounds sterling in value': 'I had a fat old silver watch in my pocket, which had been given me by my grandmother before the blacking-days, and I had entertained my doubts as I went along whether that valuable possession might not bring me over the twenty pounds. So I was greatly relieved, and made him a bow of acknowledgment as I went out.'[59] To keep possession of this watch is not just to keep in mind a remembrance of better days but to remain cognisant of what can be survived, reused and passed on. Yet to remember the moment is also to revisit the site of a trauma that can barely be spoken about. The watch is being used to say something that the writer cannot.

Several years later, after the Staplehurst Railway accident, it was Dickens's prized chronometer from the people of Coventry that kept him returning to the horrifying scene and that allowed him to find a way of expressing how it was being re-lived as well as lived through. Several correspondents received letters with confessions like this: 'my watch (a special Chronometer) has never gone quite correctly, since'; 'My watch (a chronometer) had palpitations six months afterwards'; 'Is it not curiously significant of the action of a great Railway accident on the nerves of human creatures, that my watch (a chronometer) got so fluttered in my pocket … that it has never since been itself to the extent of two or three minutes?'[60] The railways may have been the prime movers behind the shift to standardised timing, but the Dickensian clock reserves the right to be haunted by the past and to carry traces of it in its timings. The chronometer is a half-secret, confidential way of talking about himself too, of course. He's never since quite gone correctly, or gone the same, but on he goes. Five years to the day after the Staplehurst accident (9 June 1870), in an ending that came like clockwork, the writer would die of a brain haemorrhage.

Clocks in Dickens don't just tell the time; they tell of a relationship with time. One way of conceiving this relationship would be as a form of trauma. Another would be as a form of gratitude or a sense of belonging. Both options were perhaps felt when Dickens received his watch at Coventry ('chronometer, Repeater, and every other terrible Machine that a watch *can* be. It was very feelingly and pleasantly given, and I prize it highly'). In *Great Expectations*, Pip recalls of Wemmick: 'I noticed, too, that several rings and seals hung at his watch chain, as if he were quite laden with remembrances of departed friends' (*GE*, II, 2, 169). This kind of noticing is one of the great pleasures of Dickens's style – part of the way he remembers and of the way he wants to be remembered. In his will, he left Forster not only the manuscripts of his published works but an item that had played a part in the making of those works: 'I give my watch (the gold repeater presented to me at Coventry), and I give the chains and seals and all appendages I have worn with it, to my dear and trusty friend John Forster.'[61] It seems fitting that the timepiece should speak volumes by allowing the full story to remain unspoken.

NOTES

1 E. M. Forster, *Aspects of the Novel* (1927; reprinted London: Penguin, 1990), 43.
2 Virginia Woolf, *Orlando: A Biography* (1928; reprinted Oxford World's Classics, 1998), 95.
3 Georg Lukács, *The Theory of the Novel: A Historico-Philosophical Essay on the Forms of Great Epic Literature*, trans. Anna Bostock (Cambridge, MA: MIT Press, 1971), 91.
4 Ian Watt, *The Rise of the Novel* (Berkeley, CA: University of California Press, 2001), 22.
5 Frank Kermode, *The Sense of an Ending: Studies in the Theory of Fiction* (Oxford University Press, 1966), 45.
6 Kermode, *The Sense of an Ending*, 44–5.
7 Kermode, *The Sense of an Ending*, 46.
8 On earlier narratives in relation to clocks, see Stuart Sherman, *Telling Time: Clocks, Diaries, and English Diurnal Form, 1660–1785* (University of Chicago Press, 1996).
9 Quoted in *CH*, 323, and Stephen Wall (ed.), *Charles Dickens: A Critical Anthology* (Harmondsworth: Penguin, 1970), 153.
10 *Letters*, XII, 220.
11 *Life*, II, 204.
12 Samuel Richardson, *Pamela; or, Virtue Rewarded*, ed. Thomas Keymer (Oxford World's Classics, 2001), 369.
13 James Boswell, *The Life of Samuel Johnson*, ed. David Womersley (London: Penguin, 2008), 288.
14 George Eliot, *Middlemarch*, ed. David Carroll (Oxford World's Classics, 2008), 9.
15 Quoted in Mark Spilka, *Dickens and Kafka: A Mutual Interpretation* (Bloomington, IN: Indiana University Press, 1963), 76.
16 Graham Greene, 'The Young Dickens', in *The Lost Childhood and Other Essays* (London: Eyre and Spottiswode, 1954), 53.
17 G. K. Chesterton, *The Collected Works of G. K. Chesterton*, vol. XV: *Chesterton on Dickens*, ed. Alzina Stone Dale (San Francisco, CA: Ignatius, 1989), 135.

18 Letter from Charles Dickens to John Bennett, 14 September 1863, *Letters*, XII, 697.

19 Letter from Charles Dickens to John Bennett, 17 December 1857, *Letters*, VIII, 493.

20 I would like to acknowledge here my gratitude and indebtedness to Andrew Miller, whose searching responses to an earlier version of this essay were a gift.

21 *Speeches*, 286.

22 Letter from Charles Dickens to Miss Burdett Coutts, 13 December 1858, *Letters*, VIII, 718.

23 Letter from Charles Dickens to John Forster, [? mid-February 1843], *Letters*, III, 441.

24 William Carpenter, *Principles of Mental Physiology* (4th edn, 1876) (London: Routledge, 1993), 347–8.

25 Charles Dickens, *Lazy Tour of Two Idle Apprentices*, Chapter 4, *Journalism*, III, 462.

26 Lewis Mumford, *Technics and Civilization* (1934; reprinted New York: Harcourt, 1934), 14. For a superb account of the subject, see David Landes, *Revolution in Time: Clocks and the Making of the Modern World* (London: Penguin, 2000).

27 E. P. Thompson, 'Time, Work-Discipline, and Industrial Capitalism', *Past and Present*, 38 (December 1967): 56–97.

28 Benedict Anderson, *Imagined Communities: Reflections on the Origin and Spread of Nationalism* (London: Verso, 1991), 35.

29 Anderson, *Imagined Communities*, 33.

30 See John Butt and Kathleen Tillotson, *Dickens at Work* (London: Methuen, 1957), 47.

31 *Speeches*, 339.

32 *CH*, 525.

33 *Journalism*, I, 532–3.

34 *Journalism*, I, 15.

35 George Eliot, *Daniel Deronda*, ed. Terence Cave (London: Penguin, 1995), 7.

36 Charles Dickens, 'A Dinner at Poplar Walk', *Journalism*, III, 306.

37 Mark Currie, *About Time: Narrative, Fiction and the Philosophy of Time* (Edinburgh University Press, 2010), 150.

38 Lawrence Sterne, *The Life and Opinions of Tristram Shandy, Gentleman*, ed. Ian Campbell Ross (Oxford University Press, 1998), 1, 4, 8.

39 For a recent engagement with this topic, see Jonathan H. Grossman, *Charles Dickens's Networks: Public Transport and the Novel* (Oxford University Press, 2012).

40 Quoted in Derek Howse, *Greenwich Time and the Discovery of the Longitude* (Oxford University Press, 1950), 87.

41 Howse, *Greenwich Time*, 113.

42 E. Dixon, 'The Lagging Easter', *Household Words*, 19 (5 March 1859), 329.

43 Letter from Charles Dickens to John Forster, 1, 2, 3 and 4 April 1842, *Letters*, III, 181.

44 Henri Bergson, *Laughter: An Essay on the Meaning of the Comic*, trans. Cloudesley Brereton and Fred Rothwell (Rockville, MD: Arc Manor, 2008), 72.

45 Northrop Frye, 'Dickens and the Comedy of Humors', in R. H. Pearce (ed.), *Experience in the Novel* (New York: Columbia University Press, 1968), 49–81, at 81.

46 Charles Dickens, 'Out of the Season', *Household Words*, 13 (28 June 1856), 327.

47 Sue Zemka, *Time and the Moment in Victorian Literature and Society* (Cambridge University Press, 2011), 117.

48 Charles Dickens, *Memoirs of Joseph Grimaldi* (New York: Colyer, 1838), iii.

49 Thomas Dibdin, *Harlequin and Mother Goose; or, The Golden Egg!* (1807), reprinted in Andrew McConnell Stott, *The Pantomime Life of Joseph Grimaldi* (London: Canongate, 2009), 325–44, at 333.

50 Dibdin, *Harlequin and Mother Goose*, 339.

51 Charles Dickens, 'The Pantomime of Life', *Journalism*, I, 501.

52 Charles Dickens, 'Lying Awake', *Journalism*, III, 93.

53 Charles Dickens, 'A Curious Dance Round a Curious Tree', *Household Words*, 4 (17 January 1852), 386.

54 *Letters*, IX, 310, 325.

55 Edwin Eigner, *The Dickens Pantomime* (Berkeley, CA: University of California Press, 1992), 171, 177.

56 *Speeches*, 76.

57 *Letters*, IX, 403.

58 G. K. Chesterton, *Robert Louis Stevenson* (1928; reprinted London: Dodo Press, 2011), 72.

59 *Life*, I, 33.

60 *Letters*, XII, 161, 335; XI, 134.

61 *Life*, II, 522.

CHAPTER THREE

Dickens's rhythms

Robert Douglas-Fairhurst

One of the Victorian novel's finest pieces of narrative timing occurs in George Eliot's *Adam Bede*:

> But Adam's thoughts of Hetty did not deafen him to the service; they rather blended with all the other deep feelings for which the church service was a channel to him this afternoon, as a certain consciousness of our entire past and our imagined future blends itself with all our moments of keen sensibility. And to Adam the church service was the best channel he could have found for his mingled regret, yearning, and resignation; its interchange of beseeching cries for help, with outbursts of faith and praise – its recurrent responses and the familiar rhythm of its collects, seemed to speak for him as no other form of worship could have done.[1]

In his densely suggestive essay 'Redeeming the Time', Geoffrey Hill chooses this passage to demonstrate Eliot's 'fine sense of traditional rhythmic life'.[2] This sense is powerfully concentrated in phrases such as 'recurrent responses', because these responses are understood to recur not just within the limited time span of this particular evensong, following the established patterns of the *Book of Common Prayer*, but also over the weeks and months of the liturgical year. This is how 'channels' are created for 'deep feelings', as a worshipper's voice settles into these old grooves like the needle on a worn record, and we hear the process at work in the patterns of Eliot's prose, as she sinks the individual stresses and slacks of Adam's thoughts into the balanced periods of congregational call and reply: 'beseeching cries for help, with outbursts of faith and praise ... recurrent responses ... familiar rhythm'.

However, in taking for granted that these feelings are as firmly 'established' as the Church, Eliot's 'certain consciousness' risks sounding too sure of itself. After all, not everyone who utters the words of a church service will mean what they say. Thomas Hardy, for example, had far less certain responses to Anglican worship, ruefully conscious that for him, as for many of his contemporaries, Eliot's 'channels' had been silted up by doubt:

We enter church, and we have to say, 'We have erred and strayed from thy
ways like lost sheep', when what we want to say is, 'Why are we made to err
and stray like lost sheep?' …

   Still, being present, we say the established words full of the historic sentiment only, mentally adding, 'How happy our ancestors were in repeating
in all sincerity these articles of faith!' But we perceive that none of the con-
gregation recognises that we repeat the words from an antiquarian interest
in them, and in a historic sense.[3]

Many of Hardy's poems try to find shapes for 'established' forms of religious expression which he found sentimentally attractive but intellec-
tually suspect. For example, he remained fond of hymns long after he had
decided that they were chiefly of 'antiquarian interest', and his own use
of traditional hymn stanzas often conveys simultaneously a regret for the
days when they could be repeated 'in all sincerity' and a resignation to the
idea that their contents were now only of 'historic sentiment'. Consider
the opening stanza of 'The Impercipient: At a Cathedral Service':

> That with this bright believing band
> I have no claim to be,
> That faiths by which my comrades stand
> Seem fantasies to me,
> And mirage-mists their Shining Land,
> Is a strange destiny.[4]

The first four lines are in common metre, the measure in which many
popular hymns are written, but Hardy's poem skews the sense of his words
across this traditional form and then draws out the stanza for an extra two
lines, longingly and mockingly, as if wondering what his speaker still has
in common with the sentiments usually carried by this metre. It is especially in these last lines that Hardy can be heard checking how snugly
new thoughts fit into old moulds, as the rhythms of speech proclaim
their resistance to the rigid pattern imposed on them, and the thoughtless
sing-song of 'Is *a* strange *de*stiny' is pulled up short with a sudden metrical
shudder: 'Is a *strange* destiny'. A 'stanza' is literally a 'room', and with this
last line Hardy's speaker reveals that he is speaking in a room that is not
only falling behind the times but also falling into disrepair, like the bul-
ging walls and collapsing roof of an abandoned church.

   Such uncertainty has not always been heard very clearly or very kindly:
William Empson once suggested that 'Hardy often simply drops his
rhythm, as a child drops its rattle and stares before it straight at the skyline, dribbling slightly.'[5] But it is not only out of boredom or dribbling
stupidity that a child might drop its rattle, just as the breaking of a poetic

rhythm can indicate the dawning self-consciousness of a speaker who has outgrown old aural pleasures. In prose, similarly, the timing of a line on the page can show the pressures of historical circumstance coming up against those of custom, routine, habit. To borrow Gertrude Stein's distinction, prose rhythm can reveal significant overlaps and slippages between 'the time of the composition' and 'the time in the composition'.[6]

Dickens has often been enlisted in these debates over cultural change, even if in his case they sometimes amount to little more than citing Ruskin's famous description of him as 'a pure modernist, a leader of the steam-whistle party' who 'had no understanding of antiquity except a sort of jackdaw sentiment for cathedral towers'.[7] In fact, Dickens was as ambivalent about the past as he was about most of the present, and his skill at combining a tone of sturdy common sense with an unpredictable flexibility of attitude makes it hard to characterise him as 'purely' anything. This has not prevented critics from trying to map that shift from Eliot's 'familiar rhythms' to Hardy's 'strange destiny' onto the trajectory of his career. It is a cultural movement that is usually identified with different kinds of physical movement, as Dickens leaves behind the jerky progress of the stagecoaches in *The Pickwick Papers* and warily embraces the relentless advance of the railway. From here it is only a short step to seeing his novels as symptoms of what Geoffrey Hill describes as the period's 'drastic breaking of tempo'.[8] Scenes such as *Dombey and Son*'s description of the train as a 'remorseless monster' gobbling up everything in its path show an individual narrative consciousness encountering a new set of industrial rhythms: the synchronised world of railway timetables, Greenwich Mean Time, clocking on and clocking off, that we still inhabit.

> Away, and still away, onward and onward ever: glimpses of cottage-homes, of houses, mansions, rich estates, of husbandry and handicraft, of people, of old roads and paths that look deserted, small, and insignificant as they are left behind: and so they do, and what else is there but such glimpses, in the track of the indomitable monster, Death! (*DS*, 20, 276)

But, although this might be read as a passage of writing that embodies and enacts the passage of time, it is noticeable that Dickens's narrative voice refuses to settle into purely mechanical rhythms. Repeatedly, his prose baulks itself, drags its feet, as if reluctant to give itself up altogether to the democratic vistas seen through the train window. Dickens's rhythms show thoughtless mechanism encountering human doubt; they show not only his complicity with the train's advance, treating lines of print like railway tracks and words like coupled-together carriages, but also his attempt to apply the brakes.

Such uncertainty is not surprising. Though the destruction wrought
by trains made Dickens nervous, it also excited him, not least because
he sometimes enjoyed thinking of himself as a kind of human steam
engine. As early as 1835, he explained that 'my composition is peculiar; I
can never write with effect – especially in the serious way – until I have
got my steam up, or in other words until I have become so excited with
my subject that I cannot leave off.'[9] One outcome of this process was a
prose that sometimes hardened into a form of blank verse, especially when
Dickens was writing 'in the serious way'. This too is something he seems
not to have been able to leave off, even if it sometimes threatened to put
his readers off. Usually it has been passed over as a minor quirk of his
style – an audible trace of his theatricality, or a sign of how easily his hand
fell into particular rhetorical patterns – although its lofty sonorities can
be hard to ignore when they break into his fiction. At such moments,
Dickens's writing can again sound oddly like a declaration of loyalty to an
age of mechanical reproduction, as if he were not content merely to take
advantage of the newly mechanised world of printing and distribution but
actively wanted to incorporate it into his prose, to make every part of a
book's life beat in time together. However, as the rest of this chapter will
argue, Dickens's rhythms represent far more than a form of stylistic excess.
They are central to both his tone and his timing – his skill at constructing
a voice that measures the passage of time and negotiates its own passage
through time.

One problem with trying to pin down this feature of Dickens's style is
that, as a critical term, rhythm is at best loose and at worst impossibly
promiscuous. Attempting to define it is like taking aim at a moving target, not just because rhythm can only be understood *as* a movement, like
traffic flow or the circulation of the blood, but also because it shifts its
meaning as it migrates between different critical accounts. The *OED*'s definition of rhythm as 'measured recurrence' may be true of formal prosody, but it is hardly an adequate summary of the more unpredictable ways
the term has been applied in literary criticism. As D. W. Harding points
out, 'rhythm' attracts ideas of 'ordering, structure, coordination, progression, regular alternation, smoothness, periodicity'; it brings together
'the rhythm of the seasons, the circadian rhythm of animal activities, the
rhythm of work, primitive and industrial, and all the rhythms found or
talked of in literature, and most of the other arts'.[10] In bridging everything
from 'the rhythm of marching feet' to 'the rhythm of the universe', the
word has become 'a vast unsupported span'.[11]

Perhaps understandably, many critics have responded by treating this term less like a bridge than a landmine, one that is liable to explode into meaningless fragments if any sustained pressure is applied to it. Albert C. Clark's 1913 study *Prose Rhythms in English* opens by plaintively declaring that 'In spite of all the obscurities which surround the subject, no one has doubted that there are principles at work, if only we could grasp them';[12] E. M. Forster's chapter on 'Pattern and Rhythm' in *Aspects of the Novel* admits that 'both these words are vague', and, after some throat-clearing on narrative patterns, it invites the reader to 'edge rather nervously towards the idea of "rhythm"', where the term is held in quotation marks like a pair of tongs.[13]

When the same critics try to define narrative rhythm, Dickens is at once irresistible as a source of examples and stubbornly resistant to being explained away by a single theory. Thus, when Harding writes that 'It is difficult not to believe that passages we feel to be specially characteristic of a writer owe something of this to their quality of rhythm', the first writer he reaches for is Dickens: 'Some of the torrentially abundant and cumulative sentences of Dickens ... are part and parcel of his creative prodigality and expansiveness.'[14] Dickens himself seems to have been aware of this, which may be why he was so keen to scapegoat his stylistic excesses by pinning them onto comic chatterboxes such as Mrs Nickleby and Flora Finching, but as far as rhythm is concerned Harding's example only scratches the surface. Verbal repetition, symbolism, serialisation, *Bleak House*'s periodic expansion and contraction of its narrative focus: all these and more have been written about in terms of Dickens's 'rhythms'. Narratologists have found his writings an especially fertile source of examples, although they have usually been more interested in abstract ideas of narrative patterning than in the local verbal texture created by words falling into particular stress patterns. To take just one example, although Mieke Bal points out that 'Rhythm is as striking as it is elusive',[15] when she wants to demonstrate what she means by the term, namely the relationship between what a narrative dwells on and what it elides or arrests, she turns to the opening of *Oliver Twist*, which devotes three pages to Oliver's birth, just over a page to his childhood up to the age of nine and then several pages to the moment he announces, 'Please, sir, I want some more.' It is an imaginative double helix of generosity and restraint that is sunk into every level of Dickens's writing, from his syntax to his methods of serialisation. However, Bal's analysis moves a long way from the more basic question of how Oliver voices his request. Does his speech reveal a lonely child asserting his needs above those of the crowd ('*I* want some more'), or does it fall into an iambic pulse ('I *want* some *more*'), like a miniature theatrical soliloquy directed towards an audience that includes the workhouse officials, the other boys for whom he is a spokesman and, ultimately, Dickens's readers as well?

Answering such questions is not made any easier by the number of rival ideas concerning rhythm – from its origins to its effects – that were available to Dickens. Discussions of *poetic* rhythm usually resorted to legal or contractual metaphors: for Edwin Guest in 1838, metrical verse reflected 'the law of succession';[16] for Coventry Patmore in 1857, it involved 'the co-ordination of life and law'.[17] *Prose* rhythm, by contrast, wriggled free from any attempts to pin it down; it became a good example of D. H. Lawrence's later dictum that 'If you try to nail anything down, in the novel, either it kills the novel, or the novel gets up and walks away with the nail.'[18]

One significant pattern that can be traced is how closely the critical fortunes of 'rhythm' follow those of 'style'. In 1857, a *Fraser's* article on 'Literary Style' pointed out that 'A rhythmical structure ought to exist … and the warp and woof of the entire texture should be so woven as to preserve continuity of pattern, and to produce the effect of a harmonious whole.'[19] (There are shades here of Dickens's postscript to *Our Mutual Friend*, with its reference to the narrative pattern 'which is always before the eyes of the story-weaver at his loom' [*OMF*, 821].) In his 1885 essay 'On Style in Literature', Stevenson went even further by arguing that prose, like music, should involve a pattern of 'sounds and pauses',[20] although without this pattern becoming predictable, which would make reading a novel about as exciting as staring at wallpaper.

Indeed, so frequently do writers on style dwell on rhythm that, when she looked back on the period in 1917, Olive Savage found herself wondering how often modern prose rhythms were really just the fossils of previous styles that had become detached from their sources and embedded in literary habit, like someone who enjoys humming fragments of old tunes long after they have forgotten the words. 'As year by year passes', she wrote, 'it becomes increasingly difficult to have a style peculiarly one's own; so that it would seem to be desirable that writers in prose should aim at rhythm rather than at originality of style.'[21] To a large extent she was swimming against the historical current. So was the writer of a letter to the *Academy* in 1900, who earnestly explained that 'I am most anxious, as one having literary aspirations, to cultivate *style*. Would you favour me with a few hints, or tell me where I could get the hints?'[22] He would have found a more sympathetic hearing a century earlier, when it was widely assumed that the impassioned rhythms of poetry had sprung from a way of life in which, as Hugh Blair had suggested, 'cool reasoning and plain discourse' were unknown.[23] In this view, prose was part of a civilising process that replaced the savage thrill of beating drums and chanting with the more modest pleasures of sociable discourse. Like a good conversationalist, it was popularly assumed, prose style should draw attention to its subject rather than to itself. By 1900, however, the idea that style could be taught or shared would have struck most readers as curiously old-fashioned. Far more common was the idea that style was a process of individuation, a unique signature of personality. This notion that 'le style c'est de l'homme même'[24] may have had its roots in France – hence Baudelaire's dream of 'the miracle of a poetic prose' which would be 'supple enough and rugged enough to adapt itself to the lyrical impulses of the soul' – but it was hardly enough to flower across the Channel, not least in Henry James's attempts at 'Catching the very note and trick, the strange irregular rhythm of life.' 'That is the attempt whose strenuous force keeps Fiction on her feet', James concluded, the joke being that any prose that could be cut up into metrical feet would soon fall flat on its face.[25]

Dickens's career was caught between these rival models of style, and his prose takes the measure of each. In his 'Essay on Style' (1888), Walter Pater argued that prose was especially well attuned to 'the chaotic variety and complexity' of the modern world, capable of recalibrating itself from moment to moment as 'an instrument of many stops, meditative, observant, descriptive, eloquent, analytic, plaintive, fervid', which would 'exert in due measure all the varied charms of poetry, down to the rhythm'.[26] Dickens's rhythms play a complex set of variations on these 'stops'. They can express a rage for order or a desire to throw off bonds and fetters; they explore the pleasure of routine as it shades into the grip of compulsion; they measure the competing claims on his characters of order and contingency, fate and free will. They are also central to what might be described as his politics of style. It is probably only a coincidence that the *OED* dates the use of 'rhythm' in relation to prose from 1832, the year of the Reform Bill, but something more deliberate seems to be at work, or at play, in *Edwin Drood*, which contains the only two uses of the word in Dickens's published fiction. The first comes in Chapter 2:

> 'We shall miss you, Jasper, at the "Alternate Musical Wednesdays" to-night; but no doubt you are best at home. Good-night. God bless you! "Tell me, shep-herds, te-e-ell me; tell me-e-e, have you seen (have you seen, have you seen, have you seen) my-y-y Flo-o-ora-a pass this way!"' Melodiously good Minor Canon the Reverend Septimus Crisparkle thus delivers himself, in

musical rhythm, as he withdraws his amiable face from the doorway and conveys it down stairs. (*ED*, 2, 7)

The second comes in Chapter 12:

> 'Don't hurt the boy, Mister Jarsper,' urges Durdles, shielding him. 'Recollect yourself.'
> 'He followed us to-night, when we first came here!'
> 'Yer lie, I didn't!' replies Deputy, in his one form of polite contradiction.
> 'He has been prowling near us ever since!'
> 'Yer lie, I haven't,' returns Deputy, 'I'd only jist come out for my 'elth when I see you two a-coming out of the Kinfreederel. If –
> "I – ket – ches – Im – out – ar – ter – ten"
> (with the usual rhythm and dance, though dodging behind Durdles), 'it ain't *my* fault, is it?' (*ED*, 12, 11)

The narrative echo works something like an imaginary encounter between Adam Bede and Hardy's impercipient. Crisparkle's voice falls into the rhythms of an old ballad, while Deputy's voice cuts across the choric traditions of the punningly named '*Kin*freederel', but they are brought together by the checks and balances of the work in which they find themselves. In many ways, this passage from *Edwin Drood* works like a miniature version of Dickens's career as a whole, in which rhythm provides a central focus for his doubts over how far individual impulses can be or should be reconciled with larger structures – social forms as well as narrative forms.

The remaining sections of this chapter outline two of the ways in which Dickens's fiction explores this crux in his thinking. The first involves his carefully weighted response to mortality, and in particular his attempts to place the death of individual characters into a broader social context. Sometimes the death of a character such as Little Nell creates a shock that continues to reverberate in the memory of those who are left behind to mourn – a shock that also ripples uneasily through the rhythms of Dickens's prose. Other fictional deaths are less pronounced at the level of Dickens's style, as his narrators observe that similar events happen every day, even if they are not all elevated to the dignity of print, and prove their point by absorbing the rhythmical flutter of a particular character's demise into a more measured pulse of doom. In both cases, it is Dickens's rhythms that allow him to consider how much weight should be placed on the value of a single human life.

The final part of my argument develops this theme by discussing Dickens's attempts to give the social relationship between individual and group a stylistic analogue in the narrative relationship between part and whole. This is an area of his style that has often drawn adverse critical comment, as when George Orwell pithily observed that Dickens's structures were overwhelmed by his characters and jokes: 'He is all fragments, all details – rotten architecture, but wonderful gargoyles.'[27] However, while attempts to find underlying patterns in Dickens's writing usually latch onto repeated motifs and metaphors – dust heaps, the river, and so on – there is a good case for thinking that the most important connecting tissue in his fiction is to be found at an even more fundamental level than his language. In the final section of this chapter I propose that this is the level at which Dickens's rhythms operate: they are the contours of style over which narrative currents of desire and memory flow.

Dickens's sensitivity to rhythm is especially pronounced when he dramatises his characters' sense of past and passing time. In his essay on 'The Young Dickens', Graham Greene has a lovely phrase for Dickens's 'delicate and exact poetic cadences, the music of memory': 'secret prose'.[28] No novel deploys this secret prose better than *David Copperfield*, where one key question that remains unresolved is how far the narrator is trying to relive the past or relieve himself of it. Here is David returning in thought to his empty family home:

> [I]t pained me to think of the dear old place as altogether abandoned; of the weeds growing tall in the garden, and the fallen leaves lying thick and wet upon the paths. I imagined how the winds of winter would howl round it, how the cold rain would beat upon the window-glass, how the moon would make ghosts on the walls of the empty rooms, watching their solitude all night. I thought afresh of the grave in the churchyard, underneath the tree: and it seemed as if the house were dead too, now, and all connected with my father and mother were faded away. (*DC*, 17, 212)

Fad*ing* away, perhaps, but not altogether dead and gone, and we hear this in a chain of internal echoes, as a sudden gulp in the speaker's voice – 'as if the house were dead too, *now*' – is picked up and refracted through the *hows* of the passage, *hows* that centre on the *howl* of the wind. Adam Piette has helpfully drawn attention to the connective tissue of this passage, which he describes as 'prose rhymes': the little verbal self-echoes that show what the speaker hangs onto from his past and what then hangs on in his voice.[29] But rhythm is an equally important device for recreating the acoustic textures of memory, producing an extra set of chains that couple the narrator to his past: 'weeds growing tall ... winter would howl ... ghosts on the walls ... grave in the churchyard'. And this too is 'secret prose', because Dickens's rhythms occupy a threshold between conscious and repressed knowledge; they mark the stresses of childhood that give an involuntary inflection to the narrator's adult voice.

Of course, Dickens is not the only writer to have tapped rhythm as a creative resource in this way: we might compare Wordsworth's use of blank verse in *The Prelude*, which simultaneously carries his memories and underlies them like the background ticking of a clock. Because prose lacks this built-in time-beater, it also lacks a convenient way of showing objective chronological time coming up against the more unpredictable ways it can be shaped and stirred in our minds. Yet in the right hands this absence of a metrical structure can itself be a creative resource: prose rhythms can dramatise the modulations of a voice trying to retrieve meaningful patterns from time's indifferent melt. De Quincey provides some good parallels, not least because when he writes a form of 'secret prose' it is far from clear how many secrets he is keeping from us and how many from himself:

> Out of the darkness, if I happen to call up the image of Fanny from thirty-five years back, arises suddenly a rose in June; or, if I think for an instant of the rose in June, up rises the heavenly face of Fanny. One after the other, like the antiphonies in the choral service, rises Fanny and the rose in June, then back again the rose in June and Fanny. Then come both together, as in a chorus; roses and Fannies, Fannies and roses, without end – thick as blossoms in Paradise.[30]

Presumably this is what De Quincey meant in his essay on 'Style' when he spoke of the need 'to break up massy chords into running variations; and to mark, by slight differences in the manner, a virtual identity in the substance'.[31] Different rhythms carry different memories in this passage, but as the memories start to merge so the rhythms overlap until they are close to forming a single dactylic pulse – dactyls being a popular choice for staging ideas of return, from Tennyson's 'The Charge of the Light Brigade' ('Half a league, half a league, / Half a league onward') to Hardy's 'The Voice' ('Woman much missed, how you call to me, call to me').

David Copperfield is less settled than this, less orderly, and as its rhythms come and go they carry the narrator's sense that while a pattern may exist it has slipped from his grasp, or can only be heard out of the corner of his ear. It is far from an unusual case in Dickens's fiction, where rhythm often supplements his 'prose rhymes' to dramatise the workings of memory, feeding on the fact that etymologically 'rhythm' and 'rhyme' have the same root and frequently collaborate in snappy jingles like 'Remember remember the fifth of November.' Yet the process is not always as personal as it is in *David Copperfield*. When Dickens wants to articulate this

nagging sense of a pattern establishing itself in a character's life, he sometimes deploys little rhythmical phrases – shards of cultural memory – that
are already lodged in his readers' heads.

As a writer who switches unpredictably between prose and verse,
Shakespeare was especially vulnerable to this sort of piecemeal appropriation, and Dickens enjoyed borrowing the cadences of his writing as
much as the words themselves. An example is provided by the memoirs
of Grimaldi that Dickens edited (and largely rewrote) in 1838.[32] According
to this version of his life, Grimaldi rarely took to the stage without some
disaster befalling him. While playing a robber at Sadler's Wells he acci-
dentally shot himself in the foot so that his boot 'puffed out to a great
size, presenting a very laughter-moving appearance to everybody but the
individual in it, who was suffering the most excruciating agony' (*MJG*,
I, 198). During a pantomime appearance in Liverpool he fell through a
trapdoor on stage and played the rest of the scene 'as though nothing had
happened to discompose him' even though he was 'in agony' throughout
(I, 49). His life was an extended comedy of errors – a version of the idea
that 'The jest on the lip and the tear in the eye, the merriment on the
mouth and the aching of the heart, have called down the same shouts of
laughter and peals of applause a hundred times' (I, 15). Perhaps that is why
Dickens made Grimaldi part of a performance tradition that reached back
into the realms of myth. Although he is never explicitly named in the
book, Grimaldi's great predecessor in Dickens's eyes was a clown already
fixed in the alembic of memory: *Hamlet*'s Yorick. After the death of his
wife, Dickens reports, Grimaldi was summoned to the theatre 'to set the
audience in a roar' after 'chalking over the seams which mental agony had
worn in his face' (I, 169). He followed a similar route after the death of
his friend Richard Hughes, when, in order to attend the funeral, he was
forced to run from a pantomime rehearsal to the graveyard, returning just
in time 'to set the audience in a roar'. Both events remember *Hamlet*'s
graveyard scene:

> *Hamlet:* Alas, poor Yorick. I knew him, Horatio, a fellow of infinite jest, of
> most excellent fancy. He hath bore me on his back a thousand times, and
> now – how abhorred in my imagination it is. My gorge rises at it. Here
> hung those lips that I have kissed I know not how oft. Where be your gibes
> now, your gambols, your songs, your flashes of merriment, that were wont
> to set the table on a roar? Not one now to mock your own grinning? Quite
> chop-fallen?[33]

Hamlet's growing pains can be heard in his appalled returns to 'now'
and the sudden collision of his past and present in that sickening slide

of 'bore' into 'abhorred', as he does a double-take on the man who used
to carry him around and is now reduced to having bits of himself carried
around. (The chain of sounds in 'bore … abhorred … gorge … your …
your … your … roar' attunes Hamlet's voice to 'poor Yorick' in a mournful series of echoes that is as fragmented and unsettled as Yorick's body.)[34]
Most self-consciously, we hear how Hamlet remembers the regular kisses
that punctuated his childhood in a line that struggles towards but fails
to recapture an orderly iambic pulse – 'Here hung those lips that I have
kissed I know not how oft'; and again, more successfully: 'were wont to
set the table on a roar'. In Hamlet's mouth, the rhythm now seems as
ancient and battered as Yorick's grin, and it surfaces now as the relic of a
world that existed before both time and this loved body were put 'out of
joint'. Reappearing in Grimaldi's *Memoirs*, the phrase about setting the
audience in a roar sounds even more distant and hollow, but it retains the
same measured shape and so reminds us that both clowns are victims of
a world – part tragic and part slapstick – in which freedom is routinely
mastered by necessity.

Rhythm is central to this idea. In part this is because when speech
rhythms fall into metre they always risk sounding as if the speaker is in
the grip of some external force. But it is also because in English there is
no intrinsic relationship between metre and subject matter, which is why
the same metrical pulse can carry ideas of tragic inevitability, or comic
routines, or something in between. It is this in-between category that
Dickens's writing populates most thickly, particularly when little spasms
of blank verse creep into his prose. At such moments his blank verse works
like a blank look, neutral in itself but endlessly open to interpretation.
Indeed, in novels such as *Bleak House*, the narrative tends to settle into
blank verse precisely at the moments when Dickens is most concerned
with putting things historically and ethically into perspective:

> The light is come upon the dark benighted way. Dead!
>   Dead, your Majesty. Dead, my lords and gentlemen. Dead, Right
> Reverends and Wrong Reverends of every order. Dead, men and women,
> born with Heavenly compassion in your hearts. And dying thus around us,
> every day. (*BH*, 47, 677)

The chime of 'every day' with 'dark benighted way' suggests that in this
gloomy moral climate Jo's fate was written long before his own life began,
just as the line of perfect blank verse that rounds off this chapter – 'And
dying thus around us, every day' – harks back to earlier writers who had
used blank verse to similar ends. We might hear echoes of Shakespeare's

tragedies of wasted potential, with 'way/day' acting like a staggered rhyming couplet, or Milton's fables of lost innocence. We might even hear echoes of Wordsworth, whose own verse frequently applies his theory that the more 'pathetic situations and sentiments' can be better 'endured in metrical composition' – metre acting to put a formal framework around otherwise insupportable experience, allowing cries of pain to be abstracted into lyrical lamentations.[35] The fact that this cadence cannot be placed with any certainty is, of course, appropriate for the homeless Jo, just as it is for the idea that he is just one of the nameless poor – a social category that is no respecter of historical differences. And here too blank verse provides a helpful resource, because its five stresses always sound incomplete and so tend to link themselves into longer narrative units. 'And dying thus around us every day' ends the chapter with a death-knell that is also an appeal: although Jo has died, the strong implication is that the struggle against such deaths is to be continued.

Dickens was especially attracted by the open-ended quality of blank verse when he wanted to gesture towards the timeless or transcendent. This is why his description of Niagara Falls in *American Notes* drifts into blank verse, as does the final paragraph of *Nicholas Nickleby*. The potential endlessness of blank verse is equally good at capturing the sublime or the cosy routines of domestic life – a pattern that *The Old Curiosity Shop* describes as 'That love of home from which all domestic virtues spring', where 'domestic' interrupts what would otherwise be another perfect line of blank verse. Sometimes, it is true, the habit led Dickens into theatrical posturing, as in his early letters to Maria Beadnell, which can sound suspiciously like someone rehearsing his favourite lines in front of the mirror: 'I have but one word more to say', or 'the miserable reckless wretch I am'.[36] At the same time, the ambiguity of 'spring' in 'from which all domestic virtues spring' also reminds us how vulnerable such writing was to comedy. Rhythm threatened even the most solemn scenes in Dickens's fiction with the quality Bergson was to characterise as 'something mechanical encrusted on the living':

> The comic is that side of a person which reveals his likeness to a thing, that aspect of human events which, through its peculiar inelasticity, conveys the impression of pure mechanism, of movement without life … *something mechanical encrusted on the living.*[37]

Dickens's critics have sometimes reached for a similar vocabulary, as when G. H. Lewes observed that Dickens's characters were like children's wooden toys that 'run on wheels', or frogs whose brains had been removed but

could still croak or twitch their legs when tickled or jabbed with a pin.[38]
However, Dickens was capable of tapping a far richer set of imaginative
possibilities contained in 'something mechanical encrusted on the living'.
At its simplest, this can be seen in his rich confusion of people and timepieces, in descriptions that rapidly find themselves settling into a sympathetic rhythm: Betsey Trotwood 'passing in and out, along this measured
track, at an unchanging pace, with the regularity of a clock-pendulum'
(*DC*, 40, 496); or the clock in *Dombey and Son*, which Paul hears asking him 'how, is, my, lit, tle, friend?' (*DS*, 9, 145, 149), like a parody of
Dickens's own attitude towards his readers, sending out new instalments
of the novel with the regularity of a huge, slowly ticking clock; or Mrs
Gamp, whose speech rhythms have the self-assured quality of a soliloquy
even when she is talking to someone else: 'I'm easy pleased; it is but little
as I wants; but I must have that little *of* the best, and *to* the minnit wen
the clock strikes, else we do not part as I could wish, but bearin malice in
our arts' (*MC*, 49, 744). Dickens was conscious of this stylistic tic: 'I am
perfectly aware', he wrote in 1844, 'that there are several passages in my
books which, with very little alteration – sometimes with none at all – will
fall into blank verse, if divided into lines … I run into it, involuntarily
and unconsciously, when I am very much in earnest.'[39] However, he also
seems to have fallen into blank verse when he wanted to test the limits of
his earnestness, using its blankness more like the poker face of a professional stooge.

The most famous example comes towards the end of *The Old Curiosity
Shop*, as the narrator slowly edges towards Nell's grave:

> And now the bell – the bell she had so often heard, by night and day, and
> listened to with solemn pleasure almost as a living voice – rung its remorse-
> less toll, for her, so young, so beautiful, so good. Decrepit age, and vigorous
> life, and blooming youth, and helpless infancy, poured forth – on crutches,
> in the pride of strength and health, in the full blush of promise, in the mere
> dawn of life – to gather round her tomb. (*OCS*, 72, 561)

This finally liberates a grim pun that has been lurking around the heroine's
name – Nell with a silent K – turning her into a figure just as doomed
as Oedipus. When R. H. Horne reproduced the same passage in *A New
Spirit of the Age* in 1844, he helpfully set it out as a poem, noting that
Dickens's metrical prose might have been 'the result of harmonious accident', although he then went on to compare it to the 'kindly admixtures'
of serious and comic scenes that Charles Lamb had detected in Hogarth.[40]
And, listening closely to this scene, we might think that Wilde is not the
only person to have wondered whether it would take a heart of stone not

to laugh at the death of Little Nell. A similar sense of perspective is built into Dickens's writing. Elsewhere in *The Old Curiosity Shop* this takes the form of what comes before and after such scenes – Dick Swiveller's bursts of romantic doggerel, for example, or the level-headed response of Kit's children, who listen to the sad story of Nell's death but are soon 'quite merry' again. Both are typical of Dickens's skill at building little narrative heckles into the texture of his writing. The metrical prose of this funeral scene, on the other hand, contains its own potential for heckling. In some ways its stiffness is a triumph of free indirect style, accurately recreating the narrator's numbed reaction, and, as the passage develops, it finds a home for two more contradictory feelings that the bereaved might experience: the need to go on and the desire to clasp their thoughts into memorial patterns. In this way, Dickens's rhythms finally reconcile the twin senses of 'curiosity' that have worked their way through the novel: wandering movement versus static object. This is the moment at which *The Old Curiosity Shop* achieves its finest balance between being simultaneously a lively picaresque narrative and the world's longest epitaph. It is also the moment at which Dickens opens his writing up to an equally measured response – one that might include anything from violent grief to the sense that, as Beckett put it in *Endgame*, 'Nothing is funnier than unhappiness.'[41]

Dickens's flexible and creative ways with blank verse run strangely counter to what most Victorian critics understood to be the proper function of prose rhythm – a set of critical assumptions that achieved an eccentric climax in 1912 with the publication of George Saintsbury's *History of English Prose Rhythm*. Saintsbury devotes only two pages to Dickens, one of which is wholly taken up by a long quotation from *David Copperfield*, and here it is particularly Dickens's tendency to drift into blank verse that makes the critic shake his head. 'If I have marked the numerous blank-verse fragments here, it is with no *Schadenfreude*', he claims, 'But, at the same time, it must be confessed that the prevalence of much blank verse almost necessarily implies ... a certain poverty in rhythmical resources.'[42] Dickens's problem, according to Saintsbury, is that he offends against the unwritten rule that distinguishes verse from prose. Whereas verse depends upon rhythmical regularity and recurrence, prose depends upon rhythmical variety and difference: 'Its great law is that every syllable shall, as in poetry, have recognizable rhythmical value, and be capable of entering into rhythmical transactions with its neighbours, but that these transactions shall always stop short, or steer clear, of admitting the recurrent combinations proper to metre.'[43] In terms of its rhythmical structure, that is, good prose is happy to flirt but reluctant to settle down; it keeps our ears on the stretch by raising expectations and then disappointing them. To borrow Hardy's definition of 'the Gothic art-principle', in which he trained as an architect and claimed to have 'carried on into his verse', such writing rejects regularity of form in favour of 'cunning irregularity'.[44]

Dickens could produce this sort of narrative effect when he chose, as in the brilliant passage in *Great Expectations* that describes Pip wheeling Miss Havisham around while she bangs out 'Old Clem', creating a set of contrapuntal rhythms that show Dickens taking the main idea of his plot – expectations being disappointed – and working them into the smallest details of his style. However, he was equally good at deliberately restricting rhythmical variations in his writing, creating a dominant time signature that gradually gathered up alternative rhythms and subdued them to itself. I have already suggested some reasons for this, as individuals start to recognise the patterns in their lives or are forced to submit to a more general narrative pulse. Another comes when Dickens takes the underlying principle of metre – individual words being carried along by a common drive – and uses it to dramatise the anonymous power of crowds.

Many of the most compelling examples occur in *A Tale of Two Cities*. From first sentence to last, the stylistic keynote of this novel is repetition with variation: shadows; doubles; echoing footsteps; Jacques One, Two, Three. When Dickens comes to describe the French Revolution, however, it quickly becomes clear how dangerous it would be to confuse a literary style with a lifestyle, by giving up one's identity to the self-multiplying mob.

> Cannon, muskets, fire and smoke; but, still the deep ditch, the single drawbridge, the massive stone walls, and the eight great towers. Slight displacements of the raging sea, made by the falling wounded. Flashing weapons, blazing torches, smoking waggon-loads of wet straw, hard work at neighbouring barricades in all directions, shrieks, volleys, execrations, bravery without stint, boom smash and rattle, and the furious sounding of the living sea. (*TTC*, ii, 21, 265)

Dickens's writing sounds out this living sea, as individual words are swept up by the rhythmical current – 'all directions ... execrations' – even as it demonstrates his control over those who are losing control. Like the blank verse in a play by Webster, Dickens sets social and ethical collapse within a framework of order. To adapt Coleridge's discussion of metre in the *Biographia Literaria*, this is rhythm as 'an interpenetration of passion and of will, of spontaneous impulse and of voluntary purpose'.[45]

Dickens's most ambitious attempts in this vein were his public readings, during which he sought not only to bring different classes together but to orchestrate their responses as one. No doubt it is just a coincidence that one advertisement for the farewell readings appeared in *All the Year Round* on the same page as an article on musical rhythm, but many of the writer's examples would have chimed with Dickens, particularly the leader of Egyptian slaves who made them work together to build the pyramids by raising himself above them and singing, 'beating the measure with his hands'.[46] If readings such as 'Sikes and Nancy' were rhythmical in their prose style, they were even more profoundly rhythmical in their intended social effects; in fact, Dickens seems to have hoped his voice would create a unified social body that would articulate itself around him as its beating heart. In this context it is not altogether surprising that his pulse raced, rising to 114 beats a minute, then 118, then 124.[47] It was having to pump enough blood to keep his whole audience going.

There is some evidence that the success of the public readings went to Dickens's head, or at least to his hand. Afterwards, the rhythms of his sentences became more elaborately weighted and balanced, more rhetorically self-conscious, as increasingly he treated the page like a sounding-board for his voice.[48] But he never forgot the idea that writing allowed the private rhythms of the self to find themselves within, and also assert themselves against, the larger rhythms of the social world. As at the end of *Little Dorrit*:

> They paused for a moment on the steps of the portico, looking at the fresh perspective of the street in the autumn morning sun's bright rays, and then went down.
>
> Went down into a modest life of usefulness and happiness. Went down to give a mother's care, in the fulness of time, to Fanny's neglected children no less than to their own, and to leave that lady going into Society for ever and a day. Went down to give a tender nurse and friend to Tip for some few years, who was never vexed by the great exactions he made of her in return for the riches he might have given her if he had ever had them, and who lovingly closed his eyes upon the Marshalsea and all its blighted fruits. They went quietly down into the roaring streets, inseparable and blessed; and as they passed along in sunshine and in shade, the noisy and the eager, and the arrogant and the froward and the vain, fretted, and chafed, and made their usual uproar.

Just as this description returns to the 'Babel' of sounds in the opening chapter, so in a beautiful modulation from 'they' to 'their' Dickens's syntax dramatises the couple returning to the anonymous throng from which they emerged at the start of the story. And playing on and around this syntax is Dickens's rhythm: 'went down … went down … went down … went down … went quietly down … uproar'. A sequence of rising rhythms is finally crowned by a word that gestures upwards but is given in a falling cadence: 'uproar'. The married couple are not identified, but the rhythmic aftershocks of their names mean that their identity can still be heard within this anonymous crowd: 'Amy Dorrit', 'Arthur Clennam', 'uproar'. Similarly, the phrase 'up and down' does not appear – a key phrase in the novel, where it is used to describe everything from the Dorrits walking in the Marshalsea to what Rigaud does with his moustache and his nose – but this too makes itself felt in Dickens's writing. In terms of the novel's persistent concern with matters of rising and falling, the passage offers what John Hollander might describe as a transumption, at once a summing up of the narrative and a transcending of its limitations.[49] It also answers E. M. Forster's question even before he could ask it:

> Expansion. That is the idea the novelist must cling to. Not completion. Not rounding off but opening out. When the symphony is over we feel that the notes and tunes composing it have been liberated, they have found in the rhythm of the whole their individual freedom. Cannot the novel be like that?[50]

NOTES

1 George Eliot, *Adam Bede* (1858), ed. Carol A. Martin (Oxford: Clarendon Press, 2001), 18, 186.
2 Geoffrey Hill, *The Lords of Limit* (London: Deutsch, 1984), 88–9. I am drawing here on my earlier discussion of Eliot and Hardy in *Victorian Afterlives: The Shaping of Influence in Nineteenth-Century Literature* (Oxford University Press, 2002), 301–3.
3 Florence Hardy, *The Life of Thomas Hardy* (1928–30; reprinted London: Studio Editions, 1994), 1, 358.
4 Thomas Hardy, *The Complete Poetical Works of Thomas Hardy*, ed. Samuel Hynes, 5 vols. (Oxford: Clarendon Press, 1982–95), 1, 87.
5 William Empson, *Argufying: Essays on Literature and Culture*, ed. John Haffenden (London: Hogarth Press, 1988), 422.
6 Gertrude Stein, 'Composition as Explanation'; reprinted in *A Stein Reader*, ed. Ulla E. Dydo (Evanston, IL: Northwestern University Press, 1993), 493–503, at 502.
7 Letter from John Ruskin to Charles Eliot Norton (19 June 1870); reprinted in Stephen Wall (ed.), *Charles Dickens: A Critical Anthology* (Harmondsworth: Penguin, 1970), 191.
8 Hill, *The Lords of Limit*, 84.

9 *Letters*, I, 97.

10 D. W. Harding, *Words into Rhythm: English Speech Rhythm in Verse and Prose* (Cambridge University Press, 1976), 1.

11 Harding, *Words into Rhythm*, 1.

12 Albert C. Clark, *Prose Rhythm in English* (Oxford: Clarendon Press, 1913), 6.

13 E. M. Forster, *Aspects of the Novel*, ed. Oliver Stallybrass (Harmondsworth: Penguin, 1987), 146.

14 Harding, *Words into Rhythm*, 137.

15 Mieke Bal, *Narratology: Introduction to the Theory of Narrative*, 2nd edn (University of Toronto Press, 1997), 99.

16 Edwin Guest, *A History of English Rhythms*, 2 vols. (London, 1838), II, 1.

17 Coventry Patmore, *Coventry Patmore's 'Essay on English Metrical Law': A Critical Edition with Commentary*, ed. Sister Mary Augustine Roth (Washington, DC: Catholic University of America Press, 1961), 7.

18 D. H. Lawrence, 'Morality and the Novel' (1925); reprinted in *Novelists on the Novel*, ed. Miriam Allott (London: Routledge, 1959), 101–2, at 102.

19 William Forsyth (unsigned), 'Literary Style', *Fraser's Magazine*, 55 (1857), 250.

20 Robert Louis Stevenson, 'On Style in Literature: Its Technical Elements' (1885); reprinted in *The Works of Robert Louis Stevenson*, 24 vols. (New York: Charles Scribner's Sons, 1895–9), XXII, 243–65, at 246.

21 Olive Savage, *Rhythm in Prose Illustrated from Authors of the Nineteenth Century* (London, 1917), 46.

22 *Academy*, 58 (30 June 1900), 559. See Travis R. Merritt, 'Taste, Opinion, and Theory in the Rise of Victorian Prose Stylism', in George Levine and William Madden (eds.), *The Art of Victorian Prose* (New York: Oxford University Press, 1968), 3–38, at 30.

23 Hugh Blair, *Lectures on Rhetoric and Belles Lettres* (1783) (London: Cadell & Davies, 1812), 423.

24 'Style is the man himself', Comte de Buffon, *Discourse on Style* (1753).

25 Henry James, 'The Art of Fiction' (1884); reprinted in Edwin M. Eigner and George J. Worth (eds.), *Victorian Criticism of the Novel* (Cambridge University Press, 1985), 193–212, at 206.

26 Walter Pater, 'Essay on Style' (1888); reprinted in *Appreciations, with An Essay on Style* (Rockville, MD: Arc Manor, 2008), 7–25, at 10.

27 George Orwell, 'Charles Dickens', *Critical Essays* (London: Secker & Warburg, 1946), 7–56, at 52.

28 Graham Greene, 'The Young Dickens' (1950); reprinted in George H. Ford and Lauriat Lane, Jnr. (eds.), *The Dickens Critics* (Ithaca, NY: Cornell University Press, 1961), 244–52, at 246–7.

29 Adam Piette, *Remembering and the Sound of Words: Mallarmé, Proust, Joyce, Beckett* (Oxford: Clarendon Press, 1996), 17–18.

30 Thomas De Quincey, 'The English Mail-Coach', *Blackwood's Edinburgh Magazine*, 66 (1849): 485–500, at 494.

31 Thomas De Quincey, 'Style', *Blackwood's Edinburgh Magazine*, 48 (July 1840): 1–17, at 4.

32 I discuss this in more detail in *Becoming Dickens: The Invention of a Novelist* (Cambridge, MA: Belknap Press of Harvard University Press, 2011).

33 *Hamlet*, v, i.

34 I am grateful to Daniel Tyler for pointing this out to me.

35 William Wordsworth, *Lyrical Ballads*, ed. R. L. Brett and A. R. Jones, 2nd edn (London: Methuen, 1991), 252.

36 *Letters*, i, 17, 23.

37 Henri Bergson, *Le Rire (Laughter)* (1900); reprinted in Wylie Sypher (ed.), *Comedy* (Baltimore, MD: Johns Hopkins University Press, 1980), 86; Bergson's emphasis.

38 G. H. Lewes, 'Dickens in Relation to Criticism' (1872); reprinted in Stephen Wall (ed.), *Charles Dickens: A Critical Anthology* (Harmondsworth: Penguin, 1970), 191–202, at 196.

39 *Letters*, iv, 112–13.

40 R. H. Horne (ed.), *A New Spirit of the Age*, 2 vols. (London, 1844), i, 45–7.

41 Samuel Beckett, *Endgame* (London: Faber & Faber, 1958), 101.

42 George Saintsbury, *A History of English Prose Rhythm* (London: Macmillan, 1912), 381–2.

43 Saintsbury, *History of English Prose Rhythm*, 344.

44 Hardy, *The Life of Thomas Hardy*, ii, 79.

45 Samuel Taylor Coleridge, *Biographia Literaria*, ed. J. Engell and W. J. Bate (Princeton University Press, 1984), 65.

46 'Phenomena of Music', *All the Year Round*, 490 (12 September 1868): 334–6, at 336.

47 See Helen Small, 'A Pulse of 124: Charles Dickens and a Pathology of the Mid-Victorian Reading Public', in James Raven, Helen Small and Naomi Tadmor (eds.), *The Practice and Representation of Reading in England* (Cambridge University Press, 1996), 263–90, at 288.

48 See Robert Golding, *Idiolects in Dickens: The Major Techniques and Chronological Development* (London: Macmillan, 1985), 50.

49 John Hollander, *The Figure of Echo* (Berkeley, CA: University of California Press, 1981), 120.

50 Forster, *Aspects of the Novel*, 149–50.

CHAPTER FOUR

Spectres of style

Daniel Tyler

In March 1868, worn out by an exhausting series of public readings, Dickens was apprehensive of a return to writing later in the year. He wrote to the actor, Charles Fechter:

> after I have rested – don't laugh – it is a grim reality – I shall have to turn my mind to – ha! ha! ha! – to – ha! ha! ha! (more sepulchrally than before) – the – the CHRISTMAS NUMBER!!! I feel as if I had murdered a Christmas number years ago (perhaps I did!) and its ghost perpetually haunted me.[1]

Dickens's joke is good for a number of reasons, not the least of which is that his best-known Christmas ghost stories were themselves often about the difficulty of escaping the deadening grip of routine. For Dickens, Christmas was a time to stand aside from the ceaseless business of the year and, at that seasonal milestone, to reflect upon past days, on what might have been and on what might yet be, a message which his ghosts frequently espouse. In 1868, Dickens must have felt that his own life had fallen into a fixed course that he was compelled unvaryingly to pursue and that the Christmas period was as little likely to yield him any respite as it was to relieve the unregenerate Scrooge. Under the pressure of a demanding writing schedule, the approaching yuletide seemed more of a curse than a blessing.

In most years since the publication of *A Christmas Carol* in 1843, Dickens had written a ghostly tale for the festive period. There had been a prototype of Scrooge's story in the tale of Gabriel Grub for the December 1836 instalment of *The Pickwick Papers*. After *A Christmas Carol*, Dickens published four more Christmas books in the 1840s, most of them ghostly,[2] and he turned again and again to the genre in special Christmas numbers of his journals throughout the 1850s and 1860s, often enlisting the contributions of other writers to make up a round of tales. The collaborations included *A House to Let* (1858) and *The Haunted House* (1859), and Dickens himself penned several stories including, among the most noteworthy, 'To Be Taken with a Grain of Salt' in *Doctor Marigold's Prescriptions* (1865) and 'The Signal-Man' in the *Mugby Junction* stories for 1866. In the event, there was no Christmas number in 1868, and *No Thoroughfare*, his collaboration with Wilkie Collins in 1867, was his last.

In writing ghost stories as often as he did, Dickens was taking on a genre itself weighed down with a past that was all too ready to repeat itself. As his comments to his journals' contributors show, he was aware that the same well-worn conventions, the same formulae, even the same basic plots were rehearsed over and over again. This presented a challenge to writers who turned their hand to the genre, which some found insurmountable. For Dickens, however, the burdensome legacy of the ghost story seems to have provided a creative stimulus, because it meant that the genre was suited to a peculiar degree to tales that wrestled with the difficulty of breaking from customary patterns or with the possibility of bringing new life and energy where it had long been absent. In his 1850 Christmas piece, 'A Christmas Tree', Dickens wrote with mingled weariness and delight:

> There is no end to the old houses, with resounding galleries, and dismal state-bedchambers, and haunted wings shut up for many years, through which we may ramble, with an agreeable creeping up our back, and encounter any number of ghosts, but (it is worthy of remark perhaps) reducible to a very few general types and classes; for, ghosts have little originality, and 'walk' in a beaten track. ('CT', 12)

A relish for the endless possibilities of the genre comes up against a more jaded sense of its wearying conventionality. These were the terms on which Dickens approached, editorially, the ghost stories submitted to his journals. He repeatedly advised prospective contributors that innovation in conception and execution was paramount, and he consistently strove for originality in his own handling of the genre – such that he could sincerely claim in relation to *The Haunted Man* (1848) to be 'the inventor of this sort of story'.[3] Writing to Elizabeth Gaskell, who contributed several Gothic tales to his journals, he singled out the way such stories are told as of chief importance: 'Ghost-stories, illustrating particular states of mind and processes of the imagination are common-property, I always think – except in the manner of relating them.'[4] The claim comes in a letter responding to Gaskell's accusation that 'To Be Read at Dusk', a tale Dickens published in *The Keepsake* for Christmas 1851, lifted its essential plot element from a story she had once shared with him. There are clearly strongly mitigating reasons why he should want to reply that ghost stories are 'common-property'. Nonetheless, other letters support the claim that they should be distinguished by 'the manner of relating them', and while the principle was expedient on this occasion, Dickens's practice, especially in the Christmas books of the 1840s which are the focus of this chapter, bears out his emphasis on the need to find an idiosyncratic style for the tales. For it is through his style in the ghost stories that Dickens breathes new life into the conventional genre, taking style, in this case, in both its broadest sense, approximating 'mode', and in a more scriptive sense, encompassing rhetorical tropes, grammar and syntax. It is above all the inventive style of Dickens's ghost stories, enlivening the recognisable, replicable patterns of plot, that distinguished them from the ordinary productions of the genre. One of the reasons for *A Christmas Carol*'s pre-eminence among the Christmas tales is that there the exuberant performance of the writing is inseparable from the ghostly circumstances of the plot in creating the overall meaning and achievement of the work.

An important aspect of the Christmas books' innovative mode is epitomised in a single moment of *A Christmas Carol*. The Ghost of Christmas Past reveals an enjoyably chaotic domestic scene, where the husband of Scrooge's former fiancée brings heaps of presents home for his children. Tumult ensues, including:

> The terrible announcement that the baby had been taken in the act of putting a doll's frying-pan into his mouth, and was more than suspected of having swallowed a fictitious turkey, glued on a wooden platter! The immense relief of finding this a false alarm! The joy, and gratitude, and ecstasy! (*CC*, II, 40)

This episode contains in miniature the plot and tone of most of Dickens's Christmas books. It raises acute fears of events that are soon discovered to have been merely imaginary, effecting a rapid alteration from terror to unbridled joy. All of Dickens's Christmas books are structured around what is essentially a 'false alarm', a frightful prospect, not of actuality but of an imagined possibility, often presented by a quasi-imaginary agency. A 'fictitious turkey' is an apt emblem for the imaginary stimulants of such fears in the Christmas fables.

This leading characteristic of Dickens's innovation is reflected in recurrent reminders that the horror in the Christmas books is only ever imaginary. There are several such occasions in *A Christmas Carol*. Bob Cratchit is upset when his daughter, Martha, hides from him on his return home on the playful pretence that she will not be there for Christmas. Seeing his reaction, she 'came out prematurely from behind the closet door' in order not to dent the Christmas cheer, as 'she didn't like to see him disappointed, if it were only in joke' (*CC*, II, 50). After dinner, the Cratchits worry, without foundation, that the Christmas pudding may have been stolen – 'All sorts of horrors were supposed' (II, 51) – but it is immediately brought in to everyone's satisfaction and the anxiety is quelled. In this Christmas book, fears are imaginary and short-lived. Even the delighted response of Scrooge's boyhood self to remembered scenes from *Robinson Crusoe* (1719) – 'There goes Friday, running for his life to the little creek! Halloa! Hoop! Halloo!' (II, 32) – neutralises by its prevailing comic spirit the terrifying original where Friday was being chased by cannibals.[5] These hints that all the ostensible threats are fictive enabled the Christmas books to diverge from the darker and more consistently solemn tone adopted by many of the writers in Dickens's journals. It was also a way that they distinguished themselves from the serious-minded, purportedly factual, collections of supernatural sightings popular during Dickens's career that were intended to substantiate the case for the existence of an unseen world. Dickens read such works as Catherine Crowe's *The Night Side of Nature* (1848) and William Howitt's *A History of the Supernatural in All Ages* (1863), containing all manner of ghostly visions, which, like the baby with the 'fictitious turkey', more credulous readers were suspected to have swallowed whole. Dickens lightens the mood of his own ghost stories with a comic voice that offsets the Gothic strains: so that *A Christmas Carol* can 'haunt [its readers'] houses pleasantly' (Preface, 6) and all the tales induce what he calls in the passage quoted from 'A Christmas Tree' an 'agreeable creeping'.

Bringing into play a sense that these tales are merely fictitious, which gives rise to much of their distinctiveness in construction and tone, shows that the 'processes of the imagination', in the terms of the letter to Gaskell, that they illustrate are more than any other those involved in reading and writing. Throughout the tales, Dickens apprehends many connections between writing and ghosts or ghostliness. They are evident from the first line of *A Christmas Carol*: 'Marley was dead, to begin with' (*CC*, I, 9), where the ghostly double meaning links the act of beginning the narration to the returning of life to the dead. This quick wordplay recognises a truth about fiction, that to begin either to read or to write any story is in that instant to bring it to life. Several critics have taken up such insights in analyses of their own. Julian Wolfreys, in *Victorian Hauntings* (2002), explores several writers, including Dickens, from the premise that all text is ghostly. A text has a material presence but it also always conjures up something over and above the marks on the page, in a way that he finds unearthly. These enquiries have been underwritten by Jacques Derrida, whose book *Specters of Marx* (1994), and his short essay, 'Marx, c'est quelqu'un' (1997), have stimulated critical interest in the spectral and in its relations to economics.[6]

The language of ghosts came readily to mind when Dickens wrote about various aspects of the nature of fiction. His own experience of composition could feel like an encounter with a spectral power. As he began to conceive of *Bleak House*, he observed 'the first shadows of a new story hovering in a ghostly way about me'.[7] Less happily, a few months after the letter to Fechter, he disconsolately quipped to his subeditor, W. H. Wills, that he could not 'raise the ghost of an idea for a Xmas No.'[8] The same language seemed appropriate to describe a writer's distinctive style. Dickens thought that *Uncle Tom's Cabin* (1852) was imitative of major English novelists, including himself and Elizabeth Gaskell, identifying 'the ghost of Mary Barton' peeping through the pages.[9]

The narrators of fiction could seem ghostly, too. They witness numerous scenes, though the actors in them catch no sight of any watching presence. They can move with phantom ease through time and space, and their voices are disembodied, speaking from no fixed location. Maurice Blanchot has observed that narrative voice is 'a neutral voice that utters the work from a placeless place, where the work is silent', noting that in such cases it is 'ghostly, phantom-like'.[10] Dickens makes the connection himself, when, in *A Christmas Carol*, the intervening narrator announces, strikingly: 'The curtains of the bed were drawn aside; and Scrooge, starting up into a half-recumbent attitude, found himself face to face with the unearthly visitor who drew them: as close to it as I am now to you, and I am standing in the spirit at your elbow' (*CC*, ii, 28). As a way of describing one's own narrative presence in a ghost story, this is remarkably stark and full of self-conscious irony.[11] It continues the glimpsed recognitions, set in train by the opening sentence, that the ghost story itself seems frequently to offer a submerged commentary on the nature of fiction and how we read it.

It suits this self-referential dimension to Dickens's ghost stories that they repeatedly draw attention to their own process of narration by way of an exaggeratedly meticulous narrative voice. In this, they are indebted partly to an oral tradition of retelling ghostly tales, where the tales become performative acts in their own right, and partly to the reports of supernatural activity such as those collated by Crowe and Howitt. Dickens wrote a sceptical review of Catherine Crowe's collection for the *London Examiner*. (He promised readers a second discussion laying out arguments in favour of the existence of ghosts to counterbalance the first part, but it never followed.) His review perceptively identified a weakness in the spiritualist position based on the internal characteristics of the proffered narratives. He noted that they depended for their supernatural character on one factor that if differently understood undermined the whole:

> it is the peculiarity of almost all ghost stories, as contradistinguished from all other kinds of narratives purporting to be true, to depend, as ghost stories on some one little link in the chain of evidence, and that supposing that link to be destructible, the whole supernatural character is gone.[12]

Over ten years later, he emphasised the same point in a letter to Howitt, a convinced spiritualist: 'I have not yet met with any Ghost Story that was proved to me, or that had not the noticeable peculiarity in it – that the alteration of some slight circumstance would bring it within the range of common natural probabilities.'[13] With an eye for the peculiar construction of these tales, Dickens regards them as narrative curiosities.

Throughout the Christmas books Dickens consistently delights in the vulnerability of his imaginative fancies to a strong dose of remedial rationalism. He exploits the vulnerable ontological status of ghost stories in his handling of the genre. His narrators purportedly invite us to take the ghost stories on their own terms, but all the while they hint that there is a rational explanation that would make us reconceive the whole account. The tales are at any moment one 'slight circumstance' away from rendering void their own generic status. The threat of a literal-minded realism to the existence of the ghostly fictions as such is felt throughout the Christmas books. The potential collapse of the fiction is signalled in the examples of Martha pulling the plug on her practical joke, or the horrors of the Christmas-pudding theft immediately giving way to actuality. The characteristic interchange of belief and uncertainty in reading Dickens's ghost stories is suggested too in the detail of the doll's house, found among the apparitions of the piece on 'A Christmas Tree': 'though it *did* open all at once, the entire house-front (which was a blow, I admit, as cancelling the fiction of a staircase), it was but to shut it up again, and I could believe' ('CT', 5).

In this way, the ghost stories provide a heightened version of how we read any text, approaching it on its own terms but able also to think outside those terms. In this crux of his Christmas books, Dickens addresses what has been called the 'paradox of fiction', whereby we respond to fictional characters and circumstances as if they were real, without forgetting that they are not.[14] Coleridge's famous dictum – in relation to the *Lyrical*

Ballads (1798) – that reading requires the 'willing suspension of disbelief' is often taken as a universal truth, but Dickens creates in his ghost stories a more intricate interplay of belief and incredulity.[15] Disbelief is not so much suspended as brought into play, alongside or underneath our acquiescence in the fiction. Therefore, the ghost stories become subtle investigations into the process of reading fiction, into the apparent paradox of a believable story.

There is something peculiarly ghostly about Dickens's style. Across all his writing, it has a tendency to enliven and transform ordinary scenes and objects. Everyday life becomes surreal under the curious pressure of his prose. It is as if ghost stories provided the natural genre to showcase the usual effects of his style and to begin, by analogy, to dramatise and investigate its mysterious operations. The Christmas books take up not only general connections between ghosts and writing, then; they also explore elements of Dickens's idiosyncratic writing style.

A Christmas Carol, especially, is a remarkable achievement of style. Michael Slater has remarked that it is 'first and foremost a triumph of *tone*'.[16] J. Hillis Miller has praised its 'extraordinary stylistic verve'.[17] In such stylistically exuberant tales as this Dickens explores the potential effects of the techniques of his prose by turning his stylistic habits into matters of plot. Such features of his style as seeing the world as if in a waking dream, bringing inanimate things to life, effecting surprising transformations, are central plot concerns in the ghost stories. That is to say, the ghost story was particularly hospitable to Dickens's style and to investigations into it, because in the conventions of the Gothic, Dickens found his small-scale stylistic tendencies writ large.

The ontological uncertainty of the tales is typically achieved by undermining the purportedly supernatural occurrences with strong hints at rational explanations: that Gabriel Grub has been drinking, that Scrooge has eaten something that has affected his dreams, that Redlaw's phantom is a manifestation of his own troubled psychology, and so on. This frequently involves situating the ghost seers in a liminal state between waking and sleeping, as in the case of Scrooge, or Trotty Veck in *The Chimes*. It turns a recurrent interest of Dickens's fiction into an integral part of the machinery of his ghost stories, since characters in the novels, including Oliver Twist, Nell, Stephen Blackpool and Affery Flintwinch, also experience visionary transformations of reality while strangely half-asleep. As E. D. H. Johnson has stated, Dickens was 'especially original in exploiting what may be called the waking dream, in which impressions derived from the surrounding world merge with subjective imaginings'.[18] But while this was a recurrent plot element throughout his career, its fascination for Dickens lay in its concentration of a habitual aspect of his writing style: his tendency to cast a dreamlike sheen over realistic events. In Dickens's prose as much as in Oliver's dream, 'reality and imagination become so strangely blended' (*OT*, 34, 228) as to be inextricable.

The characteristic is especially significant in the ghost stories, which combine pressing social or psychological concerns with fanciful imaginings. Francis Jeffrey described this doubled vision in one of its instances when he wrote to Dickens that 'The whole scene of the Cratchetts [sic] is like the dream of a beneficent angel in spite of its broad reality.'[19] The intermingling of flights of imaginative fancy and urgent, harsh realities, typical of the Christmas ghost tales, was essential to Dickens's understanding of the nature of dreams, as well as of his own work. He claimed, in writing to Dr Thomas Stone in 1851, that in dreams we experience all manner of impossible visions which are unsettled by a nagging awareness that they must be a fiction. He suggested that some dreams are common to many people: for example, 'we all go to public places in our night dresses, and are horribly disconcerted, lest the company should observe it.'[20] But throughout such visions, there is an 'occasional endeavour to correct our delusions, made by some waking and reasoning faculty of the brain', so that the dreams are disturbed by a sense that something cannot be quite right:

> I cannot help thinking that this observant and corrective speck of the brain suggests to you, 'my good fellow how can you be in this crowd, when you know you are in your shirt?' It is not strong enough to dispel the vision, but it is just strong enough to present this inconsistency.[21]

This provides a perfect commentary on the mode of Dickens's ghost stories. It is translated into John Leech's original illustrations for *A Christmas Carol*. One depicts a diminutive Scrooge being shown the two ragged children, Ignorance and Want, with an urban skyline in the background. Another, 'The Last of the Spirits', shows Scrooge, with his head in his hands, confronted with his own gravestone in a churchyard. In both cases Scrooge is out of doors and in his nightshirt. The jarring inappropriateness of the experience prompts him and us with a doubt that he may only be dreaming. These are pictorial representations of the distinctive epistemological uncertainty of Dickens's ghost stories. Productively situated in between sleeping and waking, the tales turn a feature of Dickens's habitual style into a fundamental mechanism of their plot and into a premise for their overall effects.

A much observed aspect of Dickens's style that becomes a literal feature of the ghost stories is his trick of imparting life to inanimate objects. These are cases of the exuberance of the Dickensian imagination, which goes beyond normal limits. They register Dickens's own imaginative vitality in being able to render the ordinary in new ways, to find enjoyably new ways of looking at objects and things. J. Hillis Miller has argued that all storytelling is an act of prosopopoeia, 'the ascription to entities that are not really alive first of a name, then of a face, and finally, in a return to language, of a voice'.[22] In this sense, each local animism is a microcosm of the fiction itself, and it explains why ghost stories, which are by definition about the bringing to life of something that is dead, are intrinsically predisposed towards dramatising, more or less allegorically, the power of the creative imagination and especially Dickens's style itself.

In several such instances, the animism is prompted by catachresis – the use of words from one semantic field in an unfamiliar context. Paul de Man observed the ghostly potential latent in this property of language: 'Something monstrous lurks in the most innocent of catachreses: when one speaks of the legs of the table or the face of the mountain, catachresis is already turning into prosopopeia, and one begins to perceive a world of potential ghosts and monsters.'[23] Dickens's spectres are a natural emanation from the habitual animisms of his style and from the inherent curiosities of language. In this sense, they are not conjured up only at his own volition but are a phantom product of his idiosyncratic encounters with language.

For example, in one of his earliest Gothic fantasies, the Bagman's tale of the talking chair in *The Pickwick Papers*, Dickens observes that the legs of the chair – a promising catachresis lurking there – are 'carefully tied up in red cloth, as if it had got the gout in its toes' (*PP*, 14, 205). The humanising simile prepares for the subsequent ghostly animation of the chair, and it makes the transformation seem merely a far-fetched extension of Dickens's habitual manner; as Garrett Stewart has put it, 'the whole tale seems to have unrolled from a simple instance of his typical descriptive trick – the animation of lifeless objects.'[24] This is all the more so in the Christmas books, where the ghostly visions emerge from inanimate objects. In *A Christmas Carol*, the door knocker turns into Marley's face, and the Ghost of Christmas Yet to Come seems to have emerged from Scrooge's bedpost, or at least that is what it metamorphoses back into. In *The Chimes*, the great Bell becomes animated and speaks to Trotty.

Aside from these literal extrapolations, Dickens's well-known stylistic trait of personification or prosopopoeia is especially widespread in his ghost stories. Early in *A Christmas Carol* he writes about the vibrations of the church bell tower, 'as if its teeth were chattering' (*CC*, I, 15). He also imparts life to Scrooge's house, in a dark and dilapidated corner of London: 'one could scarcely help fancying it must have run there when it was a young house, playing at hide-and-seek with other houses, and forgotten the way out again' (I, 16). Repeatedly, these flights of fancy are prompted by a natural predisposition of the language towards personification. The personification of the bell tower follows a description of the 'gruff old bell' (I, 14). A bell can just about be gruff in its sound, but the adjective has already humanised the bell, as if it is old and irritable. The memorable personification of Scrooge's chambers succeeds mention of his 'gloomy suite of rooms' (I, 16). Rooms can be gloomy, if they lack light, but the adjective invites the sense that they have a depressed mood of their own, that Scrooge's house is down in the dumps. Dickens goes on in his description to write that 'the fog and frost so hung about the black old gateway of the house' (I, 16). Although it is accurate enough to describe fog and frost as hanging about, the verb contains the sense that the weather is like an idle youth lounging around, and the prose immediately yields to the animism: 'it seemed as if the Genius of the Weather sat in mournful meditation on the threshold' (I, 16).

A related aspect of Dickens's style that is similarly foregrounded by the plots of his ghost stories is the tendency of his books to revitalise the dead. The power of death to overcome the living at any moment is imaginatively reversed in the frequency with which the dead come back to life in Dickens's writing or can be imagined as doing so. As well as Marley, Doctor Manette is 'recalled to life' at the start of *A Tale of Two Cities*, and John Harmon comes back from the dead, as it were, in *Our Mutual Friend*. More than this, resurrection is a habit of Dickens's image-making. As John Carey and others have shown, Dickens regularly describes corpses and coffins as if they were alive.[25] It is a set of images that channel some of Dickens's long-standing concerns about how much of a person's life and influence remains posthumously and about the need to keep responsible attitudes towards mortality from the life-defeating paralysis of a morbid fear of death.

This imaginative attraction towards the resurrection of the dead, central to the Christmas books, is played out in the realm of language and idiom, particularly in *A Christmas Carol*. In a story where the spirits of the dead return to haunt Scrooge, in the form of Marley's ghost, Dickens is remarkably alert to the possibility that new life can be given even to dead metaphors. It starts on the first page, with:

Old Marley was as dead as a doornail. Mind! I don't mean to say that I know, of my own knowledge, what there is particularly dead about a doornail... But the wisdom of our ancestors is in the simile; and my unhallowed hands shall not disturb it, or the country's done for. (*CC*, 1, 9)

In a genre characterised by overused plots and worn-out conventions, into which Dickens sought to breathe new life, such staged reworkings of cliché as this, despite its mock conservatism, challenge habits of mind and speech inherited from the past. In reanimating tired idioms he rehearsed the same belief that the past is not permanently binding and that its determining power can be overturned – a conviction that his characters throughout the Christmas books are required to learn. The opportunity for old habits to be changed to new purposes is first glimpsed in these ostentatious variations on traditional speech forms.

Throughout the story, language is reanimated by the relentless energy with which *A Christmas Carol* imparts life to that which is dead, in the hope that the renewal may also encompass dead hearts and lifeless imaginations. Consistently, the idioms refuse to stay put. For example: 'Scrooge had often heard it said that Marley had no bowels, but he had never believed it until now' (*CC*, 1, 19). When the ghost corrects Scrooge's tense in referring to him, Scrooge reworks an idiom that was not unusual in the 1840s: '"You're particular, for a shade." He was going to say "*to* a shade," but substituted this, as more appropriate' (1, 21). It is still happening at the conclusion of the tale, when Scrooge sends the passing boy to go and buy the huge turkey: 'The boy was off like a shot. He must have had a steady hand at a trigger who could have got a shot off half so fast' (*CC*, v, 79). The vitality of Dickens's prose itself creates an atmosphere in which the potential for new life is immanent, hence the suitability of this style of writing to tales where spectres return from the dead and which hold out the hope of resisting the established patterns of habit and even, particularly in *The Chimes*, the settled indifference of history.

The energetic revitalisation of language and the animation of material objects are part of Dickens's ghostly, Gothic style, but they are also of a piece with that thematic preoccupation of his ghost stories: the possibility of radical change. In all the Christmas books of the 1840s, the ghosts bring about a humanising conversion: of Scrooge, of Trotty, of Tackleton in *The Cricket on the Hearth*, of Doctor Jeddler in *The Battle of Life*, and of Redlaw in *The Haunted Man*. Dickens's language is often transformative in the same way – beyond reawakening conventional idioms. A careful reading of *A Christmas Carol* reveals Dickens rehearsing, in patterns on the page, Scrooge's movement from isolated miser to generous-hearted, community-spirited benefactor. In his introduction to the Christmas Books, Robert Douglas-Fairhurst has noted the contagiousness of the vocabulary, the way in which Dickens's prose often takes up its own earlier terms, the abundance of description at the outset that provides, ahead of time, a model for Scrooge's later generosity.[26] This characteristic is often a model of change as well as of generosity. For example, in the early descriptive passages, we move from the words 'foggy withal' (*CC*, I, 10) to fog that was 'dense without' (11), which creates on the page a sense of turning outward that is here only a quirky coincidence of language but which will later be realised by Scrooge. At the same time, amid the fog, candles flare in office windows, 'like ruddy smears upon the palpable brown air' (I, 10). Dickens's prose soon activates the hopeful, heartening possibilities of the gloomy first adjective when Scrooge's nephew, Fred, arrives: 'his face was ruddy and handsome' (I, 11). So, too, in contrast to the miserable 'pelting rain' (I, 10) of the opening scene, Bob Cratchit, released from work, runs 'home as fast as he could pelt, to play at blindman's-buff' (16), where 'pelting' has become the enthused energy of a man liberated and filled with Christmas cheer.

Such writing creates a mood in which radical change seems part of the atmosphere. In *The Haunted Man*, the same sort of transformative potential is invested in the descriptive prose immediately prior to the scene in which Milly's presence reverses the curse that has afflicted the Tetterbys. As dawn arrives, it energises the urban setting with the potential for dramatic, magical change. The rising sun 'turned the smoke and vapour of the city into a cloud of gold' (*HM*, III, 388). The sundial 'shook off the finer particles of snow that had accumulated on his dull old face in the night, and looked out at the little white wreaths eddying round and round him' (*HM*, III, 388). The personification of the sundial, prompted by the anticipated catachresis of 'face', bestows life upon the scene and gives living motion to the 'white wreaths', which are variously suggestive of death, everlasting life and Christmas. Then the 'blind groping of the morning' (*HM*, III, 388) reached into the crypt and 'quickened the slow principle of life' (388) there, where it may take a second glance to appreciate the full extent of the change, as 'quickened' recovers from its false opposition to 'slow', to suggest a more thorough bringing to life in the archaic sense of 'the quick and the dead'.

Most of the lexical transformations I have discussed from *A Christmas Carol* occur immediately prior to the visitation by Marley's ghost, preparing the way for the metamorphosis of the door knocker and, more importantly, the change that will be effected in Scrooge. There, too, the scene is made to tremble with the possibility of change:

The water-plug being left in solitude, its overflowings sullenly congealed, and turned to misanthropic ice. The brightness of the shops where holly sprigs and berries crackled in the lamp heat of the windows, made pale faces ruddy as they passed. Poulterers' and grocers' trades became a splendid joke: a glorious pageant, with which it was next to impossible to believe that such dull principles as bargain and sale had anything to do. (*CC*, I, 15)

New life comes upon the street scene here. Faces are again made 'ruddy' by the transformative power of Dickens's prose, as much as by the brightness of the shops, and in this spirit the trades are deemed a 'glorious pageant'. The water-plug, 'left in solitude' and forming 'misanthropic ice', has 'sullenly congealed' – not 'suddenly', though the change of state has happened quickly, but 'sullenly', humanising the overflowings, chilly emblems of Scrooge that they are. There is a quick movement from 'its overflowings sullenly congealed' to – at the end of the next paragraph – the 'even more congenial frost' (*CC*, I, 15), where the passage from 'congealed' to 'congenial' is another of those instances that anticipate Scrooge's change, rehearsing his release from sympathetic blockage to generous conviviality, while 'congenial' itself contains a trace of ghostliness – genial, genie – without which the transformation will not be effected.

The potential for transformation is latent in Dickens's syntax, too. When the young Scrooge is set to leave school for Christmas, the prose imparts upon the schoolmaster, by a redemptive paraprosdokian (a sentence that surprises by ultimately departing from expectations), the kind of change that the adult Scrooge will soon undergo: 'A terrible voice in the hall cried, "Bring down Master Scrooge's box, there!" and in the hall appeared the school-master himself, who glared on Master Scrooge with a ferocious condescension, and threw him into a dreadful state of mind by shaking hands with him' (*CC*, II, 33). The last action, surprisingly, translates the fierceness into friendliness. More subtle in its effect, consider the sentence that introduces the schoolroom. Its string of negatives seems to describe the quietness of the scene. One wonders whether Dickens knew the first lines of 'A Visit from St Nicholas' (1823): ''Twas the night before Christmas, when all through the house / Not a creature was stirring, not even a mouse.' Dickens's sentence reads:

Not a latent echo in the house, not a squeak and scuffle from the mice behind the panelling, not a drip from the half-thawed water-spout in the dull yard behind, not a sigh among the leafless boughs of one despondent poplar, not the idle swinging of an empty store-house door, no, not a clicking in the fire, but fell upon the heart of Scrooge with a softening influence, and gave a freer passage to his tears. (*CC*, I, 31)

The delayed 'but fell' transforms the scene from one of silence and isolation to one where noises play upon the sensitive heart of the adult
Scrooge. The scene itself is brought to life across the course of the sentence, as Scrooge himself is slowly being awakened into a new vitality.

Dickens had read Tennyson admiringly since at least the autumn of
1842,[27] so it is no surprise that one 'latent echo' in this passage is from
Tennyson's 'Mariana', another near-silent scene, oddly disturbed by slight
noises, including doors that 'upon their hinges creaked' and a mouse that
'Behind the mouldering wainscot shrieked', and where the shadow of a
poplar falls across Mariana's bed – all elements that reappear in Dickens's
description.[28] Dickens here responds finely not only to that poem's
stock of images but also to its careful confusion of noise and silence: for
Tennyson has 'Unlifted was the clinking latch', where the 'clinking' of the
latch is forever and only held in potential, as it remains 'Unlifted', never
having the opportunity to clink, even while 'Unlifted' is teasingly close to
'Uplifted'.[29]

The transformations effected by Dickens's style – by his vocabulary and
his syntax – rehearse the pattern of conversion that Scrooge will later replicate. They create a climate of change in which Scrooge's story is less jarringly improbable. What happens to Scrooge is inevitable in this context
and in this genre. But these stylistic transformations raise the question
of whether these changes are only imaginative occurrences. Conversions
on the page seem easier to effect than real-life changes. Scrooge's question about whether he has free will or not is the right one not only for
someone with a history of habitual miserliness but also for a character
in a Christmas tale predestined for a happy ending. It extends Dickens's
long-held concern that his stories proposed imaginative solutions existing
in print alone that he could not rely on his readers to effect in real life.

The Christmas books, then, are exuberant displays of style such that at
every turn the ghostly potential of Dickens's characteristic style has a realised correlative in the plots of the tales. Dickens's life-giving prose anticipates the work of the ghosts, who bring about renewal in the world and
who are themselves newly raised to animation. To this extent the ghostly
tales illuminate the operations of his prose. They are extended considerations of the 'processes of the imagination' and of the ability of his own
prose style to bestow new life on his writing and his characters.

Dickens's ghost stories are parables of the imagination, and this is finally
registered by the endings of the tales. Almost without exception, Dickens
raises the conjecture that the whole story may itself have been a vision.

Scrooge may have been intoxicated. Trotty is suspected to have dreamed, and the foregoing scenes are, in a revealing choice of apparitional words, 'visions' and 'shadows' (*Chimes*, 161). The characters in *The Cricket on the Hearth* seem to have been figments of the narrator's imagination that vanish into the air. A range of rational explanations for Redlaw's visitations are proposed by a non-committal narrator.

Since characters on the page have no life of their own but are brought to life in the imaginations of the writer and the readers, we are reminded on several occasions of the apparitional quality of Dickens's characters. In *A Christmas Carol*, Fezziwig is strangely described as having light issue from his calves when he is dancing, a detail that strikes a comparison with the Ghost of Christmas Past, from whose head, we have been told, springs 'a bright, clear jet of light' (*CC*, ii, 28). Scrooge is caricatured as having his own microclimate, freezing everything around him: 'He carried his own low temperature always about with him' (i, 10). This is more literally realised by Marley's ghost which, we are told, carries about with it 'an infernal atmosphere of its own' (i, 21).

Dickens's apprehension of the phantom-like quality of literary characters, his strong hint that his ghost stories investigate the experiences of writing and reading, is best evident in the scenes of reading that he describes. When Scrooge is a boy, reading books at school before Christmas, a parade of characters appears before him, much as the ghosts will do before his adult self:

> The Spirit touched him on the arm, and pointed to his younger self, intent upon his reading. Suddenly a man, in foreign garments: wonderfully real and distinct to look at: stood outside the window, with an axe stuck in his belt, and leading by the bridle an ass laden with wood.
>
> 'Why, it's Ali Baba!' Scrooge exclaimed in ecstasy. 'It's dear old honest Ali Baba! ... And Valentine ... and his wild brother, Orson; there they go! And what's his name, who was put down in his drawers, asleep, at the Gate of Damascus; don't you see him! And the Sultan's Groom turned upside down by the Genii; there he is upon his head!' (*CC*, ii, 31–2)

The scene is a precursor to the much-discussed equivalent scene in Chapter 4 of *David Copperfield* (1849–50), where the hero is 'reading as if for life' (*DC*, 4, 48). David's reading conjures up imaginative visions that appear to him as the characters did for the boy Scrooge, and as the ghosts did for the adult Scrooge: 'From that blessed little room, Roderick Random, Peregrine Pickle, Humphrey Clinker, Tom Jones, The Vicar of Wakefield, Don Quixote, Gil Blas, and Robinson Crusoe, came out, a glorious host, to keep me company' (*DC*, 4, 48). The characters are brought to life for David in the way that ghosts are in the imaginations of Dickens's many haunted characters. It is another reminder that much of Dickens's writing is animated by the connection between ghost-seeing and reading fiction. Perhaps that is why in the quotation from *David Copperfield* the word 'ghost' seems to haunt the phrase 'glorious host'.

NOTES

1 Letter from Charles Dickens to Charles Fechter, 8 March 1868, *Letters*, XII, 68.
2 *The Chimes* (1844), *The Cricket on the Hearth* (1845), *The Battle of Life* (1846) and *The Haunted Man; or, The Ghost's Bargain* (1848). Not all of the Christmas books are ghost stories, strictly speaking, although they share similar ghostly traits and themes, and, with the exception of *The Battle of Life*, they each have a supernatural character. The subtitles indicate that *The Chimes* is a 'goblin story' and *The Cricket on the Hearth* is a 'fairy story'.
3 Letter from Charles Dickens to the Earl of Carlisle, 2 January 1849, *Letters*, V, 467.
4 Letter from Charles Dickens to Mrs Gaskell, 25 November 1851, *Letters*, VI, 547.
5 See Edwin M. Eigner, 'On Becoming Pantaloon', *The Dickensian*, 89 (3) (winter 1993): 177–83, at 180–1.
6 See also Andrew Smith, *The Ghost Story, 1840–1920: A Cultural History* (Manchester University Press, 2010).
7 Letter from Charles Dickens to Mary Boyle, 21 February 1851, *Letters*, VI, 299.
8 Letter from Charles Dickens to W. H. Wills, 30 June 1868, *Letters*, XII, 145.
9 Letter from Charles Dickens to Mrs Richard Watson, 22 November 1852, *Letters*, VI, 809.
10 Maurice Blanchot, 'L'Absence de livre', in *L'Entretien infini* (Paris, 1969), 564–6. The translations here are taken from Derrida's discussion of Blanchot's terms in 'Living On: Border Lines', translated by James Hulbert, in Harold Bloom, Paul de Man, Jacques Derrida, Geoffrey Hartman and J. Hillis Miller, *Deconstruction and Criticism* (New York, 1979), 62–142, at 86, 88.
11 See Michael Slater, 'The Christmas Books', *The Dickensian*, 65 (1969): 17–24, at 19; Graham Holderness, 'Imagination in *A Christmas Carol*', *Études Anglaises*, 32 (1979): 28–45, at 33.
12 Charles Dickens, 'Review of Catherine Crowe, *The Night Side of Nature*', *The Examiner*, 26 February 1848, 131–3, at 132.
13 Letter from Charles Dickens to William Howitt, 6 September 1859, *Letters*, IX, 116.
14 See Colin Radford, 'How Can We Be Moved by the Fate of Anna Karenina?', *Proceedings of the Aristotelian Society*, supp. vol. 69, 67–80; and the ensuing debates, as surveyed by Alex Neill, 'The Paradox of Responding to Fiction',

in Stephen Davies, Kathleen Marie Higgins, Robert Hopkins (eds.), *A Companion to Aesthetics*, 2nd edn (Oxford: Blackwells, 2009), 278–81.

15 Samuel Taylor Coleridge, *Biographia Literaria*, ed. James Engell and Walter Jackson Bate, 2 vols., in *The Collected Works* (Princeton, NJ: Bollingen, 1983), II, 6, 134.

16 Michael Slater, 'Introduction' to *The Christmas Books* (Harmondsworth: Penguin, 1971), I, xi.

17 J. Hillis Miller, 'The Genres of *A Christmas Carol*', *The Dickensian*, 89 (3) (winter 1993): 193–206, at 193. Miller identifies four predominant rhetorical features: 'lists and parataxis, prosopopoeia, facetious paronomasia, and hyperbole' (193).

18 E. D. H. Johnson, *Charles Dickens: An Introduction to His Novels* (New York: Random House, 1969), 133.

19 Lord Cockburn, *Life of Lord Jeffrey, with a Selection from His Correspondence*, 2 vols. (Edinburgh, 1852), II, 380–1, cited in *CH*, 147.

20 Letter from Charles Dickens to Thomas Stone, 2 February 1851, *Letters*, VI, 280.

21 *Letters*, VI, 280.

22 J. Hillis Miller, *Versions of Pygmalion* (Cambridge, MA: Harvard University Press, 1990), 5.

23 Paul de Man, 'The Epistemology of Metaphor', *Critical Inquiry*, 5(1) (1978): 13–30, at 21.

24 Garrett Stewart, *Dickens and the Trials of Imagination* (Cambridge, MA: Harvard University Press, 1974), 41.

25 John Carey, *The Violent Effigy: A Study of Dickens' Imagination* (London: Faber & Faber, 1973), 80–104.

26 Robert Douglas-Fairhurst, 'Introduction', in *A Christmas Carol and Other Christmas Books* (Oxford University Press, 2006), vii–xxix. The introduction includes a good discussion of the significance of Dickens's writing style in *A Christmas Carol*.

27 Noted by Kathleen Tillotson in 'A Background for *A Christmas Carol*', *The Dickensian*, 89 (winter 1993): 165–9, at 169; and see Letter from Charles Dickens to John Forster, [7 August 1842], *Letters*, III, 307.

28 Alfred Tennyson, 'Mariana', in Christopher Ricks (ed.), *The Poems of Tennyson*, 2nd edn, 3 vols. (Harlow: Longman, 1987), I, 205–9, ll. 62 and 64 at 209.

29 Tennyson, 'Mariana', l. 6 on p. 206.

CHAPTER FIVE

Dickens and the form of the historical present

Clare Pettitt

All is going on as it was wont. The waves are hoarse with repetition of their mystery; the dust lies piled upon the shore; the sea-birds soar and hover; the winds and clouds go forth upon their trackless flight; the white arms beckon, in the moonlight, to the invisible country far away.

(*DS*, 41, 554)

Dickens's extraordinary use of the historic-present tense throughout five entire chapters of *Dombey and Son*, and in parts of several other of its chapters, is one reason why this novel of 1846–8 reads so very differently to its predecessors, *Barnaby Rudge* (1841) and *Martin Chuzzlewit* (1843–4).[1] It was a stylistic shift that was noticed, although not universally welcomed, at the time. One contemporary critic described *Dombey and Son* as 'a sad falling off', regretting that Dickens 'seemed … to have had the misfortune to strike into a vein of fine writing, yielding whole pages which might have been read off into rather bombastic blank verse'.[2] Another critic, while enjoying the story, agreed in bewilderment that 'The book is … full to overflowing of waves whispering and wandering; of dark rivers rolling to the sea; of winds, and golden ripples, and such like matters.'[3] Others were more sympathetic to Dickens's new 'poetic expression', and his 'more ideal tendencies' in *Dombey and Son*, through which 'particular thoughts and phrases … run … like the leading colour through a painting, or the predominant phrase in a piece of music'.[4]

Most contemporary readers in 1847, for whom generic boundaries were far more impervious than they were later to become, were trained to hear the present tense as the 'lyric present' of poetry.[5] What troubled them was quite what such 'poetry' might be doing intruding in the middle of Dickens's new novel. What scholars of linguistics describe as a 'non-temporal use of tense … [when] … what is usually a grammatical sign for a time relation may sometimes be used for other notional purposes' is rare in English narrative writing, but I suggest that Dickens, encouraged by the powerful example of Carlyle, was experimenting with a present tense which was not in fact lyric in intention.[6] In 1847, it seems that Dickens was reaching for a tense with which to exercise a temporary withdrawal from linear time in order to contemplate the place of individual experience in a universal 'history'. The tense he uses to do this is the *historic* present tense.[7] Dickens's use of the historic present in the 1840s introduces a careful and precise rearrangement of historical narrative from a fundamentally and radically presentist viewpoint. By the time he came to write his 1859 historical novel, *A Tale of Two Cities*, Dickens had ceased to use the historic present tense so much because by then he had found a presentist structure for the narrative itself. *A Christmas Carol* (1843), *The Chimes* (1844) and *Dombey and Son*, although none of these were 'historical' fictions, were in fact the pivotal texts in which Dickens worked out his own idea of 'history'.[8]

The newly historically universalised perspective of *Dombey and Son*, corroborated by metonymic profusion (all those waves and rivers), which we might now assume to be part of a distinctively 'Dickensian' style, was in fact forged by Dickens as a response to a very specific experience of the dislocation of history. Stuttering, scattered and various in their outcomes, a series of revolutions erupted seemingly simultaneously in the mid to late 1840s. The so-called 'European Revolution' reached from the Atlantic to Ukraine, from the Baltic to the Mediterranean, catapulting millions of people across the Continent into political life and opening up Europe again to disorder and mobility after an interval of post-Napoleonic peace. By 1851, of course, most of these revolutions had 'failed', although this moment of international volatility and rebellion surely had a more lasting effect on the modern construction of a historical present than we now tend to remember.[9] If we take the political unsettlement of these years seriously, as those living through that decade undoubtedly did, we can perhaps begin to understand better the seismic stylistic shifts in British literary writing of the 1840s.

Writing to his friend John Forster just after the February Revolution and the establishment of the Second French Republic in 1848, and signing himself 'CITOYEN CHARLES DICKENS', Dickens broke enthusiastically into French, 'MON AMI, je trouve que j'aime tant la République, qu'il me faut renoncer ma langue et écrire seulement le langage de la République de France – langage des Dieux et des Anges – langage, et [*sic*] un mot, des Français!'[10] The European revolutions of February and March had 'appear[ed] synchronized' to those who lived through the exciting first months of 1848, and this synchronicity helped Dickens to imagine an expanded human fellowship, a newly politicised generation that could connect beyond national boundaries to create a universal human history.[11] Dickens continued to see the revolutions as part of an unfinished and ongoing process of social change into the 1850s. He was right. François Furet describes the establishment of the Third French Republic in 1870, the year of Dickens's death, as 'the French Revolution coming into port', nearly 100 years after its first eruption.[12] Dickens's newly Frenchified political spirit was noted with disapproval at the time by some readers of *Dombey and Son*: 'This levelling principle, frequently peeping out in Dickens's works, is ... imported from France, where that spirit is so rife', complained one reviewer.[13]

In this politically turbulent period, Dickens starts not only to experiment with the historical-present tense but also to explore the possibility of making the present historical. His journalism and his Christmas books need to be placed alongside similarly politically motivated rhetorical experiments by, for example, Augustus Welby Pugin in *Contrasts* (1836), and Thomas Carlyle in *The History of the French Revolution* (1837) and *Past and Present* (1843). These are all texts that cast around for a new grammar, lexical or visual, which is capable of dramatising the present with reference to the past (and crucially not the other way around). Carlyle famously found himself grammatically embattled in this period. Replying to John Stuart Mill's criticism of his style and his 'quarrel with the Nominative-and-verb' in *The French Revolution*, Carlyle explained:

> the common English mode of writing has to do with what I call *hearsays* of things; and the great business for me, in which alone I feel any comfort, is recording the *presence*, bodily concrete coloured presence of things; – for which the Nominative-and-verb, as I find it Here and Now, refuses to stand me in due stead.[14]

In reaching for the historic present, both Carlyle and Dickens reached for a tense that works better in French than in English. This Frenchification of their respective prose represents a significant turn outwards from the local and the vernacular at a moment of intense and urgent internationalism.

Between 1842 and 1847 Dickens covered immense distances. He travelled to America and several times to Italy, to France and Switzerland. He experienced these as not only journeys across space, but also journeys through time. The Italy he visited in 1845 was already in the throes of the Risorgimento, 'Signore Mazzini and the fiery cross were traversing Italy from end to end', as he later recalled.[15] When he arrived in Rome he was delighted by 'so many fresh traces of remote antiquity' (*PI*, 170). The *freshness* of antiquity in a period that saw not only more actual travel but also a proliferation of printed information and visual representations and reconstructions of the distant past posed a new challenge to the imagination of what it meant to be contemporary. Dickens suffered a kind of crisis of temporal calibration as he travelled around in an uncertain and politically unstable present time which seemed to occupy more space and to drag behind it more 'historical' time than ever before. The texts which respond most directly to this crisis are *American Notes* (1842), the first two of Dickens's Christmas books, *A Christmas Carol* and *The Chimes*, and *Pictures from Italy*, which first appeared as a series of letters in his own newspaper, the *Daily News* (1845–6).

But in 1841, before he set out on his peregrinations, Dickens had written his first 'historical' novel, *Barnaby Rudge*, a book so closely mapped onto London that Steven Connor suggests that the narrative suffers from a 'perspectival difficulty ... [as] ... for Dickens to see with and through the body of the city is to surrender the possibility of determinate perspective'.[16] *Barnaby Rudge* is indeed a curiously claustrophobic narrative, and we spend a lot of it locked inside its bounded spaces, from the 'snug corner' (*BR*, 3, 32) of the Maypole to the 'small room[s]' (13, 118) and 'dark winding flights of stairs' (4, 41) in Gabriel Varden's house in Clerkenwell, and Widow Rudge's house in a 'narrow ... extremely dark' street in Southwark (16, 139). The plot finally works itself out under lock and key in a series of dungeons and prison cells. It seems that even Dickens felt he could never quite escape his small party of main characters, although he tried to cut loose from them in the 'fire and smoke' of the riot scenes, which he explained that he wanted to present as 'a great mass ... all mixed up together' and 'even to lose my own dramatis personae in the throng, or only see them dimly'.[17] One of the ways he tries to 'mix up' his description of the rampaging mob is by using the image of the sea, with the crowd 'Roaring and chafing like an angry sea' (*BR*, 63, 501), and it is through the image of the sea, too, that Dickens tries to introduce some uncertainty into his 'historical' narrative, breaking into the present tense to rupture what Michael Wood has called 'the unimpeachable authority of the past tense':[18]

> A mob is usually a creature of very mysterious existence, particularly in a large city. Where it comes from or whither it goes, few men can tell. Assembling and dispersing with equal suddenness, it is as difficult to follow to its various sources as the sea itself; nor does the parallel stop here, for the ocean is not more fickle and uncertain, more terrible when roused, more unreasonable, or more cruel. (*BR*, 52, 413–14)

This is a perspectival shift in the narrative, which perhaps suggests a connection between Dickens's account of the Gordon riots of 1780 and the Chartist unrest that he was witnessing in London in the late 1830s. But this present tense is the 'gnomic' present of commonplaces, generalisations and proverbial truths and not the historic present with which Dickens will later attempt to forge a dynamic link between past and present.[19] Dickens is here introducing an *image* of uncertainty (the sea) rather than creating uncertainty in the fabric of his text.[20] *Barnaby Rudge* never breaks historiographically, or philosophically, with the past-perfect tense, the tense which Roland Barthes called 'the factitious tense of cosmogonies, myths, histories and novels' and which scholars of linguistics recognise as the normative 'unmarked tense form'.[21] That the images of the rioting crowd provide the only mentions of the sea in what is an otherwise landlocked story is also significant. 'Chroniclers are privileged to enter where they list', Dickens famously asserts at the beginning of Chapter 9, 'to come and go through keyholes, to ride upon the wind, to overcome, in their soarings up and down, all obstacles of distance, time, and place' (*BR*, 9, 79). But there is very little riding on the wind or soaring in this novel, hampered as it is by 'perspectival difficulties'. Dickens only really seems to have learnt how to make his narrative fly and soar after he himself put out to sea in 1842 and put some serious distance between himself and his London home. And even then he did not immediately strike upon his new style.

Dickens in the Old World and the New: *American Notes* and *Pictures from Italy*

'His mind is American – his soul is republican – His heart is democratic' announced the *New York Herald* on 1 February 1842, shortly after Dickens's arrival in America.[22] Of course, after Dickens's famous and repeated denunciations of American piracy of British books, the publication of his *American Notes for General Circulation* in October and the American sections of *Martin Chuzzlewit* the following spring, the *Herald*, like most of the American press, was to take an altogether different line – excoriating him for his 'lies and blackguardism'.[23]

So what happened to *this* Dickens (the republican, democratic, 'American' Dickens), the Dickens who set off from Liverpool 'in a small steamer, to board the "Merrikin"' on 3 January 1842, already disgusted with Peel's Tory administration in Britain – a government which later that year was to use increasingly authoritarian methods to put down the industrial unrest and riots that spread across the north of England and into Wales.[24] Dickens left for America with every expectation of proving to himself his theory that good institutions and an active and democratically mandated state machinery would inevitably produce a good and happy populace. His disappointment with much – although not all – of what he found in America greatly influenced his responses to Italy where he went two years later and where he and his family spent the best part of a year.[25] The Chapman & Hall 1866 Library Edition of Dickens's works followed Dickens's own instructions in publishing *American Notes* and *Pictures from Italy* together into one volume, and Dickens's responses to the New World and the Old in these two travelogues are best understood as a kind of pair, and a pair that owes much to the politically fraught context of British and international politics between 1842 and 1846.

Dickens approached the New World as 'a Lover of Freedom' with high expectations of its newness, fully expecting to find the Americans 'applying themselves in a new world to correct some of the falsehoods and vices of the old'.[26] But, almost as soon as he disembarked, he started to perceive a shallowness about this spanking newness. American scenes seemed to him to have 'no more perspective than a Chinese bridge on a tea-cup' (*AN*, 1, 5, 81), Boston was 'slight and unsubstantial in appearance' (1, 3, 34) and the houses did not seem 'to have any root at all in the ground' (1, 3, 34). America's brightness quickly became glaring and rebarbative. The light 'so intensely clear, and dry, and bright'; the

> gaudy colours; the gilded letters were so very golden; the bricks were so very red, the stone was so very white, the blinds and area railings were so very green, the knobs and plates upon the street doors so marvellously bright and twinkling; and all so slight and unsubstantial in appearance. (*AN*, 1, 3, 34)

It is striking in these descriptions that Dickens makes very little use of analogy or metaphor: the bricks are just 'very red' and the blinds just 'very green'. Dickens's enthusiasm for political transparency was, in fact, rather dampened by this unremitting visibility. America seemed a country of surfaces.[27] Inalienable freedoms and the rhetoric of Liberty, for example, allowed some people to make slaves of others: 'to the music of clanking chains and bloody stripes' (*AN*, 1, 8, 133). As he wrote to his friend, the actor Macready, 'I am a Lover of Freedom, disappointed. – That's all.'[28]

Just as he had looked forward to newness in America, in approaching Rome, Dickens is eagerly anticipating oldness, and he writes that the Tiber had 'a *promising* aspect of desolation and ruin' (*PI*, 116, [my emphasis]), but on entering Rome he was disappointed: 'There were no great ruins, no solemn tokens of antiquity, to be seen; – they all lie on the other side of the city. There seemed to be long streets of common-place shops and houses, such as are to be found in any European town' (*PI*, 116).

Even when he did finally get to the ruins next morning, he found that 'obelisks, or columns: ancient temples, theatres, houses, porticos, or for-ums … every fragment, whenever it is possible, has been blended into some modern structure' (*PI*, 151). The old 'blended' indistinguishably with the new and refused to fall into a satisfactorily sequential narrative. Dickens's inability to bring the past and the present into a meaningful relationship on his travels is manifest in his travel writing. In *American Notes* he did occasionally try using the present tense, but *Blackwood's* com-plained that he had fallen 'into the error of attempting to describe events in the present tense and first person – abruptly passing into it – moreover, from the ordinary style of the narrative in the past tense'.[29] It did not judge the experiment, which it assumed was an imitation of the Homeric epic present, to be a success.

Stephen Bann, John Plunkett and Kate Flint have shown how the imagery of photography, skiagraphy, dissolving views, dioramas and pano-ramas informs and even structures the text of *Pictures from Italy*. What is most striking, however, about the relentless vocabulary of shows and pictures in this text is the way in which Dickens places himself – most uncharacteristically – as the passive consumer of images.[30] He does not represent himself as being in control of imagining, making or interpret-ing. The technologies referenced here, then, are perhaps not themselves so important as the passivity of his response. There is a limit – one might even go so far as to say a bankruptcy – of his imagination in these two travelogues, which Macaulay recognised when, in refusing to review *American Notes* for the *Edinburgh Review*, he pronounced the book 'at once frivolous and dull'.[31] In his critique of *Les Guides Bleus* in *Mythologies*, Roland Barthes suggested that these guides can answer 'none of the ques-tions which a modern traveller can ask himself [*sic*] while crossing a coun-tryside which is real *and which exists in time*', because the guide books 'account … for nothing of the present, that is, nothing historical, and as a consequence, the monuments themselves become indecipherable, there-fore senseless'.[32] Dickens seems to have suffered, on his travels, from the tourist's incapacity to bring past and present time into a truly historical perspective. Horrified that he was able 'briefly [to] summarise … Genoa, that city of splendid history and most poetic and romantic fame, as "a

city of pink jails"', one reviewer of *Pictures from Italy* pronounced Dickens
'impertinent' and 'ignorant'.[33]

In America, Dickens complained that the 'very flatness and extent' of
the Looking-Glass Prairie 'left nothing to the imagination' (*AN*, II, 5, 201),
and he often seems to have had a sense of imaginative blankness, not only
in shallow and flimsy new America but also – and perhaps more surprisingly – in the deep shadows of the ruins of the Old World. In Rome,
for example, although he was fascinated by the Colosseum and tells us
that 'I could never get through a day without going back to it' (*PI*, 161),
his literary response to this iconic ruin is oddly platitudinous for this
most inventive of writers, and he does no better with the amphitheatre at
Verona, which he describes as like 'the inside of a prodigious hat of plaited
straw', immediately apologising for this 'homely and fantastic' image but
claiming it is all he could come up with at the time (88). Dickens is right
in calling his 'pictures' from Italy, 'faint reflections' (*PI*, 5) and 'shadows in
the water' (5) – there is something curiously second-order, recycled and
premeditated about his experience of the 'great scenes' he set out to see.[34]
One of his problems was that there was no lining up of past, future and
present in the right order: Rome had reminded him more of London than
New York had, and he had found some areas of America primitive in the
extreme: he needed to find another way of thinking about history. His aim
in November 1843 when he had planned his trip to Italy was to 'enlarge
[his] stock of description and observation'.[35] He returned with largely
second-hand stock and what he described as a 'tired memory' (*PI*, 140).

As he started writing *The Chimes* in Italy in October 1844, Dickens wrote
to Forster: 'Never did I stagger so much upon a threshold … I seem as if I
had plucked myself out of my proper soil when I left Devonshire-terrace;
and could take root no more until I return to it.'[36] It is a revealing image of
being unable to enter, to take up residence and inhabit his fiction. Being
far from home seemed to deliver him into a world of impenetrable surfaces and empty show. Displaced and imaginatively exhausted, Dickens
had to build his new story from unfamiliar materials, to use what was
around him: not in London, but in his Italian villa, where, as he wrote to
a friend, 'every inch of the walls is painted in fresco'.[37]

For in Italy Dickens had repeatedly encountered one style that fascinated him. Whenever he encountered the 'voluptuous designs' of the
high baroque style, his writing intensified.[38] The 'intolerable abortions'
sculpted by Bernini that he sees in Rome he describes as 'breezy maniacs;
whose every fold of drapery is blown inside-out; whose smallest vein, or
artery, is as big as an ordinary forefinger; whose hair is like a nest of lively

snakes' (*PI*, 146–7). Of St Peter's, 'after many visits', he concludes, 'It is an immense edifice with no one point for the mind to rest upon; and it tires itself with wandering round and round' (119). In the Palazzo Tè, 'as singular a place as I ever saw' (92), he is astonished and disturbed by the frescoed giants 'staggering under the weight of falling buildings, and being overwhelmed in the ruins; upheaving masses of rock, and burying themselves beneath' (93). The writing is swept up and fascinated as well as repelled by the movement, the hybridity and all the simultaneous knotted and entangled activities of baroque style, its figures 'wandering round and round' (119) and 'flying upward, and downward' (40). Walter Benjamin has described the vitality of the international baroque style as residing in its 'transposition of the originally temporal data into a figurative spatial simultaneity'.[39] Dickens may or may not have been struck by these 'spatial simultaneities', as he was obviously struck by the vertiginous perspectives, but he was certainly fascinated and half-appalled by the baroque as a 'style' of foreignness – a powerful and international representational code which he repeatedly encountered across Europe. And he may have claimed to object to all this breezy billowing, but it blows into his own writing after 1844. These passages surely prefigure not only the description but also the move towards a new style inspired by his exposure to the baroque in 'the host of shifting and extraordinary figures' who appear in the bell tower in *The Chimes*, with their 'restless and untiring motion' and their deliberate collapsing of different categories of time (*Chimes*, 3, 126).

The Chimes: the making of an historical present

Despite his avowed renunciation of fiction writing, Forster describes how Dickens was inspired by the bells of the Duomo in Genoa, 'the clang and clash of all its steeples' during a high wind.[40] *The Chimes; or, A Goblin Story of Some Bells That Rang an Old Year Out and a New Year In* (1844) was written at the Palazzo Peschiere where he and Catherine were sleeping under the vertiginously tumbling figure of a frescoed Phaeton.[41] As has been noticed before, in the story, Dickens transforms the pealing of the bells of Genoa into a wake-up call to the condition of England and a clamorous attack on Malthusian political economy.[42] But there remains more to say about the texture and style of Dickens's writing in this piece.

The Chimes was of far more importance to Dickens than it has ever been to Dickensians. 'All my affections and passions got twined and knotted up in it', he wrote, confessing that when he had finished the story he had had 'what women call "a real good cry"', and then left for Venice 'to recover the composure I had disturbed'.[43] So urgent was his desire to show the story to Carlyle in particular that he took the extraordinary decision to make the arduous journey back from Italy to London in wintertime across the Simplon Pass in order to do just that. He read it out loud at Forster's rooms in Lincoln's Inn Fields on 2 December 1844 to a small group which consisted of Thomas Carlyle, Laman Blanchard, Douglas Jerrold, John Forster, Frederick Dickens, Daniel Maclise, Clarkson Stanfield, William Harness, Alexander Dyce and William J. Fox.[44] Maclise reported that 'there was not a dry eye in the house' and that there were 'floods of tears'.[45] Dickens was ecstatic – even gleeful – about his friends' reaction: 'If you had seen Macready last night – undisguisedly sobbing, and crying on the sofa, as I read – you would have felt (as I did) what a thing it is to have Power.'[46] To the modern reader, this is puzzling as the story seems sentimental and somewhat insubstantial. So in what did the original power of *The Chimes* subsist?

Like the better known *A Christmas Carol*, written the Christmas before, *The Chimes* uses time travel to effect a reawakening to fuller consciousness. Here is the passage in which Trotty sees the vision of the goblins in the bell tower:

> He saw them riding downward, soaring upward, sailing off afar, perching near at hand, all restless and all violently active ... He saw some putting the hands of clocks forward, some putting the hands of clocks backward, some endeavouring to stop the clock entirely. (*Chimes*, 3, 125–6)

The goblins in *The Chimes*, with their 'shifting and extraordinary figures', literally enact Dickens's stylistic struggle to find a position from which to bring the past and present into a meaningful synthesis. While their actions are frenzied and energetic, there is also an attempt to 'stop the clock'. Similarly, despite the vertiginous air travel of *A Christmas Carol*, Scrooge notices that 'the Christmas Holidays appeared to be condensed into the space of time they [he and the Spirit] passed together' (*CC*, III, 61). In both *A Christmas Carol* and *The Chimes*, the spectral removes us into another time and then delivers us back into the uninterrupted succession of serial time as if nothing has happened. Although, of course, something *has* happened: a transformation has taken place in Scrooge, and in Trotty Veck. Anachronism and anatopism are the rhetorical figures of revolution, when time is wrested out of joint and spaces are occupied by disorder in an attempt to re-begin the world differently. Frustrated by the 'neglect, oppression, and misrule' (*PI*, 187) of Italy, which mirrored that in England, and by the shallow, forgetful newness of America, Dickens

strains towards a history that does not look backwards but rather forwards. Rather than writing 'a cry of lamentation for days which have had
their trial and their failure' (*Chimes*, 3, 128), he wants to look forward into
the future through the past and thus to 'awaken' the present. Trotty pleads
with the spirits as they show him his daughter Meg heading towards the
river to drown herself and her baby, 'For any gentle image of the Past, to
rise before her!' (*Chimes*, 4, 155) – he wants the past *before* her, not behind
her, so that she can escape the nightmarish causality that is driving her
inexorably towards infanticide. Dickens here seems to want to counter a
linear, diachronic, serial and causal historical view with a spatialised view
that makes available all times and tenses, a point of view that recalls the
vertiginous perspective of the baroque. Indeed, the illustrations to the first
edition of *The Chimes* by Daniel Maclise and Richard Doyle seem deliberately to invoke the baroque. Dickens attempts to create a fully 'historical'
present in which the past can alter the possibilities of the present. 'I will
live in the Past, the Present, and the Future' cries Scrooge at the end of
A Christmas Carol, 'The Spirits of all Three shall strive within me' (*CC*,
IV, 77).

Hannah Arendt has defined the struggle of making, imagining or creating a present thus:

> Seen from the viewpoint of man, who always lives in the interval between
> past and future, time is not a continuum, a flow of uninterrupted succes-
> sion; it is broken in the middle, at the point where 'he' stands; and 'his'
> standpoint is not the present as we usually understand it but rather a gap
> in time which 'his' constant fighting, 'his' making a stand against past and
> future, keeps in existence. Only because man is inserted into time and only
> to the extent that he stands his ground does the flow of indifferent time
> break up into tenses.[47]

In his Christmas stories of the 1840s, Dickens is not trying to dispense with
tenses altogether so much as to break the grammar of oppression by their
temporary confusion. The grammar of industrial modernity, in Dickens's
imagination, is a heartlessly linear and sequential system on which the
individual can get no purchase, and which allows no pause.[48] These short
volumes, which punctuated his uncharacteristically long break from serial
fiction writing before he returned to monthly parts in *Dombey and Son*,
must be read as experiments in this fundamental refiguring of time and,
correspondingly, the literalisation, or dramatisation, of new possibilities of
metonymy in his work.

When Dickens was actually moving himself – travelling into regions
unknown to him, his analogical imagination rather tended to fail – or at

least it was sorely tested when he reached places he did not know what to do with. But nevertheless it was Dickens's own restless movement in this period of the 1840s that renewed, as he put it, the 'old relations between myself and my readers' (*PI*, 6). Peter Fritzsche has noted that 'The sense of itinerancy in the nineteenth century was strongly related to the historicisation of the world.'[49] Fritzsche argues that increased mobility in the nineteenth century made it easier for people to build models of sequence and seriality and to understand time and history through these paradigms. But Dickens's itinerancy initially disturbed him, confusing sequences and upsetting his sense of history and progress, until he worked out how to transform this confusion into an imaginative tool which he could use to disrupt historic sequence in his own work. Certainly Dickens's experiences of 'abroad' in this period were to lead to a profound change in his sense of historical narrative. The goblins in *The Chimes* are effectively placeholders for the new style towards which Dickens was straining in his itinerant years.

It is in *The Chimes* that we first hear the churning of the sea as a figure of universalised time, a trope which Dickens will of course go on to use to powerful effect in *Dombey and Son* and in *David Copperfield*. Trotty Veck declares at the end of *The Chimes*: 'I know that our inheritance is held in store for us by Time. I know there is a sea of Time to rise one day, before which all who wrong us or oppress us will be swept away like leaves. I see it, on the flow!' (*Chimes*, 4, 157). But when Dickens crossed the sea back to London in July 1845, it was not to fiction but to a newspaper that he returned.

Breaking news and the present tense

In his Editorial Leader in the first issue of the *Daily News* on 21 January 1846, Dickens figured the abolition of the Corn Laws as inevitable – like the unstoppable chime of a clock: 'The wheels have revolved; the hands point to the hour, and the clock must strike' he wrote.[50] The repeal of the Corn Laws is about to become history, but it is not *yet* history; here it is still held in suspense as breaking news, like the whirring of a clock before it chimes. During his brief but exceedingly enthusiastic editorship, Dickens immersed himself in the evergreen present tense of the *daily* news in the *Daily News*. Musing on the restlessness and disorder of the contents of any page of newsprint, Richard Terdiman has suggested that in the newspaper, 'form *denies form*', and Kevis Goodman agrees that 'The [news]paper … testified obliquely to the contradictions and complexities of ongoing events not by mapping them faithfully but by miming them with its own incoherences or dissociations.'[51] The newspaper mimes that aspect of presentness that resists known historical categories because the terms that will describe them are not yet fully formed or known, social relations remain inchoate and in the act of becoming on its pages.

Like *A Christmas Carol* (1843) and *The Chimes* (1844), the daily newspaper also enacts the paradox of unstoppable time being temporarily stopped. The formless onrush of eventful time achieves a form in the newspaper, albeit an ephemeral one, like those of the goblins of *The Chimes*, who exist only for the duration of the clock's striking and then 'in the act of falling died and melted into air' (*Chimes*, 3, 126). Kathleen Tillotson noticed long ago that the importance of the Christmas books to the novels 'lies ... in their treatment of time'.[52] *The Chimes* is harshly divided, like the clock, into four 'quarters', and the bells chime on the hour. The narrative is full of images of remorseless time. The '[new year]'s life was parcelled out in almanacks and pocket-books, the coming of its moons, and stars, and tides, was known beforehand to the moment' (*Chimes*, 2, 108). *A Christmas Carol* is divided into five 'staves' as it is, of course, a carol, and Scrooge is visited with businesslike punctuality by the series of three ghosts. The newspaper is the record of a day, ruled into columns and divided into sections. But, at the same time, the contents of the page of news and the spirits and visions of the stories spill over, exceed and defy these artificial boundaries. What the newspaper and the Christmas stories share is the construction of a represented or mimed present through the production of spatial simultaneity.

This is better appreciated if we look more closely at a page of the *Daily News* for Wednesday, 11 March 1846. The last of Dickens's series of *Travelling Letters* 'Written on the Road' appears alongside news just arrived from France, Poland and Madrid (the *Daily News* ran, by Dickens's insistence, far more international news than any other London paper). There is an article about a poor woman in London who drowned a child she could not feed (as Meg is about to do in *The Chimes*); there are letters from Dublin opposing the new Coercion Bill for Ireland and, under the heading, 'Advances of Famine', details of the kinds of seaweed that starving Irish people are now eating along the coasts in their utter desperation. Next to this, Charles Mackay's poem, 'An Emigrant's Blessing', is spoken in the dramatic present tense by a starving English emigrant on the eve of his departure for a 'new nation'.

Dickens's *Travelling Letter* ends with a present-tense narrative. He is being shown around Bologna churchyard by a cicerone, who points to

a grassy plot in the cemetery: 'there are five of my little children buried there, Signore; just there; a little to the right. Well! Thanks to God!
It's very cheerful. How green it is, how cool it is! It's quite a meadow!'
(*PI*, 70). Jostling on the page in the shared space of the present against
seaweed-eating in Ireland, desperate infanticide in London and a poem
spoken by a poor, starving Englishman forced to emigrate, Dickens's
'little man' in Bologna is reflected in a curiously non-Anglocentric,
non-triumphalist light. The page of news that surrounds the Bolognese
guide generates a powerfully affective field of presence and creates for its
readers on that particular Wednesday morning in March a strong feeling
of involvement in the 'news', through their imagined insertion of themselves into events elsewhere. This creates a sense of historical participation
at one remove, or second-hand.[53] But the jumble of news stories also fragments a linear model of narrative. The reader cannot follow one thread
but must pass quickly and often from one to another, relativising each
one against the next. Significantly, it is reading a newspaper that prompts
Trotty's despair in the first few pages of *The Chimes*: 'I like to know the
news as well as any man ... But ... [i]t frightens me almost' (1, 93).[54]
The perspective of 'history' offered by the newspaper is an uncertain, fragmented, present-tense one. Causalities and consequences are often as yet
unclear. The experience of editing a newspaper at this politically urgent
time considerably deepened Dickens's commitment to finding a new literary style that could accommodate such uncertainty. When the *Saturday
Review* remarked somewhat unkindly in 1858 that 'Mr. Dickens's writings
are the apotheosis of what has been called newspaper English', it was, in a
sense, absolutely right.[55]

Despite his own intense desire for historical participation through
the *Daily News*, Dickens left the editorship after only three weeks on 9
February 1846, passing the role onto John Forster. He 'sent himself abroad'
once more, both physically, across the Channel to France, and artistically, obeying Marley's ghost's injunction to Scrooge that 'the spirit within
him should walk abroad among his fellowmen, and travel far and wide'
(*CC*, 1, 22). Under immense political pressure to find new analogies and
a new grammar capable of impressing the urgency of the present political
crisis upon his readers, Dickens reached for a narrative tense that could
reconnect the past to the present in ways that radically undermine the
temporal distances and perspectives of conventional 'past-historic' narrative. In *Dombey and Son*, a novel with an unusually contemporary setting,
Dickens attempts a new generalisation and mobility of meaning. The historic present tense displays past and present in a single moment while also

suggesting an irreducible repetition that underpins, and to some extent undermines, all human agency. In *Dombey and Son*, the historic present is linked to the anxious metonymic qualities of that novel: 'A few days have elapsed, and a stately ship is out at sea, spreading its white wings to the favouring wind' (*DS*, 57, 772). Walter and Florence's honeymoon journey floats down the metaphoric stream already established by a novel in which ships, streams, rivers and waves stand in for the deeper structuring concepts of the 'story': risk, time and death.[56] The novel first switches into the present tense in Chapter 18, when Paul Dombey has just died and the household is in suspension so that 'it seems like Sunday' (*DS*, 18, 238) in a 'prolonged mortuary present';[57] it returns briefly in the railway train 'roaring, rattling, tearing on', another repeated motif in this text of the unstoppability of time, the train is like 'the remorseless monster, Death!' (20, 276), and more substantially in Chapter 31 on the day of Dombey's marriage to Edith, as the 'steeple-clock [is] … emerging from beneath another of the countless ripples in the tide of time that regularly roll and break on the eternal shore' (420). The household await the happy couple's return in the present tense at the start of Chapter 35, and in Chapter 41, Florence returns to Brighton where 'the requiem of little Dombey on the waters' (554) is played in the present tense while 'all goes on, as it was wont' (563). In Chapter 51, the humiliated Dombey, after Edith's elopement, imagines the opinion of the 'World' in a nightmarish and continuous present: 'it is in his house, outside it, audible in footsteps on the pavement, visible in print upon the table, steaming to and fro on railroads and in ships; restless and busy everywhere' (682). In Chapter 57, when Walter and Florence put out to sea on their honeymoon, the waves continue 'their ceaseless murmuring, of love – of love, eternal and illimitable, not bounded by the confines of this world, or by the end of time, but ranging still, beyond the sea, beyond the sky, to the invisible country far away!' (773). Chapter 59, 'Retribution', starts in the present with the ruin of Dombey's firm and the sale of his possessions. And the final chapter returns to the present where, on a beach, a 'white-haired gentleman walks with the little boy' (62, 833).

As Steven Connor says of the resolution of the metonymic and metaphorical narrative and counter-narrative at the end of *Dombey and Son*: 'The growth in structural awareness marks the move into a metaphorical/paradigmatic dimension, replacing the purely serial, metonymic relationship of events coming one after another. The story which has been experienced temporally can now be experienced spatially, with all its elements imaginatively present at once.'[58] The experiments dramatised in *A Christmas Carol* and *The Chimes* are now projected into the patterning of the narrative. Instead of ghosts and goblins, Dickens displays a renovated rhetorical apparatus of narrative tense alternation, metaphors and metonymic chains of associative imagery. Instead of a fairy-goblin, he uses the present tense in *Dombey and Son* to stop time and deliver his readers to a place 'not bounded by the confines of this world, or by the end of time' (*DS*, 57, 773).

The present-tense chapters in *Dombey and Son* mark the crises of the action. They host a marriage, a funeral, a breakdown and another marriage, and yet their focus tends to be on a chorus of peripheral characters. The anticipatory activities of Mrs Miff the pew-opener in Chapter 31, or of Dombey's cook and the servants in Chapter 35, for example, seem deliberately to move the reader away from the main characters. By writing in the present tense and by opening up a contiguous action contemporary to the main narrative, Dickens finds a way to suggest the difficulty of ascribing value to events in the here and now, before they have been committed to the organising narrative of history. Indeed, he even suggests, through his careful use of language and tense forms in these chapters, his scepticism about the possibility of *ever* being able to incorporate the events and periods of individual human lives into a meaningful perspective of 'history'. This seems symptomatic of the pervasive political confusion of the 1840s, as revolutions and counter-revolutions unreeled with a domino effect across Europe. Bewilderingly, the 'monstrous system' of papal government in Italy, for example, could be replaced by the Roman Republic, which in turn was attacked and brought down by the 'stupendous baseness' of the very nation that, as Dickens saw it, had started the revolutionary process in the first place: France.[59]

At the opening of Chapter 31 of *Dombey and Son*, the 'dawn moans and weeps for its short reign' (420) and night 'sits upon the coffins' (421): while Dickens directs us to the single day which is Dombey's wedding day, his imagery also suggests the longer timescales of religion and politics. The historic present is a tense that returns foreboding and suspense to completed events, unravelling them and leaving them once again unfinished. The fearfulness and foreboding that permeates *Dombey and Son*, particularly in these present-tense chapters, seems to extend well beyond the confines of this largely domestic story into a grander, global perspective. It is through this that Dickens finds the way to launch what is an urgent historiographical enquiry into a pan-European state of unfinishedness. The uneven and scattered upheavals and revolutions of the 1840s represented for Dickens not completed events but the forebodings and risks of something as yet incomplete and inchoate. A decade later, in the late

1850s, he continues to feel a dangerous incompletion to these events, as is clear from *A Tale of Two Cities*.[60]

Narratologists argue that 'extended passages of the historic present tense in nineteenth-century literature typically experiment with presentification and descriptive close-ups. They may be considered as forerunners of later more extensive types of tense alternation.'[61] Linguists propose that the historic present is generally an 'internal evaluation device', which functions in alternation with other tenses to create breaks and emphases *within* the narrative.[62] While these observations are undoubtedly broadly correct, when applied to Dickens's narrative experiments in the 1840s they create a curiously ahistoric reading of his style. Rather than a 'forerunner' of something later and more 'extensive' in – presumably – the twentieth century, Dickens's new style is already a direct and complete response to the abjection and confusion of the 1840s. Dickens creates the perspective and distance he could not establish in 1841 in *Barnaby Rudge*, partly as a result of his experience of travel in the intervening years because those restless journeys had challenged his notions of time and history.

A Tale of Two Cities: history just about to happen

Twelve years later, in his only other 'historical novel', *A Tale of Two Cities* (1859), Dickens returned to his preoccupations of the 1840s with 'abroad' and with revolution. But *A Tale of Two Cities* never becomes a historical novel in the 'full immersion' sense of a Scott novel. It rather further develops the metonymic patterning of *Dombey and Son* to create a novel that rests on analogical affinities between here and there and now and then.

Mark Philp has commented of *A Tale of Two Cities* that Dickens's 'portrayal of France is not innocent of his portrayal of England, and neither is untouched by the implicit counterfactual of American liberty'.[63] Certainly, by 1859 Dickens had crossed 'salt water' (*TTC*, 1, 4, 31) many times, and, unlike the doggedly patriotic Miss Pross, he can no longer imagine Britain as an island isolated from the rest of the world. But even Philp understates the way in which *A Tale of Two Cities* is structured around the 'travelling backwards and forwards betwixt London and Paris' (1, 4, 20) rather than around a binary division between the 'two cities'. At the beginning of the novel, on the brink of one of its many cross-Channel journeys, Mr Lorry waits in Dover for a sailing packet to Calais, noticing that the 'air … [was] at intervals clear enough to allow the French coast to be seen' (1, 4, 21). The distance between Paris and London in this novel is slight, and the true centre of the narrative is the Channel. Dickens reinforces this proximity and connection by opening the novel with the international Mail Coach (*la malle-poste*) 'mash[ing ... its] way through the thick mud' (1, 2, 5) to keep to its timetabled schedule to meet the mailboat.

The Mail Coach connects the two countries by letter, and they are further connected by diasporic families: Lucy Manette is an Anglo-French hybrid who speaks English 'a little foreign in its accent' (1, 4, 23); Charles Darnay is a French 'emigrant' to England; and Miss Pross's brother Solomon is discovered under the name Barsad in Paris. Business and fiscal connections are strong too: Tellson's bank has branches both in London and in 'the Saint Germain Quarter of Paris' (III, 2, 316). Indeed, all of the main characters in the novel cross the salt water at least once, and Dickens's chapters move restlessly between the two cities. Dickens's insistence on the geographical proximity of the two countries is metonymically linked to his insistence on the proximity of the present to the past. If France is so close, so perhaps is its Revolution. The very first paragraph of the book enforces this temporal analogy, telling us that, 'in short, the period was so far *like* the present period' (1, 1, 1, emphasis added). From the outset in this 'historical novel', neither France nor its revolutionary energy are very far away at all.

Ian Duncan has suggested that 'History does not appear as a category of dynamic process in [Dickens's] narratives', because for Dickens history 'signifies not even lives passing, but a dark, blind, dead past'.[64] Certainly, Dickens's disdain for any kind of nostalgia for the 'olden days' is blatant in some of the deleted passages on 'Young England' he originally wrote in *The Chimes*, in his poem 'The Fine Old English Gentleman. New Version' that he published in the *Examiner* in 1841, in his *A Child's History of England* that he was writing in the early 1840s, and in the joke titles of his set of mock books at Gad's Hill, 'The Wisdom of Our Ancestors'.[65] But this is a political disdain for a Tory version of 'History' not an irreverence for the power of the past itself, of which he was intensely, almost superstitiously, aware.

As was also true for Carlyle, thinking 'historically' for Dickens never meant merely thinking about the past. Dickens's almost millenarian hope for the imminent arrival of a new time in the 1840s has often been read simply as his debt to Carlyle's prophetic style. But, as Gareth Stedman Jones has pointed out, even in the grim 1840s, Dickens had retained far more political faith than the gloomy Carlyle, who consistently 'degraded' the possibilities of political agency and change.[66] Carlyle's French Revolution, as seen from his vantage point in 1834 to 1836, was a unique and apocalyptic eruption. Carlyle himself explains in Book II of Part III of his gigantic *French Revolution* why he abjures the past tense in favour of the present:

> For indeed, it is a most lying thing, that same Past Tense always: so beautiful, so sad … For observe, always one most important element is surreptitiously (we not noticing it) withdrawn from the Past Time: the haggard element of Fear! Not *there* does Fear dwell, nor Uncertainty, nor Anxiety; but it dwells *here*; haunting us, tracking us; running like an accursed ground-discord through all the music-tones of our Existence; – making the Tense a mere Present one![67]

Carlyle's frequent recourse to the present tense throughout his *French Revolution* represents the attempt of an historian to restore chaos, uncertainty, fear and complexity to completed past events, even if, as Malcolm Hardman has shown, *The French Revolution* is in fact 'nearly a third' interpretation in the form of commentary and reflection by the narrator.[68] Carlyle continues to privilege the interpretative perspective of the past over the confusion of the 'mere Present', using the present tense as a device to reopen the affect and multivalency of the past whilst simultaneously retaining the control of the 'historian' looking back over the narrative. The energy generated by the collision of these two opposing narrative positions is what powers Carlyle's remarkable prose: his writing sets out deliberately to enact precisely the contradiction between event and interpretation that produces 'History'.

Vernon Lee, astonished and impressed by Carlyle's achievement of the 'lyric of prophecy' through his use of the historic present tense, claimed that, by contrast, in Dickens it becomes only 'a vulgar dodge for realization'.[69] This seems a misreading or misunderstanding of Dickens's style. It is true that Dickens's use of the present tense is different from Carlyle's in its motivation. Dickens does not represent the French Revolution as an epochal event that rents the fabric of time and creates a shockingly new sense of 'history', so much as part of a causal series of linked events. The obstinately insistent political determinism of *A Tale of Two Cities* suggests that Dickens in 1859 now saw the events of 1848 as part of a continuum of the long revolutionary process which was still unspooling across Europe after its dramatic initiation in the French Revolution. Now that there was a script, everyone knew how to stage a revolution. If the circumstances of neglect, poverty and iniquity were in place, as Dickens believed they were in Britain in the mid 1850s, then the people would know what to do: 'Sow the same seed of rapacious license and oppression over again, and it will surely yield the same fruit according to its kind' (*TTC*, III, 15, 459), he warns in the final chapter of his 'historical' novel. Dickens's historiography is less fully Hegelian than Carlyle's in that he retains a stubborn belief in individual agency and is unwilling to abandon all his political faith to the blind and inevitable processes of Hegel's philosophy of world history.[70]

A Tale of Two Cities only twice moves into extended present-tense passages: at the point of Darnay's near arrest when being smuggled out of revolutionary France (III, 13) and at the climactic execution scene (III, 15) when Sidney Carton is the twenty-third prisoner to be guillotined on one December day in Revolutionary Paris: 'The murmuring of many voices, the upturning of many faces, the pressing on of many footsteps in the outskirts of the crowd, so that it swells forward in a mass, like one great heave of water, all flashes away. Twenty-Three' (III, 15, 464). Carton is described as he stands on the guillotine in the Place de la Révolution awaiting his execution as looking 'sublime and prophetic' (III, 15, 464). But, despite the repetition of 'I see' in the final three paragraphs of the novel, what we are given at the end of *A Tale of Two Cities* is not a prophecy. Dickens takes us not into the present tense of prophecy but into the conditional perfect, 'if he had given any utterance to his [thoughts], and they were prophetic, they would have been these' (III, 15, 464). What follows is therefore not a prophecy but an imagination of what a prophecy might have been from the secure position of hindsight. Dickens knew Second Empire Paris well, and he had resided there between October 1855 and May 1856. He often walked in the Place de la Concorde, formerly the Place de la Révolution, and beheld it, 'fair to look upon, with not a trace of this day's [the Revolution's] disfigurement' (III, 15, 465). This is the scene that Lucy Manette's grandson is shown at the end of the novel. So the novel ends not in the future of prophecy but in the present in Dickens's own lifetime. Indeed, Lucy Manette's grandson is probably born around the same time as Charles Dickens himself, in the second decade of the nineteenth century, so that Dickens himself stands in the place of the grandchild of the Revolution. It was both the distance and the proximity of the bloody days of France's Terror that fascinated Dickens as he strolled in the comfortable and elegant boulevards of Paris in the mid 1850s, just as the Haussmannisation of the city was getting under way. The guillotine was only two generations behind him; the February revolution of 1848 and the June Days were less than a decade away. *A Tale of Two Cities* is never a fully 'historical' novel because Dickens's narrative never fully inhabits the past: instead, it is told self-consciously and deliberately from the perspective of the uncertain present of 1859.

Conclusion

Vernon Lee was right that Dickens does not use the present tense of prophecy, but she does not see that this is because he has no desire to fore-see an inevitable future. Instead, Dickens uses the present tense as a tense of possibility: a tense that deliberately delivers us into the parblind, inchoate and risky contemporary moment, and no further. It is important to Dickens that the future is impossible of vision, as Paul Saint-Amour says, in order 'to reawaken us to the ramifications of our *timeliness* – of our *not* being too late'.[71]

The historic present tense, for Dickens, marks the gravity of the present moment – here, now – and the serious consequentiality of our seemingly ephemeral actions, which are always just about to acquire the solidity of history. His use of the historic present tense, his metonymic repetitions and his refusal of prophecy, are there to remind us that we are all always participating in what could be called 'history' but which Dickens suggests might be better understood as the 'historical present'. For Dickens, the erstwhile newspaper editor and political commentator, history is not what has already happened, or what will inevitably happen, but the catastrophe which might be just about to happen.[72] The political disaffection and difficulty of imagining a future in the 1840s produced a peculiarly modern form of presentism, a 'regime of historicity', in François Hartog's terms, in which 'light is produced by the present itself, and by it alone'.[73] Dickens's furious attempts to reunite the past with the orphaned present were further fuelled by his struggle to understand the relationship of the old to the new on his travels in this period.

Dickens reminds us that he 'began [*Dombey and Son*] … by the lake of Geneva, and went on with it for some months in France'.[74] The trajectory of Dickens's style in the 1840s, like his own travels across oceans and seas, is marked by a slow journey out – as the landlocked eighteenth-century London of *Barnaby Rudge* gives way to the expansive world historical present of *Dombey and Son*, a novel that delivers us, on its final page, into 'Autumn days [on] the sea-beach' and back into the 'shining', momentous and crucially unfinished present (*DS*, 62, 833).

NOTES

1 The chapters in the present tense are 31, 41, 51, 57 and 62.
2 Unsigned review, '*David Copperfield and Pendennis*', *Prospective Review*, 7 (July 1851): 157–91; reprinted in *CH*, 264–6, at 265.

3 *Sharpe's London Magazine*, 6 (March 1848): 200–3, at 201.

4 *Examiner*, 28 October 1848, 692–3, at 692.

5 *Examiner*, 28 October 1848, 692.

6 Otto Jespersen, *The Philosophy of Grammar* (London: Allen & Unwin, 1924), 265.

7 The historic present is often confused in English with the dramatic present, and the two terms are often used synonymously. Raymond Williams makes a helpful distinction between the two. The dramatic present is used when things are still happening, for example, 'Whence is that knocking / How is't with me, when every noise appals me?' (*Macbeth*). The historic present narrates completed events in the present. Raymond Williams, *Writing in Society* (London: Verso 1983), 54. Simon John De Vries introduces a third type of present, the 'gnomic present', which 'is the present to which wisdom sayings pertain, hence it is repeated and repeatable as long as the sayings are true. The cultic present is very similar: it is the ongoing present to which every sort of ritual and cult legislation pertains. These two kinds of present are, together, ideologically opposite to the historical present. The essential difference is that the historical present is always unique – an experience unto itself – whereas the gnomic and cultic present is anything but unique. If the historical present is disjunctive, even irruptive, the gnomic/cultic present is repetitive, cyclical, and institutional.' Simon John De Vries, *Yesterday, Today, and Tomorrow: Time and History in the Old Testament* (Grand Rapid, MI: Wm. B. Eerdmans Publishing, 1975), 45.

8 I agree with Elizabeth Deeds Ermarth that all Victorian novels are, in fact, 'historical' novels, because 'The historical novel … has everything to do with a particular construction of time, and nothing to do with antiquarian subject matter.' Elizabeth Deeds Ermarth, *The English Novel in History 1840–1895* (London: Routledge, 1997), 82. If all Victorian novels are 'historical', there is, of course, much to say about Dickens's use of the historical present in *David Copperfield* (1849–50) and in *Bleak House* (1852–3), but *A Tale of Two Cities* is so self-consciously concerned with the French Revolution and the making of 'history' that I have singled it out for discussion here.

9 See R. J. W. Evans and Hartmut Pogge von Strandmann (eds.), *The Revolutions in Europe, 1848–1849: From Reform to Reaction* (Oxford University Press, 2000); Axel Korner, *1848, A European Revolution? International Ideas and National Memories of 1848* (Basingstoke: Palgrave Macmillan, 2000), and Jonathan Sperber, *The European Revolutions, 1848–1851*, 2nd edn (Cambridge University Press, 2005).

10 Letter from Charles Dickens to John Forster, 29 February 1848, *Letters*, v, 256–7, at 256. [MY FRIEND, I find I love the Republic so much, that I must renounce my language and write only in the language of the French Republic – the language of Gods and Angels – the language, [in] a word, of the French!]

11 Hartmut Pogge von Strandmann, '1848–1849: A European Revolution?', in R. J. W. Evans and Hartmut Pogge von Strandmann (eds.), *The Revolutions in*

Europe, 1848–1849: From Reform to Reaction (Oxford University Press, 2000), 1–8, at 5.

12 François Furet, *Revolutionary France, 1770–1880* (Oxford: Blackwell, 1992), 537.

13 'Dombey and Son', *Home and Foreign Review*, I (4) (22 January 1848): 64–6, at 65.

14 Letter from Thomas Carlyle to J. S. Mill, 22 July 1836. Available online at *The Carlyle Letters Online*, http://carlyleletters.dukejournals.org (accessed 31 March 2012); *The Collected Letters of Thomas and Jane Welsh Carlyle*, 40 vols. to date, ed. C. R. Sanders (Durham, NC: Duke University Press, 1970–), vol. IX, ed. C. R. Sanders and K. J. Fielding (1981), 14–16.

15 Only later did Dickens confess that he had carried a bottle and a message secretly to a political prisoner in Italy. 'The Italian Prisoner' first appeared in *All the Year Round* (13 October 1860); reprinted in *Journalism*, IV, 190–9, at 198.

16 Steven Connor, 'Space, Place and the Body of Riot in *Barnaby Rudge*', in Steven Connor (ed.), *Charles Dickens* (London and New York: Longman 1996), 211–29, at 228.

17 Letter from Charles Dickens to John Landseer, 5 November 1841, *Letters*, II, 417–18, at 418.

18 Michael Wood, 'Afterword', in Colin Jones, Josephine McDonagh and Jon Mee (eds.), *Charles Dickens*, A Tale of Two Cities *and the French Revolution* (Basingstoke: Palgrave, 2009), 188–94, at 189.

19 See note 7.

20 See Thomas Jackson Rice, 'The End of Dickens's Apprenticeship: Variable Focus in *Barnaby Rudge*', *Nineteenth-Century Fiction*, 30 (2) (September 1975): 172–84.

21 Roland Barthes, *Le Degré zero de l'écriture* (Paris: Éditions du Seuil, 1953), 47; Monika Fludernik, *The Fictions of Language and the Languages of Fiction: The Linguistic Representation of Speech and Consciousness* (London: Routledge, 1993), 201.

22 Madeleine House, Graham Storey and Kathleen Tillotson, 'Preface', *Letters*, III, vii–xix, at xii.

23 House et al., 'Preface', xvi, n. 7.

24 Letter from Charles Dickens to Daniel Maclise, [3] January 1842, *Letters*, III, 8–9, at 9.

25 Dickens stayed in Italy from 2 July 1844 to 3 July 1845.

26 Letter from Charles Dickens to William Macready, 1 April 1842, in *Letters*, III, 173–6, at 176; and *AN*, I, 8, 133.

27 Miles Taylor claims that political radicalism at this time 'was placed at the confluence of Benthamism, socialism, Mazzinian nationalism, anti-clericalism and Whiggery' within an essentially pre-democratic system without party alliances. Miles Taylor, *The Decline of British Radicalism, 1847–1860* (Oxford: Clarendon Press, 1995), 13.

28 Letter from Charles Dickens to William Macready, 12 April 1842, *Letters*, III, 173–6, at 176.

29 'Dickens's *American Notes for General Circulation*', *Blackwood's Edinburgh Magazine*, 52 (326) (December 1842): 783–801, at 794.

30 Stephen Bann, 'Visuality Codes the Text: Charles Dickens's *Pictures from Italy*', in J. B. Bullen (ed.), *Writing and Victorianism* (London: Longman, 1997), 202–12. John Plunkett, 'Optical Recreations and Victorian Literature', in David Seed (ed.), *Literature and the Visual Medium* (Suffolk: Boydell & Brewer, 2005), 1–28. Kate Flint, 'Introduction' to Charles Dickens, *Pictures from Italy* (London: Penguin, 1998), vii–xxx.

31 Quoted in *Letters*, III, 289, n. 2.

32 Roland Barthes, 'The *Blue Guide*', in *Mythologies*, trans. Annette Lavers (New York: Hill & Wang, 1981), 74–7, at 75–6. James Buzard discusses E. M. Forster's attempt to re-synthesise history and the present through the genre of the guidebook in James Buzard, *The Beaten Track: European Tourism, Literature, and the Ways to Culture, 1800–1918* (Oxford University Press, 1993), 330–1.

33 'Two English Novelists: Dickens and Thackeray', *Dublin Review*, 17 (32) (April 1871): 315–50, at 339.

34 Letter from Charles Dickens to John Forster, 2 November 1843, *Letters*, III, 591.

35 Letter from Charles Dickens to John Forster, 1 November 1843, *Letters*, III, 587.

36 Letter from Charles Dickens to John Forster, ?6 October 1844, *Letters*, IV, 197–9, at 199.

37 Letter to Count D'Orsay, 7 August 1844, *Letters*, IV, 166–71, at 167. This is a description of the Dickenses' first summer villa (Villa di Bagnerello). In the autumn they repaired to the more splendid Peschiere, whose frescoes were described by Dickens in a letter to John Forster on ?30 September 1844, *Letters*, IV, 195–7, at 195.

38 Here I part ways with Stephen Bann, who sees Dickens as falling neatly into line with the 'good replicas' of northern Europe and 'bad replicas' of the Catholic south. Bann, 'Visuality Codes the Text', 206–7.

39 Walter Benjamin, *The Origin of the German Tragic Drama*, trans. John Osborne (London: Verso, 2003), 81.

40 *Life*, I, 384.

41 See Philip V. Allingham, 'Charles Dickens, the Villa Pallavicino della Peschiere in Genoa, and its Frescoes (1556)', available online at www.victorianweb.org/authors/dickens/gallery/peschiere2.html (accessed 31 March 2012).

42 For a discussion of the anti-Malthusian charge of Dickens's story, see Josephine McDonagh, *Child Murder and British Culture, 1720–1900* (Cambridge University Press, 2003), 116–22. For further political contexts to *The Chimes*, see Michael Shelden, 'Dickens, "The Chimes" and the Anti-Corn Law League', *Victorian Studies*, 25 (3) (spring 1982): 329–53; and Michael Slater, 'Carlyle and

Jerrold into Dickens: A Study of *The Chimes*', *Nineteenth-Century Fiction*, 24 (4) (March 1970): 506–26.

43 Letter from Charles Dickens to Countess of Blessington, 20 November 1844, *Letters*, IV, 224–8, at 224 and 224–5. Letter from Charles Dickens to John Forster, 3 and [4] November 1844, *Letters*, IV, 210–11, at 210.

44 Dickens read *The Chimes* to Macready on 1 December 1844 in London.

45 Letter from Daniel Maclise to Catherine Dickens, 8 December 1844, quoted in K. J. Fielding, 'Two Sketches by Maclise', *Dickens Studies*, 2 (1966): 7–17, at 13. Quoted in *Letters*, IV, 235 n. There was a second reading on 5 December after dinner at Forster's.

46 Letter from Charles Dickens to Catherine Dickens, 2 December 1844, *Letters*, IV, 234–5, at 234–5. Dickens read *The Chimes* to Macready in Paris on his way back to London from Italy.

47 Hannah Arendt, *Between Past and Future: Eight Exercises in Political Thought* (1954) (New York: The Viking Press, 1968), 11.

48 Dickens was to become more interested in the potential of industrial modernity, which he portrays very differently, for example, in his 1854 novel, *Hard Times*. Tamara Ketabgian, *The Lives of Machines: The Industrial Imaginary in Victorian Literature and Culture* (Ann Arbor, MI: University of Michigan Press, 2011) makes a good case for a more fully imagined industrialism in this novel.

49 Peter Fritzsche, *Stranded in the Present: Modern Time and the Melancholy of History* (Cambridge, MA: Harvard University Press, 2004), 181.

50 Leader, *Daily News* (21 January 1846).

51 Richard Terdiman, *Discourse/Counter Discourse: The Theory and Practice of Symbolic Resistance in Nineteenth-Century France* (Ithaca, NY: Cornell University Press, 1985), 122. Kevis Goodman, *Georgic Modernity and British Romanticism: Poetry and the Mediation of History* (Cambridge University Press, 2004), 77.

52 Kathleen Tillotson, 'The Middle Years: From the Carol to Copperfield', in *Dickens Memorial Lectures 1970*, Supplement to *The Dickensian*, 65 (September 1970): 7–19, at 14.

53 Kevis Goodman has written about 'the sense of the historical present that is fostered by a nascent news culture' and the consciousness of a 'virtual historicity' engendered by it. See Kevis Goodman, 'The Loophole in the Retreat: The Culture of News and the Early Life of Romantic Self-Consciousness', *The South Atlantic Quarterly*, 102 (1) (winter 2003): 25–52, at 44 and 31.

54 When Trotty reads a story of infanticide in his newspaper, 'with an earnest and sad attention', Dickens's first readers would have recognised the case of Mary Furley which had been widely reported in the press in April 1844. Furley threw herself and her baby in the Thames after being refused poor relief. She was rescued, but her baby drowned, and Dickens joined in the protest to commute her death sentence to transportation. See Charles Dickens, *The Christmas Books* (London: Penguin English Library, 1971), ed. Michael Slater, vol. 1, 264.

55 *Saturday Review of Politics, Literature, Science and Art*, 5 (132) (8 May 1858): 474–5, at 475.

56 See Steven Connor, *Charles Dickens* (Oxford: Blackwell, 1985), 44–55; Stephen Marcus, *From Pickwick to Dombey* (London: Chatto & Windus, 1965); and Janice Carlisle, '*Dombey and Son*: The Reader and the Present Tense', *The Journal of Narrative Technique*, 1 (3) (September 1971): 146–58.

57 The phrase is Garrett Stewart's. Garrett Stewart, 'Dickens, Eisenstein, Film', in John Glavin (ed.), *Dickens on Screen* (Cambridge University Press, 2003), 122–44, at 132.

58 Connor, 'Metaphor and Metonymy in *Dombey and Son*', 54.

59 Charles Dickens, 'Appeal for Funds for the Italian Refugees', *Examiner* (8 September 1849).

60 This discussion of *Dombey and Son* was much improved by Daniel Tyler's ideas and suggestions, for which I am very grateful.

61 Monika Fludernik, *Towards a Natural Narratology* (London: Routledge, 1996), 196.

62 Michael Toolan, *Narrative: A Critical Linguistic Introduction* (London: Routledge, 1988), 162.

63 Mark Philp, 'The New Philosophy: The Substance and the Shadow in *A Tale of Two Cities*', in Colin Jones, Josephine McDonagh and Jon Mee (eds.), *Charles Dickens, A Tale of Two Cities and the French Revolution*, 24–40, at 26. Philp maintains that the politics of Dickens's French Revolution are more Painite than Carlylean.

64 Ian Duncan, *Modern Romance and Transformations of the Novel* (Cambridge University Press, 1992), 16.

65 'The Fine Old English Gentleman. New Version', *Examiner* (7 August 1841). For a discussion of the deleted passages of *The Chimes*, see Michael Shelden, 'Dickens, "The Chimes" and the Anti-Corn Law League', *Victorian Studies*, 25 (3) (spring 1982): 329–53. Dickens's series of dummy books comprised: vol. I: Ignorance, vol. II: Superstition, vol. III: The Block, vol. IV: The Stake, vol. V: The Rack, and vol. VI: Dirt. Paul Schlicke discusses the dummy books in *Dickens and Popular Entertainment* (London: Routledge 1988), 195–6. For a discussion of the *Child's History* and the dummy books, see Michael Slater, 'Carlyle and Jerrold into Dickens: A Study of *The Chimes*', *Nineteenth-Century Fiction*, 24 (4) (March 1970): 506–52. See also, Anonymous, 'Dummy Books at Gad's Hill Place', *The Dickensian*, 54 (1958): 46–7.

66 Gareth Stedman Jones, 'The Redemptive Powers of Violence? Carlyle, Marx and Dickens', in Colin Jones, Josephine McDonagh and Jon Mee (eds.), *Charles Dickens, A Tale of Two Cities and the French Revolution* (Basingstoke: Palgrave, 2009), 41–63, at 48.

67 Thomas Carlyle, *The French Revolution: A History*, ed. K. J. Fielding and David Sorensen (Oxford University Press, 1989), 204.

68 Malcolm Hardman, *Six Victorian Thinkers* (Manchester University Press, 1991), 30.

69 Vernon Lee, *The Handling of Words and Other Studies in Literary Psychology* (London: John Lane, 1927), 186.

70 As Michael Wood has noticed, this leads to the 'paradox' at the heart of *A Tale of Two Cities*, which is that 'if we fail to prevent it, the inevitable will indeed have happened'. Michael Wood, 'Afterword', in Colin Jones, Josephine McDonagh and Jon Mee (eds.), *Charles Dickens, A Tale of Two Cities and the French Revolution* (Basingstoke: Palgrave, 2009), 188–94, at 193.

71 Paul K. Saint-Amour, '"Christmas Yet to Come": Hospitality, Futurity, the *Carol*, and "The Dead"', *Representations*, 98 (1) (spring 2007): 93–117, at 100.

72 On Carlyle's use of the present tense, see Barton Friedman, *Fabricating History: English Writers on the French Revolution* (Princeton University Press, 1988), 114; and Elliot L. Gilbert's essay, 'A Wondrous Contiguity: Anachronism in *Carlyle's Prophecy* and Art', *PMLA*, 87 (1972), 432–42.

73 François Hartog, *Régimes d'historicité: présentisme et expériences du temps* (Paris: Seuil, 2003). I argue that the political disaffection of the 1840s produced a similar, although not identical, form of presentism. The translations from Hartog are Patrick Wright's from his Preface to *On Living in an Old Country* (Oxford University Press, 2009), xviii.

74 Charles Dickens, 'Preface to the Cheap Edition of *Dombey and Son* (1858)', *DS*, 834.

CHAPTER SIX

'Gigantic domesticity': the exaggeration of Charles Dickens

Freya Johnston

Exaggeration, according to G. K. Chesterton in *Charles Dickens* (1906), 'is almost the definition of art'. Or perhaps it is the hallmark of literary criticism – at least, criticism of Chesterton's rhapsodic variety – since thirteen pages later exaggeration has become, unequivocally, 'the definition of art'. For Chesterton, it was also 'The essence of the Dickens genius'.[1]

Naturally enough, we might understand countless things by that genius for exaggeration. Dickens's notorious 'leafiness'; his 'tendency to words and images, for their own sake'; his vivid, fecund, prodigal style (recently dubbed 'hyperrealism');[2] his violent, theatrical caricatures, distended plots and grotesque inflations: all of these, and more, pose flagrant challenges to reality and its advocates. The novelist's early champions praised an apparently very different quality when they singled out his alertness to 'the truth of life as it is';[3] Thomas Lister commended his watchful 'management of details'.[4] Other readers complained of a needless profusion of those same details – said to reveal, at best, Dickens's commitment to real life, at worst a vulgar inability to discriminate between what was important and what wasn't. Charles Buller felt that Dickens's 'accumulation of little details of misery and discomfort' in *Oliver Twist* (1837–8) 'positively pains, and at last harasses the reader ... The very accuracy of all these minute details of human wretchedness makes their effect more distressing.'[5] Still, this is a long way from associating Dickens with what *A Tale of Two Cities* (1859) calls 'the superlative degree of comparison only' (I, I, I). Buller may have had in mind such passages as that describing the choleric Bermondsey rookery of Jacob's Island:

> Crazy wooden galleries common to the backs of half a dozen houses, with holes from which to look upon the slime beneath; windows, broken and patched: with poles thrust out, on which to dry the linen that is never there; rooms so small, so filthy, so confined, that the air would seem too tainted even for the dirt and squalor which they shelter; wooden chambers thrusting themselves out above the mud, and threatening to fall into it – as

some have done; dirt-besmeared walls and decaying foundations; every repulsive lineament of poverty, every loathsome indication of filth, rot, and garbage; all these ornament the banks of Folly Ditch.

In Jacob's Island, the warehouses are roofless and empty; the walls are crumbling down; the windows are windows no more; the doors are falling into the streets; the chimneys are blackened, but they yield no smoke. Thirty or forty years ago, before losses and chancery suits came upon it, it was a thriving place; but now it is a desolate island indeed. The houses have no owners; they are broken open, and entered upon by those who have the courage; and there they live, and there they die. They must have powerful motives for a secret residence, or be reduced to a destitute condition indeed, who seek a refuge in Jacob's Island. (*OT*, 50, 339)

A palpable restraint governs Dickens's inventorial reportage, a bating of his own dynamic powers. The voice sometimes rises to become indignant and judgemental, even outraged ('repulsive', 'loathsome'), but he has not unleashed his battery of personifications or other animating devices on this scene. The chimes and repetitions, such as they are ('holes ... poles'; 'thrust ... thrusting'; 'fall ... falling'; 'so ... so ... so'; 'every ... every'; 'windows ... windows'; 'There they live and there they die'; 'indeed ... indeed'), don't obtrude themselves, and overall the passage lacks the brazen anaphora that Dickens favours elsewhere (take, for instance, the 'staring white houses, staring white walls, staring white streets, staring tracts of arid road, staring hills from which verdure was burnt away' in *Little Dorrit* [1855–7], 1, 1). In fact, the description of Jacob's Island, for all that it alights on physical realities, lacks detail – or rather, it details what is lacking; the writing is full of holes, losses and absences. There is no linen where you might expect it; there are no roofs, no goods in the warehouses; there is no smoke from the chimneys. Rooms are said to shelter 'dirt and squalor' rather than human tenants. Activities are described in the infinitive rather than grammatically realised by living agents, creating another vacancy: 'holes from which *to look upon* the slime beneath ... poles thrust out, on which *to dry* the linen that is never there' (this deprivation of agency is a favourite technique: compare the absence of main verbs in the opening paragraph of *Bleak House* [1852–3]). Jacob's Island is haunted by inhabitants who don't seem fully present or alive – a condition that besets all fictional characters, only here we are in territory that also exists, or subsists, outside the world of the novel. For that reason, Dickens's synecdoche harbours a threat and an urgent appeal. What does it say about the island-nation we readers inhabit if this hidden, 'desolate island' is allowed to remain as it stands (and gradually falls)? Hence the move is quietly made from one painful aberration to the moral character of the land in which things are like this: 'The true state of every nation is the state of common life.'[6]

Coketown in *Hard Times* (1854) suggests that if there is one thing worse than industry thwarted it is industry set free. In this 'severely workful' place of 'unnatural red and black', a place that repudiates the 'taint of fancy', grim uniformity prevails at the level of architecture – but Dickens's style runs riot (*HT*, I, 5, 28–9). In Jacob's Island, faced with emptiness and decay, he holds back; in Coketown, work is never-ending, and the prose lets imaginative rip on a scene of monotonous hyperactivity. The urban panorama is depicted in a series of extreme and disconcerting similes: a savage's face; interminable, uncoiled serpents; and a melancholy, mad elephant (5, 28).

These two passages seem, on the face of it, to spring from opposing impulses – on the one hand to document, on the other to hallucinate. And yet, both reality and fantasy stoke the activity of exaggerating, as the *OED* defines it, in the following four ways (the last of which enters the language around the time that Wilkins Micawber enters *David Copperfield* [1849–50]):

> To exaggerate:
>
> 1 To heap or pile up, accumulate: said with reference to both material and immaterial objects; also to form by accumulation. (1533)[7]
> 2 To 'pile up' (eulogies, accusations); to emphasize (statements); to make much of, dwell on the greatness of (virtues, faults, conditions, etc.). (1564)
> 3 To magnify beyond the limits of truth; to represent something as greater than it really is. (1570?)
> 4 To intensify, aggravate (conditions, etc.), abnormally; to make (physical features, etc.) of abnormal size. (1850)

As is made clear by this sequence, exaggeration has been historically understood, quite neutrally, as a form of accumulation or aggregation, not only as hyperbolic inflation; indeed, one may lead to the other. An exaggerative style may thus descend from vigilant attention to minutiae as well as from the excesses of oratory. David Copperfield, training to be a novelist, 'could observe, in little pieces, as it were; but as to making a net of a number of these pieces, and catching anybody in it, that was, as yet, beyond me' (*DC*, 2, 18). Here, perhaps, is a hint as to the possible motives for shifting from the first to the fourth sense of 'to exaggerate'. Exaggeration sets out to catch someone – perhaps a reader as well as a fictional creation – in order to arrest their character, and our attention.

Dickens's early aggregative style might be read as an experiment in conveying accurately the fullness of reality – although, as Chesterton pointed out, there is nothing inherently realistic about 'arresting details', 'convincing irrelevancies' or the 'impedimenta of prosaic life': mere aspects of that 'technical realism' that characterises a work as fantastical as *Gulliver's Travels* (1726).[8] Dickens was praised and ticked off throughout his career both for his close fidelity and for his rampant infidelity to life. Those apparently bifurcating tendencies fostered in their turn two kinds of dim-witted reader, summarised by Chesterton (in reverse order) as the anti-Dickensian 'who could prove that Micawber never lived' and the pro-Dickensian 'who could prove in what particular street he lodged'.[9]

What begins with local observation of material objects often ends, in Dickens, in monstrous amplification; writing on selfishness in *Martin Chuzzlewit* (1843–4), he remarks, 'what a grim giant it may grow, from small beginnings', and the comment might be applied to his own style (*MC*, Preface, 846). Exaggeration can be scrupulous or unscrupulous, but, rather than overlook the details, it initially involves that shoring up and cataloguing of trifles which Buller noticed as a discomfiting feature of Dickens's style. What we might consider divergent tendencies are, in Dickens, interdependent, and perhaps sequential, aspects of the same creative activity. James Fitzjames Stephen saw 'artistic exaggeration' and 'minute description' as twin fallacies pervading his work; William Forsyth complained that 'His characters are all exaggerations' and that Dickens had 'a marvellous talent for minute description', but neither critic saw these qualities as inherently involved with one another.[10] As points on a novelistic continuum, however, they are reflected in the long-standing critical tussle about whether Dickens is a realist or an illusionist.

Considered as a stylistic principle, exaggeration straddles truth and fiction. While it opens up a breach between them, it also highlights a process of ceaseless exchange between the two. Hippolyte Taine instinctively understood this when he wrote that Dickens 'reckons his details one by one ... this minute description has nothing cold about it: if it is thus detailed, it is because the contemplation was intense; it proves its passion by its exactness.' For Taine, Dickens lacked the ability to perceive 'great things'; rather, his enthusiasm was kindled by 'vulgar objects'.[11] Precision coexists with intensity and hence with what other readers condemn as perverse aggrandisement. Thackeray was far less enthusiastic about Dickens's passionate, emphatic licence with such objects, or indeed about any of his rival's departures from sober realism. He wrote to David Masson in 1851 that

Micawber appears to me an exaggeration of a man, as his name is of a name. It is delightful and makes me laugh: but it is no more a real man than my friend Punch is: and in so far I protest against him ... holding that the Art of Novels *is* to represent Nature: to convey as strongly as possible the sentiment of reality – in a tragedy or a poem or a lofty drama you aim at producing different emotions; the figures moving, and their words sounding, heroically: but in a drawing-room drama a coat is a coat and a poker a poker; and must be nothing else according to my ethics, not an embroidered tunic, nor a great red-hot instrument like the Pantomime weapon.[12]

If Dickens's characters are mere caricatures, grotesque distortions of reality, it is hard to work out what exactly they are caricaturing. Mr Peggotty's 'old Mawther!' (by which we are told that he meant 'old girl') presumably translates as 'old Mother' (*DC*, 3, 34). But say Micawber's name is indeed an exaggeration, what original does it exaggerate? McCabe, perhaps? (Chesterton is sure that 'Dickens ... is not at all Scottish. I cannot conceive Micawber as Macawber.')[13] If Micawber is 'No more a real man than my friend Punch', a point on which Chesterton agrees with Thackeray – '[Micawber's] kingdom is not of this world'; he has 'never taken the trouble to exist in a mere material way'[14] – he seems to be in contact, nevertheless, with an originating reality whose presence Thackeray detects behind and around the fictional character. Chesterton warned against 'the weakness of taking too literally the idea of Dickensian "originals"' because it was 'the whole point of Dickens that he took hints from human beings; and turned them, one might say, into super-human beings'.[15] Thackeray doesn't identify a candidate for the real Micawber, but he seems to imply that Micawber was once a man and became something else, just as Dickens's coat has become an embroidered tunic and his poker a pantomime weapon. It's as if Thackeray is suggesting we might perform on Micawber the sort of operation required by question 2 of the *Pickwick Club* examination paper set by C. S. Calverley in 1857:

> Translate into coherent English, adding a note wherever a word, a construction, or an allusion, requires it:
> 'Go on, Jemmy – like black-eyed Susan – all in the Downs' – 'Smart chap that cabman – handles his fives well – but if I'd been your friend in the green jemmy – punch his head – pig's whisper – pieman, too.'[16]

In the original preface to *Nicholas Nickleby* (1838–9) (*NN*, Preface, xlix–l) and in the various prefaces to *Martin Chuzzlewit*, Dickens commented on the 'curious' matter of his caricatures and their real-life originals (or the lack thereof). Immediate responses to the later novel had faulted its characterisation, the *North British Review* mentioning Jonas as a specially inept and offensive example.[17] Dickens replied that: 'On this head of exaggeration … I have never touched a character precisely from the life, but some counterpart of that character has incredulously asked me: "Now really, did I ever really, see one like it?"' (*MC*, Preface, 846). The image and activity of 'touching … precisely from the life' come from painting; Dickens has just been speaking about the author who 'colours highly' versus the reader 'whose eye for colour is a little dull' (*MC*, Preface, 846). So the truth of a portrait seems to lie in the eye of the beholder. When Dickens writes 'precisely' about life, readers antagonistic towards his target will agree that he's accurate. The victims of his 'touch', however, will always insist that he has affronted reality. To 'touch' a character 'precisely from life' is related to that sense of 'capturing' someone in a net, as David Copperfield puts it, and hence to the satirical 'hit' with which an individual is immortalised – in a way that is at once true to life and ridiculous.[18] Dickens comes close to Swift when he writes about his readers and his characters in this way; in *The Battle of the Books* (1704), satire is famously defined as 'a sort of *Glass*, wherein Beholders do generally discover every body's Face but their Own'.[19]

While the original preface to *Martin Chuzzlewit* had focused on the novel's truth to life as a defence against the charge of exaggeration, in his subsequent cheap-edition preface Dickens changed his emphasis. Here he claimed that upbringing and education can produce grotesque characters, so that the fault of exaggeration – the distortion of the natural into the unnatural – lies not with the author, but with those responsible for nurturing and encouraging vice:

> I conceive that the sordid coarseness and brutality of Jonas would be unnatural, if there had been nothing in his early education, and in the precept and example always before him, to engender and develop the vices that make him odious. But, so born and so bred; admired for that which made him hateful, and justified from his cradle in cunning, treachery, and avarice; I claim him as the legitimate issue of the father upon whom those vices are seen to recoil. And I submit that their recoil upon that old man, in his unhonoured age, is not a mere piece of poetical justice, but is the extreme exposition of a plain truth. (*MC*, Preface, 846)

There are human monsters, then, but Dickens isn't responsible for their creation; they exist in reality. There is a more basic error in perception and comprehension, he argues, than that which points out failings of character in everyone other than oneself. Society, it turns out, fosters the aberrations of heart and mind it then rejects as impossibly outlandish; such is the truth Dickens apparently sought to communicate in *Martin Chuzzlewit* in the first place. If this is the case, however, it was a truth he failed to identify in his own work until it was attacked.

To diagnose a fictional character as exaggerated may be to see it as unrepresentative, and hence as dispensable. For some readers, characters need to be more relevant to their fictions, more hard-working than Dickens seems to think, in order to earn their keep: 'There are a great number of *dramatis personae* moving about in this story, some of them exercising no perceptible influence upon its action', complained an anonymous reviewer of *Bleak House* in 1853.[20] These 'exaggerated exceptions' must be regarded 'as mere excrescences which we should like to see pruned away. Of what conceivable use, for example, is such a personage as Mr Harold Skimpole? He does not assist the story, and, apart from the story, he is simply a monstrosity'.[21]

And yet, to have certain characters appear and disappear without a perceptible influence on anything might be counted an aspect of realism, one of whose hallmarks is meant to be the inclusion of extraneous detail. On the question of usefulness and relevance, exaggeration is equally difficult to pin down. It can be an efficient conduit to truth – grim giants lead back to small beginnings. Edwin Whipple discerned even in Dickens's most exuberant portraits an author who is continually 'observing, not creating': 'Such caricature as this is to character what epigram is to fact, – a mode of conveying truth more distinctly by suggesting it through a brilliant exaggeration'.[22] But Whipple drew an intellectual distinction between various types of reader and their likely responses to such writing. Exaggeration might serve as 'a powerful stimulant to accurate perception' for coarser readers, those 'who lack fineness and readiness of intellect'.[23] Such audiences are said to require shock tactics to provoke them into realising what people and life are like.[24] In the end, this seems not so much a defence of as an apology for exaggeration.

As for the 'sentiment of reality' which Thackeray argues it is the duty of novels to convey, Dickens often seems, conversely, to be striving to present the reality of sentiment – a reality that is characterised by all sorts of distortions and inconsistencies, muddled by the whims and lapses of memory and imagination. In the 1867 Preface to *Martin Chuzzlewit*, he argued that 'What is exaggeration to one class of minds and perceptions, is plain truth to another. That which is commonly called a long-sight, perceives in a prospect innumerable features and bearings non-existent to a short-sighted person' (1867 Preface, 846). And in *David Copperfield* it is indeed hard to distinguish exaggeration from memory or fidelity of perception, especially in relation to the experience of time: 'The length of those five days I can convey no idea of to any one. They occupy the place of years in my remembrance', David writes, 'all this appears to have gone round and round for years instead of days, it is so vividly and strongly stamped on my remembrance.' (Dickens originally plumped for four days rather than five, so that the 'length' of the time in question became, on second thought, objectively longer [*DC*, 4, 51–2 and n.].)

Dickens's novel-in-the-middle and 'favourite child' (*DC*, 1867 Preface, 752) tussles in many other ways with the distinction between realism and fancy. It continues to revolve a curious observation about readers and inter-pretation which had appeared in the original preface to *Nicholas Nickleby*: 'It is remarkable that what we call the world, which is so very credulous in what professes to be true, is most incredulous in what professes to be imaginary' (*NN*, Preface, l). People don't know how to respond to works of imaginative power because they cannot establish in what sense such works might or might not be 'true'. How can readers test the validity or authen-ticity of something which openly professes to be the work of imagination? In March 1850, when *David Copperfield* had another eight instalments to go, the first issue of *Household Words* was published, introduced by a vow from Dickens to 'cherish that light of Fancy which is inherent in the human breast' and to 'show to all, that in all familiar things, even in those which are repellent on the surface, there is Romance enough, if we will find it out'.[25] This promise is echoed in the 1853 Preface to *Bleak House*, where Dickens – having taken pains to establish a factual basis for his portrayal of Chancery judges and for Krook's death by spontaneous com-bustion – signs off with the remark that 'I have purposely dwelt upon the romantic side of familiar things' (*BH*, Preface, 5–6). Realism yields, in the end, to romance. And yet, in *David Copperfield*, the narrator's sympathies appear to lie with the facts. Imagination threatens the integrity of mem-ory and hence the status of autobiographical narrative:

> When my thoughts go back, now, to that slow agony of my youth, I won-der how much of the histories I invented for such people hangs like a mist of fancy over well-remembered facts! When I tread the old ground, I do not wonder that I seem to see and pity, going on before me, an innocent romantic boy, making his imaginative world out of such strange experi-ences and sordid things! (*DC*, 11, 145)

Facts are simultaneously 'well-remembered' and veiled by the 'mist of fancy', as if the truth is at once present and inaccessible. David Copperfield seems indirectly to voice Dickens's fears about his own style and about

the act of remembering (especially in writing a form of deflected autobiography). Although David is careful to avoid descriptions of his actual
novels and stresses (as above) his recall of 'facts', he offers up some suggestive anxieties about the role of exaggeration in memory: 'I am really
afraid to recollect, lest I should seem to exaggerate' (DC, 7, 77); 'I know
I do not exaggerate, unconsciously and unintentionally, the scantiness of
my resources or the difficulties of my life' (DC, 11, 139). How much of
memory is exaggeration? If memory is sometimes indistinguishable from
imagination, is it possible to differentiate between truth and lies? To create
a novel, should the writer strive to compose something probable rather
than something true, since truth is often improbable and therefore not
credible?

Even an exaggerated, inflated style can itself be susceptible of over and
understatement, depending on the norms that have been established with
regard to a speaker – we quickly discover the level on which each of them
typically operates. Characters who speak in a high style may temporarily relax or drop it; they may choose suddenly to moderate their wordiness – as Micawber often does, giving a long and short version of what he
is attempting to communicate, or putting an end to the orotund version
of events with a plain summing up of things as they are (more or less): 'I
am at present, my dear Copperfield, engaged in the sale of corn upon com-
mission. It is not an avocation of a remunerative description – in other
words it does *not* pay' (DC, 27, 349). Here, the comic play-off is of long
against short, polysyllables against monosyllables, circumlocution against
plain speaking, luxurious words against impoverished reality. It is a linguistic deferral of the inevitable by a speaker who always trusts that something
will, eventually, 'turn up' and who plugs the time with glorious florid pat-
ter until it does (see e.g. DC, 17, 220). But it also reveals a character who is
emphatically a writer, a prolific, effusive correspondent enjoying multiple
linguistic resources of which, however, his command is uncertain – does
he reach for 'in other words' merely because he has run out of polysyllabic
steam? There is a Micawber who speaks elaborately, who turns over and
savours his words, prolonging the moment, and there is a Micawber who
speaks plainly and 'in short', but whether he is capable of translating freely
between these stylistic levels isn't always clear (see e.g. DC, 12, 149).

Garrett Stewart has written of Dickens's 'sustained send-up … of the
Johnsonian high style of journalistic and parliamentary claptrap in the
eighteenth-century Age of Rhetoric'[26] – a send-up that feeds into his life-
long fondness for adjectival triplets – but Johnson himself, like Micawber,

was often conscious of a gap between his day-to-day way of speaking and the 'Johnsonian' manner:

> He seemed to take a pleasure in speaking in his own style; for when he had carelessly missed it, he would repeat the thought translated into it. Talking of the Comedy of 'The Rehearsal,' he said, 'It has not wit enough to keep it sweet.' This was easy; – he therefore caught himself, and pronounced a more rounded sentence; 'It has not vitality enough to preserve it from putrefaction.'[27]

In truth, both of the sentences in question are voiced in Johnson's 'style'; he can choose to explode pretension and circumlocution through plain speaking as well as perform elephantine pirouettes in what he is aware may degenerate into mere Johnsonese – a form of writing with which Micawber is closely allied through his pompous speeches, but especially through his prolix epistolary manner. Micawber's type of 'faded gentility' in such compositions (*DC*, 27, 342) also surfaces in the nearly contemporaneous *Cranford* (1851–3), where Miss Jenykns tells Captain Brown that 'Dr. Johnson's style is a model for young beginners. My father recommended it to me when I began to write letters. – I have formed my own style upon it.'[28] As with Micawber, it is specifically her letters that exhibit the Johnsonian strain: 'Epistolary writing, she and her friends considered as her *forte*.'[29] In an elaborate letter condemning Heep – whose name suggests acts of observation and material accretion – Micawber writes of his own 'accumulation' in typically overloaded terms: 'In an accumulation of Ignominy, Want, Despair, and Madness, I entered the office – or, as our lively neighbour the Gaul would term it, the Bureau – of the Firm, nominally conducted under the appellation of Wickfield and – HEEP, but, in reality, wielded by – HEEP alone. HEEP, and only HEEP, is the mainspring of that machine. HEEP, and only HEEP, is the Forger and the Cheat' (*DC*, 52, 642).

David remarks of the style of this letter that:

> Mr. Micawber had a relish in this formal piling up of words, which, however ludicrously displayed in his case, was, I must say, not at all peculiar to him. I have observed it, in the course of my life, in numbers of men. It seems to me to be a general rule ... We talk about the tyranny of words, but we like to tyrannise over them too; we are fond of having a large superfluous establishment of words to wait upon us on great occasions; we think it looks important, and sounds well. As we are not particular about the meaning of our liveries on state occasions, if they be but fine and numerous enough, so the meaning or necessity of our words is a secondary consideration, if there be but a great parade of them. And as individuals get

into trouble by making too great a show of liveries, or as slaves when they are too numerous rise against their masters, so I think I could mention a nation that has got into many great difficulties, and will get into many greater, from maintaining too large a retinue of words. (*DC*, 52, 645)

Given Dickens's own fondness for linguistic 'accumulation' and 'piling up', it is unsurprising that the complaint against superfluity is not upheld throughout the novel. Young David's style has already been comically assimilated with that of Micawber (*DC*, 38, 473). It is also, perhaps, suggested that Micawber, who has (as Traddles observes) 'seen a good deal of life' (*DC*, 27, 347), teaches David how to see things too, and thus how to be a novelist: 'I looked at nothing, that I know of, but I saw everything, even to the prospect of a church upon his china inkstand, as I sat down – and this, too, was a faculty confirmed in me in the old Micawber times' (344). Yet in the passage on Micawber's denunciation of Heep there is a clear attempt to mark David off from the worst abusers of language – those tyrants who care nothing for meaning and everything for show – and thence from 'the most popular styles of writing', in the endeavour 'to create a world in which it is undeniable that [David] is the literary artist and Micawber is a common, everyday writer'.[30]

Dickens's wordiness could easily be cast as a failing along the lines of Micawber's. As Franz Kafka wrote in a diary entry (8 October 1917):

> Dickens 'Copperfield' … Dickens' Reichtum und bedenkenloses mächtiges Hinströmen, aber infolgedessen Stellen grauenhafter Kraftlosigkeit, wo er müde nur das bereits Erreichte durcheinanderrührt. Barbarisch der Eindruck des unsinnigen Ganzen, ein Barbarentum, das allerdings ich, dank meiner Schwäche und belehrt durch mein Epigonentum, vermieden habe. Herzlosigkeit hinter der von Gefühl überströmenden Manier. Diese Klötze roher Charakterisierung, die künstlich bei jedem Menschen eingetrieben werden und ohne die Dickens nicht imstande wäre, seine Geschichte auch nur einmal flüchtig hinaufzuklettern.[31]

Kafka has apparently won a victory through weakness, a weakness that is in fact superior to Dickens's show of wealth. Dickens appears, like his Circumlocution Office in *Little Dorrit* (10, 100–17), to squander his words through evasion and weariness; he lacks care, oppressing his reader with needless repetition that undoes gains he has already secured. Ruskin wrote on Dickens's death that the novelist did not possess 'the desire of truth without exaggeration', whereas Ruskin himself sought 'the pure fact and nothing less or more, which gives me whatever power I have; it is Dickens's delight in grotesque and rich exaggeration which has made him, I think, nearly useless in the present day'.[32] Like Micawber, then, Dickens is at once powerfully in charge of his linguistic medium and its powerless victim; constituted by words, both author and subject may become the slaves of their language rather than its masters. Like Micawber, Dickens can seem thoroughly irresponsible in how he deploys his literary resources; prodigality entails a waste of talent, and the result is, seemingly, enervation on all sides. Or perhaps a better comparison on this score is between Dickens and Steerforth:

> If any one had told me, then, that all this was a brilliant game, played for the excitement of the moment, for the employment of high spirits, in the thoughtless love of superiority, in a mere wasteful careless course of winning what was worthless to him, and next minute thrown away – I say, if any one had told me such a lie that night, I wonder in what manner of receiving it my indignation would have found a vent!' (*DC*, II, 265)

The complexity of this moment, which spans multiple time frames, is that it entertains the partially acknowledged truth as, simultaneously, an outright lie. The mature David recognises at some level that Steerforth *was* playing a game, but, in imagining how the young David would have felt at being told such a thing, before any proof of it existed, the claim becomes again untrue. This hovering between truth and fiction sums up the role of exaggeration in Dickens: it is simultaneously a commitment to and departure from reality.

As well as seeming to involve too much, and hence becoming wasteful, Dickensian exaggeration may be accused of involving too little; he himself suggested as much when he described the 'American portion' of *Martin Chuzzlewit* as 'in no other respect a caricature than as it is an exhibition, for the most part, of a ludicrous side of the American character' (*MC*, Preface, 847). Exaggeration depends on partial representation of the whole. Hence Dickens's recurrent use of synecdoche: he often reads characters in terms of one attribute, capturing them through single parts of the body, clothes and other props which can be made to engulf a whole person. As George Brimley put it: '[Dickens's portraits] border on and frequently reach caricature, of which the essence is to catch a striking likeness by exclusively selecting and exaggerating a peculiarity that marks the man but does not represent him'.[33] Here again is an instance of how the locally observed particular might lead to the inflated figure of fantasy.

Dickens famously liked to animate the inanimate, even to dehumanise people by personifying their lifeless attributes, possessions or surroundings; John Eagles wrote that 'every character is in extreme … The inanimate nature must be made equally conspicuous, and every thing exaggerated. And it is often as forced in the expression as it is exaggerated in character.'[34] But then, forced expressions are sometimes appropriate to the characters they describe – as, for instance, in the initial description of Thomas Gradgrind in *Hard Times*. Anaphora and repeated 'emphasis' suggest consistency of form and content, but such patterns introduce a series of lurid images which are in turn at odds with one another. As in the picture of Coketown, exaggeration serves to dismantle rather than to underscore the point apparently being made, in favour of mere fact. Instead, imagination begins to take over, and the ostensibly monotonous 'scene' becomes a jumble of wildly discordant impressions (*HT*, I, I, I–2).

For Chesterton, the most gigantic of Dickens's creations will always be Micawber, 'an immense assertion of the truth that the way to live is to exaggerate everything'; 'I repeat, and it cannot be too much repeated that the whole lesson of Dickens is here. It is better to know Micawber than not to know the minor worries that arise out of knowing Micawber. It is better to have a bad debt and a good friend.'[35] Dickens introduces him to us, and to the young David, as follows:

> The counting-house clock was at half-past twelve, and there was general preparation for going away to dinner, when Mr. Quinion tapped at the counting-house window, and beckoned me to go in. I went in, and found there a stoutish, middle-aged person, in a brown surtout and black tights and shoes, with no more hair upon his head (which was a large one, and very shining) than there is upon an egg, and with a very extensive face, which he turned full upon me. His clothes were shabby, but he had an imposing shirt-collar on. He carried a jaunty sort of a stick, with a large pair of rusty tassels to it; and a quizzing-glass hung outside his coat, – for ornament, I afterwards found, as he very seldom looked through it, and couldn't see anything when he did.
>
> 'This,' said Mr. Quinion, in allusion to myself, 'is he.'
>
> 'This,' said the stranger, with a certain condescending roll in his voice, and a certain indescribable air of doing something genteel, which impressed me very much, 'is Master Copperfield. I hope I see you well, sir?' (*DC*, II, 134)

Micawber's 'magnificent mock-heroic stature' arises from the combination of tremendous effects with trifling causes – there is a lack of definition, as well as a shabbiness, about him, but he is 'large', 'extensive', 'full', 'imposing', and impressive: 'The thing about any figure of Dickens ... is that he cannot be exhausted. A Dickens character hits you first on the nose and then in the waistcoat, and then in the eye and then in the waistcoat again, with the blinding rapidity of some battering engine.'[36] For most of the book, Micawber's oratory seems to flourish and expand in inverse proportion to his material wealth. The less he has, the more he says. And exaggeration often flares up in Dickens in relation to poverty; characters who lack other resources can afford to be rich in their vocabulary (see, for instance, Micawber, Skimpole and Dorrit). The association of wordiness with poverty comes about because exaggeration implies irresponsibility and bad linguistic husbandry – a lack of due thrift and attention to reality which is reflected in a lack of ready cash as well as in a fund of words.

Numerous characters in Dickens are recognisable by phrases they repeat, as if magically or mechanically. People give 'proof of [their] identity' (*DC*, 1, 4) through these, their idiolects or signature tunes. Characters are constituted by such repetitions, physical and verbal, for instance (in *David Copperfield*) 'Barkis is willin'', 'be 'umble', 'King Charles's head', 'I'm a lone lorn creetur' and 'I'm a mother myself.' Uriah Heep is shaped by his professions of humility. As much stress is laid on the effect of these repetitions on their auditor as on the fact of their occurrence in the speaker, so that – in a sort of echo chamber – one character's repetitions foster another set of repetitions in the audience. Jeremy Tambling remarks that *David Copperfield* 'created Dickens as the reader', as well as the writer, of his own work, so there is perhaps an aspect of authorial self-mirroring involved in this repetition of repetition. Dickens wrote of being powerfully moved by the experience of composing and returning to *David Copperfield*, just as Mr Peggotty finds that Mrs Gummidge's repetitions have a 'moving effect' on him, one that leads him to 'repeat' himself and her words to others.[37] There is, then, a generative quality to such repetition; the performance of other people's words and feelings creates a likeness between characters and those they encounter, both directly and indirectly:

> I did not quite understand what old one Mrs. Gummidge was supposed to have fixed her mind upon, until Peggotty, on seeing me to bed, explained that it was the late Mr. Gummidge; and that her brother always took that for a received truth on such occasions, and that it always had a moving effect upon him. Some time after he was in his hammock that night, I heard him myself repeat to Ham, 'Poor thing! She's been thinking of the old 'un!' And whenever Mrs. Gummidge was overcome in a similar manner during the remainder of our stay (which happened some few times), he always said the same thing in extenuation of the circumstance, and always with the tenderest commiseration. (*DC*, 3, 35)

The level of repetition in *David Copperfield* is such that stories and people don't so much move on as circle around and overlap with one another. The keywords of Micawber's vocabulary and identity are 'turn up' and 'in short' – these keywords, which concern appearing and revolving, ascending and contracting, give him an other-worldly, inhuman quality;

but they also relate him to David, who is trying to return to the past and who writes about the expansions and contractions of his own memory and experience. As he moves back and forth between childhood and adulthood, people and places increase and diminish in accordance with changes of time, scale and perception. Repetition and exaggeration are thus called upon to register sameness and difference. In Mr Peggotty's cottage, characters and interiors seem eternally unchanged but at the same time to have altered for ever in the eyes of their beholder:

> It looked just the same, except that it may, perhaps, have shrunk a little in my eyes; and Mrs. Gummidge was waiting at the door as if she had stood there ever since. All within was the same, down to the seaweed in the blue mug in my bedroom. I went into the outhouse to look about me; and the very same lobsters, crabs, and crawfish possessed by the same desire to pinch the world in general, appeared to be in the same state of conglomeration in the same old corner. (*DC*, 10, 120)

Is the repetition of words tantamount to the repetition of experience? After a while, the iterated 'same' becomes uncanny, as if David's emphasis is eliciting a difference in the observer, the sudden unfamiliarity of a familiar scene to one who has himself grown up, rather than a confirmation that nothing has moved on. Compare the 'unchanged' Micawber, introduced by 'An opportune double knock at the door'; he enters, 'not a bit changed – his tights, his stick, his shirt-collar, and his eye-glass, all the same as ever' (*DC*, 27, 347). Structurally as well as in terms of phrases, characters and images, *David Copperfield* works by recurrence: many episodes in the book are 'double knocks', or memories of remembering. David begins life in London twice; he is a pupil at two schools; as an adult, he has two kinds of job; and he marries twice. He has two fathers and is cared for by two women called Clara (his mother and Peggotty).

This set of accumulated, multilayered repetitions demonstrates the novel's fascination with the move from small beginnings to gigantic dimensions and back again. David Copperfield notes, at the moment Uriah Heep tells him he loves Agnes, that

> He seemed to swell and grow before my eyes; the room seemed full of the echoes of his voice; and the strange feeling (to which, perhaps, no one is quite a stranger), that all this had occurred before, at some indefinite time, and that I knew what he was going to say next, took possession of me. (*DC*, 25, 326)

There is a chronological see-saw effect here, as David remembers a moment in the past when he felt that something in the future had already happened. Opposites merge into sameness so that the unfamiliar becomes familiar ('strange … no stranger'), and memory seems to have become a form of imagination; facts are irrevocably allied to fancy. In other words, exaggeration – an expansion beyond natural human size and scope – is also shown to be a form of memory, or repetition. The abundance of Heep filling the room is also the abundance of a sense that this has all happened before, and not only in the personal sense of David's déjà vu, which is itself a memory – but in the larger, more general sense that all characters and people are types and relatives of one another; we are all in some way repetitions or reproductions. The world is full of human like-nesses, not-quite-samenesses. Just to underline the point, that recollection of déjà vu is itself repeated in Chapter 39: 'We have all some experience of a feeling, that comes over us occasionally, of what we are saying and doing having been said and done before, in a remote time … I never had this mysterious impression more strongly in my life, than before [Micawber] uttered those words' (*DC*, 39, 483).

Dickens shows an early fondness for what Garrett Stewart has called 'directionless vitality'; Dick Swiveller shares with Micawber 'that will-ingness to take the prevailing wind which often makes him seem as though he is merely going in circles'.[38] Hence, in part, the striking revol-vency of *David Copperfield*. It is not only Micawber who's described in terms of turning and returning (evolving, devolving and revolving on his stool at Mr Wickfield's; *DC*, 39, 482). The signal characteris-tic of David in love is his tendency to go 'round and round' (*DC*, 33, 404); in a queasy turn of phrase, Betsey Trotwood imagines David's dead mother alive again to behold her grown-up son – her 'soft little head' would be 'completely turned' (29, 234). Turning and returning are centrally involved in the acts of writing and reading, as they are in the processes of remembering – amassing particulars, repeating and enlarging on the past, exaggerating in order to produce Dickens's pecu-liar 'sort of gigantic domesticity' that is 'at once Gargantuan in its fancy and grossly vivid in its facts'.[39]

Learning to be a novelist, David finds he needs to 'look about' himself (*DC*, 29, 235); Micawber's faith in something 'turning up' is akin to the reader's appetite for event; and the actions of turning and looking 'around' are akin to those of the literary critic. If the reader tends to wait for some-thing to happen, it remains, perhaps, the central task of the critic to cir-cumambulate the characters of Dickens. Chesterton's repetitive phrasing on this score mimics that of Dickens himself, in a form of creative return that unites homage and amazement:

Dickens was a man like ourselves; we can see where he went wrong, and study him without being stunned or getting the sunstroke. But Micawber is not a man; Micawber is the superman. We can only walk round and round him wondering what we shall say. All the critics of Dickens, when all is said and done, have only walked round and round Micawber wondering what they should say. I am myself at this moment walking round and round Micawber wondering what I shall say. And I have not found out yet.[40]

NOTES

1 G. K. Chesterton, *The Collected Works of G. K. Chesterton*, vol. xv: *Chesterton on Dickens*, ed. Alzina Stone Dale (San Francisco, CA: Ignatius Press, 1989), 35, 48, 26. Henry Fothergill Chorley, reviewing *Bleak House* (1852–3), set Dickens's admirable 'progress in art' against his deplorable 'progress in exaggeration' (*CH*, 276).

2 *CH*, 250; John R. Reed, *Dickens's Hyperrealism* (Columbus, OH: Ohio State University Press, 2010).

3 *CH*, 48.

4 *CH*, 72.

5 *CH*, 54–5.

6 Samuel Johnson, *The Yale Edition of the Works of Samuel Johnson*, vol. ix: *A Journey to the Western Islands of Scotland*, ed. Mary Lascelles (New Haven, CT: Yale University Press, 1971), 22.

7 The *OED Online* describes this sense as obsolete and its last citation dates from 1676, although 'to exaggerate' is also defined in these terms in Samuel Johnson's *Dictionary of the English Language* (1755 and 1773).

8 Chesterton, *Collected Works*, xv, 23.

9 Chesterton, *Collected Works*, xv, 533.

10 *CH*, 348, 351.

11 *CH*, 338.

12 *CH*, 260.

13 Chesterton, *Collected Works*, xxxi: *The Illustrated London News: 1917–1919*, ed. Lawrence J. Clipper (1989), 358. See also Masson's review of *Pendennis* and *Copperfield*: 'It is nonsense to say of [Dickens's] characters generally, intending the observation for praise, that they are life-like. They are nothing of the kind … at most, those characters are real only thus far, that they are transcendental renderings of certain hints furnished by nature' (*CH*, 256).

14 Chesterton, *Collected Works*, xv, 192; xxvii: *The Illustrated London News: 1905–1907*, ed. Lawrence J. Clipper (1986), 57.

15 Chesterton, *Collected Works*, xv, 551–2.

16 *CH*, 39.

17 *CH*, 186–7.

18 See *OED Online*: 'To touch' sense 17a. *trans.* 'To apprehend, succeed in getting at, "hit", hit upon; to guess or state correctly. ? *Obs.*' (last citation from 1797).

19 Jonathan Swift, 'The Preface of the Author' to *The Battle of the Books*, in *A Tale of a Tub*, ed. A. C. Guthkelch and D. Nichol Smith, 2nd edn (Oxford: Clarendon Press, 1958), 215.

20 *CH*, 287.

21 *CH*, 287.

22 *CH*, 239.

23 *CH*, 240.

24 *CH*, 240.

25 *Household Words* (30 March 1850), 1.

26 Garrett Stewart, 'Dickens and Language', in John O. Jordan (ed.), *The Cambridge Companion to Charles Dickens* (Cambridge University Press, 2001), 136–51, at 136, 145.

27 James Boswell, *Boswell's Life of Johnson, together with Boswell's Journal of a Tour to the Hebrides and Johnson's Diary of a Journey into North Wales*, ed. G. B. Hill, revised and enlarged by L. F. Powell, 6 vols., 2nd edn (Oxford: Clarendon Press, 1971), IV, 320.

28 Elizabeth Gaskell, *Cranford*, ed. Elizabeth Porges Wilson (Oxford University Press, 1980), 9.

29 Gaskell, *Cranford*, 9.

30 Laura Rotunno, 'The Long History of "In Short": Mr. Micawber, Letter-Writers, and Literary Men', *Victorian Literature and Culture*, 33 (2005): 415–33, at 425. This article also notes Micawber's indebtedness to Richardson and eighteenth-century epistolary manuals.

31 Franz Kafka, *Tagebücher, 1910–1923* (Frankfurt: Fischer, 1992), 391. Dickens's 'Copperfield' … Dickens's opulence and great thoughtless prodigality, but as a result passages of terrible powerlessness, where he just wearily goes over effects he has already achieved. Barbaric, the impression of a senseless whole, a barbarism that I, in any event, thanks to my weakness and the wiser for my epigonism, have avoided. Heartlessness behind the style that overflows with feeling. These crude characterisations, which are artificially forced on everyone and without which Dickens wouldn't be able to get on with his story, even for a moment. (My translation.)

32 *CH*, 444.

33 *CH*, 286.

34 *CH*, 230.

35 Chesterton, *Collected Works*, xv, 152, 332.

36 Chesterton, *Collected Works*, xvi: *The Autobiography of G. K. Chesterton*, introduction and notes by Scott Randall Paine (1988), 313; xv, 382.

37 See *David Copperfield*, ed. Jeremy Tambling, rev. edn (Harmondsworth: Penguin, 2004), xxii–xxiii.

38 Garrett Stewart, *Dickens and the Trials of Imagination* (Cambridge, MA: Harvard University Press, 1974), 105–6.

39 Chesterton, *Collected Works*, xv, 231.

40 Chesterton, *Collected Works*, xv, 335.

CHAPTER SEVEN

Style and the making of character in Dickens

Philip Horne

The first of two obvious thoughts: style, which in Dickens is offered as a pleasure, and a value, in itself, is intimately involved with Dickensian habits of characterisation, and particularly in the way Dickens's characters talk. The second: that a person's style of talking, thinking, writing and being is a register, so overdetermined as to constitute an incalculable mystery, of a whole life of pressures, chances, losses, gains – of paths taken, and untaken.

Unlike Henry James, Dickens has seldom been criticised for having all his characters talk the same way. But Henry James does have a contribution to make. He says in the 1909 Preface to *The Golden Bowl* that, ethically speaking, language cannot be separated from, should not necessarily be subordinated to, action: 'we recognise betimes that to "put" things is very exactly and responsibly and interminably to do them. Our expression of them, and the terms on which we understand that, belong as nearly to our conduct and our life as every other feature of our freedom.'[1] To put it another way, saying is doing. Action is character; talk is action; talk is character. Let us start, then, by thinking about how characters speak – not wishing to ignore how they look, feel, move, behave and so forth, which are also part of character.

First, it may be worth briefly visiting the question of the usefulness of the term 'character' – in fiction and in life. In one sense, characters in books are all figments, are just ink and paper, black and white, mere words, only imaginary; while in actual life the word 'character' can be accused of giving a delusive fixity to something really intrinsically unstable, of presuming and installing a false unity and so forth. We must keep these kinds of unreality and instability in view, and this chapter will partly try to investigate them. But most novels – certainly Dickens's – construct their people as 'characters', through the notion that selves are defined by histories, circumstances, habits, associations, compulsions, dilemmas; so it would be perverse to ignore it as a dimension of our reading. It also has its uses when we're thinking about the friend who will always be late for an appointment or the family member from whom there's no point trying to get sympathy for one's ailments.

Speech in Dickens is, generically speaking, realist. Unlike Shakespeare's, for instance, Dickens's characters don't for the most part speak in verse, and, as a rule, their level of educational attainment and verbal dexterity are reflected pretty closely in their manner of expression.[2] And styles of speech can have large implications for character. In *Oliver Twist*, learning how to speak in thieves' cant – 'I suppose you don't know what a beak is' – very obviously constitutes an initiation into crime (*OT*, 8, 47). And other argots – those of soldiers, sailors, lawyers, doctors – bring with them the values and attitudes of professions or activities, sometimes admirably but always with the possibility of a *déformation professionelle*. My focus here falls more on characters' individualised styles of speech, ways of talking – and the extent to which Dickens's narration individualises itself as it energetically stretches the bounds of the usual in the effort to catch the peculiar trick of a character's life.

For instance, broken or broken-up sentences become variously eloquent, often comically – and experiments in punctuation render speech which is in one way or another interrupted by a physical object or event. Thus, in *Our Mutual Friend*, as he bumps along in a cart to visit the illiterate Mr Boffin and to read to him from *The Decline and Fall of the Roman Empire*, 'Mr Wegg's conversation was jolted out of him in a most dislocated state' – '"Do you know-Mist-Erboff-in?" asked Wegg' (*OMF*, 1, 5, 54). Or the systematically irresponsible Harold Skimpole in *Bleak House* heartlessly plays his piano when he speaks of a bailiff's death – as Esther tells us, mimicking his musical playfulness but carefully substituting indeterminate 'full stops':

> 'And he told me,' he said, playing little chords where I shall put full stops, 'That Coavinses had left. Three children. No mother. And that Coavinses' profession. Being unpopular. The rising Coavinses. Were at a considerable disadvantage.' (*BH*, 15, 223)

The chords doubtless play or imply a tune; the narrating Esther's stops don't, are pointedly tuneless – they put a stop to Skimpole's frivolity, or at any rate mute it. In Chapter 4 of *David Copperfield*, more feelingly, Peggotty can only speak to young David, imprisoned after biting Mr Murdstone, through the keyhole. David himself plays the same trick of inserting full stops – with a Shandean, hyperbolic claim for Peggotty's 'broken little sentences' and his inventive mimetic device for rendering them.

Then Peggotty fitted her mouth close to the keyhole, and delivered these words through it with as much feeling and earnestness as a keyhole has ever been the medium of communicating, I will venture to assert: shooting in each broken little sentence in a convulsive little burst of its own.

'Davy, dear. If I ain't ben azackly as intimate with you. Lately, as I used to be. It ain't because I don't love you. Just as well and more, my pretty poppet. It's because I thought it better for you. And for some one else besides. Davy, my darling, are you listening? Can you hear?'

'Ye – ye – ye – yes, Peggotty!' I sobbed.

'My own!' said Peggotty, with infinite compassion. 'What I want to say, is. That you must never forget me. For I'll never forget you. And I'll take as much care of your mama, Davy. As ever I took of you. And I won't leave her. The day may come when she'll be glad to lay her poor head. On her stupid, cross old Peggotty's arm again. And I'll write to you, my dear. Though I ain't no scholar. And I'll – I'll –'

Peggotty fell to kissing the keyhole, as she couldn't kiss me. (*DC*, 4, 52–3)

Peggotty 'ain't no scholar', but she is supreme for 'feeling and earnestness'. The ridiculous – in her kissing the keyhole, as if to complete her sentence, though when he's away she'll have to miss him rather than kiss him – is also touching, the mixture of affect producing a fresh, poignant comedy. Cart, piano, keyhole – these things, as props for comic, though not only comic, business, join in the conversation and enrich our sense of the speaker.

Esther's treatment of Skimpole reminds us that punctuation – as anyone knows who has had to transcribe an interview from a recording – is a potent tool, a form of editing, even a form of rewriting. In *Little Dorrit* Arthur Clennam's once-beloved Flora – a rewriting of Dora from *David Copperfield* – has her own distinctively gushing style of speech as she explains why she married Mr Finching after she and Arthur were separated by their parents.

'One more remark,' proceeded Flora with unslackened volubility, 'I wish to make, one more explanation I wish to offer, for five days I had a cold in the head from crying which I passed entirely in the back drawing-room – there is the back drawing-room still on the first floor and still at the back of the house to confirm my words – when that dreary period had passed a lull succeeded years rolled on and Mr. F became acquainted with us at a mutual friend's, he was all attention he called next day he soon began to call three evenings a week and to send in little things for supper, it was not love on Mr. F's part it was adoration, Mr. F proposed with the full approval of Papa and what could I do?' (*LD*, I, 13, 146–7)

The main joke of this, which is not as such an 'explanation', is that of punctuation, stopping and starting incoherently. The joke depends on its arbitrary selectiveness: if punctuation were altogether excluded, as (bar that one last full stop) in the last chapter of *Ulysses*, that would be modernism, and beyond a joke.[3] The scatterbrained logic of offering the mere room as confirmation of five days of lovelorn suffering (with a cold in the head) gives the pleasure of unwitting absurdity – and the whirlingly unpunctuated expansion of the time scheme in 'when that dreary period had passed a lull succeeded years rolled on and Mr. F became acquainted with us at a mutual friend's' in its droll way suggests how often Flora must have dwelt on these clichéd formulae in order to be able to pour them out so volubly. There are twenty-three unpunctuated words from dash to comma, then twenty-five without a pause before the *next* comma – and the gush of the formulaic now allows the joke of 'it was not love', giving us a millisecond of puzzlement before a richly satisfying turn to florid cliché: 'it was *adoration.*'

There is an art of the long sentence – its masters including James, Proust and Faulkner – but in this case, one might think, we only have one by virtue of Flora's unslackening delivery – and also by virtue of Dickens's manipulative, unscrupulous, even treacherous punctuation of her. His experience with shorthand of course makes him alert to peculiarities of speech, and adept at verbatim transcription. But since speech is the issue, we cannot so clearly go that step further and say this is also a *punctuatim* transcription. When we speak, we know what words we are saying, but do we always clearly decide how they should be punctuated? For a parallel issue about Dickens's treatment of his characters' speech, we might recall Mark Lambert in his stimulatingly controversial *Dickens and the Suspended Quotation*, reading Dickens's way of breaking into a character's quoted speech with a narratorial comment or qualification (e.g., 'proceeded Flora with unslackened volubility') as a mark of aggression, of hostile interruption: it is, he says, 'most deeply an expression of hostility towards his own characters'.[4] On the other hand, if we don't read Dickens as so systematically hostile to his people, we may also be thankful to Danny Karlin for nicely pointing out that interruption is not suspension, and vice versa.[5]

A small move now, from Mr F's adoration to Mr F's Aunt, and a case that makes clear how crucial to Dickens is a character's manner of speech – physical gestures, tone and address, rhythm and emphasis and reception by an interpretative community:

> A momentary silence that ensued was broken by Mr. F's Aunt, who had been sitting upright in a cataleptic state since her last public remark. She

now underwent a violent twitch, calculated to produce a startling effect on
the nerves of the uninitiated, and with the deadliest animosity observed:
'You can't make a head and brains out of a brass knob with nothing in it.
You couldn't do it when your Uncle George was living; much less when he's
dead.'

Mr. Pancks was not slow to reply, with his usual calmness, 'Indeed,
ma'am! Bless my soul! I'm surprised to hear it.' Despite his presence of
mind, however, the speech of Mr. F's Aunt produced a depressing effect
on the little assembly; firstly, because it was impossible to disguise that
Clennam's unoffending head was the particular temple of reason depreciated, and secondly, because nobody ever knew on these occasions whose
Uncle George was referred to, or what spectral presence might be invoked
under that appellation. (*LD*, 1, 23, 267)

There's no suspending a quotation from Mr F's Aunt. The contrast with
Flora is part of the point: this is very pointed; and, speaking of points,
Dickens gives her a semicolon to play up the antithesis in the second
sentence. The admirable Pancks registers the affect of this utterance and
responds in a placating way. But Pancks's 'presence of mind' is pitted
against the 'spectral presence' (in the same sentence) and cannot dispel
it. The veil of genteel fiction that swathes so many of the mercenary and
oppressive transactions in *Little Dorrit* is – for Clennam and the others
depressingly, for us refreshingly – ripped away by Mr F's Aunt and her
'deadliest animosity' (which is multiplied by the ominous plural of 'on
these occasions'). One of the ways in which Dickens's narration plays up
the effect of the Aunt's forceful Anglo-Saxon vocabulary is to produce in
contrast a battery of Latinate, euphemistic, circumlocutory terms – 'particular temple of reason depreciated', 'spectral presence', 'invoked under
that appellation'. Moreover, it's flavoured with gentlemanly allusiveness:
the narration – which in its elaborate manner seems not to be especially
marked as rendering Clennam's point of view – is recalling Henry Francis
Cary (1772–1844) and his 'Ode to General Kosciusko' of 1797, ll. 79–82:

> Britain, my country! let the blush
> Of shame thy burning cheek o'erspread
> Who dar'st with lordly foot to crush
> The Indian's unoffending head.[6]

The lightening of tone Dickens thus generates cuts two ways: turning to
communal comedy and pleasure a scene of painful discomposure (and of
mental disturbance) – and sharpening it. Clennam's 'unoffending head',
brown with foreign travel of course, is the 'brass knob with nothing in it';
the company may well blush at the crushing remark directed at him. In

the novel as a whole, Britain's shame is systematically made manifest in innumerable connections.

The style of a character is not necessarily just language but also demeanour, a style of behaviour (which Dickens evokes *in* language). One recalls *Tristram Shandy* (an influence on, for instance, the opening of *David Copperfield*) and its example of evocations of posture and gesture, even supplying diagrams of stance and manner – as for the trajectory of the 'flourish' of Corporal Trim's stick.[7] Dickens's constant recourse to '*as if*' constructions is partly connected to this. As a simile applied to an action whereas 'like' applies to a noun, 'as if' has a tendency to transform the objects *of* an action into their equivalents in some other situation. Sometimes it is low key, only insidiously transformative: when the first Spirit in *A Christmas Carol* speaks, 'The voice was soft and gentle. Singularly low, as if instead of being so close beside him, it were at a distance' (*CC*, II, 29). Sometimes it is, so to speak, Chaplinesque – it's no coincidence that the Little Tramp who eats his scavenged luncheon on an upturned crate with extreme daintiness was based on years of observation of South London poverty.[8] Bob Cratchit has 'a situation in mind for Master Peter, which would bring in, if obtained, full five-and-sixpence weekly': 'Peter himself looked thoughtfully at the fire from between his collars, as if he were deliberating what particular investments he should favour when he came into the receipt of that bewildering income' (III, 53). The weighty banker's manner – and Latinate abstraction – prompted by such a small sum brings home the Cratchits' deprivation. The 'as if' characterises Master Peter *and* the Dickensian narrator, enjoying the ironies of incongruity between the poor boy and the wealthy financiers we see in the tale – for a (Chaplinesque) combination of comedy and pathos.

The style of speech of a character can extend beyond the sphere of direct quotation and seep into the narration at times so that the prose of the quasi-omniscient narrator takes on local colour from words characteristic of the figures and texts – and places – in the vicinity. The narration comes to smack of them, in an overt, humorous, less drily sardonic parallel to the indirect free style that Flaubert was refining in *Madame Bovary* just as Dickens was publishing *Little Dorrit*. The Plornishes come to visit Clennam.

> Mr Plornish amiably growled, in his philosophical but not lucid manner, that there was ups, you see, and there was downs. It was in wain to ask why ups, why downs; there they was, you know. He had heerd it given for a truth that accordin' as the world went round, which round it did rewolve

> undoubted, even the best of gentlemen must take his turn of standing with his ed upside down and all his air a flying the wrong way into what you might call Space. Wery well then. What Mr. Plornish said was, wery well then. That gentleman's ed would come up'ards when his turn come, that gentleman's air would be a pleasure to look upon being all smooth again, and wery well then! (*LD*, ii, 27, 712)

The alternation of vocabularies and manners – 'his philosophical but not lucid manner' being the narrator's, the phonetically marked cockney-isms and grammatical deviations being Plornish's – is a tour de force of quick-change ventriloquism. Indeed, 'What Mr Plornish said was' is at the same time a narratorial formula for reporting speech (parallel to 'Mr Plornish amiably growled' at the start of the passage quoted) and, more closely hewing to Plornish's actual utterance, a bit of free indirect style – so that we may understand Plornish to say, 'What I say is, wery well then.'[9] Dickens's narrators have in fact an appetite for varieties of words and texts that can be taken into his own: his works frequently swallow other words, others' words, with allusive gusto – even when they incorporate rhyme and risk turning prose to verse. The child David Copperfield, before the advent of the Murdstones, is in church.

> I look up at the monumental tablets on the wall, and try to think of Mr. Bodgers late of this parish, and what the feelings of Mrs. Bodgers must have been, when affliction sore, long time Mr. Bodgers bore, and physicians were in vain. I wonder whether they called in Mr Chillip, and he was in vain; and if so, how he likes to be reminded of it once a week. (*DC*, 2, 13)

The interplay between David's recreated childishly literal thoughts and the chiselled rhyming epitaph is comic (especially because David's account politely substitutes 'Mr Bodgers' for the presumable 'he' in 'Affliction sore long time he bore' – the standard formula – and messes up the scansion). But there's a shadow here: the fatherless boy's interest in the tablets – perhaps via an underlying pun on the medicinal prescription of 'tablets', meaning lozenges – is imaginably connected to his sense of the feelings of Mrs Copperfield, his mother, when his father Mr Copperfield also late of this parish made his premature exit from life (when we may reasonably assume Mr Chillip *was* called in and *was* in vain).

While Dickens is using style as a mode of characterisation for the *personae* of his fiction, so he can be re-economising it to build and shape the reader's sense of the voice or person (or spirit?) who is conducting us through the created world they inhabit. I'd therefore like to turn now to a character of a different order: the narrator who is mediating all this to us, who does not just 'do the Police in different voices'[10] – the third-person narrator, not named, not always at all emphatically an 'I', whom many Victorian readers would doubtless have thought of as Dickens himself, and particularly so once he started his public readings. The theatricality of much Dickensian narration makes narration a performance – a theatrical self-presentation that suggests the narrator is consciously created as a persona. Moreover, while a narratorial description of a character's appearance or action or speech may characterise that character, it inevitably also characterises the narrator. The spectrum of styles and tones a narrator deploys may constitute *a* style and *a* tone. Ranging across different modes – satirical, sermonical (Carlylean), farcical, mock-sententious (Fieldingesque), sentimental, psychological, elegiac, encyclopaedic, sociological – a narrator takes on many of the characteristics of a character: winning our trust, keeping us entertained, moulding our judgement, stimulating our imagination and our sympathies. Narration, in fact – even when not first-person – can be understood as always implicitly characterising itself – revealing its attitudes and preoccupations, its visual habits, its rhythms, manifesting its own inner rules. Dickens also educates his reader through a certain overtness in the kinds of reading that are available, or required.

My focus in this chapter falls on what seem peculiarly Dickensian forms of verbal play as they relate to character. G. H. Lewes remarks on the constant 'drollery' that 'his language, even on the most trivial points, has, from a peculiar collocation of the words, or some happy expression', attributing the effect to a 'fine … association of idea'.[11] John Carey notes a lovely instance where the newly arrived Oliver 'washed himself: and made everything tidy, by emptying the basin out of the window, agreeably to the Jew's directions' (*OT*, 9, 53). As he says, '"Agreeably to", which looks an innocent adverbial construction, makes a disdainful comment, in passing, about people who pour dirty water out of windows.'[12] We are prepared for this comic effect by the way in which 'emptying the basin out of the window' is said to make '*everything* tidy', rather than just the room – in Fagin's world, where Number One is the only number that counts, the rest of the world had better watch out.

Little Dorrit offers another fine case, another 'peculiar collocation' or transaction between contexts:

> the paternal Gowan, originally attached to a legation abroad, had been pensioned off as a Commissioner of nothing particular somewhere or other, and had died at his post with his drawn salary in his hand, nobly defending it to the last extremity. (*LD*, 1, 17, 201)

The 'association of idea' generates a magnificent series of puns, founded on the zeugma, or syllepsis, whereby in the service of one's country one can draw a sword or a salary. Working back from this, 'died at his post', a generally heroic formula for the doing of duty in the dangerous spot where one has been posted – is transformed: where sinecures are in question, a 'post' is a well-paid, cushy billet. 'In his hand' in this new context doesn't mean heroically battling to the bitter end but greedily clutching the pay-check, while the dogged battle to defend 'it' (either 'post' or 'salary', but if the former then anyhow chiefly for the sake of the latter) – against one's own countrymen, presumably – becomes questionable. And, by infec-tion, 'nobly' carries the sense that such diehard rapacity is a characteristic activity of aristocrats like the Barnacles (Gowans are 'distant ramifications' [*LD*, I, 17, 201] of the Barnacles) – ready bitterly to fight for their vested interest. As characterisation, it also shows the narrator's readiness to judge, to give an opinion, to mock, his lack of deference (as Fitzjames Stephen would complain) and his satirical talent for mock-heroic pyrotechnics. Dazzling as it is, however, this is a *broad* effect – compared at least with a subtler one from the same novel, a more richly suggestive, point-of-view effect:

> Arthur entered the rather dark and close parlor (though it was lofty too), and sat down in the chair she placed for him.
>
> 'Not to deceive you, sir, I notice it,' said Mrs Plornish, 'and I take it kind of you.'
>
> He was at a loss to understand what she meant; and by expressing as much in his looks, elicited her explanation.
>
> 'It an't many that comes into a poor place, that deems it worth their while to move their hats,' said Mrs Plornish. 'But people think more of it than people think.'
>
> Clennam returned, with an uncomfortable feeling in so very slight a courtesy being unusual, Was that all! (*LD*, I, 12, 131)

The main point, of course, is that the Bleeding Hearts don't get shown much courtesy; but it is reinforced for us, as for Clennam, by the deliber-ately baffling device Dickens invents: there is no way we could know what Mrs Plornish means by her 'it' in 'I notice it', as we haven't been told that Clennam has taken off his hat on entering. Hat removal evidently goes without saying for Clennam, in poor homes as well as wealthy; hence the silence on the subject. And Mrs Plornish's explanation – we might note in terms of 'suspended quotations' that there are no elegant, semi-jocular tags (simply twice 'said Mrs Plornish') – achieves a surreal poetry in the way it tweaks normal usage. Her doubling of 'people think ... people think' – which verges on self-contradictory nonsense through the repetition of the undifferentiated third-person plural – actually manages to say exactly what it means, with an eloquently awkward delicacy. People care more than they think they do – and in particular poor people care more than well-off people think they do. 'Worth their while' suggests the ubiquity of the profit motive and its reach into human relations between the classes. Another point of this rich little exchange with the poor is also Mrs Plornish's sensitivity – thus shown not to be only a prerogative of the higher orders. Indeed, like her parlour, she can be 'lofty'.

The reader of Dickens is being trained by his author, or his author's narrator, to recognise and enjoy the kind of self-referential playfulness of which this moving hat moment is a luminous example. The pleasure of such recognition in jokes or comic payoffs acts as an incentive to other kinds of alertness and recognition, of non-comic strands of imagery and implication, establishing that readerly attention will be rewarded in pleasure and instruction. Next, let us examine another case from the same novel, suggesting the kinds of responsiveness we are to develop.

The housekeeper Affery, forcibly married to Flintwinch, Mrs Clennam's retainer, comes downstairs from her bedroom late at night to witness an uncanny scene. Through a doorway, she sees her husband Flintwinch.

> But what – hey? – Lord forgive us! – Mrs. Flintwinch muttered some ejaculation to this effect, and turned giddy.
> For, Mr. Flintwinch awake, was watching Mr. Flintwinch asleep. He sat on one side of the small table, looking keenly at himself on the other side with his chin sunk on his breast, snoring. The waking Flintwinch had his full front face presented to his wife; the sleeping Flintwinch was in profile. The waking Flintwinch was the old original; the sleeping Flintwinch was the double. Just as she might have distinguished between a tangible object and its reflection in a glass, Affery made out this difference with her head going round and round. (*LD*, 1, 4, 41–2)

In due course the waking Flintwinch pokes the sleeping Flintwinch with the candle-snuffers. His companion wakes.

> 'You have been asleep,' snarled Jeremiah, referring to his watch, 'two hours. You said you would be rested enough if you had a short nap.'
> 'I have had a short nap,' said Double. (*LD*, 1, 4, 42)

'Said Double' – as against 'said the double' with lower case 'd' – is the peculiarly Dickensian note, with the conversion of the noun to a name – as a culmination of the passage's pleasure in paradoxical doubling. The 'watch' Jeremiah refers to at the end doubles back to his earlier 'watching'; the parallelism of 'Mr Flintwinch awake' and 'Mr Flintwinch asleep' has been echoed and extended through the passage, conveying Affery's confusion. (She has 'her head going round and round' partly because she's looking back and forth between them, partly because the double vision makes her feel giddy.) And one effect of the parallelism of names – 'snarled Jeremiah' / 'said Double' – is to treat them both as first names, since both have been 'Mr Flintwinch' (and in fact it's true – they're twin brothers). It's a daring turn: the word 'double', and uncapitalised, has only been used once in the passage, and not for over 150 words. That said, Dickens prepares the moment so as to make sure we know who's being addressed and who's speaking. Inventive and in its way challenging as this is, it conforms to an unwritten contract with the reader. We are not yet in the grip of modernism, and we don't have to worry about encountering a gesture like Joyce's single mention of 'Mr Bloom's dental windows' in *Ulysses* – the Bloom in question being not his hero Leopold but a real dental surgeon of 1904 Joyce discovered in his researches and stuck in as a joke on the reader, only explained in passing eighty-five pages later.[13]

Dickensian wordplay can enable the reader to contemplate, and even enjoy contemplating, things in themselves miserable and oppressive, lightening the tone when necessary. Only a few pages earlier in *Little Dorrit* we can see how narratorial imagination guards against excessive grimness in a description of the desolate Clennam house – the style, a good companion, enabling us to contemplate a depressing ugliness that might otherwise be too much.

> They mounted up and up, through the musty smell of an old close house, little used, to a large garret bedroom. Meagre and spare, like all the other rooms, it was even uglier and grimmer than the rest, by being the place of banishment for the worn-out furniture. Its movables were ugly old chairs with worn-out seats, and ugly old chairs without any seats; a threadbare patternless carpet, a maimed table, a crippled wardrobe, a lean set of fire-irons like the skeleton of a set deceased, a washing-stand that looked as if it had stood for ages in a hail of dirty soap-suds, and a bedstead with four bare atomies of posts, each terminating in a spike, as if for the dismal accommodation of lodgers who might prefer to impale themselves. (*LD*, 1, 3, 37–8)

There's a careful patterning in the far from 'patternless' description here, which yields a small sample epidemiology of what Daniel Tyler nicely calls the 'contagiousness of vocabulary' in Dickens.[14] The movement from '*worn-out* furniture' to '*with worn-out* seats' to '*without* any seats' first passes 'worn-out' from phrase to phrase, then finds 'with/out' in 'with/

worn-/out' – a further reduction beyond even the threadbare. 'Atomies' is an abbreviation (a cut-down version) of 'anatomies', meaning skeletons; the maimed and crippled finally starve ('lean') and die and turn to bones. But the beauty of this passage, giving us a fillip even as it terminates in a climax of despair, is the climactic pun on 'accommodation'. That second 'as if' appears at first to qualify 'bedstead' – 'accommodation' in the sense of a bed to sleep in; but then as we read on it turns more syntactically precise, applying to the spikes and the suicidal 'preference' (a genteel, Bartleby-like word) which can thus be conveniently 'accommodated', the depressed Clennam being the latest lodger to whom this convenience is offered. This case, incidentally, in its progress from the meagre to the suicidal, bears out Henry James's suggestive remark that 'All writing is narration; to describe is simply to narrate things in their order of place, instead of events in their order of time.'[15] Because Clennam's point of view controls what we see, the last sentence, enumerating the items in the room, implicitly travels with his increasingly appalled gaze. The pun is both bathos and climax, relieving and crystallising the grimness, reminding us of the narratorial imagination that is shepherding us through this world. Maybe, too, the wit and point of this description is implicitly Clennam's own – which would suggest the resilience that keeps him going through the novel's accumulating oppressions.

As we have already seen with Esther Summerson and David Copperfield, for first-person narration the rules are different in a number of respects. These are not all completely obvious; as in reversing a car or rowing, it's somewhat counterintuitive. As Christopher Ricks says in his fine essay on *Great Expectations* of 1962:

> The effect of using the first-person is completely to reverse the normal problem about keeping a reader's sympathy. We do not, in the ordinary way, have much difficulty in liking someone who tells us how bad he has been; we are perhaps less sympathetic to someone who talks about his good deeds. And, conversely, we are likely to feel sympathy with a man seen from the outside as acting well, but not otherwise.[16]

That is, if a narrator praises a character or, better, shows the character behaving well, we esteem that character. Whereas if I tell you how virtuous I am, or expatiate on my charitable actions, you distrust me and suspect I'm a prig. Ricks quotes the proverb, *Qui s'excuse, s'accuse;*[17] he doesn't say whether it works the other way round too, but I suspect it does (at the level of rhetorical strategy and tactics). He is especially helpful on tone, and on how, under these first-person conditions, it has to be, as it were, neither too hot, nor too cold, but just right. Ricks picks out, for example, the moment late on in *Great Expectations* when the chastened Pip goes to ask Miss Havisham to help Herbert: she asks if she can do anything 'for you yourself?' Pip's answer: 'Nothing. I thank you for the question. I thank you even more for the tone of the question. But, there is nothing' (*GE*, III, 10, 394). Ricks finely comments: 'That comma after "But" must be the least careless comma in Dickens – the decent mystery of leaving the rest unsaid.'[18] Because once there seemed so much she could, and would, do for him. This reminds us how often Dickens's punctuation conveys dramatic timing rather than logical, grammatical structure (one might think of the colon experiment of the 1840s, where Dickens profusely inserts colons for emphatic pauses where one might expect commas).[19] Ricks cites Gissing: 'No story in the first person was ever better told.'[20]

An omniscient or selectively omniscient narrator is above the characters, and is permitted a corresponding latitude in displaying superior knowledge and generalising about the ways of the world she or he is mediating. In first-person narration, told by a supposedly real character in the story, too much display is quickly put down as showing off. We don't allow omniscience or even as a rule superior knowledge to first-person narrators. Certain kinds of licence are revoked. And problems arise. For the narrative to cohere, often the reader must learn of events beyond the narrator's ken – contrivances loom, convenient overhearings, even cheats and tricks of telepathy, intuition, feats of deduction. How, and how reliably, does the narrating character know the minds of other characters? How does a first-person narrator judge other characters without being found judgemental – or sly (an issue with Esther Summerson)? Or seen as envious, besotted, etc.? If they're telling of their own suffering, how can they avoid seeming excessively to pity themselves? And when the reader's trust is not a founding premise of a novel, as it mostly is with omniscient narration, it has to be earned by a first-person narrator who is a character among others, and whose reliability must not be compromised by exaggeration or too obvious an axe to grind.[21] There are fine balances to be struck, which have implications for style.

The autobiographical aspects of *David Copperfield*, Dickens's longest first-person novel, mean it brings up with special vividness questions of style and character; as well as of memory and imagination. The rule just discussed about first-person showing off manifests itself in a relative sobering down, or sobering up, of Dickens's narrative manner for *David Copperfield*. Thackeray thought Dickens had been influenced (partly by him) into 'greatly simplifying his style and foregoing the use of fine words'.[22] Michael Slater comments on the novel's shift to a new style:

> That Dickens himself was aware of having in *Copperfield* toned down some of his customary stylistic effects is suggested in his jocose reference, in a letter to Lemon of 25 June, to his just-written description of David's mother's death: 'Get a clean pocket-handkerchief ready for the close of "Copperfield" No. 3: "simple and quiet, but very natural and touching." – *Evening Bore*.'[23]

The complex self-parodic jocosity in the letter, squirming away from the anticipated terms of the critics' praise, shows us Dickens flexing his stylistic muscles against the constraints of first-person proprieties. The decorum of styles dictates the choice of the 'simple and quiet' or plain style (as far as Dickens can restrain himself to that) for a work that takes the fictional form of an autobiography.

Particular issues arise in this regard from Dickens's own much-discussed 'autobiographical fragments', as so much is transferred into *David Copperfield* with minimal revision. The fragments particularly suggest the inextricability of questions of style from other matters – of memory, imagination, responsibility and judgement. The most striking effect in many passages is that so *little* revision seems thought necessary by Dickens: a number of passages go in verbatim, others almost untouched. That pieces of autobiographical confession can be just slotted into a large-scale, artistically ambitious work of fiction without any adjustment is remarkable.

Here is a passage as it occurs in the fragment:

> It is wonderful to me how I could have been so easily cast away at such an age. It is wonderful to me, that, even after my descent into the poor little drudge I had been since we came to London, no one had compassion enough on me – a child of singular abilities, quick, eager, delicate, and soon hurt, bodily or mentally – to suggest that something might have been spared, as it certainly might have been, to place me at any common school. Our friends, I take it, were tired out. No one made any sign. My father and mother were quite satisfied. They could hardly have been more so, if I had been twenty years of age, distinguished at a grammar-school, and going to Cambridge.
> The blacking warehouse was the last house on the left-hand side of the way, at old Hungerford-stairs. It was a crazy, tumble-down old house.[24]

And now as it appears in *David Copperfield* – where it is the beginning of Chapter 11. Making his own experience that of a fictional character, and subject to the rules of fictional first-person narration, Dickens has to get the tone right.

CHAPTER II. I BEGIN LIFE ON MY OWN ACCOUNT, AND DON'T LIKE IT

    I know enough of the world now, to have almost lost the capacity of being much surprised by anything; but it is matter of some surprise to me, even now, that I can have been so easily thrown away at such an age. A child of excellent abilities, and with strong powers of observation, quick, eager, delicate, and soon hurt bodily or mentally, it seems wonderful to me that nobody should have made any sign in my behalf. But none was made; and I became, at ten years old, a little labouring hind in the service of Murdstone and Grinby.

    Murdstone and Grinby's warehouse was at the waterside. It was down in Blackfriars. Modern improvements have altered the place; but it was the last house at the bottom of a narrow street, curving down hill to the river, with some stairs at the end, where people took boat. It was a crazy old house. (*DC*, II, 132)

The openings are strikingly different. The fragment passage follows straight on from a paragraph ending 'on a Monday morning I went down to the blacking warehouse to begin my business life';[25] the *David Copperfield* chapter-end immediately before sees David in a coach leaving his birthplace. So for the novel this is a fresh start; for the memoir it is an indignant continuation, full of grief and grievance. The strong statement by Dickens in his own person, yeasting himself up with the repeated 'It is wonderful to me', moreover, refers to his living, indifferent parents; whereas the novel needs to adjust to the fact that the orphan David's fate is determined by a tyrannical stepfather (Murdstone) and Murdstone's sister. 'Cast away' becomes 'thrown away': the first suggests Cowper's damned, drowning victim in his poem 'The Castaway'; 'thrown away' seems more casual, more thoughtless – on the part of the adults responsible, not as a word choice by the remembering David. The second comma, after 'that', in 'It is wonderful to me, that' makes a weighty pause, registering an expressive rather than a grammatical pressure in a plangent sentence which groans with self-compassion, with weight on 'even', 'enough', 'something', 'might' and 'any' making the case that this was cruel and unusual neglect. The second sentence in the novel reverses the fragment's order of elements: 'A child' first, *then* 'it seems wonderful to me'; and it's '*seems* wonderful', not *is* wonderful. The level of talent Dickens first claims for himself (not unreasonably, but for winning our sympathy, maybe unseasonably) is taken down a notch from 'singular' to 'excellent'; the emphatic comma after 'soon hurt' is briskly removed as if to fit the cooler distance of retrospect; and yet both versions in their own way fuse the present remembering self and the past remembered self in the kind of absolute continuity the novel insistently claims. In the fragment's version of the passage, we find 'it is wonderful to me, that, … no one had compassion enough on me', with first adult 'me' and then childhood 'me'; the novel's grammar, producing a momentary confusion of temporalities, seems suddenly to speak, in the present, in the voice of the *young* David: 'A child of excellent abilities, … it seems wonderful to me that …'.

The paragraphs just compared have widely distinct destinations: the memoir needs to render justice to the perversity of living parents who in effect choose to orphan their son, whereas the novel has, much more tidily, made David a real orphan who really has 'nobody' to make any sign (except perhaps Betsey Trotwood). The end of the fragment paragraph has the force of one of Dickens's 'as if' constructions ('hardly … more so, if') and makes the confident statement of his parents' feelings of high complacency. The collision between 'Cambridge' at the end of the first paragraph and 'The blacking warehouse' at the start of the next makes its forceful point. The novel has no such surprise: the repetition of the formula 'Murdstone and Grinby' (which seems to ask us to find in it, Spooneristically, 'Grindstone and Murby') launches us into David's grim fate. And the blacking warehouse is shifted East, from Hungerford-stairs to Blackfriars, perhaps for plausible deniability of the episode's autobiographical basis.

There's a chapter to be started and a different plot situation to be accommodated, so this cannot be one of the passages that are transferred quite *verbatim* – unlike that recounting Dickens's autobiographical account of his sales of books to the second-hand dealer, which Forster notes is 'reproduced word for word in his imaginary narrative'.[26] Even so, it is, as I've already noted, disconcerting how directly the autobiographical material is being used. It's all the more disconcerting when one remembers the first-person narration's need to get the tone just right.

The reason for the compatibility of the fragment passages with the structure of the novel, I would suggest, is their common thrust – not just the closeness of real to fictional *event* but the closeness of argumentative emphasis on the boy's neglect as a failure of a duty of care and on the serious dangers he has narrowly escaped. Dickens is preoccupied throughout his career by the possible other case – by the thought of having been corrupted where he came through intact, of sinking where he actually rose; of falling into excessive familiarity with Bob Fagin and the others in the blacking warehouse; of not becoming a writer. The dismal might-have-been, for the practised plotter-out of lives, is brought back from a dead past into the freshness of recreated risk and peril. And this giddying sense of possible other outcomes involves also a sharpened sense of possible other characters a person might have become, ignorant instead of learned, rich instead of poor, debauched instead of innocent, damned instead of saved.

In *David Copperfield*, despite its heart-rending depiction of childhood suffering, we get only partial glimpses of these abysses. Agnes Wickfield becomes the approved muse of the novelist David in a work that, as has often been noted, never really becomes the *Künstlerroman* it seemed to promise. The emphasis in the mentions of David's career falls mainly on his hard work and his morally improving purpose. When Dora has died and David has lost his sense of direction, Agnes persuades him that, 'As the endurance of my childish days had done its part to make me what I was, so greater calamities would nerve me on, to be yet better than I was; and so, as they had taught me, would I teach others' (*DC*, 58, 698). This official version, with its stress on 'endurance' as engendering virtue, is heroic, and admirable, but it does rather accentuate the positive. The novel wants to say that no harm has been done – but the lingering doubt remains, what if he had been, what indeed if he *has* been, warped?

The appalling exposure of the child-narratee to moral risk must be established; but for the adult narrator to retain the reader's trust and respect, in the domesticated economy of *David Copperfield* it seems that this moral risk must also be asserted emphatically to have produced no moral damage. Forster, in *The Life of Charles Dickens*, quotes David Copperfield insistently claiming that the eighteenth-century books he read 'did me no harm; for, whatever harm was in some of them, was not there for me; *I* knew nothing of it'.[27] However, Forster, prompted by Dickens, also remarks that as a boy Dickens had 'a dangerous kind of wandering intelligence that a teacher might turn to good or evil, happiness or misery, as he directed it'.[28] It is a preoccupation that surfaces in the 1853 essay 'Gone Astray', where, as a small, lost child in London, Dickens goes to the theatre on his own and has to wait outside among the common people. The chapter dwells on what might have been.

> The greater part of the sailors and others composing the crowd, were of the lowest description, and their conversation was not improving; but I understood little or nothing of what was bad in it then, and it had no depraving influence on me. I have wondered since, how long it would take, by means of such association, to corrupt a child nurtured as I had been, and innocent as I was. ('Gone Astray', *Journalism*, III, 162)

Such wondering drives *Oliver Twist* also, of course; the ease with which Oliver could be turned to the bad is so central to that novel. Character, under this searching light, is the product of contingency – or at least is ultimately subject to contingency – with the reliving of earlier crises producing a vertigo of personality in which the roads not taken come to preoccupy the individual with the vision of other fates that might have come to pass. And such issues of character register, inevitably, as issues of style.

Certain moments in the memoir cannot get into *David Copperfield*. For obvious reasons (David's parents are dead), Dickens cannot reuse the excruciating moment when, after a paternal quarrel with the proprietors of the blacking warehouse, his father says he can go back to school, but his mother disagrees.

> I do not write resentfully or angrily: for I know how all these things have worked together to make me what I am: but I never afterwards forgot, I never shall forget, I never can forget, that my mother was warm for my being sent back.[29]

Qui s'excuse, s'accuse: despite its protestation, this powerful sentence seems fuelled by resentment and unforgiving anger. The resentment and anger seem justified, but the claim protests too much altogether to convince. That produces its own effect, however: the creditable *attempt* to escape resentment and anger is part of what gives this sentence its poignancy. Knowing 'how all these things have worked together to make me what I am' – a success, but in any case 'what I am' is simply a fact – does not exculpate his selfishly thoughtless mother. 'All these things' acknowledges multiplicity; beside it, 'The endurance of my childish days had done its part to make me what I was' – the Agnes version of the issue, quoted above – comes to sound too bland and singular. The triple impossibility of forgetting his mother's attitude – 'I never afterwards forgot, I never shall forget, I never can forget' – overwhelms the equanimity claimed. 'My mother was warm for my being sent back.' The great, chilling word in this is 'warm' – a perversion of the maternal warmth an unhappy child craves. 'What I am' – the product of this personal history – inevitably includes a personal style; so the very style of the sentence which so eloquently points up this cruel injustice is in part, and inextricably, a result of it.

The very process of growth and change which has made character – by accretions of thought and experience – is recoverable by memory, and thus permits, or enforces, a measure of fluidity between present and past. 'Character' cannot become a fixed or stable quantity; memory can always return it to its origins, unsettling it with what might have been – the descent into the world of the criminal, the low, the inarticulate. Would the self – 'what I am' in some sense – still be there? One way of feeling the movements of Dickens's style as they explore and negotiate different registers might be as a continuing exploration of his own escape into authorship, constructing fictional worlds that keep renegotiating the relation between the made and the unmade self.

NOTES

I would like to thank Oliver Herford, Danny Karlin, Karl Miller, Adrian Poole and Rebekah Scott for all their help and encouragement.

1 Henry James, *Literary Criticism: French Writers, Other European Writers, The Prefaces to the New York Edition*, ed. Leon Edel and Mark Wilson (New York: Library of America, 1984), 1, 340.

2 In Shakespeare, there is a more open question about how far, how profoundly, the way characters speak is to be credited to them or treated as informing about them – it is an effect of blank verse, and of the way Shakespeare's imagination has for the most part no outlet save through the speech, and by implication the imagination, of his characters. It's a suggestive question about the mass murderer and memorable poet Macbeth, to go no further than that: is he in any sense conscious of speaking in verse? If he *is*, isn't that strange? But if he *isn't*, that's surely strange too, for it seems to beg the question merely to say that we have to accept the convention of blank verse. How far can we take his choice of words as telling and responsible?

3 Danny Karlin points out that there are many precedents for Dickens's imaginative deployment of punctuation comically to express a process of self-undoing, one notable instance being Jane Austen's bravura editing down – through dashes and syntactic elisions – of at least an hour's worth of speech into a pungent brief paragraph, as Mrs Elton progressively collapses from ebullient stridency to crotchety heat exhaustion during the strawberry-picking at Donwell Abbey in *Emma* (1815; vol. III, Chapter 6).

4 Mark Lambert, *Dickens and the Suspended Quotation* (New Haven, CT: Yale University Press, 1981), 35.

5 In a marginal note in his copy of Lambert, which he graciously gave me. Let me offer a pedestrian, more conventional, repunctuation of Flora's speech with the comedy sucked out to throw into relief not only the brilliance and possible cruelty of Dickens's version but also its relish in and delight at Flora's way of being, thinking and speaking:

> 'One more remark,' proceeded Flora with unslackened volubility, 'I wish to make; one more explanation I wish to offer. For five days I had a cold in the head from crying, which I passed entirely in the back drawing-room – there is the back drawing-room, still on the first floor, and still at the back of the house, to confirm my words.
>
> 'When that dreary period had passed, a lull succeeded. Years rolled on; and Mr F. became acquainted with us at a mutual friend's. He was all attention. He called next day; he soon began to call three evenings a week; and to send in little things for supper. It was not love on Mr F.'s part, it was adoration. Mr F. proposed, with the full approval of Papa – and what could I do?'

6 Henry Francis Cary, 'Ode to General Kosciusko', *Ode to General Kosciusko* (London: Cadell, Junior & Davies, 1797), 3–6, at 5.

7 Laurence Sterne, *The Life and Opinions of Tristram Shandy, Gentleman* (1759–67), ed. Graham Petrie, intro. Christopher Ricks (Harmondsworth: Penguin, 1967), IX, 4, 576.

8 Chaplin's biographer David Robinson remarks on Chaplin's 'peculiar genius for perceiving in any object the properties of another object, which was the basis of a life-time of "transposition" gags'. David Robinson, *Chaplin: His Life and Art*, rev. edn (London: HarperCollins, 1992), 340. Thus breakfast rolls become feet, bootlaces spaghetti and so on.

9 I owe this point to Oliver Herford.

10 T. S. Eliot originally considered Dickens's line 'He do the Police in different voices' as a title for his epic of different voices, *The Waste Land* (1922). It comes from *Our Mutual Friend*, where the semi-literate Betty Higden praises the boy Sloppy for his powers of vocal impersonation: 'And I do love a newspaper. You mightn't think it, but Sloppy is a beautiful reader of a newspaper. He do the Police in different voices' (*OMF*, I, 16, 198).

11 G. H. Lewes, review of *Sketches by Boz, The Pickwick Papers* and *Oliver Twist* (December 1847), in *CH*, 63–8, 67–8.

12 John Carey, *The Violent Effigy: A Study of Dickens' Imagination*, 2nd edn (London: Faber, 1991), 73.

13 'As he strode past Mr Bloom's dental windows the sway of his dustcoat brushed rudely from its angle a slender tapping cane and swept onwards, having buffeted a thewless body'. James Joyce, *Ulysses: The 1922 Text*, ed. Jeri Johnson (Oxford World's Classics, 1993), 'Wandering Rocks' episode, 240. As *Ulysses Annotated: Notes for James Joyce's Ulysses* by Don Gifford with Robert J. Seidman tells us, this is 'Marcus J. Bloom, dental surgeon to Maynooth College, former lecturer on dental surgery, St. Vincent's Hospital, and ex-surgeon, Dental Hospital, Dublin, and St. Joseph's Hospital for Children, 2 Clare Street. No relation to Leopold Bloom.' Don Gifford with Robert J. Seidman, *Ulysses Annotated: Notes for James Joyce's Ulysses*, revised and expanded edn (Berkeley, CA: University of California Press, 2008), 282.

14 See Chapter 4 in this volume.

15 Henry James, 'Review (January 1865) of *Azarian: An Episode* by Harriet Elizabeth (Prescott) Spofford', in *Literary Criticism: Essays on Literature, American Writers, English Writers*, ed. Leon Edel and Mark Wilson (New York: Library of America, 1984), 603–13, at 610.

16 Christopher Ricks, '*Great Expectations*', in John Gross and Gabriel Pearson (eds.), *Dickens in the Twentieth Century* (London: Routledge & Kegan Paul, 1962), 199–211, at 203–4.

17 Ricks, '*Great Expectations*', 205.

18 Ricks, '*Great Expectations*', 207.

19 See Philip Horne, 'Selected Textual Variants', in *Oliver Twist*, ed. Philip Horne (London: Penguin Classics, 2002), 533.

20 Ricks, '*Great Expectations*', 207.

21 There is as well, more generally, a tension in the Victorian novel between the claims of first- and third-person narration – between the immediacy of first and the mediation of third; the eyewitness is pitted against the judge (see, for example, 'Janet's Repentance' in George Eliot's *Scenes of Clerical Life*, where the combination of methods can strike the reader as relatively artless).

22 Quoted in Michael Slater, *Charles Dickens* (New Haven, CT: Yale University Press, 2009), 291.

23 Slater, *Charles Dickens*, 291.

24 *Life*, I, 25.

25 *Life*, I, 25.

26 *Life*, I, 21: the passage indeed recurs *verbatim*: *DC*, II, 141.

27 *Life*, I, 9–10.

28 *Life*, I, 12.

29 *Life*, I, 38.

CHAPTER EIGHT

Snarling Charles: a Saxon style of restraint

Rebekah Scott

Is there an English-language poem as scornful of the English language as Byron's *Beppo*? Midway through, the chatty narrator indulges in a digression that gives us a brilliant sample of his trademark chiaroscuro. A set piece of the poem, it offers a contrastive picture of Italy and England. To Italy he awards sunshine, wine and bronzed women; to England he cedes dung, sorrow, borrowed candles, smoke, bad weather, frigid women, taxes, debt and beef-steak. It is not hard to see where his preference, and by extension Byron's preference, lies, even without this unflattering comparison of Italian with his mother tongue:

> XLIV
> I love the language, that soft bastard Latin,
>   Which melts like kisses from a female mouth,
> And sounds as if it should be writ on satin,
>   With syllables which breathe of the sweet South,
> And gentle liquids gliding all so pat in
>   That not a single accent seems uncouth,
> Like our harsh northern whistling, grunting guttural,
> Which we're obliged to hiss, and spit, and sputter all.[1]

Tellingly, his denunciation comes in the Italian verse form of *ottava rima* – the poem was an early experiment in the form for Byron – and the pleasing words 'satin' (which gives an easy, unstressed feminine ending to the line) and 'liquids' are both Old French and ultimately Latin in origin. By contrast, the words so offensive to the ear – 'uncouth', 'harsh', 'whistling', 'grunting', 'hiss', 'spit' and 'sputter' – are Old or Middle English (or Middle Dutch). The line beginning 'Like our harsh', which follows on from 'uncouth', invites either an unnatural emphasis on 'our' to maintain the iambic pentameter (so that the adjective 'harsh' takes a weak stress) or else disrupts it with three equally stressed syllables before resuming its rising rhythm. To prove his point Byron really lays it on 'thick' – to use another Old English word.

Dickens is the master of such tricks. His own prose medleys – like Byron's poetic ones, exaggerated for comic effect – were one reason he was regarded by his contemporaries as 'grotesque' and 'monstrous', while twentieth-century critics have described his sudden shifts in language and register as 'manic' and 'neurotic'.[2] Indeed, a striking continuity in the criticism of Dickens of the past 150 years is that his style is deemed 'excessive'. (Ditto his plots, characterisation and dialogue.) One of the things I'll be considering in this chapter is the converse of Dickens's excessive style: his style of restraint. Restraint is, after all, only manifest beside what it is not, or what it terrifyingly might be.[3] I won't be looking at restraint as 'silence' or 'stoppage', subjects both admirably dealt with elsewhere,[4] but as 'self-mastery' and 'austerity', the indications of which are in those accumulations of the guttural one hears so often in Dickens – in reported speech and, more curiously, in free indirect speech. Specifically, I am interested in restraint as a defining feature of Dickens's 'Englishness', and indeed of his 'Saxon-English', and shall be focusing on those 'native' qualities of maintaining 'a stiff upper lip', 'holding back', 'swallowing it' and 'keeping it down', all of which are expressed in tones of masculine gruffness or bluffness – as lexical *and* phonological means of restraint. As far as the genealogy of this style goes, I'll be suggesting that Dickens is the inheritor of a terse, post-Romantic 'rudeness' that is not without an eloquence of its own, a style whose Victorian parallels might be found, say, in the poetic 'growls' of Robert Browning. This style may be detected in phrases in which the high and low coalesce, in a kind of counterpoint, or in what might be termed the aural grotesque – in collocations, variously, of the foreign and the home-grown, the oratorical and the colloquial, the standard and the non-standard, the straight and the devious. Itself neither high nor low, neither human nor animal, Dickens's style of restraint resides most revealingly in those compounds of the literate and the semi- or even the *sub*-literate.

A native style

A defining feature of Dickens's Englishness is his use of the vernacular, particularly in situations where a strong contrast is in order. The most memorable example must surely be from *Our Mutual Friend* (1865): Podsnap's dinner party in honour of his daughter Georgiana's eighteenth birthday, at which an unnamed 'foreign gentleman' is present. Podsnap begins by making the usual mistake, that foreigners are if not stupid then deaf, as may be observed in the capitalisations of his leading question, 'How Do You Like London?'

'You find it Very Large?' said Mr Podsnap, spaciously.

The foreign gentleman found it very large.

'And Very Rich?'

The foreign gentleman found it, without doubt, enormément riche.

'Enormously Rich, We say,' returned Mr Podsnap, in a condescending manner. 'Our English adverbs do Not terminate in Mong, and We Pronounce the "ch" as if there were a "t" before it. We Say Ritch.'

'Reetch,' remarked the foreign gentleman. (*OMF*, I, II, 132)

No doubt the foreign gentleman, at this point, finds 'it' to be affluent *and* heavy, indigestible, sick-making. Possibly, he even finds the whole conversational tenor 'a bit rich'. The irony of this is further brought home by the proximity of the foreign gentleman's response ('reetch') to 'retch'. Undeterred, Podsnap sets aside his elocution lesson in favour of a lecture on Britain's political infrastructure, beginning, as all civilised lectures surely must, in the Abstract: 'And Do You Find, Sir, ... Many Evidences that Strike You, of our British Constitution in the Streets Of The World's Metropolis, London, Londres, London?' Meeting bafflement, Podsnap pursues:

'I Was Inquiring,' said Mr Podsnap, resuming the thread of his discourse, 'Whether You Have Observed in our Streets as We should say, Upon our Pavvy as You would say, any Tokens –'

The foreign gentleman with patient courtesy entreated pardon; 'But what was tokenz?'

'Marks,' said Mr Podsnap; 'Signs, you know, Appearances – Traces.'

'Ah! Of a Orse?' inquired the foreign gentleman.

'We call it Horse,' said Mr Podsnap, with forbearance. 'In England, Angleterre, England, We Aspirate the "H," and We Say "Horse." Only our Lower Classes Say "Orse!"'

'Pardon,' said the foreign gentleman; 'I am alwiz wrong!'

'Our Language,' said Mr Podsnap, with a gracious consciousness of being always right, 'is Difficult. Ours is a Copious Language, and Trying to Strangers. I will not Pursue my Question.' (*OMF*, I, II, 132–3)

Podsnap, with his insistence on the Teutonic 'horse', remains deaf to the foreigner's unintentionally Byronic insult that London streets are 'rich' in yet another sense: full of 'dung'. What's more, the veneration of the English language that lies at the heart of Podsnap's patriotic pride conceals a marked ignorance of etymologies: 'Copious Language', 'Trying to Strangers' and 'Pursue my Question' are made up of phrases consisting of Old French and Latin elements. If Podsnap's conversation with his guests is as 'heavy' as his tableware, it is more for such ponderous Latinisms than any peculiar traits of 'the English langwidge' (as Sam Weller might say), any abrupt glottals or throaty gutturals.

Podsnap aside, there are many characters who *do* possess such a lang-widge. Indeed, our English vernacular, with its stock of words from Old English and Low German, contains, as Byron rightly identifies, a glut of the guttural, those throaty sounds that occur when the back of the tongue pushes against the soft palate: g, k, x, ŋ [ng]. While such sounds may be shown to characterise the phonotactics of English in general, it is the vulgar- or rough-tongue, or so we like to think, that is especially associated (in a kind of spurious portmanteau) with both the *gutter* and the best*ial* (= *guttural*). Vulgar or rough characters, typically illiterate or semi-literate, incline not only to a 'grunting guttural', which they're 'obliged to hiss, and spit, and sputter all', but often to a sub-literate language of *mere* hissing, spitting and spluttering – to which catalogue may be added snarling, snorting, groaning and growling. More often than not, however, these characters 'grunt' and 'hiss' their very locutions; indeed, they are typically 'interrupted' in these acts by the narrator, who 'pauses' them to remark on their delivery ('he snarled' / 'she spat').[5] Having doomed them to mono-tones, the narrator seems to take further pleasure in the competitive par-ticipation that the onomatopoeic qualities of a tag such as 'snarled' or 'growled' lends to his own prose narration.[6]

It is in such verbal minutiae that Dickens's Englishness most overpower-ingly resides. Dickens's contemporary reviewers have more or less intui-tively sensed this about his style. Richard Ford, writing in the *Quarterly Review* (June 1839), is representative of mid-century reviewery when he asserts that 'Boz is a truly national author – English to the backbone.'[7] The consensus during this period is that Dickens's Englishness has some-thing to do with his reportorial ear for the people's language. (Ford chris-tens him 'regius professor of slang'.)[8] Thomas Henry Lister, writing in the *Edinburgh Review* the previous year (October 1838), describes Dickens's 'style' as 'fluent, easy, spirited, and terse' – all conversational qualities.[9] Indeed, there is a peculiar emphasis on modes of 'address' in the popular press of this time, particularly the forms of address one could or should adopt towards one's readers. On this topic *Household Words* wasn't slow to join in the agitation. An article such as 'Slang' clearly demonstrates the house policy of the journal towards the conventions of 'speech' – and not just between scribblers and their readers, but between members of all walks of society.

'Slang' was published as a leader on 24 September 1853, and is often wrongly attributed to Dickens in online versions of the text. In fact, it was written by George Augustus Sala, an acolyte and mouthpiece of Dickens who often submitted to invasive editorial procedures at the hands of the man he knew as 'the master'.[10] In 'Slang' Sala makes this appeal to his readers:

> [I]f we continue the reckless and indiscriminate importation and incorporation into our language of every cant term of speech from the columns of American newspapers, every Canvas Town epithet from the vocabularies of gold-diggers, every bastard classicism dragged head and shoulders from a lexicon by an advertising tradesman to puff his wares, every slip-slop Gallicism from the shelves of the circulating library; if we persist in yoking Hamlets of adjectives to Hecubas of nouns, the noble English tongue will become, fifty years hence, a mere dialect of colonial idioms, enervated ultramontanisms and literate slang.[11]

It is the 'literate slang' to which Sala particularly objects, rather than, say, regional dialects or the sociolects of the working classes, whose slang terms he seems rather to savour as he reels them off for opprobrium. One can imagine Dickens taking great relish in this spirited rant of Sala's, egging him on at the sidelines even. Yet the younger man's droll catalogue loses its buoyancy and bite as soon as he starts making moral pronouncements on the defilement of the English language. These pronouncements come distastefully close to the Victorian discourse of social engineering and social cleansing.[12] Witness:

> The fertility of a language may degenerate into the feculence of weeds and tares: should we not rather, instead of raking and heaping together worthless novelties of expression, endeavour to weed, to expurgate, to epurate [sic]; to render, once more, wholesome and pellucid that which was once 'a well of English undefiled' and rescue it from the sewerage of verbiage and slang? The Thames is to be purified; why not the language?[13]

The tone of this piece is very difficult to judge. The glitch of his own 'bastard classicisms' and 'ultramontanisms' is surely one of the redeeming ironies of the piece, as is the muted allusion to the Parable of the Wheat and Tares, in which Jesus indicates the futility of man's attempt to separate the fallen (represented by the tares or weeds) from the saved (represented by the wheat), a task which, come Judgement Day, can only belong to God Himself.[14] Yet the patriotic preference for Anglo-Saxon language and literature, for Spenser and through him Chaucer ('a well of English undefiled'), generally accords with what is known of editorial preferences at this time.

A native gruff style

In the front-page manifesto of the first issue of *Household Words*, the editors supply this rationale for their choice of title and, indeed, for their wider endeavour: 'The mightier inventions of this age are not, to our thinking, all material, but have a kind of souls in their stupendous bodies which may find expression in Household Words.'[15] That ordinary 'household words' may also have 'a kind of soul' is a sentiment that must have found favour among the journal's contributors and readers alike; here the truism holds that the popular press doesn't mould the opinions of the age, it merely reflects them. As Garrett Stewart has remarked:

> It must not be thought that Dickens stood alone in his day as a champion of native English in all of its resource and vernacular energy. He was part of a strong nineteenth-century movement away from unquestioned deference to the classical standards of language, and he wrote a piece called 'Saxon-English' for his periodical *Household Words* on the history of English, with an expressed bias towards native rather than imported diction, a preference for what we might in fact call 'household words'.[16]

It is certainly the case that Dickens showed a 'bias towards native rather than imported diction'; yet, as tempting as it is to attribute 'Saxon-English' to Dickens, the essay is in fact the product of two of Dickens's sub-editors, William Rushton and Henry Morley.[17] Stewart's point, however, stands. 'Saxon-English', which ran in *Household Words* on 10 July 1858, was quite vocal on the subject of the superiority of the English (or Saxon) tongue:

> When a man has anything of his own to say, and is really in earnest that it should be understood, he does not usually make cavalry regiments of his sentences, and seek abroad for sesquipedalian words. We all know that an Englishman, if he will, is able to speak easily and clearly; also he can, if he please, write in such a manner as to send the common people to their dictionaries at least once in every page. Let him write Saxon, and the Saxons understand him.[18]

The authors' surely ironic taunt at those who 'seek abroad for sesquipedalian words' echoes Sala's jibe at those who favour 'enervated ultramontanisms'; such echoes were so common in the pages of the journal that potential contributors were occasionally deterred by what they felt to be an authorial-editorial homogeneity. (Douglas Jerrold memorably quipped that not only were the contributions to *Household Words* anonymous – they were '*mon*onymous' too.)[19] Although the authors of 'Saxon-English' don't succeed in setting us an example of the way in which we might restore our native diction, they do muster up a few examples of Saxon terminology to get us under way. These include terms that fall into the categories of domestic and pastoral subsistence: 'house', 'roof', 'home', 'hearth', 'earth', 'flail', 'plough', 'sickle', 'spade', 'wheat', 'rye', 'oats', 'ox', 'steer', 'cow', 'calf', 'sheep', 'swine', 'deer', 'fowl'.[20] It is worth mentioning here that Henry Morley, who went on to become a Professor of English Language and Literature at University College London (1865–89), was a great scholar of Anglo-Saxon; earlier that year he had persuaded Dickens to run his 5,000-word prose précis of *Beowulf*, entitled 'A Primitive Old Epic', in the 1 May 1858 issue of *Household Words* – one of a series of articles on British literature that Morley proposed to Dickens in 1858, beginning with 'The Celtic Bards' and including 'Anglo-Saxon Bookmen'. According to Nicholas Howe, Morley's summary of *Beowulf* was designed to show up the excessive Latinity of Benjamin Thorpe's 1855 standard edition.[21]

A native gruff plain style

One gets the impression that Dickens didn't have much time for classicists, although it is tricky to tell exactly whose position any given narrator of his is occupying at any given time. Take Cornelia Blimber, the Headmaster's daughter, in *Dombey and Son* (1848). Of her we are told:

> There was no light nonsense about Miss Blimber. She kept her hair short and crisp, and wore spectacles. She was dry and sandy with working in the graves of deceased languages. None of your live languages for Miss Blimber. They must be dead – stone dead – and then Miss Blimber dug them up like a Ghoule. (*DS*, 11, 143)

Dickens's own 'translations' of Latinate words and phrases into the vulgar tongue are less systematic than those of Morley and more occasional, more tongue-in-cheek, in the manner of eighteenth-century satirists such as Swift, Sterne and Fielding, whose 'best' characters are always chasing (and dropping) that holy grail of 'plain English'. Dickens certainly pokes fun at the national fantasy of a pure sociolect. This may be seen on those many occasions when his characters chide each other for not speaking 'plain English' – often falling back on Latinate terms in the process, viz. Podsnap in *Our Mutual Friend* (1865), and before him Mrs Plornish and Mr Meagles in *Little Dorrit* (1857), Mr Bounderby in *Hard Times* (1854) and Mr Bucket in *Bleak House* (1853). Mr Bounderby, for example, castigates Jupe in the following decidedly Latinate terms: 'He is a runaway rogue and a vagabond, that's what he is, in English' (*HT*, 1, 6, 36) – when all that is properly 'English' is 'runaway', since 'rogue' derives from Latin (*rogare* = beg, ask) and 'vagabond' is a Middle English term with Old French/Latin origins (*vagabundus*, from *vagari* = wander).[22] Then there is the supposedly frank discussion between the mercenary Lammles about the benefits of pooling their resources in cunning (since they have no other) in *Our Mutual Friend*: 'You have called me an adventurer, Sophronia. So I am. In plain uncomplimentary English, so I am. So are you, my dear. So are many people. We agree to keep our own secret, and to work together in furtherance of our own schemes' (*OMF*, 1, 10, 126). Alfred Lammle seems oblivious to the fact that the 'uncomplimentary', which insinuates itself between his 'plain' and 'English', stems from a Latin word (*complementum* = completion, fulfillment), with the suggestion of a pun on 'uncomplimentary' as not simply 'unflattering' but also 'costly, at a price'; neither is he aware that 'adventurer' comes from the French (*aventurer* = venture upon) and is not 'plain English' at all.

Dickens's peculiar specialty, as has been observed before, is the collocational send-up, or what Robert Golding calls his 'contrast manner', citing as prime examples Dick Swiveller and that other arch-swiveller, Mr Micawber, since both characters routinely switch between the highfalutin and the colloquial.[23] In his own day, Dickens's critics couldn't resist making particular mention of his collocational couplings. One critic was so piqued at their frequency that he was driven to respond in kind, christening Dickens 'the very Avatar of chaff'.[24] Thomas Cleghorn, writing in the *North British Review* (May 1845), was outraged at the 'striking declension from purity' increasingly exhibited by Dickens's 'style' and cites the following instances in *Martin Chuzzlewit* as 'gross offences against the English language':

> For instance, many words, in themselves good and classical, are used in such a collocation, that to make any sense of them at all, we must suppose that the author has imported some new meaning of them from America during his transatlantic trip. Thus, we have *impracticable* nightcaps, *impossible* tables and *exploded* chests of drawers, *mad* closets, *inscrutable* harpsichords, *undeniable* chins, *highly geological* home-made cakes, *remote suggestions* of tobacco lingering within a spittoon, and the *recesses and vacations* of a toothpick.[25]

The attack here is launched on two fronts: the grammatical and the lexical. On one side, the intention is to demolish the unruly animism of Dickens's adjective–noun amalgamations. This signals the broader affront at Dickens's tendency to catachresis. On the other side, the aim is to bring negative attention to the irresolvable friction between a classical and a native idiom. This too signals a bigger offence: Dickens's bent towards all kinds of miscegenation. Not all critics fought Dickens on these fronts, of course: the year before Cleghorn's review was published R. H. Horne declared his secret love of Dickens's collocational style in his book *The New Spirit of the Age*

(1844), in which the 'jingling anatomy' of a harpsichord (from the newly serialised *Martin Chuzzlewit*, 1843–4) gets a special mention.[26] My interest here isn't in contrastive diction per se, a topic treated elsewhere for what it reveals about Dickens's irony and exuberance,[27] but in situating these bizarre pairings as an extension of the Dickens grotesque.

Dickens's aural grotesque

David Lodge makes a very good case for the reason why 'rhetoric seems a particularly useful term in discussing Dickens's work': 'Not only is the "author's voice" always insistent in his novels, but it is characteristically a public-speaking voice, an oratorical or histrionic voice; and it is not difficult to see a connection between this feature of his prose and his fondness for speech-making and public reading of his works.'[28] Clearly, the 'oratorical' style is wonderfully embodied in a Gregsbury or a Slackbridge, a Chadband or a Veneering; however, 'the oratorical' leaves a whole range of characters unaccounted for – something Ian Watt goes some way towards correcting under his more inclusive designation, 'the oral style'. Watt's essay of this name treats not simply the talkers but also the eaters, drinkers, biters and suckers of Dickens; although he too is quick to fall back on his training in stylistics: 'Rhetorical analysis ... reveals Dickens's great reliance on many of the features of epic style: repetition, apostrophe, stock formulae of phrase and sound, extended similes, parataxis; and these features are constant in abundance, if not exactly in kind, throughout his writing life.'[29] In fairness to Watt, he does point the way for psychoanalytic and phonotactic readings:

> as regards speech, it seems that there is still much to say about the way Dickens makes speaking itself both a directly physical reality in his novels, and also an infinitely symbolic activity; more generally, ... there is still much to learn about the physical, physiological and psychosexual functions of the act of speech.[30]

If we are to regard Dickens's texts *qua texts*, then his gutturals and his growls, even more than his orally fixated or oratorical characters, embody the paradox of being intensely physical and yet symbolical too. One might say that as Wordsworth invokes 'the inward eye' of the poet creating, Dickens invokes the inward *ear* of the reader reading, what has elsewhere been called 'subvocalisation'.[31] Beyond Lodge and Watt, a more primal notion of orality needs to be addressed: the association not so much between speechifying and meaning, or even speech and meaning, but between heard or imagined *sound* and meaning.[32] When Michael Hollington stresses that 'in general there is something non-verbal about Dickens's conception of the grotesque',[33] this non-verbal element should really extend beyond startling facial expressions and wild gesticulations to take in the *sub*-verbal: the grunts, the growls and the groans.

The Browning growl

In *Robert Browning* (1903), G. K. Chesterton dwells at length on the nature of the grotesque and its appeal to Browning, whom he discovers to be a 'philosopher of the grotesque'.[34] Curiously, Chesterton refuses to credit Browning's most energetic 'grotesques' – Fra Lippo, Bishop Blougram, Sludge, to name a few – with any philosophical or truth-telling capacity, except when they rise above their baseness to speak in lofty verse. When, in 'Mr Sludge, The Medium' (*Dramatis Personae*, 1864), Sludge concludes the last part of his tortuous, erratic monologue with these lines:

> R-r-r, you brute-beast and blackguard! Cowardly scamp!
> I only wish I dared burn down the house
> And spoil your sniggering![35]

Chesterton remarks: 'Whence came this extraordinary theory that a man is always speaking most truly when he is speaking most coarsely? The truth about oneself is a very difficult thing to express, and coarse speaking will seldom do it.' [36] There may be less 'nobility' of diction in 'coarse speaking', but is there less dignity? There may be less 'poetic feeling', but is there less poetic force? And 'coarse speaking' doesn't capture all there is to say about these impassioned passages, with their disrupted syntax and ecstatic punctuation (as when Sludge is asphyxiating during his forced confession), their untoward growls and howls of protest. After all, 'Men are not angels, neither are they brutes', as Bishop Blougram says in a moment of truth;[37] they are somewhere in between, an idea often expressed by Browning in his mixed diction and style.

Perhaps the most crystalline example of this is found in 'Soliloquy of the Spanish Cloister' (*Dramatic Lyrics*, 1842), a poem that is both launched and rounded with a growl. At the end of the poem the vespers intrude on the wicked monk's dark meditations: 'there's Vespers! *Plena gratia* / *Ave, Virgo!* Gr-r-r – you swine!' – a fabulously unsettling union of the Latin apostrophe to Holy Mary ('Full of grace / hail, Virgin') and the vicious, scurrilously Saxon oath against the speaker's nemesis, Brother Lawrence: 'Gr-r-r – you swine!'[38] These several instances go some way towards demonstrating the real breviloquence of the Browning gruff, something Elizabeth Barrett praised in a letter to the poet (dated 17 February 1845):

> You have taken a great range – from those high faint notes of the mystics which are beyond personality – to dramatic impersonations, gruff with nature, 'gr-r-r – you swine'; and when these are thrown into harmony, ... the combinations of effect must always be striking and noble – and you must feel yourself drawn on to such combinations more and more.[39]

Chesterton may have been blind to it, but Elizabeth Barrett saw what is 'striking and noble' in Browning's tonal contrasts – and in the very 'gruff' itself.

At home in The Growlery

Just as Browning draws on the Homeric conceit of teeth acting as a fence for unregulated thoughts,[40] Dickens too imagines the impasse of lips, teeth, tongue and throat, in a series of guttural utterances and noises at once constrained and yet startlingly communicative. In the space that remains I'll concentrate on some significant growls and snarls in Dickens, mainly because, more than the grunt, the squeal, the bark, or the groan, these most expressive of sounds suggest passion held at bay (but by no means stifled or checked) by the intellect. It appears to be the case that Dickensian snarls and growls are not so much verbal substitutions (in the manner of 'grrrrrrr') or distortions (in the manner of 'growwwup!') as verbal *intensifiers*. Take the moment in *Great Expectations* (1861) when Joe Gargery's hireling, the 'slouch' Dolge Orlick, lunges at Pip with a hot poker from the forge. Mrs Joe steps in with a barrage of insults ('I couldn't be a match for the rogues, without being a match for you, who are the blackest-looking and the worst rogue between this and France'), to which slur Orlick responds in kind: '"You're a foul shrew, Mother Gargery," growled the journeyman, "If that makes a judge of rogues, you ought to be a good'un"' (*GE*, 1, 15, 114).

Here, the growl is merely reported, pendant in the midst of a suspended quotation. This growl supplies an additional guttural consonant, which augments the four already present in Orlick's speech: 'Gargery', 'makes', 'rogues', 'good'. It shows us what the guttural may do to engender an impassioned (if imprecatory) eloquence, the gruffness and onomatopoeia of which are as much a measure of its aptness and force as more elevated (and less instinctive) rhetorical devices and effects. Aside from his simian 'slouch', his doglike 'growl' and his 'snarl like a tiger', the narrator tells us that 'the only thought [Orlick] ever had, was, that it was rather an odd and injurious fact that he should never be thinking' (*GE*, 1, 15, 112). Injurious indeed, since Orlick is no fool. Orlick's rhetorical flourish, 'If that makes a judge of rogues, you ought to be a good 'un', proves that he has as good a grasp of the silencing effects of the 'If … then' construction as he does of the throttle ('I'd hold you under the pump, and choke it out of you!').

Charles Darwin was increasingly convinced that human beings were not just like animals but showed an unmistakable continuity with animals, as became evident to him in certain shared physical and behavioural characteristics. In *The Expression of the Emotions in Man and Animals* (1872) he writes in a chapter entitled 'Means of Expression in Animals':

> Rage leads to the violent exertion of all the muscles, including those of the voice; and some animals, when enraged, endeavour to strike terror into their enemies by its power and harshness, as the lion does by roaring, and the dog by growling… Rival males try to excel and challenge each other by their voices, and this leads to deadly contests.[41]

The anthropomorphism of Darwin's 'voices' only reinforces his point about there being 'family' traits shared by humans and animals. This is the sense in which Riderhood, and Orlick too, is not simply *like* a vicious beast but distinctly, if distantly, *bestial*. The designated 'growlers' in Dickens – like Bill Sikes, Grimwig and Gamfield (*Oliver Twist*); Scrooge (*A Christmas Carol*); Quilp (*Old Curiosity Shop*); Hugh the handyman and Ned Dennis the hangman (*Barnaby Rudge*); Jonas Chuzzlewit (*Martin Chuzzlewit*); Mr Murdstone (*David Copperfield*); Coavinses (*Bleak House*); Rigaud and Flintwinch (*Little Dorrit*); Orlick and Compeyson (*Great Expectations*); Riderhood and Wegg (*Our Mutual Friend*) – remind us of this bestiality to which we all have access.

None of this is to suggest that the growl is inexpressive. As G. L. Brook rightly says, 'Whenever Dickensian characters are deeply moved, they are liable to make speeches, and this habit is not confined to those who have mastered the principles of English grammar. There are many speeches in which poetic eloquence shines through sub-standard syntax.'[42] Brook cites as examples Mr Plornish and Flora Finching in *Little Dorrit* (1857) and Mr Kenwigs in *Nicholas Nickleby* (1839), but one might just as well cite one of the rogues, a character such as Hannibal Chollop, the pistol-toting, knife-wielding anarchist in *Martin Chuzzlewit* (1844) who terrorises Eden and who, significantly, describes himself in terms of intellect *and* passion, human *and* animal nature:

> 'We are the intellect and virtue of the airth, the cream Of human natur, and the flower Of moral force. Our backs is easy ris. We must be cracked-up, or

they rises, and we snarls. We shows our teeth, I tell you, fierce. You'd better crack us up, you had!' (*MC*, 33, 523)

What has got Chollop's hackles up on this occasion is Mark Tapely's irony, his 'free' way of speaking to (and insulting) his gruff interlocutor, who somehow doesn't believe in freedom of speech ('for the genuine Freedom is dumb, save when she vaunts herself'). Chollop may not realise it, but his expressions are well chosen: both 'teeth' and 'fierce' are words that expose the teeth, vividly animating his barely contained threat.

Then there is the arch-rogue of *Our Mutual Friend* who goes by the name of Rogue Riderhood. He too is a fearsome mishmash of man and beast:

> As the Rogue sat, ever and again nodding himself off his balance, his recovery was always attended by an angry stare and growl, as if, in the absence of any one else, he had aggressive inclinations towards himself. In one of these starts the cry of 'Lock, ho! Lock!' prevented his relapse into a doze. Shaking himself as he got up, like the surly brute he was, he gave his growl a responsive twist at the end, and turned his face down-stream to see who hailed. (*OMF*, IV, 1, 629)

The Rogue is so accustomed to growling that he growls at himself. He not only sounds like a dog, but he moves like one too, 'shaking himself' and sniffing the air in a state of animal alertness. His growl, like that of any intelligent dog, is 'responsive', reactive. When Bradley Headstone comes upon him, hot on the trail of Eugene Wrayburn, the Rogue's 'coolly growled' replies are not *merely* responsive (Bradley himself is wont to grimace and groan); they are a means of regulating a potentially lethal exchange with the schoolteacher, as though his throat were one of the riverine locks that he mans (*OMF*, IV, 1, 631–2). As for Bradley Headstone, despite his basic 'decency' and his 'mechanical' facility, he still has much that is animal in him. Recall, in our first introduction to him, that 'Suppression of so much to make room for so much, had given him a constrained manner, over and above. Yet there was enough of what was animal, and of what was fiery (though smouldering), still visible in him' (II, 1, 217–18).

It is often the case that the 'growlers' in Dickens demand coherency from their interlocutors, which isn't so much a hypocrisy on their part as a demand for the verbal equivalent of the growl – which, in the instantaneity and force of its message, is the shortest cut to communication. Daniel Quilp in *The Old Curiosity Shop* (1841) is able to make himself intelligible *through* his growls, and not *despite* them, as in this characteristic exchange between him and his miserable wife:

'No, but please, Quilp – do hear me speak,' urged his submissive wife, in tears. 'Please do.'

'Speak then,' growled the dwarf with a malicious grin. 'Be quick and short about it. Speak, will you?' (*OCS*, 67, 523)

Abel Magwitch, whose introduction to the reader is without ceremony, makes a comparable demand upon Pip in the opening passages of *Great Expectations*:

> A fearful man, all in coarse gray, with a great iron on his leg. A man with no hat, and with broken shoes, and with an old rag tied round his head. A man who had been soaked in water, and smothered in mud, and lamed by stones, and cut by flints, and stung by nettles, and torn by briars; who limped, and shivered, and glared, and growled; and whose teeth chattered in his head as he seized me by the chin.
>
> 'O! Don't cut my throat, sir,' I pleaded in terror. 'Pray don't do it, sir.'
>
> 'Tell us your name!' said the man. 'Quick!'
>
> 'Pip, sir.'
>
> 'Once more,' said the man, staring at me. 'Give it mouth!' (*GE*, 1, 1, 4)

It is as though the reader (in addition to Pip) needs reminding that this strange creature is indeed 'a man', since the narrator repeats this fact three times in quick succession. This passage is memorable for its nettled, flinty, guttural prose, its paratactic clauses acting as so many stiles for the reader to haul a heavy leg-iron over, its breathless tempo that mimics Pip's experience in order to create a chased narration. The growls of Magwitch literalise his directive to 'give it mouth' – his own mouth (or set of teeth) is just about all we can make out, given his chthonic cover of mud and darkness.[43]

The surprising expressiveness of Dickens's sub-literates is finally revealed in the case of those growlers with a heart of gold, characters such as Magwitch, or Barkis (*David Copperfield*), or Boffin (*Our Mutual Friend*); or, in the case of the gentlemen growlers, Mr Jarndyce (*Bleak House*), the muscular vigour of whose gruffly uttered, participle-rich speeches on the daily grind of Chancery ('We are always appearing, and disappearing, and swearing, and interrogating, and filing, and cross-filing, and arguing, and sealing, and motioning, and referring, and reporting, and revolving' [*BH*, 8, 108]), made to his ward Esther Summerson in 'The Growlery', amount to wooing. (It is worth mentioning here that the female of the species almost never 'growls' in Dickens, with the memorable exception of Mrs Pipchin in *Dombey and Son*, though they certainly do 'screech' and 'hiss'.) In fact, there are a number of gruff, sub-literate courtships in Dickens: the cucumbers lobbed like outsized Cupid's arrows over the fence of the widow Mrs Nickleby;

or, in *Our Mutual Friend*, the nervous overtures made by the mangler Sloppy, whose 'polysyllabic bellow' (*OMF*, I, 16, 202) and 'mellifluous howl' (II, 9, 325) don't deter Jenny Wren from meeting her match in him (IV, 16, 808–11). But perhaps no courtship of this kind is more memorable than that of Peggotty and Barkis, her doggedly persistent suitor, as it is facilitated by young David Copperfield. As Barkis, who 'seemed gruff, and answered drily', explains to David:

> 'When a man says he's willin',' said Mr. Barkis, turning his glance slowly on me again, 'it's as much as to say, that man's a waitin' for a answer.'
> 'Well, Mr. Barkis?'
> 'Well,' said Mr. Barkis, carrying his eyes back to his horse's ears; 'that man's been a waitin' for a answer ever since.'
> 'Have you told her so, Mr. Barkis?'
> 'N – no,' growled Mr. Barkis, reflecting about it. 'I ain't got no call to go and tell her so. I never said six words to her myself. *I* ain't a goin' to tell her so.' (*DC*, 8, 92–3)

It is not just Mr Barkis's eyes that are directed at his horse's ears, but most of his speech too. Nevertheless his message is eventually 'got', and he and Peggotty come together in a union of her thick dialect and his thickly 'growled' 'reflecting'.

The breviloquence of brusque

As a sign of emotional constriction, the growl offers direct access to the channels of communication and, indeed, communion. 'Semantic stoppage' may well have 'engrossed Dickens', as David Trotter powerfully argues, and 'unintelligibility (or mystery)' may have been 'an object of compelling horror' to him.[44] Yet it remains to be said that verbal 'unintelligibility' is not necessarily a block to communication. The strangled medium of the growl *is* more often than not the message. In extraordinary cases, the growl even exceeds the expressive potential of words. Take Pancks, Mr Casby's rent-collector in *Little Dorrit*. Pancks's idiosyncratic 'snarls' and 'snorts' are inventoried by the narrator almost every time Pancks appears – and he appears often. In the course of the novel they undergo a transformation that parallels the moral reformation of their owner, something which can be put down to his blossoming friendship with Arthur Clennam. His snorts, whether 'nasal or bronchial' (*LD*, II, 13, 565), modulate from being 'portentous' (I, 23, 271) to being 'expressive' of 'injury and impatience' and 'a demand for payment' (I, 24, 279), until at last they become 'genuine' (II, 13, 566), so that by the time Clennam announces his destitution, Pancks 'fill[s] up a pause with a groan that came out of the very depths of his soul' (II, 26, 693).

It is certainly true, as John Kucich has suggested, that Dickens's style is excessive, prodigal, ostentatious, and that it signals or 'generalises' the larger unrealities of his work;[45] but it is equally true that there is a style of restraint in Dickens, embodied in the growl/snarl, to which he just as often seeks recourse, and which has become as distinctive as his style of excess. Of course the growl/snarl doesn't have a monopoly on 'restraint'. Vocal restraint in its many varieties – from being lost for words to being all choked up, from holding oneself back to being forcibly held back by means of slapping, or strangling, or even paralysis – emerges in disturbances to syntax and punctuation too, as we have seen. So marked is this tendency in Dickens that Sheila M. Foor has reckoned: '[i]n virtually every case, a person *is* his or her voice.'[46] Even London itself is asphyxiating, according to Robert Alter, on a 'gigantic catarrh' (*OMF*, III, 1, 420) of Dickens's manufacture.[47]

Dickens proves wrong his many critics who charge him with the kind of limited grotesquerie that is built merely on exaggeration, the kind of grotesquerie that fails to unite human and animal, chthonic and angelic, passion and intellect, the manifest and the suppressed, the Latinate and the localised. Remarkably, Dickens, like Byron and Browning, maintains the paradox of man's 'mix'd essence', 'half dust, half deity',[48] and not merely by means of random or casual adjacency but by a conscious effort at aural grotesqueness. To end, I'd like to invoke the wonderfully grotesque Mr Plornish, who has 'a prolix, gently-growling, foolish way' about him (*LD*, I, 12, 137). Plornish must be one of the few 'prolix' growlers in Dickens; however, being the composite creature that he is, he is also truly representative of the lot of them. For which other group can, like Plornish, 'amiably growl' in a 'philosophical but not lucid manner' (II, 27, 712)? For Dickens, to allow the guttural to become a growl or snarl is not to thwart meaning and unleash the animal within; it is to harmonise; it is to philosophise; it is, finally, to fence in what is best left behind the teeth while at the same time treating one's auditor to more than a little taste of it.

NOTES

I would like to express my sincere thanks to Daniel Tyler and Alex Dougherty for reading drafts of this chapter and making very helpful suggestions.

1 George Gordon Byron, *Beppo* (1818), in *The Poetical Works of Byron*, ed. Robert F. Gleckner (Boston, MA: Houghton-Mifflin, 1975), 440–52, at 445.

2 The critics who refer to Dickens's style as 'grotesque' or 'monstrous' are legion. See *CH*, 140, 228, 257, 338, 350–1, 406–7, 444, 455, 470, 491, 494, 573. Garrett Stewart, in his monograph *Charles Dickens and the Trials of Imagination* (Cambridge, MA: Harvard University Press, 1974), discusses Dickens's alternation between the 'lyric' and the 'neurotic' styles (xv).

3 See John Kucich, *Excess and Restraint in the Novels of Charles Dickens* (Athens, GA: University of Georgia Press, 1982).

4 See Sheila Foor's chapter on 'Sympathy: The Silent Rhetoric' in her monograph *Dickens' Rhetoric* (New York: Peter Lang, 1993), 127–34; and David Trotter, 'Circulation, Interchange, Stoppage: Dickens and Social Progress', in Robert Giddings (ed.), *The Changing World of Charles Dickens* (London: Vision Press, 1983), 163–79.

5 See Mark Lambert, *Dickens and the Suspended Quotation* (New Haven, CT: Yale University Press, 1981) for an account of what occurs within this internecine space of suspension – typically an arena for the competitive assertions of an oftentimes jealous narrator.

6 The *OED* tells us that 'snarl' and 'growl' both have Germanic origins and are, respectively, 'probably of imitative origin' and 'probably an echoic formation'.

7 *CH*, 81.

8 See *CH*, 81, 83.

9 *CH*, 72.

10 See Anne Lohrli's *Household Words: A Weekly Journal, 1850–59* (Toronto: University of Toronto Press, 1973), 114. This volume is a typescript of the *Household Words* office book, which chronologically lists the names of contributors as well as their payments. See also Lohrli's biographical sketch of Sala in this volume (421–3), in which she quotes from a letter by Dickens to William Henry Wills about Sala: 'There is nobody about us whom we can use, in his way, more advantageously than this young man' (27 September 1851), 422.

11 George Sala, 'Slang', *Household Words*, 24 September 1853, 73.

12 See the introduction to Josephine M. Guy (ed.), *The Victorian Age: An Anthology of Sources and Documents* (London: Routledge, 1998), 19, in which she pinpoints the 'introduction of a new kind of vocabulary into explanations of social behaviour – one of health and disease, progress and degeneration'.

13 Sala, 'Slang', 73.

14 For the Parable of the Wheat and Tares, sometimes called the Parable of the Weeds, see Matthew 13:24–30. I am grateful to Daniel Tyler for bringing this allusion to my attention.

15 'A Preliminary Word', *Household Words*, 1 (1) (30 March 1850), 1.

16 Stewart, *Dickens and the Trials of Imagination*, 12.

17 Consultation of Lohrli's *Household Words*, 182, reveals that Rushton and Morley co-authored this article. Technically, the error is not Stewart's, but rather W. F. Bolton's and David Crystal's, whose anthology *The English Language: Essays by Linguists and Men of Letters*, vol. II: *1858–1964* (Cambridge University Press, 1969) opens with 'Saxon-English' *by Charles Dickens* [sic]. See 1–7.

18 [William Rushton and Henry Morley], 'Saxon-English', *Household Words*, 18, 10 July 1858, 89–92, at 89.

19 Quoted in Edgar Johnson, *Charles Dickens: His Tragedy and Triumph* (New York: Viking, 1977), 358.

20 [Rushton and Morley], 'Saxon-English', 91. The authors drew this information from Richard Trench's *On the Study of Words*, 2nd edn (1851) (London: Parker, 1855).

21 Nicholas Howe, '*Beowulf* in the House of Dickens', in Katherine O'Brien O'Keeffe and Andy Orchard (eds.), *Latin Learning and English Lore: Studies in Anglo-Saxon Literature for Michael Lapidge*, 2 vols. (University of Toronto Press, 2005), I, 421–39. See especially 421–3.

22 The editor uses the text of 1868. For further instances of characters who criticise each other's speech habits, see G. L. Brook, *The Language of Dickens* (London: André Deutsch, 1970), 66–71, 176.

23 Robert Golding, *Idiolects in Dickens: The Major Techniques and Chronological Developments* (New York: St Martin's Press, 1985), 10.

24 Most likely James Fitzjames Stephen, *Saturday Review* (8 May 1858), quoted in *CH*, 383.

25 Quoted in *CH*, 187, 188.

26 Quoted in *CH*, 200.

27 See, respectively, Stewart, *Dickens and the Trials of Imagination*, 11–12; and Jon Mee, *The Cambridge Introduction to Charles Dickens* (Cambridge University Press, 2010), 24. Both acknowledge that such pairings are not coincidental but part of the larger attempt of the novels to marry the 'high' and the 'low'.

28 David Lodge, 'The Rhetoric of *Hard Times*', in *The Language of Fiction: Essays in Criticism and Verbal Analysis of the English Novel* (London: Routledge & Kegan Paul, 1966), 147.

29 Ian Watt, 'Oral Dickens', *Dickens Studies Annual*, 3 (1974): 165–81, at 176.

30 Watt, 'Oral Dickens', 179.

31 See Malcolm Andrews, *Charles Dickens and His Performing Selves* (Oxford University Press, 2006), 237: 'Some research has detected minute tremors in the musculature of the throat in studies of the activity of silent reading – so-called subvocalization of the text being read.' Andrews is describing what he calls the 'affective' (as distinct from the 'interpretative') 'energy' of reading/ reading to oneself, which he likens to the orientation of the actor to his or her script.

32 See Mee, *The Cambridge Introduction to Charles Dickens*, 21, and Patricia Ingham, 'The Language of Dickens', in David Paroissien (ed.), *A Companion to Charles Dickens* (Oxford: Blackwell, 2008), 126–41, at 126.

33 Michael Hollington, 'Dickens's Conception of the Grotesque', *Dickensian*, 76 (1980): 91–9, at 95.

34 G. K. Chesterton, *Robert Browning* (London: Macmillan & Co.; New York: St Martin's Press, 1967), 151.

35 Quoted in Chesterton, *Robert Browning*, 198.

36 Chesterton, *Robert Browning*, 199.

37 Robert Browning, 'Bishop Blougram's Apology' (1863), l. 864, in *Poems of Browning*, eds. John Woolford, Daniel Karlin and Joseph Phelan, vol. III: *1847–1861* (London: Pearson-Longman, 2007), 153–213, at 205. The poem was originally published in *Men and Women* in 1855; however, in 1863 Browning revised this line, which in the first edition read: 'Men are not gods, but, properly, are brutes.'

38 Robert Browning, 'Soliloquy of the Spanish Cloister', in *Poems of Browning*, eds. John Woolford and Daniel Karlin, vol. II: *1841–1846* (Harlow: Longman, 1991), 167–172, at 172.

39 *Robert Browning and Elizabeth Barrett: The Courtship Correspondence, 1845–1846*, ed. Daniel Karlin (Oxford University Press, 1990), 19. See also Danny Karlin's introduction to Robert Browning, *Selected Poetry*, ed. Daniel Karlin (London: Penguin, 1989), 14.

40 See Browning's poem 'Donald' (*Jocoseria*, 1883), in *Selected Poetry*, ed. Daniel Karlin (London: Penguin, 1989), 291:

> For, as Homer would say, 'within grate
> Though teeth kept tongue', my whole soul growled
> 'Rightly rewarded, – Ingrate!'

41 Charles Darwin, *The Expression of the Emotions in Man and Animals* (London: John Murray, 1872), 85.

42 Brook, *The Language of Dickens*, 171.

43 I owe thanks to Alex Dougherty for pointing out to me the proximity of the chthonic and the 'grotesque' (from the Italian *grottesco* or *grotta* = grotto, cave).

44 Trotter, 'Circulation, Interchange, Stoppage', 170.

45 John Kucich, 'Dickens's Fantastic Rhetoric: The Semantics of Reality and Unreality in *Our Mutual Friend*', *Dickens Studies Annual*, 14 (1985): 167–89, at 174.

46 Foor, *Dickens' Rhetoric*, 104. See also Ingham, 'The Language of Dickens', 127–8.

47 Robert Alter, 'Reading Style in Dickens', *Philosophy and Literature*, 20 (1) (1996): 130–7, at 136.

48 George Gordon Byron, *Manfred*, I, ii, ll. 302, 301, in *The Poetical Works of Byron*, ed. Robert F. Gleckner (Boston, MA: Houghton-Mifflin, 1975), 478–97, at 482.

CHAPTER NINE

Compound interest: Dickens's figurative style

Jennifer Gribble

The improvisatory self-delighting flamboyance of Dickens's style does not always unequivocally delight his readers. The style is the man, and the man, more often than not, is a showman, who seems to intrude on his fictional world and give the game away. What's more, the pleasure he takes in self-presentation seems to set at odds Dickens the popular entertainer and Dickens the man with a message. This, according to Robert Garis, has always been 'the Dickens problem'. George Gissing, whom Garis enlists in his own rather sterner judgements, reads the opening of *Bleak House* as a case in point: 'This darkness visible makes one rather cheerful than otherwise, for we are in the company of a man who does nothing to baulk his enjoyment of life.'[1]

Much of the brio of the famous opening is generated by what Hillis Miller describes as the novel's 'deep grammatical armature': the metaphor, metonymy and synecdoche unfolding in its dense figural play.[2] Brought into instantaneous connection are the live issues and contending discourses of the day, in a series of interrelated metaphors that build the overarching metaphor of Chancery, yielding interest-bearing deposits, if no secure foothold, for a readership fascinated by the hypotheses of geology, palaeontology and cosmology, while inclined to believe in the God who sent the Flood.

This ground has proved as fertile for deconstruction as for the matrix-of-analogy-affirming New Criticism of an earlier Hillis Miller. The mud accumulating at 'compound interest' in the streets of London seems to make an ambivalent metaphor, signifying not only the defilements of a 'great (and dirty) city' (*BH* I, II), the money-grubbing of grandfather Smallweed ('the name of this old pagan's God was Compound Interest' [21, 307]), and the 'mountains of costly nonsense' documenting the 'family misfortune' of the Jarndyces. It signifies, as well, the polysemous life of the novel itself.

If the deep grammatical armature carries an argument, it seems full of puzzles and paradoxes. A Megalosaurus waddling up Holborn Hill makes a surprise appearance in 'the mud left by the deluge that should have exterminated him'.[3] The High Court of Chancery may by association represent 'the darkest abyss of ancient blindness and primitive futility',[4] but it will become 'the organizing metaphor of the novel'.[5] The pervasive November fog, now substance, now process, seems an unstable signifier for Chancery's carceral power.[6] Hillis Miller's influential account of *Bleak House* concludes that its style confesses that meaning is only 'a tissue of loose ends and questions'.[7]

Discussion of the polysemy of Dickens's style has been enlarged by Mikhail Bakhtin's theory of the inherently dialogic or polyphonic play of novelistic discourse. Underlying that theory, however, is a philosophy of creation articulated in his earliest essays and returned to in late revisions, elaborating a theological subtext that draws on a Judaeo-Christian world view.[8] Based on the inherently evaluative nature of perception,[9] and in specificity of context and uniqueness of being, it involves the mutually ethical development of author, character and reader.[10] In his 'responsible consciousness',[11] the author displays his activity and agency in 'questioning, provoking, answering, agreeing', entering onto the stage of his creation as a participant, one who is 'the reader's authoritative guide present in the work'.[12] This sounds remarkably like the 'guide, philosopher and friend' Dickens aimed to be for his readers.[13] In the later novels, metaphor operates with increasing complexity and allusiveness to engage the reader's interpretative activity in the dynamic 'thinking more' it stimulates.[14] The polysemy of metaphor may be, in this regard, difficult to control and liable to search out and entertain ambivalent feelings in the writer. But in *Bleak House* metaphor sustains a coherent, ethically engaged argumentative play during which the reader is directed by the witty and well-informed authorial personality conveyed stylistically: a 'third presence' affirming the Judaeo-Christian world view Dickens shares with Bakhtin, invoked in the novel's network of biblical allusions. Bakhtin's insights suggest how the teleological work of metaphor might connect with the 'Christian Humanism' Hillis Miller notes in John Jarndyce and Esther Summerson and with what he takes to be unresolved authorial belief in 'some extra-human source of value, a stable centre outside the human game'.[15]

This chapter considers Dickens's figurative style as 'responsible consciousness', the third presence Bakhtin finds indispensable to the realisation of dialogue. Strongly characterised by recognisable authorial personality, the mature style represented in *Bleak House* functions as companion and guide through the novel's physical and discursive landscape. It identifies The Inimitable wearing the flimsy mask of 'omniscient narrator', bringing together his roles as journalist, reformer and upholder of Christian beliefs and values.[16] The rhetorical insistence of rhythm and repetition, crescendo and diminuendo, the alternations of sympathy and satire, the transformation of observed detail and recollected phrase into the metaphoric and thence into the sequencing of metonymy, all display a presence it seems only right to call 'Dickens'. Essential to the enjoyment of the self-presentation is the democratic and populist appeal to an assured audience in the public space Dickens has made his own and the intellectual energy he brings to its debate. The narrator who would take off the rooftops in Chapter 47 of *Dombey and Son* now commands an expansive view of the city and the home counties, flying as the crow flies, penetrating with the fog, floating higher than Asmodeus, that avatar of omniscience, 'in a balloon, and hanging in the misty clouds' (*BH*, 1, 11).[17] But if we find ourselves in the company of an observer getting high on his own conceits, we are also required to engage with the process of analogical thinking announced in its opening staccato reportage: 'LONDON. Michaelmas Term lately over, and the Lord Chancellor sitting in Lincoln's Inn Hall. Implacable November weather' (1, 11).

Brought into association by the transferred epithet 'implacable' are November's mud and fog, annual visitations aggravated by industrial pollution, as well as the 'implacable' dispensations of the supreme Lawgiver brooding over the face of the waters and the sitting in judgement of his parodic deputy, the Lord Chancellor. This specificity of context grounds in the local and temporal the figural play that shapes Chancery as a representation of the human condition. Dickens's own recent experience of the systematised injustice and procrastination of the court,[18] and his support of *The Times* campaign for its reform, inflects a sustained grumble about the weather in the streets with a degree of score-settling and fuels its hyperbole. Brooding over his scene, Dickens homes in on the metaphoric possibilities of the public institution, initiating that phase of his late writing in which metaphor is exploited as a mode of social enquiry and a way of structuring the expanding universe of his novels.

Humankind is held subject, from the outset, to a threefold system of laws: the laws of nature (in which natural theology, in the wake of *The Bridgewater Treatises*, is still attempting to discern the 'Power, Wisdom and Goodness of God Manifested in his Creation'),[19] together with the law that so conspicuously fails to deliver equity in the Court of Chancery

and the now disputed laws of a Creator God. The ground of the analogy
is inescapable condition, but its work is to make out of local topography
a revelation of assured destination. In a climate suspicious of analogy as
a producer of stable meaning, analogy is nevertheless indispensable to
emergent scientific discourse, as Gillian Beer has demonstrated.[20] The
laws of a normative nature provide metaphor with a stabilising ballast,
for Dickens as for the natural theologians who feed his opportunistic
imagination and whose traces are everywhere apparent in this opening
chapter. Fresh in his mind as he begins to write the novel is his review
of Robert Hunt's *The Poetry of Science*, with its beguiling story of 'the
great stone book which is the history of the earth itself', guaranteed to
awaken, as the reviewer astutely sees, 'an interest and spirit of enquiry in
many minds ... a reading public – not exclusively scientific or philosophical'.[21] Chambers's *Vestiges of the Natural History of Creation* (1840), which
Dickens's review defends against Hunt, and John Pringle Nichol's *Views
of the Architecture of the Heavens* (1836), from which Hunt quotes, provide
ways of thinking about the environmental nuisance of mud and fog that
are informed by evolutionary theory. Competing views of the world's creation are absorbed and set in play in the novel that follows. But whereas
in the law-governed universe of Nichol, for example, the 'supernatural',
unlike the natural, could not be understood,[22] the Almighty has made
Himself reasonably clear to Dickens in the Bible. This does not prevent
a quizzical look at what implacable weather reveals about divine intentions for our comfort: the genial mood that lightens the 'darkness visible'
is sufficiently confident in its theology to enjoy 'questioning, provoking,
answering, agreeing'.

In the grasped instant of local time begins the figural play Gissing finds
incompatible with the intended Miltonic solemnity of 'darkness visible'.
But the making visible is entirely compatible with the degrees of freedom available within apparently determining condition. The *medias res* of
Chancery, the human misery of 'being-in-time',[23] is experienced as lived
moment, created in the succession of present-participial verbs beating
their way through the passage: 'sitting', 'waddling', 'lowering', 'lying', 'jostling', 'adding' (*BH*, 1, 11). The 'chance' element in Chancery, embodied in
the 'chance people' who compete for urban space, proleptic of the novel's
myriad plot connections and coincidences, suggests openness to possibility. As though prompted by instantaneity, the aeons of time opened up by
new scientific speculation initiate the questioning process of responsible
consciousness. The street mud, 'which is made of nobody knows what,
and collects about us nobody knows whence or how' grounds solemnity

in a sly scatological humour, preparing the way for the 'kindred mystery' of law and equity (10, 150), that polysemic recycling of civilisation's waste.

Complaint escalates into hyperbole: 'As much mud in the streets as if the waters had but newly retired from the face of the earth, and it would not be wonderful to see a Megalosaurus, forty feet long or so, waddling like an elephantine lizard up Holborn Hill' (*BH*, 1, 11). Shifting backwards and forwards in time, heuristic fiction lightens the gloom, in a simile holding simultaneously in view humankind's *fons et origo*[24] in the sea (a reminder that London, too, has been, and still is, one of the dark places of the earth), and the discursive climate in which that origin is disputed territory. Awash with metaphor, this swampy expanse of contemporary discourse provides Dickens with the makings for metaphors of his own. Indeed, metaphors of his own are recycled from the mud and the fog that figure in the *Mudfog Papers* (1837–8). The compound mud-fog, coined in an article for *Bentley's Miscellany* in 1837, develops from the descriptive for a seaside town, in the January edition, to a metaphoric representation of systematised absurdity and obfuscation by the October edition, in 'The Mudfog Association for the Advancement of Everything'. Anticipated in the doings of the Pickwick Club, this early satire on the British Association for the Advancement of Science is not prepared to give to such advancement the focused attention Dickens gives it in the opening of *Bleak House*. The separated components of the waters, the mud and the fog, have now become productive sources of enquiry. The allusion to 'newly-retired waters' invokes the *terra firma* of biblical authority, though its orderly phrase accommodates both the creator God who separates land from sea in Genesis 1:3 and the admonitory God who causes the flood to retreat in Genesis 17. But it also accommodates the debate about whether the successive violent inundations proposed in Lyell's *Principles of Geology*, for example, might somehow be reconciled with universalist claims for the biblical deluge.[25]

The Megalosaurus appears in the modern metropolis as an apparently incidental improvisation. Yet it ushers in one of Dickens's most sustained and complex sequences of thought, effectively challenging the persistent view that 'the world of thought' lay beyond his horizon.[26] There is reason to believe that he purloined from his friend Leigh Hunt the association of prehistoric monster, mud and the London streets, a belief supported, perhaps, by his appropriation of aspects of Hunt's personality in the depiction of Harold Skimpole. Hunt's book on London, *The Town: Its Memorable Characters and Events* (1848), which imagines London before the Deluge, writes of a pedestrian who notices nothing 'except the mud through which he has passed'. It invites its readers to step back 'to a period before the creation of man, when creatures vaster than any now on dry land trampled the earth at will'.[27]

Dickens may be seen to comply with this invitation, though his figuration domesticates the monster. Comic animation, that staple of Dickensian style, fashions a figure the syntax allows us to see that it both would and 'would not be wonderful' to meet face to face: a figure of topical awe and wonder in its way, though quite devoid of the threat to secure belief posed for the near-contemporaneous Tennyson, whose 'dragons of the prime' 'tare each other in their slime'.[28] The Megalosaurus sculptures made by Benjamin Waterhouse Hawkins for the Great Exhibition of 1851 (based on the papier-mâché mock-ups made by Robert Owen, following the discovery of its bones, and its naming, by Willliam Buckland) have already transformed the dinosaur into an emblem of scientific progress, in line with the national forward-thinking celebrated in the Exhibition.[29] A certain ambivalence about that great celebration is perhaps reflected in the way the dinosaur's amiable waddling gait mocks the March of Mind. Drawing on Buckland's description of an 'elephantine lizard' estimated to 'exceed forty feet' in length,[30] Dickens stages a resurrection of his own. Tamed by its kinship with those more highly evolved descendants, the elephant and lizard, this reptile is street-wise as well, successfully negotiating one of London's notorious traffic black spots, Holborn Hill.[31] Its journey to the top of the nearest hill enjoys a witty engagement with the theories of Cuvier. Natural theology's embattled position with regard to fossil bones, mountain tops and Noah's flood was addressed by Cuvier's conjecture of a final 'general subsidence of the sea level ... which left, in northern countries, the bodies of great quadrupeds encased in ice and preserved with their skin, hair and flesh down to our own times'.[32] Thawed by the incessant rain, Dickens's Megalosaurus is imaginatively disinterred, surviving the flood that should have annihilated it because it is essentially a whimsical representation of uncertain and disputed chronology. And while it belongs in the narrative of 'the great stone book', updating and upstaging the serpent in God's garden, and the animal life that survives Noah's flood, it is co-opted by the irrepressible and well-informed consciousness that makes a third presence in the debate, waddling into the eternal present of evolving interpretation. If the Megalosaurus makes a pre-emptive strike against Chancery's anachronism and its gargantuan mindlessness, it is also quite at home in the biblical narrative that begins to shape the Chancery metaphor.

As the Megalosaurus waddles upwards, the fog is 'lowering down', in a verb animated with dark intent. Inherently evaluative, as Bakhtin proposes, perception is conveyed in the upward-downward, backwards-forwards, in-and-out movement sustained throughout the chapter, as in each of its metaphors. The dark matter of primeval swamp now becomes airborne, in a metaphor generated by London's notorious November fogs: 'Smoke lowering down from chimney-pots, making a soft black drizzle with flakes of soot in it as big as full-grown snowflakes – gone into mourning, one might imagine, for the death of the sun' (*BH*, 1, 11). This abrupt reversal of the divine *fiat lux* continues to hold in focus the threefold system of laws evoked at the outset, in which natural laws that should reveal the creator's law-governed universe are violated by the failure of man-made laws apparent in the fog. Fed by furnaces and coal fires, these November fogs produced such quantities of soot and black smoke that they had become, as Mayhew reports, the subject of a House of Commons enquiry.[33] This interchange is magically suggested in the conceit of 'flakes of soot … as big as full-grown snow-flakes – gone into mourning', a transaction in which blackness is irradiated by the pristine white of snow, that purest and gentlest of fallings, and snow is perverted at source, in the very moment of precipitation. There is a pastoral world beyond this London November, metonymically evoked throughout the novel and brought to the forefront of consciousness here as a world we are losing. The natural authority of the sun, seen in the third paragraph 'to loom by husbandman and ploughboy' in the 'spongey fields', is usurped in the city by the premature lighting of the gas, 'two hours before its time', 'as the gas seems to know, for it has a haggard and unwilling look' (1, 12). The 'London particular' that greets Esther Summerson, fresh from the country, and bringing into prevailing bleakness the warmth of 'summer' 'sun' makes 'night in the day-time' (3, 38) in the guttering candles of Kenge and Carboy. The black drizzle that lowers down here will generate a whole procession of synecdochic legal sad-sacks and obfuscators, including Chizzle and Mizzle.

The 'death of the sun' has more sinister implications, of course, though the pun on 'mourning' ('morning', 'tiers') seems to continue the whimsy of the conceit. Dickens clearly has in mind the work of Nichol and Chambers, and makes use of it again in the second paragraph. Chambers, in his evolutionary model of creation, relies as Nichol does on the 'nebular hypothesis' of Laplace, in which the solar system emerges from clouds of magellanic vapour to which it will eventually return. Dickens follows Chambers in reconciling the sun's unimaginable ending with natural law, to which he adds biblical prophecy. The case against industrial pollution is empowered by contemporary scientific discourse, and it is also supported by the biblical grand narrative. The opening of Revelation's Sixth Seal, 'when the sun became black as sackcloth of hair' (Revelation 6:12), is anticipated in Old Testament apocalyptic imagery: in the 'pillar of smoke' that accompanies the darkening of the sun in Old Testament prophesies of the destruction of cities, foretelling the coming of 'the great and terrible day of the Lord', and the sackcloth and ashes of Job, 'mourning without the sun' (Job 30:28).[34] Apocalyptic warning is continued in the metonymies of Miss Flite's troubled understandings of 'the Great Seal' and her expectations of 'judgement', in the death of Lady Dedlock, sun of the solar system of fashionable intelligence, in the *memento mori* of Krook's sacks of the hair of dead ladies, hoarded in a room 'nearly black with soot, and grease, and dirt' (*BH*, 10, 151), and in the transformation of 'the sheep … into parchment, the goats into wigs, and the pasture into chaff' (42, 611).

Present-day survivors of the deluge, armed with umbrellas, experience their survival at the end of the first paragraph, in evolutionary metaphors of struggle and competition: in endurance, continuity, adaptation. Well before Darwin, Malthus had found the workings of nature in population's 'iron law'. Competing for urban space are foot-passengers, dogs and horses, sustaining a capitalist economy at compound interest, sharing a biological inheritance as well as a physical environment. Like the horses, 'splashed to their very blinkers' by foul weather, pedestrians at the mercy of the elements suffer the blinkered vision of their 'general infection of ill-temper', a metaphor that prepares the way for the fever that spreads as physical and moral contagion from Chancery's neglected property, Tom-all-Alone's. The battle enacted in the warfare of jostling umbrellas responds to the bustle of the streets, but it is weighed against 'losing their foothold'. Included, syntactically, in the muddy accretions that stick at points 'tenaciously', the foot-passengers and the 'tens of thousands of other foot-passengers who have preceded them' will shortly become the 'tens of thousands of stages in an endless cause' as the High Court of Chancery is discovered at its business in the 'very heart of the fog'. 'Slipping and sliding since the day broke (if this day ever broke)' (*BH*, 1, 11), humankind is prone to falling, because of, or despite, the litigiousness and the tenacity of purpose that feeds its restless energy. The hyperbole of grumble seems to question, and then to reverse, the creation story, fast-backwarding from the death of the sun to the moment of creation in Genesis 1:3, when God separates land from sea, day from night ('evening and morning were the first day'). But the creation story is also the story of the Fall, and it begins to inflect the Chancery metaphor with all the questions about moral accountability generated by foul conditions and existential bewilderment.

Emerging from the slime, and barely distinguishable from it and each other, these descendants of the Megalosaurus represent the more complex organisms in the evolutionary process Chambers reads in the geological record. Dickens follows Chambers in dignifying mud as the material composition legible in 'the great stone book', but he also seizes with delight on mud as the great leveller. The blow Chambers dealt to 'special creation' gave to the animate life of the biblical ark a kinship too close for the comfort of the British Association for the Advancement of Science. The struggle in the streets anticipates both the victims and the perpetrators of Chancery's interminable process. In making his case against the systematised neglect and destitution of children in the Chancery world, Dickens enjoys the hypothesis that made Chambers's name anathema to the religious establishment of his time: that mental, and even moral, powers are not unique to humans.

The dogs that share the mud with foot-passengers are individuated as the dog that shares urban space with Jo, a 'human boy' (dignified as such by the Revd Chadband) (*BH*, 25, 377), whose work is to sweep away the mud left on a crossing, enabling foot-passengers to survive in 'dirty weather' (16, 235). The drover's dog is 'probably on a par' with the boy, both of them listening to music played by the band on market day and 'with much the same amount of animal satisfaction' (16, 238). For this is a dog who rejoices in evolutionary upward movement: 'a thoroughly vagabond dog, accustomed to low company and public-houses; a terrific dog to sheep', but also 'an educated, improved, developed dog, who has been taught his duties and knows how to discharge them' (16, 238). The political radicalism feared by the opponents of Chambers is knowingly exploited by the juxtaposition. Jo, who 'don't know nothink', to whom the higher-order activities of meaning-making are indecipherable, is more closely aligned to 'the other lower animals' (16, 237) that pass him by, 'blinded ... over-goaded, over-driven, never guided' (237) and destined for imminent slaughter.

As with the metaphoric expansiveness of mud, so with the fog. Splenetic complaint is prolonged at the start of the second paragraph by the hammer blows of repetition: 'Fog everywhere ... Fog ... Fog ... Fog ... Fog ... Fog' (*BH*, 1, 11). Fog, too, is a great leveller. Its tentacular reach penetrates the smallest of human spaces, levels of the social hierarchy and ages of man: from the 'eyes and throats of ancient Greenwich pensioners, wheezing by the firesides of their wards', to 'the stem and bowl of the afternoon

pipe of the wrathful skipper down in his close cabin' (*BH*, I, II) and the
interstices of the fingers and toes of his shivering little 'prentice boy on
deck. It is carried in a cruel alliance between November weather and urban
pollution. The coal fires that warm the pensioners infect their lungs; the
untreated sewage that transforms river mist into noxious vapour makes
the arterial system of London's great river a running sewer.[35] The fog that
is defiled by the riverside industry of collier-brigs, barges and small boats,
defiles in turn the tiers of shipping that will colonise the 'green aits and
meadows' of the Essex marshes and the Kentish heights, and beyond, into
the furthest reaches of Empire. The Dickens who marvels during an 1850
visit to the Bank of England at 'the mighty heart of active capital, through
whose arteries and veins flows the entire circulating medium of this great
country',[36] finds a very different use for the metaphor of circulation in the
fictional context of the novel he is about to write. In stark contrast with
Wordsworth's view from the bridge in 1802, the river now glides not 'at
its own sweet will', but is propelled by that very 'active capital' Dickens is
sometimes disposed to salute.[37]

For the 'chance people on the bridges peeping over the parapets into a
nether sky of fog, with fog all round them, as if they were up in a balloon,
and hanging in the misty clouds' (*BH*, I, II), the effect of the fog is as disorienting as the entropic pull of the mud. But the enchanted cloudland created by the fog searches out further ambivalence in the consciousness of
the writer. The simile of the balloon, which seems as whimsically imported
into the scene as the Megalosaurus, precisely recalls the exhilaration of
'Ballooning', in R. H. Horne's recent article for *Household Words*,[38] and
the new perspectives and vantage points made available by technological
advance: the gas fuelling this aerial 'progress' is by no means 'haggard and
unwilling'. On the other hand, the metaphor of a newly created world
of clouds, a 'nether world' of magellanic vapour, drawing almost directly
on the metaphors of Nichol, is a land of 'clouds and doubts', an image of
metaphysical speculation in which 'the solid ground of fact and observation is rapidly retiring from beneath us'.[39] Caught up in foggy pollution,
suspended in a narrative they are unable to understand, in competing
stories of origins that tell of endings, yet still committed to 'progress' and
buoyed up by expectation, the foot-passengers and chance people are, like
the whole population of Victorian England, 'in Chancery' from the very
beginning.

In a final flurry of hyperbole, responsible consciousness rests its case:
'never can there come fog too thick, never can there come mud and mire
too deep, to assort with the groping and floundering condition which

this High Court of Chancery, most pestilent of hoary sinners, holds, this day, in the sight of heaven and earth' (*BH*, 1, 12). As descriptive and allusive overview narrows to close focus, the metaphors of mud and fog are re-energised as weapons of satire. And the associative process through which figural play has been shaping the Chancery metaphor, and guiding the reader to a stabilising teleology, is now triumphantly elaborated: 'On such an afternoon, if ever, the Lord Chancellor ought to be sitting here – as here he is – with a foggy glory round his head' (1, 12). The rhetoric exults in its crowning syllogism: the 'ought to be – as here they are', 'ought-to-be – as are they not' (1, 12) formulation and the subsequently repeated 'well may', invests the professional and moral obligation of 'ought' with the inevitability of befoggment. It carries the judgement that the 'groping and floundering condition' of the foot-passengers in the streets and the chance people on the bridge belongs in the same inescapable narrative of fallen humankind as Chancery, 'most pestilent of hoary sinners'. That narrative, privileged in the play of metaphor in the opening paragraphs, becomes the vantage point from which the satiric representation of Chancery unfolds.

Contested biblical authority is invoked in the 'foggy glory' that deifies the Lord Chancellor and invests his court and its rituals with religious mystery. Dickens's satire responds to the perception that by the early nineteenth century, religion is being replaced as supreme ideology by the rule of law in which property is deified and made the measure of all things.[40] Established to dispense equity and to defend the property rights of those emblematic biblical figures the widow and the orphan, Chancery has become legendary for its 'decaying houses and its blighted lands in every shire' (*BH*, 1, 13). And the reach of the Chancery metaphor is equally tentacular, bringing with it the compound interest of a diversity of people and places, transforming Victorian England into one vast Bleak House, a decaying property housing a dysfunctional human family. The falling tenements of Tom-all-Alone's breed 'a crowd of foul existence that crawls in and out of gaps in walls and boards; and coils itself to sleep, in maggot numbers, where the rain drips in; and comes and goes, fetching and carrying fever' (16, 236). The history of the property, which is, of course, 'in Chancery', is popularly linked to the Tom Jarndyce who blew his brains out but is now home to Jo the crossing-sweeper. And it is a repository for the hidden history of Lady Dedlock, her lover Nemo and their illegitimate daughter Esther, all of them infected by the misfortunes of Jo. The pollution spread through mud and fog will bring the fever that kills Jo and disfigures Esther, enabled by the neglect of England's lords and gentlemen and their factotums, the whole tribe of ineffectual self-serving lawyers who 'lie like maggots in nuts' (10, 145).[41]

Hard by Temple Bar, enclosed in his sanctuary of crimson cloth and curtains, the Lord Chancellor presides over a failed *fiat lux,* in which 'wasting candles' are losing their battle against the darkness and stained-glass windows can only let the darkness in. Looking upwards, as Christ has commanded ('look up, for your redemption draweth nigh', Luke 21:28), he peers into a lantern that 'has no light in it', 'where he can see nothing but fog' (*BH*, 1, 12). Looking down, the synecdochic 'silk gowns' (1, 12) seem in their repeated address ('Mlud', 'Mlud') to splash at him the very street mud. Devoid of significant agency, they are ranged in a 'long matted well (but you might look in vain for Truth at the bottom of it)' (1, 12). On home ground with the clubbable self-important pomposities and theatrics of the courtroom, Dickens enjoys its 'pretence of equity' (1, 12). But the eloquent and learned Mr Tangle, and the 'eighteen of Mr Tangle's learned friends, each armed with a little summary of eighteen hundred sheets' (1, 15), who 'bob up like eighteen hammers in a pianoforte, make eighteen bows, and drop into their eighteen places of obscurity' (15–16), 'as players might' (12), are occasionally known to issue a warning: '"Suffer any wrong that can be done to you, rather than come here!"' (13). Responsible consciousness sees the absurdity of Chancery's procedures, while the faint echo of Dante's *Inferno* ('Abandon hope all ye who enter here') invokes the cultural authority of grand narrative to condemn its soul-destroying effects. Echoed, as well, are Dickens's reflections on his own recent Chancery experience ('My feeling ... is that it is better to suffer a great wrong than to have recourse to the much greater wrong of the law')[42] and the resounding judgement of *The Times* on 28 March 1851: 'To the common apprehension of Englishmen the Court of Chancery is a name of terror, a devouring gulf, a den whence no footsteps return.'[43] Abstracted from the comic play, an escalating sequence of nouns – 'trickery, evasion, procrastination, spoliation, botheration' (1, 15) – carries the Chancery process from 'the outermost circle of such evil' (15) to the 'devouring gulf', from 'the pretence of equity' (12) to its utter defeat.

Chancery is reformable and will be reformed. But what it comes to represent about foot-passengers and other chance people is perennial. In the *Jarndyce* v. *Jarndyce* suit, their 'slipping and sliding' extends the allegorical suggestiveness of the first chapter's figural play, which engages with the perplexity of a whole culture suspended in a narrative it no longer understands: 'no man alive knows what it means' (*BH*, 1, 14). Based on the scandalously long-running cases to which Dickens alludes in the Preface, the suit's 'endless cause' reflects natural history's search for the *verae causa*.[44] It has become synonymous with uncertain and disputed origin, its 'interminable brief' (1, 12) calling up the anxieties about time stirred by Chambers and Nichol and their forerunners. As John Jarndyce explains it to Esther, 'The Lawyers have twisted it into such a state of bedevilment that the original merits of the case have long disappeared from the face of the earth' (8, 108). It also holds the prospect of unimaginable ending:

> the last Lord Chancellor handled it neatly when, correcting Mr Blowers the eminent silk gown who said that such a thing might happen when the sky rained potatoes, he observed, 'or when we get through Jarndyce and Jarndyce, Mr Blowers' – a pleasantry that particularly tickled the maces, bags and purses. (*BH*, 1, 14)

Synecdoche shrinks 'the lawyers' at their bedevilling work to their function of vapid sycophancy and an airy cynicism in the matter of potatoes.

John Jarndyce wrestles with what it means to be in Chancery, attempting a reading of the narrative consistent with that of our authorial guide: 'How mankind ever came to be afflicted with Wigglomeration, or for whose sins these young people ever fell into a pit of it, I don't know; so it is' (*BH*, 8, 111). The sins of the fathers are visited on the children of England's Bleak House as biological and environmental inheritance and existential expectations: 'it's about a Will, and the trusts under a Will – or it was, once. It's about nothing but Costs, now' (8, 108). 'Original merit', 'original sin': these are the outlines of the biblical narrative of creation, fall and apocalypse, in terms of which the three remaining members of the Jarndyce family will find a redemptive meaning in the 'Will' and the 'costs' they have inherited:

> Innumerable children have been born into the cause; innumerable young people have married into it; innumerable old people have died out of it. Scores of persons have deliriously found themselves made parties in Jarndyce and Jarndyce, without knowing how or why; whole families have inherited legendary hatreds with the suit. The little plaintiff or defendant, who was promised a new rocking-horse when Jarndyce and Jarndyce should be settled, has grown up, possessed himself of a real horse, and trotted away into the other world. Fair wards of court have faded into mothers and grandmothers; a long procession of Chancellors has come in and gone out; the legion of bills in the suit have been transformed into mere bills of mortality; there are not three Jarndyces left upon the earth perhaps, since old Tom Jarndyce in despair blew his brains out at a coffee-house in Chancery-lane; but Jarndyce and Jarndyce still drags its dreary length before the Court, perennially hopeless. (*BH*, 1, 14)

Dickens's metaphoric thinking here may well find its source in the columns of *The Times* (14 June 1851):

> it is usual to speak of lawsuits as embittering the lives of those who embark
> on them; but such an expression does but little justice to the hereditary
> curse which a suit in equity on the present system hands down to the children
> who inherit it. We leave our suits to our children just as we bequeath
> to them too often our mental peculiarities and bodily infirmities. The little
> plaintiffs and defendants grow up for the benefit of Chancery; and she
> adopts them as naturally as they succeed to us.[45]

Again, Dickens breathes new life into hand-me-down metaphors, assimilating them into his case against Chancery and his unfolding design for the novel. Like some Megalosaurus, the slow-moving Jarndyce case has dragged 'its dreary length before the court' from time immemorial. 'Legions of bills in the suit' are transformed into 'mere bills of mortality' as the misery of being-in-time is measured in the rapid vivid life his sentences give to passing generations. The 'family misfortune' is endlessly protracted and reiterated in the cumulative effect of temporal process.

But it is also possible to see that the Jarndyce and Jarndyce suit gives Dickens the metaphor he has been waiting for. As early as *Nicholas Nickleby*, he entertains speculations that anticipate the theological dimensions put in place in the opening of *Bleak House*. Nicholas, pacing the streets of London, is oppressed by his sense of repetitious law and indifference to the individual case:

> Now, when he thought how regularly things went on, from day to day,
> in the same unvarying round; how youth and beauty died, and ugly griping
> age lived tottering on; how crafty avarice grew rich, and manly honest
> hearts were poor and sad; how few they were who tenanted the stately
> houses, and how many those who lay in noisome pens, or rose each day
> and laid them down each night, father and son, mother and child, race
> upon race, generation upon generation, without a home to shelter them or
> the energies of one single man directed to their aid; ... how much injustice,
> misery and wrong there was, and yet how the world rolled on, from year
> to year, alike careless and indifferent, and no man seeking to remedy or
> redress it ... he felt, indeed, that there was little ground for hope, and little
> reason why it should not form an atom in the huge aggregate of distress or
> sorrow, and add one small and unimportant unit to swell the great amount.
> (*NN*, 53, 693–4)

There are pre-echoes, here, of *Bleak House*: of Miss Flite's imprisonment of 'youth and beauty' in her crazed mission to protect vulnerable life by imitating its entanglement in law, of the 'ugly griping age' of the

Krook-Smallweed family, of the 'manly honest hearts' of Richard Carstone and Gridley, 'the man from Shropshire'. The unvarying condition of mortality and systematised indifference that is the subject of *Bleak House* is anticipated in the housing of 'generation upon generation', whether their inheritance is 'stately houses', 'noisome pens' or homelessness. Nicholas, denied 'remedy or redress', finding no grounds for 'hope', unites himself in misery with the whole family of man.

But to place the somewhat languid melancholy of these reflections beside the densely allusive, imaginatively charged writing of *Bleak House* is to see how far the associative consciousness of Dickens the man with a message and Dickens the popular entertainer has come since 1839. And John Jarndyce, 'the one single man' who will remedy and redress the familial dysfunctioning and social irresponsibility represented in Chancery, brings to such earlier stereotypes as the Cheeryble brothers a compelling psychological complexity.

In the metaphor of the family, as George Levine points out, Darwin will draw on 'the greatest of Christian metaphors' in making his case for the evolution of species.[46] The 'family misfortune' of the Jarndyces is representative of humankind's subjection to the threefold system of laws in which the novel's descriptive overview and its figural play begin. Genetic inheritance, entanglement in Chancery and trust in 'Divine providence' makes an ad-hoc family in the desolation of Tom Jarndyce's Bleak House. In resolute contrast with his young cousin Richard, John Jarndyce attempts to dissociate himself from the suit, inheriting its 'legendary hatreds' all the same. Acting *in loco parentis* for Chancery, he is drawn into its divisive and all-consuming process, and suffers its consequences. But among the foot-passengers and chance people whose lives are connected by the suit, John Jarndyce models a way of being in Chancery that is ethically responsible, and, in its necessarily limited way,[47] that ameliorates its apparently determining conditions.

In Aunt Barbary's extreme Protestant doctrine, it is a vengeful Old Testament God who visits the sins of the fathers on their children. She is struck down for visiting them on her god-daughter Esther, with the full force of Christ's compassion for the woman taken in adultery (John 8:3–11), read out by Esther from 'quite another part of the book' (*BH*, 3, 28). This battle of proof-texts at the start of Esther's narrative elaborates the biblical narrative invoked in the figurative play of the opening chapter and sets ethical directions for the novel's plot. If the biblical parables of the *parousia* provide Aunt Barbary with a justification for her loveless adherence to 'the law', they connect the expectation of judgement and apocalyptic warning with the coming of the kingdom. It is John Jarndyce who fulfils as best he can the commandment to 'watch and pray'. The parable images that define his Bleak House, the lamps burning and the welcoming house kept in good order, signify his living in readiness.

As Charley Neckett, thirteen-year-old washerwoman and mother to her siblings, disappears into the London streets, to 'melt into the city's strife and sound, like a dewdrop in an ocean' (*BH*, 15, 233), the simile is supplied by the watchful Esther. Yet it requires to be read in the whole context of Dickens's figurative style, powerfully on display in the opening chapter of *Bleak House*. Attracting compound interest, the dewdrop becomes part of the internalised 'Mems' that signpost Dickens through the composition of his vast and complex novel. Distilled from the novel's implacable weather, and its discursive oceans, as ephemeral as the soapsuds barely dry on her arm, Charley seems of no more consequence than 'a thaw-drop from the stone porch' (3, 31) of Esther's miserable childhood home. Yet Charley's parental love has done much to remediate the visitation of the sins of their father on this orphaned family. The glimpsed moment suggests both the sheer chance, and the limitations, of John Jarndyce's philanthropic intervention in the destiny of the Necketts. But it also expresses the hope that a course set by individual striving, guided by a trust 'in Providence and your own efforts' (13, 196), has the power to rescue lives held in Chancery from meaningless contingency and inescapable determinacy. It also represents unfolding possibility, the 'thinking more' of metaphor. Entertaining ideas, the active process of Dickens's style, is the expression of his unique personality engaged in the life of his times. In *Bleak House,* metaphor becomes the very figure of Victorian cultural narrative, of evolutionary process in search of ontological stability.

NOTES

1 George Gissing, *Critical Studies of the Works of Charles Dickens* (New York: Greenberg, 1924), quoted in Robert Garis, *The Dickens Theatre* (Oxford University Press, 1965), 15.
2 Hillis Miller, Introduction to *Bleak House* (Harmondsworth: Penguin Books, 1971), 11–29, at 14.
3 Adam Roberts, 'Dickens's Megalosaurus', *Notes and Queries*, 40 (4) (1993): 478–9, at 478.
4 Morton Dauwen Zabel, '*Bleak House*', in George H. Ford and Lauriat Lane, Jnr. (eds.), *The Dickens Critics* (Ithaca, NY: Cornell University Press, 1961), 325–48, at 326.
5 Terry Eagleton, *Criticism and Ideology* (London: Humanities Press, 1976), 129.

6 Steven Connor, *Charles Dickens* (Oxford: Basil Blackwell, 1985). But see also his wonderfully suggestive afterthoughts in 'Consequential Ground: The Foot Passengers of *Bleak House*', a lecture given 30 September 2000 at the Birkbeck College Dickens Study Day. Available online at www.stevenconnor.com/foot (accessed 12 January 2013).

7 Miller, Introduction to *Bleak House*, 32.

8 Alexander Mihailovic, *Corporeal Words: Mikhail Bakhtin's Theory of Discourse* (Evanston, IL: Northwestern University Press, 1977); Katarina Clark and Michael Holquist, *Mikhail Bakhtin* (Cambridge, MA: Belknap Press of Harvard University Press, 1984); and Ruth Coates, *Christianity in Bakhtin: God and the Exiled Author* (Cambridge University Press, 1998) persuasively argue this case.

9 Coates, *Christianity in Bakhtin*, 33, paraphrasing the 1920s essay 'Towards a Philosophy of the Act': 'in personally submitting to a theoretical truth, the agent rescues it from rootlessness and empty determinism by locating it, not only spatially and temporally, but also axiologically, since every responsible act must take up an evaluative stance towards the world in which it finds itself.'

10 Mihailovic, *Corporeal Words*, 217, paraphrasing Bakhtin's 'Towards a Reworking of the Dostoevsky Book' (1961), late revisions to *Problems of Dostoevsky's Creation* (1929).

11 Coates, *Christianity in Bakhtin*, 30, quoting the 1920s essay 'Towards a Philosophy of the Act'.

12 Coates, *Christianity in Bakhtin*, 41, paraphrasing the 1920s essay 'Author and Hero in Aesthetic Activity'.

13 The phrase is heavily ironised, however, when he applies it to the moral super-intendence of a William Dorrit, for example, as Robert Douglas-Fairhurst notes in *Becoming Dickens: The Invention of a Novelist* (Cambridge, MA: Belknap Press of Harvard University Press, 2011), 315.

14 Cf. Paul Ricoeur: 'Metaphor is living by virtue of the fact that it introduces the spark of imagination into the "thinking more" at the conceptual level. The struggle to "think more," guided by the "vivifying principle" is the "soul" of interpretation.' Paul Ricoeur, *The Rule of Metaphor* (London: Routledge & Kegan Paul, 1978), 302.

15 Miller, Introduction to *Bleak House*, 32.

16 On many occasions, and in many contexts, Dickens emphasises the religious dimensions of his novels, see, for example, his letter to Revd David Macrae, quoted by Dennis Walder, 'Dickens and the Reverend David Macrae', *The Dickensian*, 81 (spring 1985): 45–51, at 48.

17 The lame demon of Le Sage's fable *Le Diable boiteux* becomes a serviceable figure of urban overview in the 1840s, as Jonathan Arac suggests in *Commissioned Spirits: The Shaping of Social Motion in Dickens, Carlyle, Melville and Hawthorn* (New Brunswick: Rutgers University Press, 1979), 112. Dickens uses the figure in Chapter 33 of *The Old Curiosity Shop*, and again in Chapter 47 of *Dombey and Son*.

18 Noted in the Preface to the First Edition, *Bleak House* (Harmondsworth, Penguin, 1971), 41–2, at 41.

19 The project of the Bridgewater Treatises, 1833–40, owned and read by Dickens, as suggested by the subtitle of Buckland's essay on *Geology and Mineralogy* (1836).

20 Gillian Beer, *Darwin's Plots: Evolutionary Narrative in Darwin, George Eliot and Nineteenth-Century Fiction* (London: Arc Paperbacks, 1985).

21 Charles Dickens, 'Review of Robert Hunt's *The Poetry of Science, or Studies of the Physical Phenomena of Nature*', *Examiner*, 9 December 1848, 787–8.

22 As K. J. Fielding and Shu Fang Lai note in 'Dickens's Science, Evolution and "The Death of the Sun"', in Anny Sadrin (ed.), *Dickens, Europe and the New Worlds* (Houndsmills: Macmillan, 1999), 200–11, at 208.

23 Paul Ricoeur sees the discontinuity between time as a succession of 'instants' and the immensity of cosmic time as the misery of the human condition. Paul Ricoeur, *Time and Narrative*, 3 vols. (Chicago University Press, 1983), vol. III.

24 Erasmus Darwin quoted in Beer, *Darwin's Plots*, 129.

25 Charles Coulston Gillispie, *Genesis and Geology: A Study in the Relations of Scientific Thought, Natural Theology and Social Opinion in Great Britain, 1790–1850* (Cambridge, MA: Harvard University Press, 1996), 35–183, provides a useful account of this controversy.

26 G. H. Lewes, 'Dickens in Relation to Criticism', *Fortnightly Review*, 17 (February 1872), reprinted in Stephen Wall (ed.), *Charles Dickens: A Critical Anthology* (Harmondsworth: Penguin, 1970), 191–202, at 199.

27 Roberts, 'Dickens's Megalosaurus', 478–9.

28 Alfred Tennyson, *In Memoriam A. H. H.* in Christopher Ricks (ed.), *The Poems of Tennyson*, 2nd edn, 3 vols. (Harlow: Longman, 1987), II, 304–459, at 374.

29 John Sutherland, *Inside Bleak House* (London: Duckworth, 2005), 53–4, suggests that this reconstructive process, culminating in the Great Exhibition, was the beginning of the popular idea of dinosaurs.

30 As Susan Shatto notes, in 'Byron, Tennyson, and the Monstrous Efts', *The Yearbook of English Studies*, 6, 1976: 144–55, at 145, a precise description is given by Henry Morley in *Household Words* in late November 1851.

31 Sutherland, *Inside Bleak House*, 51.

32 Quoted in Gillispie, *Genesis and Geology*, 98. Cuvier's *Discourses sur les révolutions de la surface du globe* was translated by Robert Kerr and published in four editions, 1817–27. Dickens's library contained a number of books that attempted to reconcile science and religion, including *The Bridgewater Treatises*, and the works of Cuvier and Buffon, see John H. Stonehouse (ed.), *A Catalogue of the Library of Charles Dickens from Gadshill* (London: Piccadilly Fountain, 1935).

33 Susan Shatto, *The Companion to Bleak House* (London: Unwin Hayman, 1989), 35.

34 Janet Larson, *Dickens and the Broken Scripture* (Athens, GA: The University of Georgia Press, 2008), notes the Joban imagery here and throughout, though she argues that Dickens increasingly abandons what she takes to be his project, the literary reclamation of the Bible for his time.

35 Shatto, *Companion to Bleak House*, 36.

36 On 6 July 1850, quoted in David Trotter, *Circulation: Defoe, Dickens, and the Economies of the Novel* (Houndsmills: Macmillan, 1988), 102.

37 William Wordsworth, 'Composed upon Westminster Bridge, September 3, 1802', in *William Wordsworth: The Major Works*, ed. Stephen Gill (Oxford University Press, 2000), 285.

38 Shatto, *Companion to Bleak House*, 37.

39 Quoted in Lawrence Frank, *Victorian Detective Fiction and the Nature of Evidence: The Scientific Investigations of Poe, Dickens and Doyle* (Houndsmills: Palgrave Macmillan, 2003), 75.

40 Douglas Hay, 'Property, Authority and the Criminal Law', in Douglas Hay, Peter Linebaugh and John G. Rule, *Albion's Fatal Tree: Crime and Society in Eighteenth-Century England* (London: Allen Lane, 1975), 17–63, makes this case.

41 John Butt and Kathleen Tillotson, *Dickens at Work* (London: Methuen, 1957), 179, note that 'Tom-all-Alone's: The Ruined House' was the first title drafted for the novel in manuscript.

42 Letter from Charles Dickens to John Forster, [?October–November 1846], *Letters*, IV, 650.

43 *The Times*, 28 March 1851, quoted in Butt and Tillotson, *Dickens at Work*, 185.

44 Charles Lyell's *Principles of Geology* advances the view that to understand any natural phenomenon one must confine consideration to laws recognised as *verae causae*, i.e. true causes recognised now to be in operation. George Levine, *Realism, Ethics and Secularization: Essays on Victorian Literature and Science* (Cambridge University Press, 2008), 218.

45 Quoted in Butt and Tillotson, *Dickens at Work*, 186.

46 Levine, *Realism, Ethics and Secularization*, 272.

47 Much has been made, by Marxist critics in particular, of the conservatism of Dickens's representations of social reform. A last word might be permitted the late Gerry Cohen, 'who described himself as having moved from historical materialism to a belief that what is needed to bring about equality are changes to individual attitudes and choices – a position, he said, so near to Christianity that it would have shocked his younger self.' Jane O'Grady, Obituary, *The Guardian*, 10 August 2009.

CHAPTER TEN

Reading the book of himself: The Uncommercial Traveller *and 'Dickensian' style*

Bharat Tandon

That G. K. Chesterton had a sharp eye and ear for the 'Dickensian' is now almost an article of folk wisdom; and his reputation as one of the pioneering twentieth-century Dickens critics may owe much to his capacity for being inward with Dickens's style, even when he was commenting on works about which he had significant reservations, among them the *Uncommercial Traveller* essays. In *Criticisms and Appreciations of the Works of Charles Dickens* (1911), for example, he remarked:

> *The Uncommercial Traveller* is a collection of Dickens's memories rather than of his literary purposes; but it is due to him to say that memory is often more startling in him than prophecy in anyone else ... All these works of his can best be considered as letters; they are notes of personal travel, scribbles in a diary about this or that that really happened. But Dickens was one of the few men who have the two talents that are the whole of literature – and have them both together. First, he could make a thing happen over again; and second, he could make it happen better.[1]

The contrast which Chesterton's preface draws between the retrospective pull of 'memories' and the prospective energy of 'literary purposes' is particularly germane to my discussion here, as is his stress on Dickens's skill in making 'a thing happen over again', and making it 'happen better'; however, his 'rather than' may be overly schismatic, suggesting as it does that Dickens's personal memories and his 'literary purposes' could ever be cleanly divided from one another. On the contrary, what I would like to explore here, in looking at Dickens's 1860s journalism, are some of the ways in which *The Uncommercial Traveller*'s literary purposes draw creatively on the stylistic resources of memory – especially the writer's memory of his own fictional style. If it has become a truism to think of Dickens in the 1830s as a journalist who 'became' a novelist, then the later phases of his journalistic writing offer a rather different picture – that of a journalist reporting back on a real world that can often read as if it has been transfigured by style into one of his own fictions.

The truth of Dickens's literary apprenticeship, of course, is not as simple as any linear narrative sketch would suggest; indeed, as shown admirably by Robert Douglas-Fairhurst in *Becoming Dickens*, the writer's trajectory in the 1830s was not so much a clean developmental line as a garden of forking paths, a demonstration that 'the facts of history can be seen clearly only when viewed against a background of counterfactuals'.[2] However, the fact that Dickens discovered himself (or his selves) imaginatively in the unpredictable transit between different modes of being and writing also came to be a fertile resource for a career in which reality and its fictional portrayals continually influenced, interrogated and shaped each other; one result, for example, was that style – as both a mappable linguistic quality and a mode of aesthetic conduct – could often work as the common language in which the different facets of Dickens spoke to and comprehended each other. Writing about literary style has frequently resorted to variations on the adage propounded by Robert Burton ('It is most true, *stylus virum arguit*, our stile bewraies us, and as Hunters find their game by the trace, so is a mans *Genius* described by his workes'),[3] but in Dickens's case, the old saying may be justified: style may not necessarily have 'bewraied' or 'made' Dickens, but it did keep him (as it did for the fictional David Copperfield and Pip) in some kind of meaningful relation to himself, even as it breached the porous membrane between his work and the world outside it.

But such an emphasis needs to be qualified and justified a little; after all, many writers echo and reproduce elements of their recognisable style in later works, and not always to productive or edifying effect. Wendy Doniger has noted that '[i]ndividuals are often driven to self-impersonation through the pressure of public expectations',[4] and it remains an unpalatable fact of the commerce of public reception that artists' most assertive creations, once they become established as parts of popular consciousness, can turn in time into prisons, as an initial chorus of approval declines into a request for the same, worn-out old tune, over and over again. Can one ever distinguish comfortably between a style that creatively reworks earlier stages of itself, and that process by which artists (from Hemingway to Oasis) have unwittingly become their own deadliest parodists, their own 'tribute acts'? In this chapter, I'd like to suggest that as a result of the unusual nature of Dickens's style, and its specific relation to its subjects and the wider reading public, the social-surrealist narrative mode that he had brought to such a distinctive pitch in the novels from *David Copperfield* onwards works in *The Uncommercial Traveller* not as an obstruction, nor as an unthinking reproduction of accustomed modes, but as an enabling way of seeing and reading the reality of the 1860s.

The styles of *The Uncommercial Traveller* papers – as is perhaps inevitable with a series of occasional pieces written intermittently over an eight-year period – are not singular or uniform, but they do have a certain consistency of pitch, as witnessed by one of the most famous of the early papers, the account, first published on 18 February 1860, of the Uncommercial's wanderings through the East End to investigate the true state of affairs at Wapping Workhouse:

> Long before I reached Wapping I gave myself up as having lost my way, and, abandoning myself to the narrow streets in a Turkish frame of mind, relied on predestination to bring me somehow or other to the place I wanted if I were ever to get there. When I had ceased for an hour or so to take any trouble about the matter, I found myself on a swing-bridge, looking down at some dark locks in some dirty water. Over against me, stood a creature remotely in the likeness of a young man, with a puffed sallow face, and a figure all dirty and shiny and slimy, who may have been the youngest son of his filthy old father, Thames, or the drowned man about whom there was a placard on the granite post like a large thimble, that stood between us. ('Wapping Warehouse', *UT*, 44)

One of the remarkable aspects of this passage at a stylistic level is that, taken in isolation, it could be a long-lost passage from either of Dickens's two great London novels of the previous decade, *Bleak House* and *Little Dorrit*. There is that distinctive quality of mock-heroic circumlocution, slightly over-dressing phrases so as to be just too formally Latinate for the occasion, which Dickens draws from eighteenth-century antecedents such as Fielding and Smollett, and which surfaces here in the Uncommercial's relying 'on predestination' and his description of the 'creature remotely in the likeness of a young man'. There is the technique of stretching a metaphor or an analogy until it ceases to be simply a point of comparison, taking on a life of its own, in the 'figure … who may have been the youngest son of his filthy old father, Thames'; and, as I shall go on to discuss, that 'placard' about the drowned man points towards one of the distinguishing features of the contemporary city that Dickens was documenting in the 1860s.

More important than any individual trope of narrative rhetoric, though, are the strange and sometimes unsettling combinations of those figures, in which so much of Dickens's comic and aesthetic work takes place. For example, the passage repeatedly plays precision against blurriness: specific actions ('I gave myself up', 'abandoning myself') give way to the non-specific 'for an hour or so', only for the Uncommercial to snap back to himself, as if suddenly coming to after a reverie, with 'I found myself on a swing-bridge'; similarly, the two explicit figures of likeness ('a creature remotely in the likeness of a young man', 'the granite post like a large thimble') serve at once to clarify resemblances and to defamiliarise the things being compared. Thus, by this stage of Dickens's career, while the recognisable, topographical London cityscape is clearly present in his account, the writing has moved far beyond any dualistic notion of style, in which Dickens simply overlays the solid, factual city with his own linguistic inventions. To put it another way, there is no Gradgrindian, zero-degree alternative version that one could set against this, after the manner of Bitzer's 'factual' account of the horse in Book I, Chapter 2 of *Hard Times* ('Quadruped. Graminivorous. Forty teeth, namely twenty-four grinders, four eye-teeth, and twelve incisive' [*HT*, 1, 2, 9–10]). Rather, the world of *The Uncommercial Traveller* offers an augmented reality in which imaginative representations appear to have become parts of the real, observable, landscape. Compare this extract with, for instance, the descriptions of Mr Cripples' Academy in Book 1, Chapter 9 of *Little Dorrit*, and the Uncommercial's stylistic lineage is manifest: Arthur Clennam observes that '[t]here were so many lodgers in this house, that the door-post seemed to be as full of bell-handles as a cathedral organ is full of stops' (*LD*, 1, 9, 88), and as he makes his way further up the building, '[t]he little staircase windows looked in at the back windows of other houses as unwholesome as itself, with poles and lines thrust out of them, on which unsightly linen hung: as if the inhabitants were angling for clothes, and had had some wretched bites not worth attending to' (89). It is as if the force of Dickens's imagination, drawing on his empirical observations of the social circumstances of the 1840s and 1850s, has reworked them into a style which he then projects back out into the lived experience of his final decade. As such, the style of *The Uncommercial Traveller* militates against any easy identification of style with a retreat from salient realities – on the contrary, it insists that to share a language is, *de facto*, to share a world. 'What connection can there be', asks the third-person narrator of *Bleak House*, 'between many people in the innumerable histories of this world, who, from opposite sides of great gulfs, have, nevertheless, been very curiously brought together!' (*BH*, 16, 235). As is so often the case in Dickens, one answer to that question is right there on the page, in the very narrative in which the question is being asked.

For a writer so frequently described as having created an entire world – a popular image crystallised in the title of Humphry House's *The Dickens*

World (1941)[5] – there is, in fact, precious little direct continuity of character and incident between that world's published documents, unless one counts the not-particularly-successful resurrection of Pickwick and the Wellers in *Master Humphrey's Clock*, or the decision to follow *Mrs Lirriper's Lodgings* in the Christmas 1863 number of *All the Year Round*, with *Mrs Lirriper's Legacy* a year later. However, especially when Dickens's writing involves London, one can discern a continuity of style: not a one-size-fits-all stylistic mannerism or tic that remains fixed from book to book, but a more mobile, less easily defined artistic 'watermark' that remains visible (or audible) beneath the varying textures of the novels' narrative surfaces. This is not to say, of course, that there aren't more overt echoes and allusive links between the 1850s novels and the *Uncommercial* essays; take 'Night Walks' from 21 July 1860:

> Under a kind of fascination, and in a ghostly silence suitable to the time, Houselessness and this gentleman would eye one another from head to foot, and so, without exchange of speech, part, mutually suspicious. Drip, drip, drip, from ledge and coping, splash from pipes and water-spouts, and by-and-by the houseless shadow would fall upon the stones that gave the way to Waterloo-bridge. ('Night Walks', *UT*, 151)

The Uncommercial mentions 'ghostly silence' and almost immediately afterwards imagines the rain going '[d]rip, drip, drip, from ledge and coping', summoning up as he does so the spectral, textual trace of the rain falling on the Ghost's Walk at Chesney Wold in *Bleak House* ('the heavy drops fall, drip, drip, drip, upon the broad flagged pavement' [*BH*, 7, 95]) – and that deathly 'drip, drip, drip' also attends a corpse in the Paris morgue from 'Travelling Abroad' on 7 April 1860 ('an old grey man lying all alone on his cold bed, with a tap of water turned on over his grey hair, and running drip, drip, drip, drip, down his wretched face until it got to the corner of his mouth' [*UT*, 88]). Even more blatantly, in 'The Great Tasmania's Cargo' from 21 April 1860, the great agent of governmental obfuscation from *Little Dorrit* appears *in propria persona*, as 'that great Circumlocution Office, on which the sun never sets and the light of reason never rises' (*UT*, 99). Nevertheless, the specific echoes are perhaps not as important as the sheer existence of a stylistic bridge between Dickens's novels and journalism in the 1860s. Matthew Bevis has commented cogently that '[t]here is frequently the sense of an audience in Dickens (he imagines himself *as* an audience as he composes), a sense of words being heard as well as read.'[6] In *The Uncommercial Traveller*, Dickens's style, a style growing out of a sensitive echo-sounding of public events and voices, and one which had, by the end of the 1850s, gained a position of extraordinary public pre-eminence, resounds back into the world of his reading public to emphasise that there can be a productive commerce between them. However, as I shall go on to discuss, such a commerce, by its very nature, must work in both directions.

One reason for the particular quality of this transit between word and world can be seen more clearly, if one examines the history of Dickens's engagements with external conditions and public expectations across his career. It is one of the fertile paradoxes of his working life that, when one tries plotting the lines of force, influence and causality within his *oeuvre*, it becomes difficult to distinguish chicken from egg, since Dickens frequently takes a subject or a material circumstance and reworks it so thoroughly that he comes to be the referent for subsequent versions of it; as Frederic Schwarzbach has pointedly remarked, 'when one turns to specialized studies to check the accuracy of Dickens' observations, as often as not, Dickens is quoted as the leading witness on that very matter.'[7] One need only think of Dickens and Christmas: Chesterton could look back from 1906 on Dickens as the poet of Christmas comfort ('it belongs peculiarly to Christmas; above all, it belongs pre-eminently to Dickens'),[8] but this identification dated back as far as the 1840s, while the Christmas Books were still being published. The anonymous reviewer of *The Haunted Man* in *Macphail's Edinburgh Ecclesiastical Journal* may already have been getting vexed by the regularity of, and the perceived repetitions in, the Christmas Books, but he did, ironically, alight on a fundamental aspect of Dickens's identification with Christmas:

> Christmas *was* Christmas ... many, many centuries before Charles Dickens began to celebrate him in *Carols* and *Chimes*. But, as it is, a Christmas book from him is as regular as a Christmas goose; and the one is not more certain of being devoured than the other is of being read, extensively and with strong relish.[9]

Harold Bloom's famous theoretical narrative in *The Anxiety of Influence* plots a trajectory in which the strong poet has to pass through six phases or 'revisionary ratios' before achieving their full artistic being; Dickens, on the other hand, has clearly not read that particular script, and his writing frequently short-circuits directly to the last stage described by Bloom – *Apophrades*, or the return of the dead, in which 'the new poem's achievement makes it seem to us, not as though the precursor were writing it, but as though the later poet himself had written the precursor's characteristic work.'[10] This has many ramifications for Dickens's work, but for the rest of this chapter, I shall concentrate on a conjunction of circumstances that bears significantly on *The Uncommercial Traveller*: Dickens's return to reporting the city streets and the growing recognition of a style that could be identified adjectivally as peculiar to him.

It is a notable aspect of literary canonisation that the adjectives that come to define authors' styles for posterity frequently do not come into common usage until some time after their deaths: according to the *OED*, for instance, the first recorded usage of 'Keatsian' dates from 1845, twenty-four years after Keats's death, and the specific adjective 'Dickensian' only appears for the first time in an *Athenaeum* review of Bret Harte from 1881: 'he has trained his imagination to walk with a Dickensian gait; he observes with a Dickensian eye.'[11] Nevertheless, the second half of the 1850s saw some unsuccessful prototypes for 'Dickensian' come glancingly into use, witnessing to a growing conviction among Dickens's readers that his writing thus far could now be spoken of as a body of work with an identifiable style. In 1856, the *Saturday Review* wrote of 'a Dickenesque description of an execution',[12] and writing to Charles Eliot Norton on 9 March 1859, Elizabeth Gaskell (with a passing swipe at Dickens's perceived editorial absolutism, and his marital troubles) lamented that her current work in progress, probably *Lois the Witch*, was 'fated to go into this new Dickensy periodical',[13] namely *All the Year Round*. Therefore, by the time Dickens came to begin the first *Uncommercial Traveller* pieces, his style was not only established as adjectivally describable but it also had the ability to define, or at least to influence, how its subjects might be perceived by readers – and both of these elements have an important influence on how he composes and pitches the Uncommercial's travels back through the city streets.

There is an incident, more precisely a class of incident, that recurs in many of the essays, especially those ones set explicitly in London: a moment where the Uncommercial, or one of the characters he encounters, stops to read (and is sometimes required to decipher) a placard, poster or bill. I mentioned earlier the conceit from 'Wapping Workhouse', in which the 'apparition' at the lock is imagined as an emanation of the placard about the drowned man, but there are numerous other examples: in 'Two Views of a Cheap Theatre' (25 February 1860), 'those streets looked so dull, and, considered as theatrical streets, so broken and bankrupt, that the FOUND DEAD on the black board at the police station might have announced the decease of the Drama' (*UT*, 54); surveying Gray's Inn in 'Chambers' (18 August 1860), the Uncommercial notes 'the bills To Let To Let, the door-posts inscribed like gravestones' (*UT*, 160); and in 'An Old

Stage-Coaching House' (1 August 1863), he offers a graphically performative image of the faded, posthumous life of the old building:

> In a fit of abject depression, it had cast whitewash on its windows, and boarded up its front door, and reduced itself to a side entrance; but even that had proved a world too wide for the Literary Institution which had been its last phase; for the Institution had collapsed too, and of the ambitious letters of its inscription on the White Hart's front, all had fallen off but these:

L   Y INS   T

  – suggestive of Lamentably Insolvent. (*UT*, 273)

Throughout his work, Dickens displays a keen feeling for the visual textures and idiosyncrasies of writing, even in texts which arrive at their readers' eyes in the smoothed and standardised medium of print. Of course, as someone whose apprenticeship had taken in the ciphers of Gurney shorthand, he was only too aware of the mysterious presence and 'character' of graphemic signs[14] – David Copperfield's 'most despotic characters I have ever known; who insisted, for instance, that a thing like the beginning of a cobweb, meant expectation, and that a pen and ink sky-rocket stood for disadvantageous' (*DC*, 38, 465) – and, as many critics have noted, the novels are repeatedly drawn to textual hermeneutics for elements of plot business. If, in *The Pickwick Papers*, the wilful overinterpretation of the inscription 'Bill Stumps, his mark' (Chapter 11) can be played as broad intellectual slapstick, by the time of *Bleak House*, matters have become much more serious. As J. Hillis Miller's brilliant, influential reading of the novel has emphasised, textual interpretation is the narrative figure at the heart of *Bleak House*,[15] and for characters such as Nemo/Hawdon and Krook, it becomes a matter of life and death, with 'Nemo' writing himself out of existence and Krook eventually becoming a greasy smear alongside the letters scrawled on the walls of his room.

In the early 1860s, Dickens's fiction and journalism regularly invite a reader to imagine the real look of words beyond the uniformity of print, almost to 'see through' print to the idiosyncratic textual physique beyond – as witnessed by the novel that is closest in time to the early *Uncommercial* pieces, *Great Expectations*. At the very opening of the narrative, as Pip surveys the family gravestones ('From the character and turn of the inscription, "*Also Georgiana Wife of the Above*," I drew a childish conclusion that my mother was freckled and sickly' [*GE*, 1, 1, 3]), the italics offer a subliminal hint that the carved letters out of which the narrator's fantasies are being spun are more 'characterful' than can possibly be rendered by the printed page, which must partly extenuate Pip's speculations. This draw-ing attention to the act of reading also works, of course, as a subtle, ironic alerting device, heightening a reader's consciousness of how grievously Pip may be *mis*reading his own plot. In addition, Dickens's greater emphasis in the early 1860s on imagining the act of reading ministers to one of the more pressing realities of urban experience.

At the most basic level, all these signs surrounding the Uncommercial and his characters testify to a rapidly changing aspect of the physical being of the Victorian city (especially Victorian London): by the middle of the century, the bricks and mortar of the urban landscape were supplemented by a profusion of bills, posters and placards in the inhabitants' line of sight, with the result that the visual phenomenology of Victorian London inevitably became a matter of text as well as topography. Lynda Nead has described this effect brilliantly:

> Advertisements not only covered the walls and temporary hoardings of the city, they also circulated on the roads and pavements. Businesses and shops sent out their sandwich-board men and advertising vans; even advertise-ments had to be on the move within the metropolitan ethic of unceas-ing mobility ... The advertisement is the ultimate synthesis of the central themes of the modern metropolis: movement, exchange and the image. It is part of the visual fabric of the city; it speaks to the eye and sustains the exchange of money and goods. Walked round the streets and pulled on carts, the advertisement creates an alternative mapping of the city, tracing the contours of commodity capitalism.[16]

One can even see in Dickens and his contemporaries the beginning of that sense for the increasing textuality (and intertextuality) of urban experience that finds fuller expression in early twentieth-century works such as *Ulysses*, *Manhattan Transfer* and the poetry of William Carlos Williams. What dis-tinguishes Dickens in this regard, however, is the presence and influence of his own style; other writers in Dickens's circles produced extraordinary non-fictional accounts of London – G. A. Sala's *Twice Round the Clock*, from 1859, for instance, or Blanchard Jerrold and Gustave Doré's *London: A Pilgrimage* from 1872 – but neither Sala nor Jerrold can call upon their own work as part of the texture of what they are describing. Sala offers a suggestive image for London as a place layered with and haunted by its own literary history when he remarks:

> It is not my fault, dear reader, if the spot which your author and artist to command have selected for illustration of the eighth hour ante-meridian, be so rich in historical and literary recollections; that we may fancy every inch of its surface trodden and re-trodden till the very soil has sunk, by

the feet of the departed great; that the student, and the lover of old lore, must arrest himself perforce at every tree, and evoke remembrance at every pace.[17]

That said, his 'remembrances' are restricted to the likes of Whitman ('the booming sound that fills the city every morning, and ... "utters its barbaric youp over the house-tops of creation," is the great Public Voice'),[18] *Hamlet* ('See in your mind's eye, Horatio, how the shadows of the old frequenters of the Mall come trooping along'),[19] and *The Tempest* ('Prospero must get a new man, for Caliban has got a new master: Fashion, in Regent Street').[20] Jerrold's persona in *London: A Pilgrimage* does not inhabit its narrative present with the same raconteurish confidence as Sala's – an effect furthered by the quality of Doré's apocalyptic plates – and it therefore feels less immediately time-locked than its predecessor. Nevertheless, when Jerrold comes to enumerate the literary and historical 'ghosts' of Pall Mall and Piccadilly, the roll-call is a relatively familiar one:

> The club gossip of generations; the scandals of the great; the lives of the wits, and beaux, and beauties; the impertinences of Brummell and the mots of Sheridan; the gambling bouts of the last generation in Jermyn Street, and the learned evenings of the peaceful Albany; the histories of Almack's and the disasters brought about at Crockford's.[21]

Dickens, in contrast, has the advantage of being able to summon up himself: a rare advantage, for sure, but one that presents any number of temptations to authorial narcissism, and it is to his credit that his late writing largely bypasses such temptations. Schwarzbach offers the image of a Dickens who was 'so much a part of the national cultural life of England from the 1830s onward that his contemporaries absorbed him whole, as they did the Bible, breathing in the very rhythms and stuff of his prose ... as they did their first breaths of learning';[22] and while his phrasing may be a little rhapsodic, he still touches on a truth about the scale of the novelist's residual influence (as well as chiming felicitously with *The Uncommercial Traveller*'s account of breathing in the 'snuff' of the dead in 'City of London Churches' from 5 May 1860 [*UT*, 110]). As Dickens noted in a letter of 8 July 1861 (in a tone pitched right on the cusp of true and false modesty),

> I hope you may have seen a large-headed photograph with little legs, representing the undersigned, pen in hand, tapping his forehead to knock an idea out. It has just sprung up so abundantly in all the shops, that I am ashamed to go about town looking in at the picture windows – which is my delight.[23]

Thus, for Dickens, unlike for Sala or Jerrold, walking through London at the beginning of the 1860s would have carried an extra, uncanny resonance, since, as I have been exploring, he had become part of the very landscape he traversed, part of the urban 'text' that he was reading, and, thanks to the influence of his fictional style, a major interpretative template for any such reading of the city.

Now, such a situation (especially given the spread of the 'author photograph' that Dickens describes in his 1861 letter) could easily minister to self-love, with the whole of the real city transformed by style into some giant vanity-mirror in which the writer can preen and admire himself; the great achievement of *The Uncommercial Traveller* is that the stylistic bridge that it creates from the novels of the 1850s works instead to implicate Dickens's fiction in the real world that the Uncommercial ventures back out to observe, and, by association, to implicate it in the sheer *intractability* of so many of that world's problems, consonant with Edward W. Said's critical version of 'late style' ('what of artistic lateness not as harmony and resolution but as intransigence, difficulty, and unresolved contradiction?').[24] If, at the end of *Little Dorrit*, it is clear that the marriage of two people, however 'inseparable and blessed', will never silence or outweigh the 'usual uproar' of social indifference and casual mortality that is the last sound in the novel (*LD*, II, 34, 688), the issue is much more difficult in the *Uncommercial Traveller* papers, where Dickens doesn't even have the recourse of a clearly fictional denouement to suggest an alternative to what the Uncommercial observes. In one of his fine analyses of the late journalism, John Drew has commented that

> the "uncommercial" perspective is not one which promises easy solutions to complex problems. Rather, it involves the much harder process of accepting a private share of the public's responsibility for the welfare of those who are judged in need of it, in the face of an economic and political climate which sets them at naught.[25]

And one of the major means by which Dickens negotiates between private and public responsibilities in his Uncommercial persona is via the continuity of style – a shared medium that works to guarantee to readers that the essays belong not only in the same world as the problems they document but in an imaginative continuum with his earlier fictional treatments of related topics. In a slightly earlier piece, Drew also pinpoints the specific running metaphor that allows style to link these discrete areas together, the metaphor of travelling itself: 'a literary representation of the author's self-image which is given public life and mobility only through travel

narratives, specially adapted for periodical publication'.[26] Companionable
travelling is called upon repeatedly as a suggestive analogy from early on
in Dickens's published career: from the characteristic blend of sentimental prompt and commercial sales pitch that he gives to Master Humphrey
in 1840 ('if I should carry my readers with me, as I hope to do, and there
should spring up, between them and me, feelings of homely affection and
regard')[27] to the opening of *Household Words* in 1850, an appeal much more
explicitly attuned to the relations between writer-reader intimacy and the
new technologies. ('The traveller whom we accompany on his railroad or
his steamboat journey, may gain, we hope, some compensation for incidents which these later generations have outlived, in new associations with
the Power that bears him onward; with the habitations and the ways of life
of crowds of his fellow creatures among whom he passes like the wind.')[28]
In *The Uncommercial Traveller*, though, the analogy between sympathetic
social relations and physical travel around the social world is brought to
an extraordinary imaginative pitch – not least because space is not the
only dimension through which Dickens's style moves.

Dickens's developments in plotting readers' movements through time
and space can be seen most clearly if one sets some of the early *Sketches'*
depictions of the city alongside the Uncommercial's treatments of comparable scenes and topics. A consistent quality of the style of the London
Sketches, for instance, is their adherence to conventions of chronological
sequence, whether they are being told in the past tense or the historic
present. As befits a description of the soundscape that gave the world
'Oranges and Lemons', 'The Streets – Night', like Sala's masterpiece after
it, takes its narrative tempo from the hours of the night and the chimes of
the city clocks, marking out a sequential progression. ('After a little conversation about the wretchedness of the weather and the merits of tea', 'After
a little prophetic conversation with the policeman at the street-corner',
'It is nearly eleven o'clock', 'One o'clock!', 'Scenes like these, are continued until three or four o'clock in the morning'.)[29] In 'Shops and Their
Tenants', too, Boz declares that '[o]ne of our principal amusements is to
watch the gradual progress – the rise and fall – of particular shops' (*SB*,
61), and a reader's attention is, accordingly, drawn to the markers along
the sketch's ironic trajectory of 'gradual decay' (*SB*, 63) and commercial
decline:

> Its decay was slow, but sure. Tickets gradually appeared in the windows;
> then rolls of flannel, with labels on them, were stuck outside the door; then
> a bill was pasted on the street door, intimating that the first floor was to be

let *un*furnished; then one of the young men disappeared altogether, and the other took to a black neckerchief, and the proprietor took to drinking. The shop became dirty, broken panes of glass remained unmended, and the stock disappeared piecemeal. (*SB*, 62)

Comparing these early examples with *The Uncommercial Traveller* indicates the greater freedom with which Dickens's late style can move illuminatingly back and forth in time, even as it plots out the physical topography of 1860s London. 'Night Walks', for example, may share some elements of its larger narrative structure with the equivalent piece from *Sketches*, but the differences are even more telling. As the Uncommercial makes his journey through the London night, time unfolds sequentially; however, as he stops at certain points, the histories of those locations unfurl into the narrated present, like time capsules being opened up. The Uncommercial even suggests in passing some link between the patterns of individual citizens' life-stories and the larger life of the city itself, when he observes that 'it was always the case that London, as if in imitation of individual citizens belonging to it, had expiring fits and starts of restlessness' (*UT*, 150). Perhaps as a result of this perception, many of the places the Uncommercial comes to tell part of their tale, or reveal part of their history, before he moves on. As he walks over Waterloo Bridge, 'the river had an awful look, the buildings on the banks were muffled in black shrouds, and the reflected lights seemed to originate deep in the water, as if the spectres of suicides were holding them to show where they went down' (*UT*, 151); as he passes the theatre, '[t]he ground at my feet where, when last there, I had seen the peasantry of Naples dancing among the vines, reckless of the burning mountain which threatened to overwhelm them, was now in possession of a strong serpent of engine-hose' (*UT*, 152); and walking past Bethlehem Hospital sparks, in turn, a memory of a past visit to a mental institution: 'Said an afflicted man to me, when I was last in a hospital like this, "Sir, I can frequently fly"' (*UT*, 153). These unpredictable shifts, from the immediate past of the narrator's memory to the less personal memories that spin out of the places he visits, find a creative match in a style that also makes a virtue out of staging sudden flickers of the past – including, as I have been exploring here, the past of Dickens's own writing. If his style provided the author himself with a determinedly eclectic common ground which his disparate selves might meet, it could also provide his readers with a medium that imaginatively comprehended both its immediate subjects in the real world and the whole history of Dickens's responses to those subjects, ministering to that blending of private and public perspectives and responsibilities that Drew sees as so central to the late non-fiction.

So it is that one of his most accomplished late Uncommercial pieces achieves its meeting of private and public by reviving and revising a metaphor from which he has drawn much varied creative energy throughout his writing life. If many of the problems the Uncommercial views are, as Drew suggests, intractable ones, Dickens can still note the isolated instances of virtue, as he does with the East London Hospital for Children in 'A Small Star in the East' from 1868, a piece whose title and tone convey an enduring astonishment at the thought that such a place can exist at all. After a harrowing description of the privations of Ratcliffe and Stepney, which rivals (and echoes) the toughest parts of *Household Words* and *Bleak House* ('I stood opposite the woman boiling the children's clothes, – she had not even a piece of soap to wash them with' [*UT*, 358]), the essay turns a corner and bumps into the area's one redeeming feature:

> Down by the river's bank in Ratcliffe, I was turning upward by a side street, therefore, to regain the railway, when my eyes rested on the inscription across the road, 'East London Children's Hospital.' I could scarcely have seen an inscription better suited to my frame of mind; and I went across and went straight in. (*UT*, 360)

It is, however, only a 'small star', afforded significantly less textual space than the miseries that surround it, and the Uncommercial is not naive enough to imagine that the hospital can somehow outweigh those miseries all by itself. Nevertheless, Dickens has at his disposal in 1868 something few writers can call upon – a style that opens the essay's concerns out for public scrutiny, sending them back out into the world of lived experience and possible political action in the very act of being read. For as 'A Small Star in the East' ends, throwing down a challenge to its readers' philanthropic sensibilities (and, by implication, to some of their chequebooks), Dickens also reworks creatively that stylistic association between companionable travelling and social sympathy that has become part of his recognisable stylistic signature. If, in an early sketch like 'The Pawnbroker's Shop' from 1835, the repetition of footsteps only signifies the repeated degradations of poverty ('How many females situated as her two companions are, and as she may have been once, have terminated the same wretched course, in the same wretched manner! One is already tracing her footsteps with frightful rapidity. How soon may the other follow her example!' [*SB*, 192–3]), *The Uncommercial Traveller* reverses the polarity of the figure. The crossover between the writing and the world in 'A Small Star in the East' allows Dickens to prompt his reader to join him in the activity of observation, however limited its efficacy might be, as he maps their future steps on to his own present ones: 'I came away from Ratcliffe by the Stepney railway station to the Terminus at Fenchurch-street. Anyone who will reverse that route, may retrace my steps' (*UT*, 364). That retracing might not change the world, but the continuity of Dickensian style means that the social concerns of the 1850s novels do live on as part of the world to which they have helped to give an imaginative shape.

In the 1868 Charles Dickens Edition of the first series of *The Uncommercial Traveller*, G. J. Pinwell's illustration to 'Travelling Abroad' figures the Uncommercial explicitly as the bearded Dickens of the portraits and public readings, just as Cruikshank deliberately placed the likeness of the young Boz in the 1836 *Sketches*. However, the essays themselves do not need the illustration to make the identification explicit; rather, it is all there already in the style of the original *All the Year Round* texts. There is a strange moment in 'Travelling Abroad', when the Uncommercial encounters 'a very queer small boy' on the road to Gad's Hill Place:

> 'Bless you sir,' said the very queer small boy, 'when I was not more than half as old as nine, it used to be a treat for me to be brought to look at it. And now, I am nine, I come by myself to look at it. And ever since I can recollect, my father, seeing me so fond of it, has often said to me, "If you were to be very persevering and were to work hard, you might some day come to live in it." Though that's impossible!' said the very queer small boy, drawing a low breath, and now staring at the house out of window with all his might. (*UT*, 86)

This is, of course, the ghost of the young Dickens, admiring the house in which the successful public Dickens does, indeed, now live; but it is only the most explicitly visualised example of his ongoing encounter, at once enabling and chastening, with his own past selves and styles over the course of the Uncommercial's travels. Sala wrote in *Twice Round the Clock* that '[t]here are two cities in the world, London and Paris, so full of these footstep memories, so haunted by impalpable ghosts of the traces of famous deeds, that locomotion, to one of my temperament, becomes a task very slow, if not painfully difficult, of accomplishment.'[30] For Dickens in *The Uncommercial Traveller*, among those ghosts was the presence of his own style – his ongoing companion back out in the real world as he walked the streets of London by night once more, reading the book of himself.

NOTES

1 G. K. Chesterton, *Criticisms and Appreciations of the Works of Charles Dickens* (London, J. M. Dent & Sons, 1911; reprinted 1933), xxvii.

2 Robert Douglas-Fairhurst, *Becoming Dickens: The Invention of a Novelist* (Cambridge, MA: Belknap Press of Harvard University Press, 2011), 14.

3 Robert Burton, *The Anatomy of Melancholy* (1621), ed. Thomas C. Faulkner, Nicholas K. Kiessling and Rhonda L. Blair, 6 vols. (Oxford: Clarendon Press, 1989–2000), I, 13. See also Geoffrey Leech and Michael Short, *Style in Fiction*, 2nd edn (Harlow: Pearson Longman, 2007).

4 Wendy Doniger, *The Woman Who Pretended to Be Who She Was: Myths of Self-Imitation* (New York: Oxford University Press, 2005), 12.

5 Humphry House, *The Dickens World* (London: Oxford University Press, 1941), *passim*.

6 Matthew Bevis, *The Art of Eloquence: Byron, Dickens, Tennyson, Joyce* (Oxford University Press, 2007), 86.

7 F. S. Schwarzbach, *Dickens and the City* (London: Athlone Press, 1979), 2.

8 G. K. Chesterton, *Charles Dickens* (London: Wordsworth, 2007), 83.

9 *Macphail's Edinburgh Ecclesiastical Journal*, January 1849; reprinted in *CH*, 179.

10 Harold Bloom, *The Anxiety of Influence: A Theory of Poetry*, 2nd edn (Oxford University Press, 1997), 16.

11 'Review of *The Complete Works of Bret Harte*', *The Athenaeum*, 2786, 19 March 1881, 390.

12 'Our Civilization', *Saturday Review*, 35 (2) (28 June 1856), 196.

13 Letter from Elizabeth Gaskell to Charles Eliot Norton, 9 March 1859, in *The Letters of Mrs Gaskell*, ed. J. A. V. Chapple and Arthur Pollard (Manchester and New York: Mandolin, 1966), 538.

14 See Bevis, *The Art of Eloquence*; and William John Carlton, *Charles Dickens, Shorthand Writer: The 'Prentice Days of a Master Craftsman* (London: Cecil Palmer, 1926).

15 See J. Hillis Miller, *Charles Dickens: The World of His Novels* (Cambridge, MA: Harvard University Press, 1958), 160–224.

16 Lynda Nead, *Victorian Babylon: People, Streets and Images in Nineteenth-Century London* (New Haven, CT: Yale University Press, 2000), 58.

17 George Augustus Sala, *Twice Round the Clock; or, The Hours of the Day and Night in London* (London: Houlston and Wright, 1859), 73.

18 Sala, *Twice Round the Clock*, 26.

19 Sala, *Twice Round the Clock*, 70.

20 Sala, *Twice Round the Clock*, 142–3.

21 Gustav Doré and Blanchard Jerrold, *London: A Pilgrimage* (London: Grant & Co., 1872), 82.

22 Schwarzbach, *Dickens and the City*, 221.

23 Letter from Charles Dickens to the Hon. Mrs Richard Watson, 8 July 1861, *Letters*, IX, 438.

24 Edward W. Said, *On Late Style* (London: Bloomsbury, 2006), 7.

25 John M. L. Drew, 'The Nineteenth-Century Commercial Traveller and Dickens's "Uncommercial" Philosophy (Part Two)', *Dickens Quarterly*, 15 (2) (June 1998): 83–110, at 86.

26 John M. L. Drew, 'Voyages Extraordinaires: Dickens's "Travelling Essays" and *The Uncommercial Traveller* (Part Two)', *Dickens Quarterly*, 13 (3) (September 1996): 127–50, at 132.

27 Charles Dickens, *Master Humphrey's Clock*, 3 vols. (London: Chapman and Hall, 1840), I, I.

28 Charles Dickens, 'A Preliminary Word', *Household Words*, I (30 March 1850), I.

29 Charles Dickens, 'The Streets – Night', *Bell's Life in London*, 17 January 1836; *SB*, 57, 58, 59, 60.

30 Sala, *Twice Round the Clock*, 67.

CHAPTER ELEVEN

Lived death: Dickens's rogue glyphs

Garrett Stewart

If the skimming eye were either to compress my title into 'livedeath' via a dental elision at the double(d) *d* (as in 'live his own death through'), or were to vary that subvocal fusion with the aural and grammatical ambiguity of long versus short *i* in the first syllable, springing an adjective rather than a verb ('live death' in the sense of 'dead alive'), neither phonemic slippage would do damage to the argument thus begun. In fact, such elicited transformations by the reader's silent ear could only help to explain the ensuing gesture of my subtitle in allusion to a famous episode in late Dickens whose mortal brinksmanship precipitates narrative prose into a prolonged critical condition of its own, not feverish but stretched at times to the edge of coherence. It does so, however, only by exacerbating a Dickensian norm – and by summoning up in the process an underlying assumption about reading his prose. For it is frequently the case that the signifying mark, the glyph, departs from itself in the event of its textual production by the reader: a scriptive self-departure in the slippage not only from word to(ward) word but from stroke to subvocal audition. The alphabetic rather than strictly pictographic glyph becomes in this way a rogue element in even silent enunciation, overstepping the letter of a particular wording into unscheduled linguistic and ultimately narrative energy – or in other words put in play beyond its designated (and designating) scriptive service.

This is all to say that I anticipate by my subtitle the famous scene of Rogue Riderhood's near death by drowning in *Our Mutual Friend*, a chapter whose interest as an ontological crux in recent philosophical discussion becomes even more revealing, and more typically Dickensian, when it is understood as the crisis not just of a body dredged from the reflux of the Thames but of a lexical materiality surfaced from the immersive slipstream of narrative grammar itself. For what Dickens activates in this scene from his last completed novel, as so often before, is a calculated vehiculation of plot on the shunts of enunciation – as vivid in evoking a dramatic scenography as if they were almost hieroglyphic increments of the pictured scene. Graphing the transit of Riderhood's liminal predication as character – now live, now dead, now neither, now live again – the rogue glyphs in question are the audiovisual traces of Dickens's syntactically flexed and uniquely oralised writing, drafted not for the public podium necessarily, but always for the stage of the inner ear.

On which stage there is not only an aura of noises off but sometimes, rushing in from the wings, the press of grammatical second thoughts that skew a given semantic gesture in mid-delivery, replacing one emergent sense by the alternate interpretation of its phrasal 'understudy'. In the theatre of Dickensian grammar, rogue glyphs find in this way their scalar equivalents in the overlaps of syntax, where a delayed cue or dropped beat may cause a phrasing's sudden entrance upon some new usage to step on expression's previous line. Apart from explicit grammatical syllepsis – that duplex figure of speech so dear to Dickensian comedy – I'm reflecting here on the more general and pervasive paradigm of sylleptic byplay in his writing: a phrasing no sooner sprung than undone and rerouted, thus bringing to a head the incomparable dexterity of Dickens as syntactician. It is the two-ply stylistic model developed in part by that local syntactic figure of syllepsis on which I will be concentrating.

And when I mentioned in the first paragraph an 'unscheduled linguistic and ultimately narrative energy', I meant that linkage between language and narrative in the sense explored as a stylistic 'microplot' in my most recent book on Victorian fiction, *Novel Violence*, the keyword of whose own subtitle, 'narratography', is meant to resist the increasingly medium-blind categories of cognitive narratology in a return to the narrative drive of phrasing itself.[1] Discussion attempts, in so doing, to codify a long-standing emphasis in my work on fiction. As it happens, the invitation to contribute to *Dickens's Style* coincided with the fortieth anniversary of my first completed manuscript on the novelist, namely 'Style and Imagination in Charles Dickens', a doctoral dissertation filed in triplicate at Yale in the spring of 1971. In literary-critical terms, the writing was already *on the wall* rather than just in the dated technology of carbon copies when, in going to print a few years later, the revised manuscript's title was changed at the urging of the Harvard Press marketing department to *Dickens and the Trials of Imagination* (1974). Ordeal was in, style out. Agon, not linguistics. Harold Bloom rather than Morton Bloomfield. And so it has gone, with one generation's hobby horse put out to pasture by the next.

Academically, Dickens remained unusually bankable for a good while, of course, even though critical scrutiny could no longer be cashed out in the coin of appreciation for the fibre and vibrancy of his prose. But after weathering phenomenology and even deconstruction in fine fettle, his stock was rapidly devalued, whether as an avatar of the panopticon or a card-carrying Orientalist. Sometime in the 1980s, a friend serving on a search committee for a Victorianist opening at a major American university, frustrated by the lack of literary traction in the conversation to that point, asked a candidate 'what comes first to mind in thinking of Dickens?' Back came the answer without a beat dropped: 'misogyny, homophobia, and imperialism'. Yes, the trials of imagination. And scarcely abated lately when a hermeneutics of suspicion has been replaced by a suspicion of hermeneutics altogether in a preference for the 'distant reading' advocated by Franco Moretti.

Let me confess to unrepentance in a very different line of work. Indeed, I must admit that for the last decade, in between projects on visual art, itching intermittently for the look and feel of words, I've been working away at a single syntactic trope lifted by Dickens from his Augustan and comic-novel predecessors. For want of a less contested term in contemporary Anglo-American rhetorical theory, I'm calling it syllepsis, what used to be (and often still is) called zeugma: a forking grammar that goes two ways at once in a split predication that usually diverges from itself along the alternate pulls of direct objects or indirect ones. In the tradition of the Dickensian novel, these effects run from Mr Pickwick, punch drunk on punch, who 'fell into the barrow, and fast asleep, simultaneously' (*PP*, 19, 280), down through the dozens of such turns in the overtly Dickensian style of John le Carré and on to the very different prose rhythms of Toni Morrison, whether in the cadences of satire or melancholy. Compare, for instance, the transdiurnal beat of Dickens's wedding-eve cadences in *Little Dorrit* – 'And the day ended, and the night ended, and the morning came, and Little Dorrit … [brief ellipsis] came into the prison with the sunshine' (II, 34, 893) – to the more wrenching cognitive dissonance of temporality and physical presence when Morrison's half-literate heroine apostrophises her absent lover: 'I know you will come but morning does and you do not.'[2]

The variety of this trope allows for effects as tender or melancholic there as they are more often farcical elsewhere. So deeply are its parallel tracks laid down in Dickens's verbal imagination that, two years before *Pickwick*, they cut an almost obsessive swath through one of his earliest sketches. In the brief nine paragraphs of 'Shops and Their Tenants', a muted shift within parallel grammar from a literal to a metaphoric plane, in observation of street traffic 'steadily plodding on to business, or cheerfully running after pleasure', is followed by a satire of unimaginative city gents (across a silent prepositional shift) 'in all the dignity of whiskers, and gilt-watch-guards'.[3] As if to reciprocate the mismatch of this vainglory, the female object of their gaze 'sits behind the counter in a blaze of adoration and gaslight' (*SB*, 61), exaggerating such phrasing's classic textbook divide between figurative and factual reference. The particular storefront property to which the rest of the short sketch is devoted is first described in a rolling double syllepsis when 'the landlord got into difficulties, the house got into Chancery, the tenant went away, and the house went to ruin' (*SB*, 62). The pattern of bent or broken predicates is relentless, for in the next doomed 'letting' of this real estate, a clerk formerly dressed in crisp white 'took to a black neckerchief, and the proprietor took to drinking' (62). The apogee of these effects arrives (at the firm's commercial nadir) with another twofold syllepsis: 'At last the company's man came to cut off the water, and then the linen draper cut off himself, leaving the landlord his compliments and the key' (62–3). And after a brief sentimental and polemic interlude about working-class conditions, the jauntier tone returns in a punning comedy akin to syllepsis when the latest defaulter on his rent 'very coolly locked the door, and bolted himself' (64). Such logical implosion makes of syllepsis what we might term, in contemporary audio parlance, a grammatical mash-up – or call it a syntactic portmanteau. My interest in accounting for its typical collision of abstract and concrete, often its psycho/somatic division of labour, has involved the metalinguistic philosophy of both Anglo-American and European traditions, from Ludwig Wittgenstein to Stanley Cavell, including the anti-Cartesian theory of mind in Gilbert Ryle, who actually quotes Dickens's joke from *The Pickwick Papers* about Miss Bolo going 'straight home in a flood of tears, and a sedan chair' (*PP*, 35, 553), seeing it as exposing the category mistake of insisting on parallel predications for mind and body.[4] I've also found it useful to put syllepsis under the lens of Giorgio Agamben's post-ontological poetics. In his studies of literature rather than his more influential work on state violence and biopolitics, in a volume called *The End of the Poem*, Agamben's stress on the definitive twin features of poetry in its deferral of sense by sound – namely caesura and enjambment, cut and splice – suggests a way to reconceive the simultaneous rupture and overlap of sylleptic syntax, its fracture and ligature.[5] At the same time, Agamben's own philosophical wordplay in the equivocation of subjective and objective genitives – across both book and chapter titles (as, for instance, the 'Dream of Language', the 'Thought of Voice' and the 'Dictation of Poetry') – does a related syntactic work, and this in the same mode of bidirectional possessive grammar mobilised unnoticed by Agamben, along with syllepsis, at the fulcral moment of that chapter in *Our Mutual Friend*, which, as we're now to see, Agamben joins fellow Italian philosopher Roberto Esposito, as well as Gilles Deleuze, in glossing from their separate if overlapping perspectives. Picking up the dropped stitches and loose ends of these converging treatments allows me to revisit and extend my previous claims for stylistic deviance in Victorian fiction as a violence in the lexical and syntactic register that often finds itself timed to some extreme and potentially lethal turn of plot.

The chapter of *Our Mutual Friend* in question is given over entirely to the near death by drowning of Rogue Riderhood, which, for Deleuze, in the sudden fascination that the man's unconscious body generates, isolates the idea of 'a life', immanent but detached from all subjectivity.[6] But Deleuze proceeds without the slightest mention of Dickens's actual phrasing in this chapter. When Agamben turns to Deleuze and Dickens, he himself singles out only one word from the episode for its legal overtones, as we'll see.[7] And when Esposito turns to Agamben on this Deleuzian proof text, no return to Dickens seems necessary at all. For him the guttering life of Riderhood offers a Deleuzian case study in 'potentializing and depotentializing flow' that moves, in Agamben's terms, between *zoe* (sheer animation) and *bios* (human life) and that engages therefore the 'classic and controversial Deleuzian theme of the "virtual"',[8] with its overtones in this case, for Esposito, of an 'affirmative biopolitics'.[9] This may be a reading of his philosophical predecessors, but it is not a reading of Dickens, for whom more is virtualised in this chapter than the ebbing life – or even the ebbing and 'flowing' life – of a solitary human body. By a dense pattern of syntactic and lexical equivocations, we probe there instead, I hope to show, the linguistic virtuality of character itself in fiction, and hence, by the route of philosophy after all, the reciprocal vanishing point, for Agamben elsewhere, of ontology and linguistics.[10] This is the metaphysical limit that defines, if one can put it this way in a double grammar all its own, the human subject's *being in language*, existing within if not constituted by it. For which prose narrative, especially when couched in a style as intrepid as Dickens's, is among our most convenient cultural laboratories. And for which a single isolated character's coming to consciousness, or back to it, across a tight mesh of linguistic and ontological ironies, closely interlinked, is an irresistible proof text.

This episode yields dozens of those ad-hoc wrinkles and double folds whose induced reflex action in reading, whose requisite second thoughts, even when far from the comic variety we see when the retiring Mary Ann Peacher 'resumed her seat and her silence' (*OMF*, II, 11, 340), are nonetheless on a continuum with the cognitive feedback loop of its splayed grammar. So it is, this chapter assumes, that a merely intermittent appearance of either marked or subtly deflected sylleptic patterns around and across its pages doesn't prevent that device's specialised bifurcating logic, its yoking of tangible and intangible, literal and metaphoric registers, from offering a pattern of considerable syntactic leverage, and at times unique thematic purchase, on the breached antitheses and finessed dichotomies that more openly organise the chapter – and this across a whole array of linguistic devices that a 'narratographic' response would dial up in tracing the 'microplot' of narrative at the level of word and phrase. Beyond that assumption, probably this much more is necessary as well: a taking for granted – and where else to risk counting on it lately than in an anthology on style – that literary reading is still first and foremost a verbal process. In a professional epoch one of whose latest trends is a so-called ethical turn that often, according to various agendas, turns us completely away from the written page and towards the imagined moral valences of character interaction, or really more like human interaction unmediated by text, my chapter is, to speak sylleptically, meant to hold out for, and an example of, something else: something like the ethics, or at least the morale, of actually reading.

So one more irresistible pair of examples, these from *Bleak House*, where we can note the sylleptic operation both in concentrated satiric form and, closer to the Riderhood chapter in *Our Mutual Friend*, as a gradual downshifting of rhetorical gears in mortal transit. First, there is the anti-colonialist joke linking agriculture to imperial culture across the hypocritical phrasing that lumps together under philanthropy 'a view to the general cultivation of the coffee berry – *and* the natives', where plunder and the white man's burden unabashedly collapse upon each other (*BH*, 4, 44). Next, anticipating our extended encounter with life on the cusp of oblivion in *Our Mutual Friend*, there is Lady Dedlock's very different ordeal, poised on the verge of her own annihilation when brought to certain death by, so to say, weather and enervation. Except in her case Dickens actually says it otherwise. Maybe this is because it is actually Lady Dedlock writing, rather than the narrator, in a letter posthumously read: 'Cold, wet, and fatigue, are sufficient causes for my being found dead; but I shall die of others, though I suffer from these' (*BH*, 59, 841).

While putting the suff-ering back into suff-iciency, Lady Dedlock also inverts a sylleptic mismatch of objective and subjective, outer and inner. Without mentioning the causal link between shame and fatal weather in the unwritten pun on 'exposure' – that matrix or structuring absence of the whole passage – she dies by displacement of snow and exhaustion. But the sylleptic split is less muted in her further clarification, with its striking shift from present tense to the mortal fait accompli of a death already transpired in the future perfect: 'It was right … that I should die of terror and my conscience', a phrasing with further overtones of an imagined Shakespearian hendiadys like those illogical twinnings so brilliantly smoked out by Empson as the limit case of double grammar, as if one were to say 'the terror and conscience of My Lady's guilt', or calling up an actual Shakespearian contortion, from another text of ghosts that walk, when the dead Buckingham appears to Richard III, urging him to 'die in terror of thy guiltiness'.[11]

A decade after *Bleak House*, we arrive at *Our Mutual Friend*, where one may well ask whether its language does indeed, as Henry James felt, represent the novelistic 'poverty … of permanent exhaustion' rather than some new depth probed in the matter of language's life-positing energies.[12] Book 3, Chapter 3, then: almost exactly midway between drownings at either end, first Harmon's supposed one, later Wrayburn's near (and Riderhood's actual) one. As prelude to the man's eventual death in kind, once Riderhood's body is discovered in the Thames and deposited upstairs in the local ale house from whose precincts he has otherwise been barred for his loutish behaviour, that body, at the novel's midpoint, rivets the neighbourhood clientele with its passive struggle for life: its life, its marginal vitality, not really *his* at all, the man named Rogue Riderhood, short for Roger. What the pub denizens, turned physician's assistants, are explicitly drawn to in the ordeal of that liminal organic form is humanity degree zero, bare (and barely) animate life, not only impersonal but virtually disembodied – made indeed merely virtual in its continued existence, speculative, invisible, at best presumptive. This withdrawn node of vitality is a residuum of being, no longer self, that is not even to be confidently located in the water-rat's saturated remains, but that retreats instead, as Dickens stresses metonymically, to unknown depths. Finally, though, the ebbing flicker of existence is reignited there in the inert rogue body by the intervention of a local doctor who also, like the others, knows the brutish man too well to care for him (in that other sense) personally. What even those who despise life's incarnation in this crude form are nonetheless magnetised by, in short, is simply the tension within which, radically impersonal, 'a striving human soul' (*OMF*, III, 3, 444) – mortal strife, not human purpose yet – is caught 'between' life and death. Or between figuration and absence. In regard to this founding divide, there is an apparently digressive joke on metaphoric ambiguity that actually hits home. Mr Tootle, speaking of Riderhood's collision with a steamer, remarks that 'she cut him in two', and the narrator is quick to intervene for clarity: 'Mr Tootle is so far figurative, touching the dismemberment, as that he means the boat, and not the man. For the man lies whole before them' (III, 3, 443). Not exactly, though, as we will soon learn, since the man is in fact sundered on the brink of extinction between personification and somatic remains – as the complexities of the passage wrench into view and sometimes torture into equivocation from here out. For his is a life force 'curiously separable from himself' (III, 3, 443) – oddly, uncannily, that is, but 'curiously' also with the hint of a lodestone, in the adverb's other sense, for neighbourhood fascination.

Well before the dead metaphoric 'strife' hidden in the variant cliché of 'mortal striving' is reduced from existential tug-of-war to waterside fisticuffs, as it will explicitly be in the chapter's final and in some ways definitive trope, with death as spectral opponent, Dickensian style has served – as if by contrast in its own beckoning and contagious high spirits, a full thirty chapters earlier – to exclude Riderhood's inveterate sociopathology from the cosy welcome of the public house, the Six Jolly Fellowship Porters. The writing there, early on, like the place itself, is too good for him. Introduced with the delectable snug echoism of 'biscuits in baskets', followed by the personification of 'polite beer-pulls that made low bows when customers were served beer' (*OMF*, I, 6, 62), such evocations set a typical Dickensian scene from whose dockside purlieus, in one meaning of this early chapter's title, Riderhood is decidedly 'cut adrift'. He is certainly cut by the proprietor, Miss Abbey Potterson – and cut off from his drink: 'The Fellowships don't want you at all' (I, 6, 63). The boorish drunk has reached his allowed limit in any case – even 'if you were as welcome here as you are not' (I, 6, 63), with that negating predication underscoring a communal exclusion and social erasure soon to be manifested in a mortal limit case.

Beyond the ironies of grammatical parallelism, the split between hospitality and an exiling spite takes in fact a passing sylleptic shape. For Riderhood is ushered out by an insistence that the cramped bar of the Fellowship 'would rather by far have your room than your company' (*OMF*, I, 6, 63). Long before his displacement by threatened death rather than disgust, his absence would make for a more convivial few cubic feet than his presence. And he is later marginalised by another sylleptic forking around the grammar not of *have* but of *give*. This happens after we've heard by ludicrously euphemistic circumlocution that his immediate neighbours are 'rather shy in reference to the honour of cultivating the Rogue's acquaintance' (II, 12, 350) with the capital R of his nickname turned further accusatory by the definitive article. As a result, to keep clear of the man, these neighbours are found 'more frequently giving him the cold shoulder than the warm hand' (II, 12, 350), substituting a metaphor of chill distance for the literal intimacy of friendly touch.

With Riderhood recently forbidden to cross the threshold of the public house, the communal circle closes around him only when he is removed from his body to death's invisible door, thus launching the highfalutin rhetorical antecedence of the later chapter's facetious title, 'The Same Respected Friend in More Aspects than One'. Among these 'aspects', implicitly, is that of villainy dispersed from personhood towards oblivion under the sign of marginal animation – and then returned again to the state of an incarnate pariah. 'In sooth', the chapter begins, the found body 'is Riderhood and no other, or' – with the alternative inserted as if in recognition of a dubious predication in the body itself 'being' Riderhood – 'it is the outer husk and shell of Riderhood and no other' (*OMF*, III, 3, 443). Within this deliberate heavy parallelism, with the internal lexical stiffening from 'other' to 'outer', waits a wordy hendiadys – as if 'husk and shell', organic and inorganic at once, were an idiomatic compound inviting a singular rather than plural verb (and with the added portmanteau suggestion, for this flotsam of the Thames, of 'husk' + 'shell' as 'hull'). Prose infers at this turn a generalised biological carapace within which life remains in question because entirely in suspension.

It is just this husky shell, this hardened husk, this hull of a hulk, that (not 'who') – inanimate now to all eyes – must ironically be 'borne' into a bedroom where only a few interested parties can assemble. Once taking up our own places there, gathered around with the others, we are confronted, out of the blue, by a direct address that one recognises, only a sentence later, as ventriloquised, without quotation marks, from a doctor summoned to the scene: 'If you are not gone for good, Mr. Riderhood', apostrophises the sentence with a professional euphemism ('gone'), only for this phrasing to turn epistemological (and so ontological) almost at once – if not gone 'it would be something to know where you are hiding at present' (*OMF*, III, 3, 444). The irony of apostrophe is in this case metaphysical, not just rhetorical. If there is a 'you' retained in this body, it has retreated beyond discernible reach, deaf to all interrogation. Reference to it seems as much a grammatical as a human impossibility. 'This flabby lump of mortality that we work so hard at with such patient perseverance, yields' – the coming phrase, as a variant of 'sign of life', being not quite idiomatic – 'yields no sign of you' (III, 3, 444): no symptom of life, but also no *signifier* of presence, where the latter seems more abstract and symbolic than the former. The next sentence reiterates the uncertainty with a grammar of being reduced to nondescript modal forms. 'If you are gone for good, Rogue' – as if, ironically, with more pressure this time on the chimed idiom, since the only place for good this creature could ever be is gone – 'it is very solemn, and if you are coming back, it is hardly less so' (III, 3, 444). Hardly indeed. The urgency in all this doesn't concern the immortality of the soul and its euphemised 'departures' rather than erasures, but instead the condition of being itself in its waning and return.

But since there is no knowing at this point, there is only a concerted superficial doing. Prose now takes up the clipped, stenographic notations of a medical case study logged in present-tense reportage: 'Doctor examines the dank carcase, and pronounces, not hopefully, that it is worth while trying to reanimate the same' (III, 3, 443) – worth trying to revive not 'him', but rather the inert and bureaucratic 'same'. The hovering present tense here is sustained across the rest of the chapter as if to dilate the suspended moment this side of death's timeless advent. 'All the best means are at once in action, and everybody present lends a hand, and a heart and soul.' The loathsome man typically 'given' a cold shoulder instead of a warm hand is now, as mere body, metaphorically 'lent' that hand by anyone 'present' to his current absence, as well as – in a favoured Dickensian syllepsis dividing body from assumed inner motive, affective and spiritual both – lent not just a hand but 'a heart and soul'.

'Stay! Did that eyelid tremble?' (*OMF*, III, 3, 444). There the self-diverging idiom 'Stay!' commands both the equivalent of 'Wait, wait, look there!' (addressed to what we might call the choric eye) and the more directly vocative 'Don't go!' (to the pending corpse), an address continued later when the 'artificial respiration' (III, 3, 444) applied by the doctor has already been interrogated in its effects, as if by osmosis, through his own 'breathing low' in apostrophising the body before him. Certainly the case isn't decided as yet between life and death. 'Nay, in the suspense and mystery of the latter question' – that is, about whether or not Riderhood still is at all, still has being enough to be viable for return – we find our doubts manifested (an uncertainty put with deliberate, rationalising stiffness in the doctor's borrowed cadences) in a question 'involving that of where you may be now' (III, 3, 444), which thus entails 'a solemnity even added to that of death' (444). The more expected 'where you are now' turns suggestively ontological in its subjunctive phrasing as 'where you may be' – with the mood of conjecture covering not just location but existence itself: if you any longer can be said to 'be'. And as if to mark further the violence done to language by the proximate silence of death, the normal dichotomy of look *on* or *at* a body versus look *away*, perhaps to the thought of life's absence, is instead rotated towards an almost ungrammatical zeugma in the idiomatic stumble of look *on* versus look *off.* For such is the unnerving nature of this episode that it renders 'us who are in attendance alike afraid to look on you and to look off you' – *off* as if into some far ineffable distance, thereby rehearsing the drastic break of the life/death toggle in the dissonant key of reception.

Alluding to the 'spark of life' (*OMF*, III, 3, 443) where the subjective genitive plays against the equative genitive – the electrical spark belonging or inherent to life and the metaphoric spark that is or amounts to life – is now, again, the same 'spark' that 'may sm*ou*lder and *go* out, or it may *glo*w *and* exp*and*' (444). In this phrasing across the hinge of a syllabic chiasm and mortal switchpoint, the disyllable 'smoulder' breaks down along the groove of assonance into two monosyllables ('go out') – only then, alternately, to be fanned up (from 'go' to 'glow') into the further animation that might mount from 'and' itself into 'expand' rather than end expended. Mimetic form – in that seemingly effortless and intuitive way Dickens is prone to mobilise it – isn't merely surplus effect in this chapter, as we will come to recognise, but catches instead the very pulse of attendance on the life it has vested in the first place.

With Riderhood 'struggling to come back', we read that 'Now he is almost here, now he is far away again' (*OMF*, III, 3, 444). Spatial euphemisms (lifted from the Victorian sociolect) like 'he is no longer with us' or 'he is passed on', detonate around that 'almost here' – life's vaguest adverb of 'presence'. And if, in the systole and diastole of this mortal oscillation, Dickens may more specifically have had the famous seventh stanza of Tennyson's *In Memoriam* in mind, it might well have been in part for the ambivalent enjambment that no sooner, tomb-side, points 'far away' towards the drowned Hallam's posthumous fate than it leaves him behind in the wake of the ongoing: 'He is not here; but far away', we read, until the adverbial phrase, end-stopped only by the unpunctuated line's end, topples forward to identify that wider sphere where 'The noise of life begins again.'[13] In the broadest sense, this is a quasi-sylleptic forking of reference for which Dickens finds repeated equivalents in the dovetailed semantics of his own prose enjambments, both in and beyond this episode, an episode in which the 'noise' of Riderhood's 'life' is soon to begin again in his growling return to consciousness. Moreover, in the passage before us – with Riderhood's immediate retreat again to 'far away' – distance in this case, by association with near-drowning, is given to us not just in hazy terms but in a marked final metaphor, figured explicitly as a depth. With animate generality finally personified once more in a single vilified form, the 'low, bad, unimpressible face is coming up' – the contrast of up to low down – 'up from the depths of the river, or what other depths, to the surface again' (III, 3, 446). In this way, the nether world is plumbed only by metonymic association with watery submergence – and this, as we note next, with a final twist of rhetoric in reprisal for this miserable, no longer socially wished-for reprieve.

For at just this point the earlier syllepsis of communal bonding and mind–body harmony – hand at one with 'heart and soul' in service to the ebbing life force – has been reversed in a return to repugnance and ostracisation, represented at once in a physical stiffening and emotional recoil: a kind of ethical rigor mortis seizing up a momentary and impersonal human identification: 'As his lineaments soften with life, their faces and their hearts harden to him' (*OMF*, III, 3, 446). In a dyadic yoking far less idiomatic than 'heart and soul', spiritual ossification has come to the fore in the image of a group physiognomy set rigidly against this recovered outcast. The coldness extends, now, well beyond the given shoulder and the withheld hand; in the thermodynamics of empathy tracked by this passage across the shift from adjectival to predicate form, or in other words from clinical to ethical register: 'As he grows warm, the doctor and the four men cool' (III, 3, 446). Again in the sense, as with 'harden', of cool *to*: all response no longer abstract, self-contained or meditative, but directed at and against, social rather than philosophical.

But look again at the splicing of the 'and' grammar in as 'their faces and their hearts harden', a process knotted off in the echoic clench of 'heart'/'hard'. This phonetic play aside, we have here a case of syllepsis in its classic form, if in the nominative rather than objective case. The parallelism is inferential, behaviorist in cast, moving from one physical fact toward, by deduction, another and more spiritual one across a metaphoric drift from features stiffening in recognition to an empathy petrified in revulsion. Yet again a simple conjunction provides the fulcrum between psychic and material notations, spiritual and somatic response: 'and' in these bifold linkages not just marking a bracket but tightening a yoke, often (as here) between presumed cause and manifest effect, or condition and symptom. The hardening of heart is invisible, intangible, implicit only by somatic symptom, or say *featured forth* as figuration. This kind of syllepsis simply spells out syntactically what is true otherwise in Dickens: the spirit manifested in body. In its hovering – or shunting – between metonymy and metaphor, syllepsis is the Dickensian trope of tropes, in that it turns characters not into people but into embodied meaning, agencies of the semiotic, vessels of inference. And with Rogue no less than the others, as we will see, what accompanies his vivification, what personalises him again if you will, is his embodiment of a trope.

Notwithstanding how often by now in this chapter the language of identity and presence has been split between the grammar of deixis ('here', 'there') and that of existence ('is', 'be'), each equally tentative, the climactic sentence of repealed death is put through its paces by being made to wheel round on itself in spelling out once more these divided terms – though now in close and reconsolidated proximity. To this end, a restorative grammar must first build up a clause-compounded head of steam in a serial run of conjunctions: 'And now he begins to breathe naturally, and he stirs, and the doctor declares him to have come back from that inexplicable journey where he stopped on the dark road' – until this burst of metaphoric cliché is cut short after a comma, and one last conjunction, in arriving – as if by jolting the brakes on – at the supposedly nonfigurative point of rest: 'to have come back, ... and to be here' (*OMF*, III, 3, 446), with its strained compression around the elongated *e* of the earlier phrasing, 'Now he is almost here' (444).

What is the prosody of this deliberately flat-footed metaphysics? To be *here*? To *be* here? To be, not there on the dark journey any longer, but here again at last? To *here* be? Nearly dead for so long, Rogue comes back to being, comes to himself, comes back to being who it is that he is. So the long shadow again of the sylleptic paradigm. Narrative progress contorts its own logic by getting forked between parallel clauses; quoting again: 'to have come back and to be here', as if 'to have come back to life and the world'. Lurking there, too, is a further sense that drives syllepsis into the crevices rather than the ligatures of the lexeme (or in other words, as Agamben might have it, that summons unlicensed caesura from within the invisible enjambment of a sound stream). On this skewed understanding, this undermined lexical standing, Riderhood is seen to have come back 'and', across a slippage between locative adverb and fugitive pronoun, 'to be he – ' as well as 'here': to, as we say, be *himself* again as well as here now, biography impinging again to subsume biology.

But there is as yet no apparent *will* to be, and the torquing force of existential irony now shifts to the genitive. For when Rogue is first prodded back to his languishing anthropoid mass, enlisted to help transform corpse again to inhabited body, it is not without resistance that he grudgingly resubmits (rather than recommits) to life. For 'like us all, when we swoon – like us all, every day of our lives when we wake – he is instinctively unwilling' (*OMF*, III, 3, 444) – unwilling, that is, to lift (himself) into consciousness. Psychoanalysis will arrive half a century later to call this resistance the death instinct fighting against life-sustaining libidinal drives; followed by psychopoetics more than half a century later, in the writing of Peter Brooks, to identify such clutched quiescence as a binding up and knotting off of energies come too soon for plot's sake and needing remotivation in progress towards a more proper end.[14] Rogue must be rescued for his right death, a deserved rather than an accidental drowning (arranged by plot later) that needs at this point only a strategic deferral to prepare for its later repetition and working-through.

What follows now, though, in the passage at hand, is the Cartesian lynchpin and sticking point in Dickens's chosen reflexive phrasing for the return of and to sentience. Unmentioned by the triangulation of philosophical work on this passage (Deleuze, Agamben, Esposito), prose itself bursts forth in metaphysical irony across a linked complication of genitive and copulative grammar when what Riderhood is 'unwilling to be' – so the sentence actually continues – is 'restored to the consciousness of this existence', so as to 'be left dormant, if he could' (*OMF*, III, 3, 444–5). He would rather 'be left dormant' than 'be'. In even that surface riptide of predication, the deeper ontological undertow is felt. Recalling the bivalve 'of' in Agamben's titles, we see here, in the circular phrase 'consciousness of this existence' (what? – versus 'this existence of a consciousness'?) a similar spread of the genitive across objective and subjective grammar – and across the whole spectrum from merely animate to actually conscious existence, or in Agamben's terms elsewhere, from *zoe* to *bios*: first, self-recognition in the objective case; second, that facet of existence which is consciousness itself (a kind of 'partitive genitive'); and third but not least, via the equative genitive again, that sense of life which is defined as nothing less than consciousness per se.

Soon enough, though, Dickens returns us to the fallen world of standard clausal grammar, where consciousness (like other nominated states) is not circular and self-confirming, like the Cartesian *cogito*, even if resisted, but instead social, anxious, besieged by otherness. 'Presently' – the faintly spatial as well as temporal locative – 'Presently they all return, and wait for him to become conscious' (*OMF*, III, 3, 447). Syntax allows us to pause there over a coherent predicate adjective. But only for the transitional moment of revived personality, at which point the adjective precipitates its own dependent clause; for Riderhood is not just to become aware again in a general sense but, as the clause unrolls, 'to become conscious that they will all be glad to get rid of him' (III, 3, 447). As will plot need to be finally and more fully rid of him – but only when he is later drowned by his enemy Headstone. Until now, the mortal risk to his *existence* has elicited the same degree of collective sympathy that is ultimately repelled by his retrieved *presence*.

What the lout has already begun leaving behind in his grudging, surly return is the philosophical yield of the episode as it must have silently appealed to Agamben (quite apart from the engagement with Deleuze). For the first chapter of Agamben's *Idea of Prose*, alluding by its odd title to the *potentiality* of expression as the absolute and founding limit of all thought – the very *idea of prose* before the ideas it inscribes – speaks of the near-death experience (with no mention whatever of Dickens, and no link to these concerns in his later turn to Riderhood) as a signal moment in the relation of thought to language. Going out-of-body puts matter(s) into perspective, even if only for the lookers-on – and of course for readers-in. The speechless lurch towards oblivion can, when recovered from, be the opposite of vitiating. Under the title 'The Idea of Matter', such moments confront the subject with its reduction to sheer matter, to corpse, even while enhancing at times that other sense: as in, say, 'the matter of my being' (paraphrasing Agamben) – or (Dickens getting here first again, with an essentialising alliteration) in Mr Tootle's speaking contemptuously, in regard to Riderhood, of the deep-seated (even phonetically self-embedded) 'manner of the man' (*OMF*, III, 3, 443).[15] For 'those who return to life after an apparent death', so Agamben argues, have seen something real besides the appearance (both senses, and too close for reflective comfort) of death.[16] They have encountered the apparition, the making apparent, of life itself as a thing distinct, curtailed, bounded. Though 'in reality they were never dead at all (otherwise they wouldn't have returned), nor are they rid of the necessity of dying some day' – in this, very much like Riderhood – 'they are, however, free from the representation of death.'[17] They have been made present to it instead. Attending upon their own death as potential, they may return potentiated to life. The philosophical clarity this can bring is of course squandered even while allegorised with the bargeman cad in Dickens: allegorised, or at least displaced, onto the innocent and suddenly more knowing bystanders, who – among them certain renowned philosophers rushing to the scene of the accident – know death's limit by proxy; and know also a fellow-feeling beneath community, the potential new ethics (Agamben again) soon eclipsed in Dickens by the specifics of social characterisation and their attendant moralisation.

Until now as well, across the distended span of Riderhood's flickering revival, his daughter has harbored false hopes for his reformation, spurred by the fact that the former self-dehumanised outcast, long-time 'object of' repugnance, is now, as an inert body rather than a personality, an 'object of sympathy and interest' (*OMF*, III, 3, 445). *Object* because, in short, not yet again a subject. Hoping as she does that the drowning will have been metaphoric only, a quenching of his anti-social 'evil', this fantasy, buoying her spirits, 'floats' across her mind in its redemptive scenario and associated aquatic conceit. Grammatically as well as figuratively, the daughter's false hopes are embedded by indirection in the canted, off-kilter prose of her desire. Ministering to his chill body, an 'empty form' in which life has not yet returned to occupancy, Pleasant 'quite believes that the impassive hand she chafes' – as if devotion itself would rub off on him – 'will revive a tender hand, if it revive ever' (III, 3, 445). What was that? In the delegation of her fantasy, the transitive grammar of her tender friction is infused as a new intransitive mode of the father's being, this when 'revive a tender hand' takes its noun as a predicate nominative, or complement, rather than object. We might think of this as a case of counter-mimetic form. Only a self-transformation as abrupt and surprising as that down-shifted grammar could turn such a hand soft – and won't. Hovering there, another phantom syllepsis: the impossible reclamation of the man as tender of hand and heart: the non-Cartesian dream of a renovated mind wholly realised in its restored body.

Instead, the water rat essentialised by death in the river comes back a grudging belligerent revived by epitome in his squaring off with his fate. For Riderhood pulls himself together 'exactly as if he had just had a Fight' (*OMF*, III, 3, 448), an 'as if' that closes out the chapter in an expanded trope – almost an extended metaphysical conceit – figuring the 'struggle' for life. Battered and dazed, as if knocked cold by an opponent, Riderhood *comes to*, comes to himself, in typical aggressive form. Sponsored unsaid by the stalest cliché, the proverbial 'fight for life', Rogue examines his hands to see what 'punishment' he had received in it, his 'pugilistic manner' extending to 'an appearance of great malevolence toward his late opponent and all the spectators' (III, 3, 448). His so-called 'late opponent' has almost rendered Rogue the late Riderhood. But to recall Roland Barthes' famous distinction, the 'figure' of pugnacity and embattlement in this revived villain is the way to extricate him, as 'character', from a leveling fate.[18] He has sparred with non-being and returned bruised and, as ever, brutal. In Dickensian ethics, Riderhood has thus returned from death as less (again) than fully human, with an ironic emphasis on first words that recalls Agamben's sense elsewhere, derived from Heidegger yet unnoted in his comments on Deleuze and Dickens, of the meeting of man and animal in the voice before meaning.[19] It's not just that Riderhood's rough movements are 'dogged' (III, 3, 448), but that, in his scoffing at the doctor's moralistic words of welcome-back, his daughter must interpret the familiar gist of his mumbled 'don't want no Poll Parroting' (448) – his tagline of contempt for any formulaic human sentiment, phrased in terms of an animal voicing without real speech. She must, that is, make out these words from amid the sheer noise of what is this time a 'growl' so 'unintelligible' (III, 3, 447) that it hasn't in its own right reached back into earthly language.

After three repetitions of 'fight' in the sense of fisticuffs, finally the unspoken cliché 'battle with death' (enlisting, via intertext, Dickens's own 1846 Christmas book title, *Battle of Life*) surfaces across the dismissive irony of the chapter's last move, Rogue's exit line. For it is there that he 'takes his departure out of that ring in which he *has* had' – the present-tense frame right to the last, here shifted into the present perfect when all drama is finally put behind him – 'in which he has had that little turn-up with Death' (*OMF*, III, 3, 448). The last paragraph has in fact taken its spur from a telling (because ultimately metanarrative) grammatical fragment: 'Thus, Mr. Riderhood:' – a phrasing angled back to his latest sulky remark and forward, through the turnstile of the colon, towards a further description that operates as a kind of extended quasi-syllepsis in its own right, bracketing the not-quite-symptomatic wordplay by which cap and its owner are each in different senses 'lent', the former *from* the hands of the daughter and latter *on* her yielding body as crutch, that daughter on whom he always in every sense leans: 'Thus, Mr Riderhood: taking from the hands of his daughter, with special ill-will, a *lent* cap, and grumbling as he pulls it down over his ears. Then, getting on his unsteady legs, *leaning* heavily upon her, and growling' (III, 3, 448). Arcing across this grammatical off-echo or syntactic slant rhyme is, I would want to add, the phantom syllepsis of his taking her help and his departure at once, always take and no give.

Yes: 'Thus, Mr. Riderhood'. Not just up to his old tricks after his bout with death. But 'thus' posited again, vested with existence, offered up herewith. Back both in action and in true form. That sort of anticlimax. Or say: born again from and by the tropes that have always conjured the defensiveness and belligerence of his personality, born again as character

from the backwash of figuration. This prolonged exercise in vitalisation
has therefore a marked allegorical overtone. 'Thus' any character, brought
to life before us by characteristics: a character whose denotation, as
Barthes would have it, is at base merely a cluster of connotations, as a
nickname like Rogue makes unmistakable. And there have been earlier
linguistic clues to this laboratory of life's vesting by figuration, including
the one dead metaphoric turn that catches Agamben's ear. As close as the
socially expelled and nearly expunged Riderhood comes in this passage to
that untouchable status of the outcast known famously as *homo sacer* elsewhere in Agamben – the 'bare' life for whom there can be no 'biopoliti-
cal' or sacrificial ritual, just brute extermination – here the literary ear of
the philosopher, leaving this unmentioned, latches instead onto a passing
trope in the language of being itself.[20]

  After citing Deleuze's quotation from the Dickens passage, that is,
Agamben bears down momentarily on a single node of its diction, but
lets up again too soon. On the score of suspended animation, quoting
Agamben, 'Dickens refers to this state as "abeyance", using a word' – here
the early student of juridical theory as well as the seasoned literary reader
in Agamben, rather than the philosopher, tips his hand – 'that originates in
legal parlance and that indicates the suspension of rules or right between
validity and abrogation' – a momentary state, so to say, of exception.[21] It
applies in particular, one might want to add, when the facts of a case, as
in a deceased's estate, are not clearly 'established' (Dickens's own coming
word, in a twisted context). In abeyance for Riderhood is a state of being
that must (almost in the medical sense) be stabilised before the locus of
animation can draw other verbs, like 'developed', into its field of predication across the mock-euphemistic legalese of Dickensian circumlocution:
'The spark of life was deeply interesting while it was in abeyance, but now
that it has got established in Mr. Riderhood, there appears to be a general
desire that circumstances had admitted of its being developed in anybody
else, rather than that gentleman' (*OMF*, III, 3, 446–7). And that spark
echoes of course the earlier iteration of this idiom, where it offers the neutral antecedent for the paragraph's penultimate clause in 'because it *is* life',
a phrasing whose italics tilt it further in the unmistakable direction of
grammatical tautology rather than synecdoche: the spark that defines life
and is recognised to do so, offered up by Dickensian grammar as a case of
the verb of *being* squared, raised reflexively to its own power.

  Further pursuant to the stuffy legal jargon of 'abeyance', though, the
localised suspension of vital spark marks something else held in explicit
'abeyance' by the novel – and anticipates its release as narrative climax:

not the return to life of a villain but, across a larger narrative arc, the return to social presence of the hero, who, after complications of the plot so faked and Byzantine that they seem deliberately mounted to vanish into allegory, has falsely encouraged the presumption of his own death by drowning, returned incognito to the workplace, and only at the end found reclamation for his desire and his name, each bestowed now not on a corpse found drowned but on a comely wife and her chastened vanity. So begins the novel's penultimate chapter, where the newly amalgamated bourgeois couple seeks out legal help in making any necessary amends, the prose itself levitated by the slant echoes of assonance in a lexical as well as social harmonics staged to ventilate the residue of legal overkill: 'Mr and Mrs John Harmon's first delightful occupation was to set all matters right that had strayed in any way wrong, or that might, could, would, or should have strayed in any way wrong, while their name was *in abeyance*' (*OMF*, IV, 16, 803).

But there's something more in the narrative bargain, paid out by way of a deeper textual investment. For again the phrasing of a crisis and its denouement catch the conscience of an entire fictional agenda – or say the ethics of virtuality in narrative characterisation. John Harmon's 'fictitious death' (*OMF*, IV, 16, 803), as it is finally called, may have kept his legal name in 'abeyance' (803), suspended without a reference. But the model for such 'suspended animation' has already been set halfway through the text, in the chapter on which we've joined the philosophers in concentrating. As we have seen in Riderhood's return from oblivion, the mordantly denominated 'respected friend' (III, 3) – shadow eponym of the hero as mutual friend to so many – has ultimately returned to the 'aspect' of a character rather than a vitalist abstraction. But of course in this novel, in any novel, all deaths are 'fictitious'. And all lives figurative. In this regard, it is the character we like least with whom Dickens has chosen to experiment most: reducing not just personhood to its mere organic immanence, in Deleuze's terms *this life* reduced instead to *a life*, but, closer to the bone of narrative invention, distilling embodied being to its mere potential, character to figure, vitality to virtuality.

And – a last but ultimately axiomatic point – there is the further and no doubt unnerving sense that we may occasionally all but peer through, or hear through, the shapes of narrative language to the invisible recess of its actual grounding – or groundlessness – in the virtualisation of human lives. This ontological false bottom can be signalled at times by the very look of words on the page, not only their sound as speech but their graphic alterations and adjustments (as in the italic lunge into emphasis of '*is* life'). And even by what is held in abeyance – and abyssal negation – by their gaping and vacancies. So a final example to this effect, reprised from its previous citation. That early pivotal paragraph about dormancy and the death drive, with the mind in feeble resistance against the 'consciousness of this existence' (*OMF*, III, 3, 445), begins with Riderhood's 'struggling to come back', or in other words with his battle for being (446). 'Now, he is almost here', we remember, 'now he is far away again' (III, 3, 444), the comma splice transfiguring the very caesura to an enjambment, with any sequence all but simultaneous in this place beyond human time. And then again: 'Now he is struggling harder to get back' (III, 3, 444). The pugilist's unsaid but ultimately suggested 'come back' is in fact a return to existence all told.

But the longer one looks at the tripled parallelism of 'Now he' (and I do mean looks), with the phrasing's wordy attentiveness to every wax and wane of vitality stretching the moment by wavering iterations – the more one looks, the more chance there is that the spaced words will themselves be distended into blank countersigns for the void over which, as is the character himself, they are suspended. There is no case of syllepsis here, of course; there is instead that self-difference internal to language for whose submarine iceberg syllepsis offers only here and there the double tip. This is what the trope models for me in Dickens: writing entertaining its own alternatives in process, or ghosted by them. In this spirit, close reading can get so close that it looks through, as in this final example, to its twin abrogation, morphemic and ontological at once, beneath the 'gaps' of lexical 'abeyance' in process. Or put it that, with characterisation's trial by ordeal in the Riderhood chapter, the gestalt oscillation between fictitious death and fictitious life is taken up in the figure/ground switch of graphophonemic inscription itself. All we need do is imagine the suspended scrape of Dickens's pen over the blanks of the lines as he, yet again, works to vest life in his characters through sheer scribal drive. 'Now, he is here ... now he is [not] ... Now he is ...', the pivotal middle iteration turning in fact on the negating monosyllabic undertone of *no he isn't*; he's far away – and nowhere we can know. Thus is the struggle to 'be here' (and therefore to be he) a struggle lexicographic and ontological both. It is waged at times, and by no doubt unconscious lexical risks and wagers, from a place beneath speech sounds altogether – with in this case the obliquely conjured haze of 'nowhere' broken up – and out of – in the very moment of the character's reemergence as once again, according to that earliest phrase for the novel's hero himself, a man from 'some' rather than no 'where'. At the level of morphology and lexical juncture, to borrow Agamben's dyad one last time, the poetics of enjambment blur the word form's own constitutive caesura. Such a cross-lexical spectre ('now he is here' cancelled in lexical process by a phantasmal 'nowhere') rears its antonymic force in these clauses – only for a split second each time – across the threefold downbeat of a syllabic split that rebunches the graphemes against the pace of the phonemes. As usual, though, enunciated language quickly overcomes, overrides, the very lapses that articulate its junctures, the emptiness it manipulates, the slack it capitalises on, its lack in action.

Be this as it may about the hinted non-being of a yawning 'nowhere' in a syncopated 'now he', any such sense of a spectral scriptive ripple operating potentially – in negative potential, as it were – across Dickens's audiovisual text is only meant, in closing, to inflect a claim at the far edge of the examples that have preceded it in our focus on this chapter's hair's-breadth divide between life and death. For, as usual, the very enterprise of close reading, and however extreme at times, however localised and contingent, can – as in this multi-plotted novel equilibrated across various durations of abeyance – carry us in the direction of *a* reading after all. To speak sylleptically one last time, this is how a narratographic attention can hope to keep up, faith or at least contact with the writing it sets out to read.

NOTES

1 Garrett Stewart, *Novel Violence: A Narratography of Victorian Fiction* (University of Chicago Press, 2009). For an earlier study more narrowly focused on the 'microplot' of the death moment in its purely figurative valences, with a chapter on Dickens, see Garrett Stewart, *Death Sentences: Styles of Dying in British Fiction* (Cambridge, MA: Harvard University Press, 1984).

2 Toni Morrison, *A Mercy* (New York: Vintage, 2008), 33, discussed along with John le Carré's prose in 'Syllepsis Redux' (n. 4 below).

3 Charles Dickens, 'Shops and their Tenants', *SB*, 61–4, with gratitude to Daniel Tyler for alerting me to its sylleptic features.

4 Gilbert Ryle, *The Concept of Mind* (London: Hutchinson, 1949), 22, as discussed in Garrett Stewart, 'The Ethical Tempo of Narrative Syntax: Sylleptic Recognitions in *Our Mutual Friend*', *Partial Answers*, 8 (1) (January 2010): 119–45, with a follow-up essay on further implications of this same trope, Garrett Stewart, 'Syllepsis Redux and the Rhetoric of Double Agency', *Partial Answers*, 10 (1) (January 2012): 93–120.

5 Giorgio Agamben, *The End of the Poem*, trans. Daniel Heller-Roazen (Palo Alto, CA: Stanford University Press, 1999).

6 Gilles Deleuze, 'Immanence: une vie …', *Philosophie*, 47 (1995): 3–7; reprinted in Gilles Deleuze, *Pure Immanence: Essays on a Life*, trans. Anne Boyman (Cambridge, MA: MIT Press, 2001), 25–34, at 30.

7 Giorgio Agamben, 'Absolute Immanence', in *Potentialities: Collected Essays in Philosophy*, ed. and trans. Daniel Heller-Roazen (Palo Alto, CA: Stanford University Press, 1999), 220–39.

8 Roberto Esposito, *Bíos: Biopolitics and Philosophy*, trans. Timothy Campbell (Minneapolis, MN: University of Minnesota Press, 2008), 193.

9 Esposito, *Bíos*, 191–4.

10 Giorgio Agamben, 'Philosophy and Linguistics', in *Potentialities: Collected Essays in Philosophy*, ed. and trans. Daniel Heller-Roazen (Palo Alto, CA: Stanford University Press, 1999), 62–76.

11 *Richard III*, v. iii. 170.

12 *CH*, 470.

13 Alfred Tennyson, *In Memoriam A. H. H.* in Christopher Ricks (ed.), *The Poems of Tennyson*, 2nd edn, 3 vols. (Harlow: Longman, 1987), II, 304–459, at 326.

14 Peter Brooks, *Reading for the Plot: Design and Intention in Narrative* (New York: Knopf, 1984).

15 Giorgio Agamben, *Idea of Prose*, trans. Michael Sulliven and Sam Whitsity (Albany, NY: State University of New York Press, 1995), 37.

16 Agamben, *Idea of Prose*, 37.

17 Agamben, *Idea of Prose*, 37.

18 See Roland Barthes, 'Character and Figure', in *S/Z: An Essay*, trans. Richard Miller (New York: Hill & Wang, 1974), 67–8.

19 Giorgio Agamben, *Language and Death: The Place of Negativity*, trans. Karen E. Pinkus with Michael Hardt (Minneapolis, MN: University of Minnesota Press, 1991), which begins with a quotation from Heidegger on the incapacity in animals either for language or, and therefore, for the genuine experience of their own death (xi).

20 Giorgio Agamben, *Homo Sacer: Sovereign Power and Bare Life*, trans. Daniel Heller-Roazen (Palo Alto, CA: Stanford University Press, 1998).

21 Agamben, 'Absolute Immanence', 229.

CHAPTER TWELVE

Dispensing with style

Helen Small

'I dispense with style', M. Blandois/Rigaud tells Abel Flintwinch, with a Gallic wave of the hand (*LD*, I, 30, 345). He does and does not mean it. The lack of any stylistic attractions, any marks of fashion or elegance, about the Clennam house is irrelevant to Blandois's purposes there, and no obstacle to pressing an entry; he is, at the same time and in his own person, an excrescence of style – a florid incursion of melodramatic mannerism into the mix of styles that constitutes and troubles Dickensian realism – one that must ultimately be '*squashed*' (to borrow Garrett Stewart's apposite verb)[1] to permit a harmonious narrative conclusion for *Little Dorrit*.

Critics standardly observe that Dickensian stylistic excess has a companion principle, a kind of counterweight in restraint or adherence to 'limits'.[2] It is a less obvious proposition that there might be, beyond this tension or contest between the unleashing and the control of expressive energy, and outside the specific acts of repression required for Dickens's novels to conclude, any effort towards 'plain style'. Applied across the whole career, the proposal would not (to invoke one of Dickens's favoured objects of humour) have legs. But the first part of this essay tests the claim that, in so far as he had a worked-out theory of style (he had clear principles and gave consistent advice to others, but never spelled out a complete 'theory'), he afforded a high place to Hazlitt's definition of 'plain style'. The virtues expressed in the idea of 'plain style' were at the heart of his sense of how good writing is to be distinguished from bad, and in many aspects of his writing he both abided by them himself and encouraged (or directed) others to do so. The second part of the essay pursues a related but distinct claim that, in his last published work, *The Mystery of Edwin Drood* (1870), Dickens put up some resistance to the kinds of performative stylistic exuberance that had become known in his own circle and beyond as 'Dickensese'.[3] Both in the manner of that novel's engagement with the familiar stylistic features of Dickens's prose, and – more obliquely – in its representation of the psychology of a musician who resents the monotony of his public performances, *Edwin Drood* encourages reflection on what Richard Wollheim has influentially described as a difference between 'style' and 'signature'.[4] Among the important characteristics of an individual style, Wollheim observes, with reference to painting, are that such a style has 'psychological reality, ... is acquired and formed', that it includes a way of conceptualising and evolving 'rules and principles for operating' (though it need not amount to a cohesive theory), that it is 'highly internalized' (in the painter's case, 'encapsulated in the artist's body') and, finally, that 'it can be grasped through its consequences', that is, it permits expression.[5] Signature, by contrast, he describes as a 'merely taxonomic conception of style' – a list of characteristic, predictable stylistic features employed to establish authorship.[6]

A problem for Dickens, especially from the later 1850s onwards, I want to suggest, is that the taxonomic features of his own 'signature' had become so recognisable, so exploitable as a commodity (not least by himself) that preserving a place for an evolving and more internalised 'style' required a confrontation with his own 'signature'. Letting go of the marks of signature was not the aim – could not be the aim, given considerations of audience, of commercial (self)-interest and, not least, of a certain pride and pleasure in his own distinctiveness. So, in this case, there is no categorical demarcation between early 'signature' Dickens and a late Dickens 'style'. And yet there are clear signs of his resisting his own signature stylistic features, as he endeavours to avoid mere repetition and to develop the technical and psychological aspects of his art. *Edwin Drood*, I shall be arguing, is the most revealing instance of such a confrontation with his own signature, but the confrontation is partial, imperfectly integrated and remains unresolved – and not only because the novel was abrupted by Dickens's death. If my description of how style is put to work in that novel is correct, it is not clear that there could have been a satisfactory resolution.

Dickensian style, in its most exaggerated journalistic manifestations, was an easily recognisable commodity in the literary marketplace of the 1850s and 1860s, reproduced and marketed for 2d weekly in *Household Words*[7] and (less exuberantly) *All the Year Round*. In part, Dickens's aim, in conducting these periodicals, was to take control of a problem arising from the success of 'signature Dickens': the more and less competent imitators who had caused him intermittent vexation ever since *The Pickwick Papers*. To take two instances, from different phases of his career: his 'object', he writes of *Master Humphrey's Clock* in January 1840, is 'to baffle the imitators and make it as novel as possible';[8] and again, correcting a mistaken message of congratulation, in 1854, 'The Walk is not my writing. It is very well done by a close imitator.'[9] Conducting his own magazines was, in tandem with more direct political efforts to obtain the extension of copyright protection, a means of reclaiming ownership of his own signature.

'Dickens ... practically trained up quite a new school of writers', his protegé and friend Percy Fitzgerald later claimed, 'insensibly moulding them to his own peculiar pattern and style'.[10] 'Words were the counters' in a form of stylistic play whereby Dickens's young men showed their proficiency at copying the master and thus their aptitude for careers in the literary marketplace (though few among them became novelists of any recognised merit).[11] 'Dickens and water' was one 'droll' description of the 'imitating followers'.[12] Fitzgerald's claims were made more than forty years after Dickens's death, in the belated, discomfiting tribute entitled *Memories of Charles Dickens* (1913): an odd mix of homage, critical demurral and feline jealousies towards all other contenders for Dickens's patronage and friendship.

That initial description, 'practically trained up quite a new school', sits oddly athwart the subclause, 'insensibly moulding' (depending on whether one reads 'practically' as 'in practice', or, hamming it up a little, 'all but', 'virtually'). How far did Dickens really want a school of imitators? And did the imitators themselves welcome or resist incorporation into Dickens Inc.? Fitzgerald is at odds with himself on these matters, wanting to boast of the cleverness of 'Dickens's young men',[13] but resenting the implied denial of stylistic independence and uncertain how far he wants to condemn his younger self along with the rest. 'Brighten it' was Dickens's standard advice to his 'bright' young men,[14] and 'They were only too eager and apt at imitation', Fitzgerald confirms: 'even clever enough to pick up a sort of mock Dickensese dialect, a kind of forced smartness with a sustained design of being funny and of making everything funny. It became really a perfect knack, and quite easy to acquire': grotesque nicknaming, exaggeration as a sustained principle, flamboyance as the norm.[15] But it was 'all mechanical'.[16] Pick up a copy of *Household Words*, fifty years after its demise, and one is, Fitzgerald judges,

> conscious of a certain flatness, as of champagne left long uncorked.... The writers were compelled, owing to the necessity of producing effect, to adopt a tone of exaggeration. Everything, even trivial, had to be made more comic than it really was. This was the law of the paper ... As I can testify from my own experience, this pressure became all but irresistible. A mere

natural, unaffected account of any transaction, it was felt, was out of place; it would not harmonise with the brilliant, buoyant things surrounding it. I often think with some compunction of my own trespassings in this way, and of the bad habit one gradually acquired of colouring up for effect, and of magnifying the smallest trifle.[17]

Similar statements, sharing Fitzgerald's ambivalence and his wish to be understood as an exception to the rule, can be found in the memoirs of other regular contributors to the periodicals, including John Hollingshead, who adds to Fitzgerald's taxonomy of 'signature Dickens' a 'tricky' way with titles: typically, punning or 'raising curiosity in the mind of the reader, [while] concealing the subject: 'A Piece of China', 'A Curious Dance Round a Curious Tree', 'Where We Stopped Growing'.[18] Hollingshead took particular pride in the success of his second submission to *Household Words*, an essay on 'the rich and unbridled imagination of City traders': 'Leaders were written about it, and one in the *Daily Telegraph* saw in it the powerful hand of Dickens.'[19] Like Fitzgerald, he responds with ambivalence:

> All Dickens's 'young men' were supposed to be imitators of the master, and the master was always credited with their best productions. I hope this was so in my case, but I am afraid it was not. My subjects were not very much *à la Dickens* – and I wrote a great quantity – having sometimes two [articles per issue], and, bad or good, I had a blunt plain style of my own.[20]

The view that Dickens's strong stylistic imprint would be better resisted than succumbed to was often aired. Among the frankest discussions of the problem came from an anonymous reviewer of the first issue of *All the Year Round*, in 1859, convinced that the widespread imitation of Dickens's style within the pages of *Household Words* was the main cause of that periodical's 'degeneracy' in its later stages. The young imitators of Dickens had adopted 'the peculiar sentiment, the peculiar humour, or the peculiar word-painting, as the case may be, of their celebrated teacher' to such an extent that a posturing mannerism had done damage to the freshness and variety of tone most readers were presumed to want in a magazine: 'A mannerism which a single great genius finds it difficult to sustain at its highest level was certain to become ere long unbearable in the hands of his professed imitators.'[21] Mrs Gaskell, looking for a berth for her new novel, *Lois the Witch*, in the same year, feared that the new periodical would be no different from the old. She had fought to preserve her own sense of style when contributing to *Household Words* and now coined her own adjective to capture the problem: 'I *know* it [*Lois*] is fated to go in this new Dickensy periodical, & I did so hope to escape it.'[22]

Of all Dickens's authors, Edmund Yates and Robert Brough perhaps deserve most credit for having the temerity to perform their anxiety of influence in Dickens's plain sight. They produced a very funny parody of *Hard Times* as part of a collection of parodies and lampoons published in 1856,[23] homing in on the hallmark Dickensian sentimentalism, the theatrical tendency to relatively under-directed dialogue exchanges, the exaggerated dialectal flags and the habit of self-reference[24] – which declares itself, in their handling, as a form of brand promotion.

> 'Ay, Stephen' [Rachel asks the bruised and battered man retrieved from the mineshaft, who now lies before her with a cloth placed over his face]; how dost thou feel?'
> 'Hoomble and happy, lass. I be grateful and thankful. I be obliged to them as have brought charges o' robbery agin me; an' I hope as them as did it will be happy an' enjoy the fruits. I do only look on my being pitched down that theer shaft, and having all my bones broke, as a mercy and a providence, and God bless everybody!' [etc.][25]

'It is surprising', Philip Collins notes, 'that Dickens, who resented attempts to parody him [as distinct from imitating him], apparently forgave Yates his association with this skit. Brough, too (the sketch bears his initials) continued after 1857 as an occasional contributor to *Household Words*.'[26]

'The Inimitable' was, in short, if not a misnomer, an invitation to a bullish young journalist to prove otherwise. The competence of a young writer's Dickensese was a fairly good gauge of how far he would prosper on *Household Words* and *All the Year Round* and how successful he would be thereafter in the literary marketplace. One of the reasons why George Augustus Sala stands out from the Dickens office crowd is that, all the bohemian irregularities of his career notwithstanding, he managed the two-stage achievement of at first sounding very like Dickens (consequently causing some trouble for later editors wanting to distinguish Dickens from imitation Dickens)[27] and then establishing a distinctive mature style of his own. When *Time* devoted a portion of its first issue to Sala, under the title 'A Journalist of the Day', he was exasperated by their decision to reprint what he now considered embarrassing juvenilia:[28]

> one ought not to look the gift horse in the mouth; but surely a better specimen of my style might have been selected for quotation than the screed of turgid verbosity about 'Day Break' which was written just <u>Twenty Seven years ago</u>, when I was a raw novice, unlicked, untrained, and with no style save one based on a slavish imitation of Dickens. Full ten years dating from that period elapsed before I found out a way of putting things in my own

fashion, … He was a wonderful genius; but as a 'stylist' he did all of us, as young men, much harm.[29]

The vehemence seems excessive, not least because Sala goes on to describe years of immersion in other styles, as distinctive in their own way as Dickens's, at the end of which he was finally competent to achieve a manner and an idiom of his own. It is a fair description of how Dickens's own style or styles had been formed. Immersion in the characteristics of other voices, attuning one's ear to distinctivenesses of manner and idiom and genre, refining one's critical sense of what constitutes a good or a bad style for particular purposes, is surely (as Sala urged) the only means to forming a style of one's own.

Much has been said about Dickens's formative literary debts (Shakespeare, Fielding, Smollett), and more particularly about that 'small collection of books … which nobody else in our house ever troubled … Roderick Random, Peregrine Pickle, Humphrey Clinker, Tom Jones, The Vicar of Wakefield, Don Quixote, Gil Blas, and Robinson Crusoe' (DC, 4, 48).[30] In so far as there is an accepted genealogy of Dickensian style, it is, predominantly, a genealogy with two major strands: one that leads back through the great humorists of the eighteenth century; the other, complementary but longer and perhaps deeper, running back through English drama to Congreve and Shakespeare.[31] Relatively little has been said about the writers who helped to form anything approaching a conscious theory of style, with the partial exception of Tom Paulin's work on the influence upon Dickens of William Hazlitt's 'radical style'.[32]

Dickens frequently expressed his admiration and affection for Hazlitt's writing.[33] The catalogue of the library at Gads Hill contains thirteen works by Hazlitt, the earliest an 1822 edition of the Political Essays and the latest a copy of the third edition of Table-Talk (1845–6), edited by Hazlitt's son, whom Dickens befriended and for whom he acted, on at least one occasion, as a referee.[34] Paulin rightly observes 'an imaginative kinship' between Hazlitt Snr. and Dickens, both of whom were parliamentary shorthand reporters in their youth, trained to observe (and adept at parodying) the rhetorical and oratorical modes of public 'speechifying'.[35] They were alike in many matters of taste and interest, each having a fine 'impatien[ce] with the established order', a 'love of inns, long country walks, inner London, and the life of the common people', and a fascination with 'the psychopathology of criminals'.[36] Paulin hazards one direct point of connection regarding style: he suggests that the description of Bradley Headstone's mind as 'a place of mechanical stowage' like a 'warehouse salesman' reaches back to Hazlitt's discussion of Coleridge, where he dismisses the Scottish jurist Sir James Mackintosh as a 'ready warehouseman of ideas', an unimaginative logician, who would never attain 'a style that can properly be called good'.[37] Paulin does not, however, push the connections at the level of conceptualising style – perhaps because Hazlitt's and Dickens's *practice* of style was sufficiently distinct, and Hazlitt wrote no fiction; and perhaps because Dickens's cast of mind was not in the main theoretical. Nevertheless, the idea of influence here seems worth pressing.

There are numerous points in Dickens's public and private reflections on what makes for a good or a bad style at which one can hear echoes of the older writer's regard for a 'plain unperverted English idiom'.[38] The Dickens of many of the letters and speeches is, indeed, about as good an example as one could hope to find of Hazlitt's conception of 'Familiar Style': a style that 'avail[s] [itself] of the true idiom of the language', writing 'as any one would speak in common conversation, who had a thorough command and choice of words, or who could discourse with ease, force, and perspicuity, setting aside all pedantic and oratorical flourishes'.[39] Puncturing afflatus is, for Dickens as for Hazlitt, a principle of good style. For Hazlitt, it required something like the 'marrowy vein' of Charles Lamb's antiquated English to justify departures.[40] Dickens, of course, had the free rein offered by novelistic characterisation. In other words, as Robert Douglas-Fairhurst argues in this volume, he could displace pedantry, oratory, incoherence, gush and so forth by putting them in the mouths of others.[41] Or, as George Gissing expressed the same thought in reverse, he could wield the 'power of appropriating a style utterly unlike his own'.[42] For Dickens and Hazlitt, as for another writer to whom both were consciously indebted, Henry Fielding, deflation of affectation is a basic impulse to comedy: sometimes a moral imperative but always an opportunity to frame style *as* style, open to parody and burlesque and (though the word does not seem to have entered the English critical vocabulary until almost the end of Dickens's lifetime) pastiche.[43]

'Subtlety', 'ease', 'simplicity', 'wholesomeness', 'reality', 'honesty', are all prominent among the stylistic qualities that Dickens, like Hazlitt, admired and recommended to his fellow writers. More gender-specifically, he praises 'vigour', 'force', 'manliness'. To write without affectation was not for Dickens, as it seems to have been for John Hollingshead (who published a collection of essays in 1880 entitled *Plain English*), a synonym for John Bull bluntness. Rather, he shares Hazlitt's conviction that

> It is not easy to write a familiar style. Many people mistake a familiar for
> a vulgar style, and suppose that to write without affectation is to write at

random. On the contrary, there is nothing that requires more precision …
than the style I am speaking of. It utterly rejects not only all unmeaning
pomp, but all low, cant phrases, and loose, unconnected, *slipshod* allusions.
It is not to take the first word that offers, but the best word in common
use; it is not to throw words together in any combinations we please, but
to follow and avail ourselves of the true idiom of the language … Any one
may mouth out a passage with a theatrical cadence, or get upon stilts to tell
his thoughts; but to write or speak with propriety and simplicity is a more
difficult task.[44]

Remove the word 'propriety' (which, as Hazlitt remarks of 'elegance', seems
much less in evidence in the critical vocabulary of the mid-nineteenth
century than it had been in the early decades of the century), and one
has a close parallel with Dickens's stipulation (in 1853) that the 'true' man
should 'deliver himself plainly of what is in him';[45] also a source of his
[undated] self-defence against a gentle query from Edward Bulwer-Lytton
as to whether 'the modesties of art were not a little over-passed' by him,
with the insistence that 'I … never give way to my invention recklessly,
but constantly restrain it'.[46]

Restraint, in the sense of a pulling back from performative excess
towards plain style, is discernibly a principle to which late Dickens shows
increasing attachment. In the early years, simplicity of style tends to be
espoused more as a theoretical good, and an approved attribute of most
men in their private character, than a committed public practice of his
own. Take, for example, a speech given in Boston in 1842, in which
Dickens hopes that it is 'natural and allowable for each of us, on his own
hearth, to express his thoughts in the most homely fashion, and to appear
in his plainest garb', but immediately launches on an elaborately fanciful
extension of the metaphor:

> I have a fair claim upon you to let me do so tonight, for you have made
> my home an Aladdin's Palace. You fold so tenderly within your breasts that
> common household lamp in which my feeble fire is all enshrined, and at
> which my flickering torch is lighted up, that straight my household gods
> take wing, and are transported there.[47]

The Dickens of 1869 is more inclined to confine fancy to brief gestures:
'Well, ladies and gentlemen … I could not say to myself, when I began
just now, in Shakespeare's line – "I will be bright and shining gold," but I
could say to myself, and I did say to myself, "I will be as natural and easy
as I possibly can."'[48]

Of course, the speeches are one thing, the fiction another. But a similar
and growing inclination over the years to curb his own characteristic and

expected excesses is certainly traceable in the fiction. George Augustus Sala
was among the sharpest early observers of the change, remarking in 1868
that, from the vantage point of many years' close collaboration, 'I have
been able to trace the successive phases of development through which
his genius has passed, ... the chastening of his style.'[49] One conventional
way of distinguishing late from early and mid-period Dickens is to agree
with Forster that from *Little Dorrit* onward there was a discernible 'strain
upon his invention'.[50] Symptomatic of that strain, as Forster sees it, was
the unprecedented recourse, between [*Bleak House* and *Little Dorrit*], to
'"Memoranda" of suggestions for characters or incidents' – 'proof that he
had been secretly bringing before himself, at least, the possibility that what
had ever been his great support might some day desert him'.[51] Forster's
assessment is essentially psychological: it has to do with the perceived tax-
ing of physical and mental resources arising from overwork, a tendency to
'rush at existence without heeding the cost of it' in accelerated ageing and
ill-health.[52]

Percy Fitzgerald's reflections on late Dickens are on similar terrain but
locate the problem more in style itself. For Fitzgerald, exhaustion is something to which style is necessarily prone,[53] especially if the style is as 'pyrotechnical' as Dickens's.[54] Fitzgerald's most substantial reservation about
the commercial exploitation of Dickensese in *Household Words* and *All the
Year Round* emerges when he speculates about the toll of twenty years and
more of such 'unreal writing' on the 'true *métier*', fiction.[55] There must have
been, he urges, a '*dissipation*' of powers.[56] The 'deceptive, rather pyrotechnical style' of the periodicals was so 'utterly opposed to the concentrated
and deliberated character of the monthly part'; the '*habit*' of ephemeral
treatment' can only have impaired Dickens's ability to sustain the longer,
more serious form of writing.[57] Then, having seeded his doubts about the
late work, Fitzgerald characteristically, backtracks: 'These are interesting
speculations, which indeed might be considered disposed of by the evidence of his last story, unfinished as it is.'[58]

As the difference between Forster's and Fitzgerald's readings of late
Dickens demonstrates, style may be an explanation for writerly change
as well as its symptom. But we need something less mechanical here than
Fitzgerald's description of style as a pyrotechnical display that inevitably
runs out of powder; or Hollingshead's theory (oddly advanced at a banquet where Charles Dickens Jnr. was guest of honour) that 'every literary man – certainly myself – [is] like a barrel-organ which ha[s] a certain
number of tunes to play, and when the tunes are played the organ ought
to leave off'.[59] A conception of style that, as Wollheim urges, allows for

conscious adoption of certain principles rather than others, for ongoing
psychological evolution, and for changing requirements of expression, as
distinct from the taxonomy of repeated characteristics that is signature,
may have something more interesting and more accurate to tell us about
late Dickens than one that looks for signature repetitions and finds only
evidence that they are growing tired.

Edwin Drood is, as Fitzgerald suggests, the logical place to test the explana-
tory power of a late exertion of pressure against signature. Stylistically, it
is a curiously dislocated and dislocating text. Its generic and tonal shifts
between mystery, different kinds of comedy, melodrama and different
kinds of romantic realism, as well as between 'signature Dickens' and
something openly at odds with it, are not contained by any defined narrating personality. So dislocating can these shifts be that one sometimes
suspects Dickens of having recourse to the historic present (and not even
that consistently)[60] as much by way of a minimal assertion of stylistic continuity as for dramatic immediacy.

There is plenty of 'signature Dickens' in the novel. No one would mistake the following passage as being by any other author, or a very competent imitator of Dickensese:

> [Mr. Grewgious's clerk] Bazzard returned, accompanied by two waiters –
> an immoveable waiter, and a flying waiter; and the three brought in with
> them as much fog as gave a new roar to the fire. The flying waiter, who
> had brought everything on his shoulders, laid the cloth with amazing rap-
> idity and dexterity; while the immoveable waiter, who had brought noth-
> ing, found fault with him in secret nudges. The flying waiter then highly
> polished all the glasses he had brought, and the immoveable waiter looked
> through them. The flying waiter then flew across Holborn for the soup,
> and flew back again, and then took another flight for the made-dish, and
> flew back again, and then took another flight for the joint and poultry, and
> flew back again, and between whiles took supplementary flights for a great
> variety of articles, as it was discovered from time to time that the immove-
> able waiter had forgotten them all. But let the flying waiter cleave the air
> as he might, he was always reproached on his return by the immoveable
> waiter for bringing fog with him, and being out of breath. At the conclu-
> sion of the repast, by which time the flying waiter was severely blown, the
> immoveable waiter gathered up the tablecloth under his arm with a grand
> air, and having sternly (not to say with indignation) looked on at the fly-
> ing waiter while he set clean glasses round, directed a valedictory glance
> towards Mr. Grewgious, conveying: 'Let it be clearly understood between
> us that the reward is mine, and that Nil is the claim of this slave', and
> pushed the flying waiter before him out of the room. (*ED*, 11, 92–3)

This has all the hallmarks of what Fitzgerald describes, demurringly, as 'brilliant, buoyanc[y]' and 'colouring up for effect': the comic oppositions ('immoveable'/'flying', 'fog'/'fire', 'everything'/'nothing'), the mock-heroic inflation ('cleave the air as he might') followed by the bathetic descent into city slang ('the flying waiter was severely blown'), the grandiloquent attributed speech ('Nil is the claim of this slave'), above all the stringing out of verbal repetitions within an extravagant polysyndeton so that the central and final sentences ('The flying waiter flew ... At the conclusion') become performative feats of grammar to rival the performance of the flying waiter. What marks this writing as not just signature Dickens but an invitation to contemplate it *as* signature Dickens is the pointed super-erogatory reflection that follows: 'It was like a highly-finished miniature painting representing My Lords of the Circumlocutional Department, Commandership-in-Chief of any sort, Government. It was quite an edify-ing little picture to be hung on the line in the National Gallery' (*ED*, ii, 93). Something other than brand promotion is happening here, though it is not incompatible with brand promotion – invoking earlier Dickens performances in similar vein (*Bleak House* and, especially, *Little Dorrit*), it holds those performances at arm's length, viewing them with an irony not very far from disavowal. 'Quite an edifying little picture': this is Dickens framing his own signature prose as a national exhibit or museum piece. Such echoes are characteristic of the prose of *Edwin Drood* and can extend to the smallest and most self-conscious phrases – as with 'far, far better' in Chapter 13, which, at the level of both narrative voice and (speculatively) plot, resonates oddly with its source in *A Tale of Two Cities*, recalling the past to life. Indeed, so much of *Edwin Drood* seems to be a recapitula-tion of fragments of Dickens's earlier novels at arm's length that one can fairly hypothesise (on the available evidence of plot and style) that he was attempting something like a stylistic equivalent for the plot device of the return of the repressed. Cloisterham Cathedral, a jumble of the old and new, starts to look like an architectural analogy for the Dickens house of fiction at the end of Dickens's career.

There are other ways in which the reader is repeatedly asked to see sig-nature Dickensian style in *Edwin Drood* as not repudiated but held up to a kind of scrutiny that suggests a measure of reserve or irony on Dickens's own part. Many of the most striking stylistic effects of the novel involve rumination on the value of old things, including old and once-honoured forms of speech, still circulated in the present: the *Book of Common Prayer* (repeatedly invoked in the Cathedral scenes), Shakespeare (who ghosts so much of the novel's prose), popular song. This is not in itself new (*Our*

Mutual Friend, for example, is full of such scraps of the literary past),
but, time and again, references back to Dickens's own earlier writings are
caught up in wider broodings on whether the persistence of an individual signature in the language is unqualifiedly a sign of stylistic worth (as
Shakespeare's example would suggest), or whether it is rather indicative of
a threatening debasement (as the tired repetitions of service in Cloisterham
Cathedral imply – a 'feeble voice, rising and falling in a cracked monotonous mutter, ... at intervals ... faintly heard' while 'Old Time heave[s] a
mouldy sigh' [*ED*, 9, 73]). (Part of Dickens's interest in song attaches to its
having, often, no strong signature in the sense of authorship: hence Silas
Wegg pedaling his ballads, in *Our Mutual Friend*, and the 'hideous small
boy', Deputy, mocking Jasper with the playground song warning of the
hangman's noose – 'Widdy widdy wen' [*ED*, 5, 32].)[61]

The sense of depreciation comes into sharp focus when Edwin Drood,
on what is probably the last night of his life, closes his hand upon the
ring and case once belonging to Rosa's mother and resolves that Rosa will
never know that this was the intended symbol of their marriage, as their
respective parents imagined it happening. Let these withered hopes be,
Edwin decides:

> He would restore them to her guardian when he came down; he in his turn
> would restore them to the cabinet from which he had unwillingly taken
> them; and there, like old letters or old vows, or other records of old aspira-
> tions come to nothing, they would be disregarded, until, being valuable,
> they were sold into circulation again, to repeat their former round.
>
> Let them be. Let them lie unspoken of, in his breast. However distinctly
> or indistinctly he entertained these thoughts, he arrived at the conclusion,
> Let them be. Among the mighty store of wonderful chains that are for ever
> forging, day and night, in the vast iron-works of time and circumstance,
> there was one chain forged in the moment of that small conclusion, riveted
> to the foundations of heaven and earth, and gifted with invincible force to
> hold and drag. (*ED*, 13, 118)

The meditation on jewels ungiven becomes (by a series of imperfect but
plangent analogies) a meditation on letters, vows, aspirations unfulfilled:
the jewels, 'being valuable', will always have currency; personal letters, 'old
vows', 'old aspirations' may lose theirs. 'Let them be' (echoing the final
paragraph of *Hard Times*) is especially evocative in this context, as it suggests an interruption of a different kind of pledge: 'Let them be offered' or
'Let them be taken' cut off as simply 'Let them be'. But, again, what makes
Edwin Drood a departure from comparable scenes in earlier Dickens (*Bleak
House* on the circulation of love letters; or Arthur Clennam repressing an

unspoken love) is the way in which Dickensian style itself becomes part of what is put aside, to be circulated elsewhere, or at another time. The 'wonderful chains that are forever forging', and of which 'one chain is forged' at this moment, are a direct reprise of the 'long chain of iron or gold, of thorns or flowers' whose 'first link' is formed on the 'memorable day' when Pip first sees Miss Havisham and Estella (*GE*, 1, 9, 73). Pip's version draws on the image of the single blacksmith, in the village forge; *Edwin Drood*'s is imaginative ironmongery on a more than industrial scale – 'wonderful chains', but formed in a 'vast' metaphysical 'iron-works'.

The recurrent impression given, in *Edwin Drood*, that Dickens's signature prose is as much an object of attention in its own right as a vehicle for the narrative is perhaps most obvious in the set-piece quality of the comic and sentimental scenes: the account of the Tartar's Staples Inn attic rooms, for example, replicates not only the interior of a ship but also Captain Cuttle's home, in *Dombey and Son*; Durdles repeats Quilp's boy Tom, and Trabb's boy, and the Artful Dodger, and so many other resilient vagabonds in Dickens; the landlady Mrs Billickin reprises Sairey Gamp and many a Dickensian termagant. Often the effect of such scenes is of a sudden slotting into a familiar groove, in a surrounding text that is oddly angular and unwilling to fit expected stylistic patterns. No previous Dickens novel makes such prominent use of inversions that momentarily throw the ear and require one to reread for sense – '"Mr. Jasper was that, Tope?"' (*ED*, 2, 4) – or of sentences that are suspended across long interpolated clauses for other than comic or obvious dramatic effect.

The sense of dislocation in *Edwin Drood* is more than an effect of style, or of style reflecting upon itself: it is also a principle of plot and psychology. Virtually everything that happens in this novel happens by virtue of sudden removals of people from habituated or expected walks of life and channels of behaviour – and at its centre is a psychological portrait of a man painfully at odds with his public style. The governing 'new idea' of Dickens's last novel, so far as one can tell, was the psychological portrait of a criminal (John Jasper) whose ungoverned passion for a young woman and indulgence in opium alike threaten to destroy the respect he derives from the public performance of his art. That Jasper is a villain is not in doubt (though many readers have disputed that he is Edwin Drood's murderer – or that Drood is, in fact, dead).[62] The object of John Jasper's desire, Rosa Bud, is to be pitied, comments the narrator: '(for what could she know of the criminal intellect, which its own professed students perpetually misread, because they persist in trying to reconcile it with the average intellect of average men, instead of identifying it as a horrible wonder apart)' (*ED*, 20, 175). The novelty of this terrain for Dickens evidently did not lie in contemplating the criminal intellect. (Almost all his works contain at least one close portrait of a criminal.) Nor did it consist in the notion of the criminal intellect as 'a horrible wonder apart' (Bill Sikes, Fagin, Ralph Nickleby, Compeyson, Bradley Headstone, would all fit that delineation). The notion of the criminal's self-division was not a new theme, either: he had already pressed hard at that idea, especially in *Our Mutual Friend*. In so far as one can tell, the newness claimed for the depiction of John Jasper had to do with extending and deepening the idea that one kind of criminal intellect might involve an exaggerated perception of operating at a perceptual distance from one's own agency: a pathological and criminal development of an ordinary enough, and not always criminal, tendency. Dickens had played with the idea in its more benign forms many times – '*Barkis is willin'*' (*DC*, 5, 56); '"there's a pain somewhere in the room … but I couldn't positively say that I have got it"' (*HT*, III, 9, 185); '"Mrs Harris … leave the bottle on the chimley-piece, and don't ask me to take none, but let me put my lips to it when I am so dispoged"' (*MC*, 19, 316) – but in *Edwin Drood* it was (apparently) to have been the central subject. In this (as it turned out) his last novel, Dickens seems to have wanted to probe the extreme distancing of a man from his own agency that might lead a man to kill the thing he loves.

The representation of psychology, under such conditions, becomes also a vehicle for scrutinising the cost to the artist of routinised performance.[63] An early clue to Jasper's character is the mismatch between the control of his voice and the suspected turmoil of his thoughts. Fearing that Ned has discerned a darkness of purpose in him, then relieved to find otherwise, he exhibits 'a tone of voice less troubled than the purport of his words – indeed with something of raillery or banter in it' (*ED*, 2, 10). Very many of his interactions with others are conducted in a distinctively 'low' voice – a quality especially remarked upon when he is in the presence of Rosa (accompanying her singing, 'watch[ing] the pretty lips, and ever and again hint[ing] the one note, as though it were a low whisper from himself' [7, 51]) and when he moves to smear Neville Landless's reputation in the city ('in a low distinct suspicious voice: "What are those stains upon his dress?"' [15, 134; see also 8, 62]; 'low' takes on the colour of a bad joke – a heavy hint). Technical control of voice is, of course, his professional ambit as Lay Precentor of Cloisterham Cathedral – but the control is precarious: 'His nervous temperament is occasionally prone to take difficult music a little too quickly' (14, 128). Right at the start of the novel, his irritation with the repetitions of the chorister's performances leads him to confess to

Edwin both his sense of the 'monotony' of his art (2, 12) and (though he conceals much here) his dependence on opium. When Edwin assures him that he finds the choral service 'Beautiful! Quite celestial', Jasper responds with vehemence: 'It often sounds to me quite devilish. I am so weary of it! The echoes of my own voice among the arches seem to mock me with my daily drudging round' (2, 11). Only in the immediate aftermath of the (presumed) murder does Jasper appear with 'grand composure' in his chosen vocation: 'in beautiful voice … In the pathetic supplication to have his heart inclined to keep this law, he quite astonishes his fellows by his melodious power. He has never sung difficult music with such skill and harmony' (14, 128). On this sole occasion he seems no longer the unwilling 'mechanism' or 'grinder' of the performance, but (having presumably dispatched his rival) the author and controller of the performance.

I am not, of course, suggesting that John Jasper is an avatar for Dickens (though several critics have seen points of connection between Jasper's overbearing interest in Rosa Bud and Dickens's relationship with the young Ellen Ternan). But the sceptical framing of 'signature Dickens' in *Edwin Drood* certainly acquires psychological depth from the novel's pre-occupation, at the levels of plot and characterisation with the figure of a man tired – more than tired, feeling himself bedeviled – by the obligation to go on grinding out technically adept performances for public consumption when he is, at heart, 'troubled with some stray sort of ambition, aspiration, restlessness, dissatisfaction, what shall we call it?' (*ED*, 2, 12).

Is there any evidence of an active effort on Dickens's part towards a less signature performance of his own style, beyond the sceptical framings of 'Dickensese', and the thematic pressure to scrutinise the relationship between the routinised public performance of an art and the psychological need to go beyond what has become merely routine? Such evidence, if it exists, would be found in the manuscript revisions to *Edwin Drood*. When Forster reflected, in *The Life of Charles Dickens*, on the condition of Dickens's last manuscript, he thought the 'final page of manuscript that ever came from [Dickens's] hand' of sufficient interest to warrant fac-simile reproduction.[64] He placed it alongside a manuscript page of *Oliver Twist* in order to highlight the 'excessive care of correction and interlineation'.[65] Such care was, he noted, characteristic 'of all [Dickens's] later manuscripts'.[66] He might have added that the *Edwin Drood* manuscript is, however, of all Dickens's manuscripts the most difficult to read because it bears the strongest signs of Dickens's failing health and of the extreme pressure of time under which he was writing. The Clarendon editor justifiably remarks that 'Many of the original words are irrecoverable and ascertaining the final reading and word order is frequently difficult' (*ED*, xlvii). Particular difficulties have been placed in the way of modern editors by Dickens's use of deletions 'in the form of curly lines' (xlvii) – that is, of overwriting in close circling patterns, rather like old-fashioned telephone cable, rather than a single strikethrough that would permit the underlying text to be detected. Even Forster conceded that some passages were 'so interlined as to be illegible'.[67] To all this can be added the tendency, on many pages, of the script to run downhill to the right, so that the bottom lines are crammed into a triangulated space on the left. Dickens's printers were familiar with his hand, but – until his death – he must, as in the past, have stood over the typesetters or worked closely with their foreman.[68] The majority of the textual variants in the *Edwin Drood* manuscript do not appear in the Clarendon edition, for the simple reason that there are so many, and a very large number are irretrievable. No editor to date has considered a full variorium edition practicable.

Within these constraints, enough can be made of the manuscript text to give tentative support to a claim that it indicates a conscious effort to restrain 'signature Dickens'. By way of example, consider the passage that attracted particular displeasure from the critic who reviewed *Edwin Drood* for the *Saturday Review*. He quotes a paragraph from the late scene (Chapter 19) in which John Jasper secures a private interview with Rosa Bud in the garden of the Nunnery House and forces her to listen to his unwelcome declaration of love. She is in mourning for Drood, who was until a few nights ago her fiancé, and is now missing, presumed drowned. The Clarendon version reads:

> 'Rosa, [says Jasper,] even when my dear boy was affianced to you, I loved you madly; even when I thought his happiness in having you for his wife was certain, I loved you madly; even when I strove to make him more ardently devoted to you, I loved you madly; even when he gave me the picture of your lovely face so carelessly traduced by him, which I feigned to hang always in my sight for his sake, but worshipped in torment for yours, I loved you madly. In the distasteful work of the day, in the wakeful misery of the night, girded by sordid realities, or wandering through Paradises and Hells of visions into which I rushed, carrying your image in my arms, I loved you madly.' (*ED*, 19, 170–1)

In this 'precious oration', grumbled the *Saturday Review* critic,

> we recognise the worst style of Mr Dickens, 'ticking off' each point ... by the burden of 'I loved you madly'. But do we recognise anything like the language of a passionate and blackhearted villain trying to bully a timid girl? It is the sort of oration which a silly boy, nourished on bad novels,

might prepare for such an occasion; but it is stiff and artificial and jerky to a degree which excludes any belief in real passion. It is rounded off prettily enough for a peroration in a debating society; or it might be a fair piece of acting for a romantic young tradesman who fancies himself doing his love-making in the high poetic style; but it has an air of affectation and mock-heroics which is palpably inappropriate to the place. It is really curious that so keen an observer should diverge into such poor and stilted bombast whenever he tries the note of intense emotion.[69]

One can see the point, and yet it is surely not right. There is an immediate defence available along the lines of appropriateness of style to speaker: a 'bad style' befits a 'bad man'. But, more to the point, if we are hearing something a reviewer might want to call 'bad style', it is not 'the worst style of Mr Dickens'. Indeed, though the reviewer rightly discerns the 'stiff … artificial … jerky' quality of the speech, he or she seems to be wanting this passage to be 'Dickensese', when it is, on careful inspection, resisting being so. A nearer model than 'bad novels', or mock-heroics, and one specifically alluded to in the same scene, is Richardson's *Clarissa*, and behind it all those Restoration dramas by which Lovelace so flamboyantly styles himself. But, as repackaged here, even the verbal evocation of the Restoration rake involves some effort against excess.

The most obvious aspect of restraint involves the play of style with and against the dramatic situation: this scene takes most of its dramatic force from the strategic and self-consciously extravagant exploitation of menacing rakishness by a man whose external appearance is calculated to deflect all suspicion. 'I do not forget how many windows command a view of us', Jasper tells Rosa. 'I will not touch you again, I will come no nearer to you than I am. Sit down, and there will be no mighty wonder in your music-master's leaning idly against a pedestal and speaking with you, … Sit down, my beloved' (*ED*, 19, 170). This is aggravated stalking in full public view. Rosa is a Victorian forerunner of the female protagonist in the horror movie who is forced to mimic normality with a knife at her back. Jasper, for his part, repeats and reverses the melodramatic stage convention of keeping up appearances in public while openly confessing his dark heart to the audience. The 'ticking off' of points is part of the menace – the structuring repetition 'even when … even when … even when', which is the verbal expression of his insistence, being set against the rhythmic disarray or distress of 'wandering through Paradises and Hells of visions into which I rushed' and the near incoherence of 'carrying your image in my arms' (not heart), coming as it does after the reference to an actual 'traducing' portrait of Rosa.

But the kind and quality of the stylistic restraint here can be better gauged by reading the Clarendon text against the manuscript evidence of Dickens's first thoughts and alternative thoughts rejected along the way. The closest this critic can get by way of a transcription is:

a view of us   says

"I do not forget how many windows command ~~the garden~~," he ~~said~~, glancing

towards them. "I will not touch you again, I will come no nearer to you than I am. Sit down,

and there will be no mighty wonder in your music-master's leaning idly against a pedestal and

~~remembering~~? after   and our shares in it.

speaking with you, ~~after~~ all that has happened, Sit down, my beloved."

– was ~~all but gone~~ all but gone

She would have gone once more^ and once more his face darkly threatening what would

~~stops~~ has stopped   the expression of the instant frozen on her

follow if she went, ~~stopped~~ her. Looking at him with ~~a frozen~~ face, she ~~sat~~ down on the seat again

sits

"Rosa, even when my dear boy was affianced to you, I loved you madly. Even when I

having   for his wife

thought his happiness in ~~receiving?~~ you^ was ~~xxxx~~ certain, I loved you ~~madly?~~ madly. Even when I

to make

strove ~~to assist? him to xxx~~ him ~~a more enthusiastic lover?~~ more ardently ~~and enthusiastically?~~ devoted

so

to you, I loved you madly. Even when he gave me the picture of your lovely face^~~that he had~~ carelessly

by him

traduced^ and which I ~~put?~~ feigned to ~~accept for his sake but worshipped~~ hang

always

~~ever?~~^in my sight for his sake, but worshipped

fol. 150

distasteful work

in torment for yours, I loved you madly. In the ~~solitary labours?~~ of the day, in the wakeful misery of the

~~ground gui~~ guided on by sordid ~~sordid mercenary?~~ or

night ~~grinding in a world? of mercenary~~ realities ~~and~~ wandering through Paradises and Hells of

carrying

visions into which I rushed ~~with~~^ your image in my arms, I ~~was?~~ loved you madly.[70]

There are two main kinds of legible revision in manuscript here: the most obvious and frequent involves a choice to favour the historic present over the perfect tense, adding dramatic immediacy and diminishing the impression of an interposing authorial perspective (offering that modicum of stylistic continuity across the novel). The second is a recurrent local reining in of possible rhetorical inflations, so that when one does get an amplification such as 'in torment', 'Wandering through Paradises and Hells', or the bourdon 'I loved you madly' to which the reviewer objected, they have the effect of sinister glimpses of a force not fully unleashed but threatening to be so.

The naturalising touches in the style ('command the garden' brought down to 'command a view of us', 'solitary labours[?] of the day' altered to 'the distasteful work of the day', 'always' substituted for the somewhat more elevated 'ever') are not necessarily the habitual or obvious course for Dickens to take. Some are revisions that go against the temptation to a more signature exertion of rhetorical power. When the text does allow itself a Dickensese pull towards iambics at a point where the 'feelings [are] deeply engaged' (an aspect of Dickens's style that irritated Gissing)[71] it is limited to the bourdon, but in such a way as to frame or ironise the staged excess. Dickens clearly troubled over that effect: 'madly' is on one occasion struck out then reinstated; it is avoided, near the end ('I was?') then accepted after all. The effect is not so much tonal instability in this instance as an effort to control full-blown melodrama and turn it, instead, to a theatre of latent menace.

The problem with identifying such local and strategic efforts towards restraining signature Dickensian moves in the pursuit of a new kind of psychological portraiture, is that *Edwin Drood* remains overall stylistically highly uneven. Some critics have, not without cause, seen much of the unevenness as symptomatic of a writer no longer fully in control.[72] Whether or not one concedes so much to Dickens's illness, age and the particular strains he was working under, the stylistic choices that seem designed to hold *Edwin Drood* together (tense and grammatical mood) may not be enough to make any given reader feel other than jarringly dislocated by the moves between signature Dickens and a less predictable, evolving style. And yet being disconcerted is itself a defensible artistic effect, and, had the novel been completed, it might have achieved greater stylistic coherence on the larger scale. On the other hand, it may be that we are seeing here the limited extent to which even Dickens himself, so late in his career, could resist (or wanted to resist) the force of his own signature.

NOTES

1 Garrett Stewart, 'Dickens and the Narratography of Closure', *Critical Inquiry*, 34 (3) (2008): 509–42, at 525; see also *Novel Violence: A Narratology of Victorian Fiction* (University of Chicago Press, 2009), especially 31–60. (Stewart's italics.)

2 Influential explorations of this duality include John Kucich, *Excess and Restraint in the Novels of Charles Dickens* (Athens, OH: University of Georgia Press, 1981) and John Carey, *The Violent Effigy: A Study of Dickens' Imagination* (London: Faber & Faber, 1973).

3 Percy Hetherington Fitzgerald, *Memories of Charles Dickens* (Bristol: J. W. Arrowsmith, 1913), 249. For other examples in the decades immediately after Dickens's death, see the anonymous review of John Hollingshead, *Miscellanies: Stories and Essays*, *The Athenaeum*, 2419 (7 March 1874), 319–20 (describing Hollingshead as 'less flashy than Sala, who takes precedence of all other Dickensese essayists' [320]); 'Old Friends', *Saturday Review*, 69 (10 May 1890), 582; 'Literature', *The Athenaeum*, 3510 (2 February 1895), 141–2 (reviewing and quoting Percy Fitzgerald, *Memoirs of an Author*); Philip Kent, 'A Maeander', *Gentleman's Magazine*, 286 (1899), 444–58, at 454; Frederic Harrison, 'Obiter Scripta: IV', *The Fortnightly Review*, 66 n.s. (1918), 481–90, at 488. 'Dickensese' means a variety of things, in these examples, but chiefly performative excess, *faux* Cockney and the deliberate use of comical circumlocution or failed elevation of the manner of speech.

4 Richard Wollheim, 'Style in Painting', in Caroline van Eck, James McAllister and Renée van de Vall (eds.), *The Question of Style in Philosophy and the Arts* (Cambridge University Press, 1995), 37–49.

5 Wollheim, 'Style in Painting', 41–3.

6 Wollheim, 'Style in Painting', 40.

7 See Catherine Waters, *Commodity Culture in Dickens's* Household Words*: The Social Life of Goods* (Aldershot: Ashgate, 2008). Waters comments only very briefly on the style of the magazine as an aspect of its commercial appeal (21; cf. 6–7, where she argues for the dialogic, multivocal aspects of the journal, notwithstanding).

8 Letter from Charles Dickens to George Cattermole, 13 January 1840, *Letters*, II, 7–9, at 7.

9 Letter from Charles Dickens to the Hon. Mrs Richard Watson, 1 November 1854, *Letters*, VII, 453–6, at 453.

10 Fitzgerald, *Memories of Charles Dickens*, 254.

11 Fitzgerald, *Memories of Charles Dickens*, 249.

12 Fitzgerald, *Memories of Charles Dickens*, 248.

13 The phrase is taken from John Hollingshead, *My Lifetime*, 2 vols. (London: Sampson & Low, 1895), I, 104. See also Peter David Edwards, *Dickens's 'Young Men': Augustus Sala, Edmund Yates, and the World of Victorian Journalism* (Aldershot: Ashgate, 1997).

14 For one example among many, see Letter from Charles Dickens to W. H. Wills, 5 August 1853, *Letters*, VII, 124–6, at 126.

15 Fitzgerald, *Memories of Charles Dickens*, 254.

16 Fitzgerald, *Memories of Charles Dickens*, 254.

17 Fitzgerald, *Memories of Charles Dickens*, 170–1.

18 Hollingshead, *My Lifetime*, I, 104. See also Ella Ann Oppenlander, *Dickens' All the Year Round: Descriptive Index and Contributor List* (Troy, NY: The Whitston Publishing Co., 1984), 38: 'no clever paper clever enough unless it had an enticing title, possibly a title "quaint with meanings"'.

19 Hollingshead, *My Lifetime*, I, 104.

20 Hollingshead, *My Lifetime*, I, 96.

21 *Press*, 12 November 1859. Quoted in Anne Lohri, *Household Words: A Weekly Journal 1850–59 Conducted by Charles Dickens, Table of Contents, List of Contributors and Their Contributions, Based on the Household Words Office Book in the Morris L. Parrish Collection of Victorian Novelists, Princeton University Library* (Toronto University Press, 1973), 23.

22 Letter from Charles Dickens to Charles Eliot Norton, 9 March 1859, in *The Letters of Mrs. Gaskell*, ed. J. A. V. Chapple and Arthur Pollard (Manchester University Press, 1966), 534–9, at 538.

23 Robert Brough, 'Hard Times (Refinished)', in *Our Miscellany (Which Ought to Have Come Out, but Didn't)*, ed. E. H. Yates and R. B. Brough, et al. (London: G. Routledge, 1856); reprinted in *CH*, 309–13.

24 See Bharat Tandon's essay in this volume.

25 Brough, 'Hard Times (Refinished)', 310.

26 *CH*, 309.

27 See Harry Stone, *The Uncollected Writings of Charles Dickens:* Household Words *1850–1859*, 2 vols. (London: Allen Lane, 1979), ix–x; Oppenlander, *Dickens' All the Year Round*, 37 (giving, as an example, the misattribution of Yates's 'Pincher Astray', 30 January 1864, to Dickens); *Journalism*, III, xi–xii; and Edwards, *Dickens's 'Young Men'*, 14, where Edwards uses Sala's 'Dumbledowndeary' (*HW*, 5 [19 June 1852], 312–17) to illustrate how difficult it is sometimes to 'distinguish Dickens's editorial interpolations from Sala's own pastiche of the approved "Dickensy" style'.

28 T. H. Escott, 'A Journalist of the Day', *Time*, 1 (April 1879), 115–21, at 119–20.

29 Letter from George Sala to Edmund Yates, 25 March 1875, in *Letters of George Augustus Sala to Edmund Yates, in the Edmund Yates Papers, University of Queensland Library*, ed. Judy McKenzie (St Lucia: Victorian Fiction Research Unit, Department of English, University of Queensland, 1993), 239. He continues: 'I must have copied out and translated into French and Italian, and then re-rendered again into different English hundreds upon hundreds of pages of Jeremy Taylor, South, Barrow, Tillotson and Sir William Temple before I could rid myself of the Dickensian fascination.'

30 *Life*, i, 9.

31 Contemporary commentators regularly placed Dickens in these traditions –
   prominent examples being Leigh Hunt, Walter Savage Landor and Algernon
   Swinburne. Modern studies of the nature and extent of the influences include
   (on Shakespeare) Valerie L. Gager, *Shakespeare and Dickens: The Dynamics of
   Influence* (Cambridge University Press, 1996); Adrian Poole, 'The Shadow of
   Lear's "Houseless" in Dickens', *Shakespeare Survey* 53 (2000): 103–13; Adrian
   Poole and Rebekah Scott, 'Charles Dickens', in *Scott, Dickens, Eliot, Hardy:
   Great Shakespeareans*, ed. Adrian Poole (London: Continuum, 2011), 53–94;
   Barbara Nathan Hardy, 'Shakespeare in Dickens', in *Dickens and Creativity*
   (London: Continuum, 2008), 145–56; and, on the eighteenth-century influ-
   ences, Francis O'Gorman and Katherine Turner (eds.), *The Victorians and the
   Eighteenth Century* (Burlington, VT: Ashgate, 2004).

32 See Tom Paulin, *The Day-Star of Liberty: William Hazlitt's Radical Style*
   (London: Faber & Faber, 1998). On Hazlitt's importance for Dickens more
   widely, see Paul Schlicke, 'Hazlitt, Horne, and the Spirit of the Age', *Studies
   in English Literature, 1500–1900*, 45 (4) (2005): 829–51 – treating Dickens as
   Horne's idea of 'the Spirit of the Age' personified. Also Archibald C. Coolidge,
   Jnr., 'Dickens' Use of Hazlitt's Principle of the Sympathetic Imagination',
   Mississippi Quarterly: The Journal of Southern Culture 25 (1962): 68–73.

33 See especially Letter from Charles Dickens to Alexander Ireland, 13 May 1868,
   Letters, XII, 123.

34 With regard to any more direct connections, it is known that Dickens was
   friendly with Hazlitt's son, but he seems never to have met Hazlitt himself.

35 Letter from Charles Dickens to Mrs Storrar, 15 May 1864, *Letters*, X, 395–6, at
   395. See Matthew Bevis, *The Art of Eloquence: Byron, Dickens, Tennyson, Joyce*
   (Oxford University Press, 2007), 86–144.

36 Paulin, *The Day-Star of Liberty*, 191, 43. I omit Paulin's claim that they were
   both Republicans, which seems to me incorrect in relation to Dickens.

37 Paulin, *The Day-Star of Liberty*, 28.

38 William Hazlitt, 'On Criticism', in *The Complete Works of William Hazlitt*,
   ed. P. P. Howe, after an edition of A. R. Waller and Arnold Glover, 21 vols.
   (London: J. M. Dent and Sons, 1930–4), VIII, 215–26, at 222.

39 William Hazlitt, 'On Familiar Style', in *Complete Works of William Hazlitt*,
   VIII, 242–8, at 242. A copy of the 3rd edn of *Table-Talk*, 2 vols., edited by
   Hazlitt's son (1845–6) was among the extensive collection of Hazlitt's writings
   in Dickens's library.

40 Hazlitt, 'On Familiar Style', 245.

41 See Chapter 3.

42 George Gissing, *The Immortal Dickens* (London: Cecil Palmer, 1925), 110–11.

43 The *OED* dates the first usage to 1866 (a review of Charles Kingsley's
   Hereward, in the American periodical, *Nation*). See 'pastiche, n. and adj'
   (1a).

44 Hazlitt, 'On Familiar Style', 242–3. This line of investigation into Dickens's
   theoretical influences seems to me entirely consistent with Harvey Peter

Sucksmith's examination of the probable influence of Edward Mangin's *Essays on the Sources of the Pleasures Received from Literary Compositions* (1809) on Dickens's narrative art. While Mangin stresses 'intensity' and 'unity' of effect, he also lays emphasis on the need for extreme care in 'selecting and bringing forward the circumstances which are conducive to [the writer's] purpose, and concealing as much as may be those which are unfavourable, or even superfluous'. Quoted in Sucksmith, *The Narrative Art of Charles Dickens: The Rhetoric of Sympathy and Irony in His Novels* (Oxford: Clarendon Press, 1970), 76.

45 Speech at a banquet to Literature and Art, Birmingham, 6 January 1853, in *Speeches*, 154–61, at 158.

46 Exchange quoted in *Life*, II, 341.

47 Speech at a banquet in his honour, 1 February 1842, in *Speeches*, 17–22, at 19.

48 Speech to the Birmingham and Midland Institute, Annual Inaugural Meeting, Birmingham, 27 September 1869, in *Speeches*, 397–408, at 406.

49 George Augustus Sala, 'On the "Sensational" in Literature and Art', *Belgravia* 4 (February 1868): 449–58; reprinted in *CH*, 487–91, at 487.

50 *Life*, II, 240.

51 *Life*, II, 240.

52 *Life*, II, 239.

53 Fitzgerald is not alone in this view of style, sometimes expressed in terms that suggest vitalist ideas of a limited supply of energy or life force available to any individual organism but also more straightforwardly presented in terms of the necessity of change and variety to sustain human interest. See, for example, Owen Jones, who argues, in the Preface to *The Grammar of Ornament* (1856), that as soon as style enters 'some fixed trammel' it will perforce be 'sudden[ly] throw[n] off ... till the new idea, like the old, become again fixed' (London: Dorling Kindersley, 2001), 18.

54 Fitzgerald, *Memories of Charles Dickens*, 119.

55 Fitzgerald, *Memories of Charles Dickens*, 248, 119.

56 Fitzgerald, *Memories of Charles Dickens*, 118.

57 Fitzgerald, *Memories of Charles Dickens*, 119, 249.

58 Fitzgerald, *Memories of Charles Dickens*, 250.

59 Hollingshead, *My Lifetime*, II, 147.

60 See Monika Fludernik, *Towards a Natural Narratology* (London: Routledge, 1996), 262–3, on Dickens's use of tense alternation, with specific reference to the use of the historic present in *The Mystery of Edwin Drood*. The term 'historic present' has, of course, questionable authority in English. It is used here to refer to the use of the present tense to narrate events that are clearly in the past.

61 See Iona Opie and Peter Opie, *Children's Games in Street and Playground* (New York: Oxford University Press, 1969), 94.

62 For critical reflections on the debate, see Simon J. James, '*The Mystery of Edwin Drood*', in David Paroissien (ed.), *A Companion to Charles Dickens* (Oxford:

Blackwell Publishing, 2008), 444–51; Gerhard Joseph, 'Who Cares Who
Killed Edwin Drood? or I'd Rather Be in Philadelphia: An Essay on Dickens's
Unfinished Novel', *Nineteenth-Century Literature*, 51 (1996): 161–75; Wendy S.
Jacobson, *The Companion to* The Mystery of Edwin Drood (London: Allen &
Unwin, 1986), 3–4. For myself, I accept Luke Fildes's statement that Dickens
required him to depict John Jasper with a doubled 'necktie' or scarf 'because
it is the murder weapon' as sufficient to cancel any doubts one might have.
See Jane R. Cohen, *Charles Dickens and His Original Illustrators* (Columbus,
OH: Ohio State University Press, 1980), 224.

63 On linguistic style as a vehicle for the exhibition of personality in Dickens,
see especially Karen Chase, *Eros and Psyche: The Representation of Personality
in Charlotte Brontë, Charles Dickens, and George Eliot* (London: Methuen,
1984).

64 *Life*, II, 454.

65 *Life*, II, 454.

66 *Life*, II, 454.

67 *Life*, II, 454.

68 See John Butt and Kathleen Tillotson, *Dickens at Work* (London: Methuen,
1957), 20–1. Having noted the extreme difficulties presented by Dickens's
manuscripts, they add: 'But the compositors were picked men [as recalled
by Dickens's daughter, Mamie], clean, quick, and accurate. To ensure rapid
despatch they were accustomed to distribute copy amongst several hands
by dividing each slip across the centre and endorsing the lower half with
a starred numeral corresponding to the number of the original slip. Their
accuracy cannot be properly attested until the manuscripts have been carefully collated with the proofs by some future editor of a standard text of the
novels; but it may be said that neither Dickens nor Forster, who also read
the proofs, found much to need correction' (21). See also Robert L. Patten,
Charles Dickens and His Publishers (Oxford: Clarendon Press, 1978), 323–4;
Allan C. Dooley, *Author and Printer in Victorian England* (Charlottesville,
VA: University Press of Virginia, 1992), 50 (on Dickens's punctuation style,
as asserted at proof stage), and 128 (on the 'greater textual authority' of the
printer's copy, over 'the assembled segments of a compositional manuscript',
in Dickens's case).

69 *Saturday Review of Politics, Literature, Science and Art,* 30 (17 September 1870),
369.

70 *The Mystery of Edwin Drood*, autograph manuscript, 1870, Forster Collection,
Victoria & Albert Museum Library, MSL/1876/Forster/167, installment
5, fols. 16–17 in Dickens's numbering. The lineation of the manuscript
has been preserved. 'xxx' marks an illegible word; '?' an uncertain reading.
^ is Dickens's insertion mark, not an editorial introduction. A digitised
copy of the manuscript is available at www.vam.ac.uk/content/articles/c/
charles-dickens-edwin-drood. It shows the general appearance of the manuscript, but the quality is not good enough for editorial purposes. (Accessed 21
December 2011.)

71 Gissing, *Immortal Dickens*, 217.
72 For a critical consideration of this view see Martin Dubois, 'Diverse Strains: Music and Religion in Dickens's *Edwin Drood*', *Journal of Victorian Culture*, 16 (3) (2012): 347–62, at 351–2, 354–5.

Select bibliography

Alter, Robert, 'Reading Style in Dickens', *Philosophy and Literature*, 20 (1) (1996): 130–7.

Bevis, Matthew, *The Art of Eloquence: Byron, Dickens, Tennyson, Joyce* (Oxford University Press, 2007).

Bowen, John, *Other Dickens: Pickwick to Chuzzlewit* (Oxford University Press, 2000).

Brook, G. L., *The Language of Dickens* (London: Deutsch, 1970).

Carey, John, *The Violent Effigy: A Study of Dickens's Imagination* (London: Faber, 1974).

Douglas-Fairhurst, Robert, 'Charles Dickens: Going Astray', in Adrian Poole (ed.), *The Cambridge Companion to English Novelists* (Cambridge University Press, 2010), 132–48.

    Becoming Dickens: The Invention of a Novelist (Cambridge, MA: Harvard University Press, 2011).

Garis, Robert, *The Dickens Theatre: A Reassessment of the Novels* (Oxford University Press, 1965).

Golding, Robert, *Idiolects in Dickens: The Major Techniques and Chronological Development* (London: Macmillan, 1985).

Lambert, Mark, *Dickens and the Suspended Quotation* (New Haven, CT: Yale University Press, 1981).

Newman, S. J., *Dickens at Play* (London: Macmillan, 1981).

Newsom, Robert, 'Style of Dickens', in Paul Schlicke (ed.), *Oxford Reader's Companion to Dickens* (Oxford University Press, 1999), 553–7.

Partlow, Robert, Jnr. (ed.), *Dickens the Craftsman: Strategies of Presentation* (Carbondale, IL: Southern Illinois University Press, 1970).

Quiller-Couch, Arthur, *Charles Dickens and other Victorians* (Cambridge: The University Press, 1925).

Quirk, Randolph, *The Linguist and the English Language* (London: Arnold, 1974).

Reed, John R., *Dickens's Hyperrealism* (Columbus, OH: Ohio University Press, 2010).

Sørensen, Knud, *Charles Dickens: Linguistic Innovator* (Aarhus: Arkona, 1985).

Stewart, Garrett, *Dickens and the Trials of Imagination* (Cambridge, MA: Harvard University Press, 1974).

Death Sentences: Styles of Dying in British Fiction (Cambridge, MA: Harvard University Press, 1984).

Dear Reader: The Conscripted Audience in Nineteenth-Century British Fiction (Baltimore, MD: Johns Hopkins University Press, 1996).

'Dickens and Language', in John O. Jordan (ed.), *The Cambridge Companion to Charles Dickens* (Cambridge University Press, 2001), 136–51.

Novel Violence (University of Chicago Press, 2009).

Sucksmith, H. P., *The Narrative Art of Charles Dickens: The Rhetoric of Sympathy and Irony in his Novels* (Oxford: Clarendon Press, 1970).

Index

CAMBRIDGE STUDIES IN
NINETEENTH-CENTURY LITERATURE AND CULTURE

General editor
GILLIAN BEER, *University of Cambridge*

Titles published

Printed in Great Britain
by Amazon.co.uk, Ltd.,
Marston Gate.